Evaluating Children's Writing

A Handbook
of Grading Choices
for Classroom Teachers

Second Edition

Evaluating Children's Writing

A Handbook of Grading Choices for Classroom Teachers

Second Edition

SUZANNE BRATCHER
With
LINDA RYAN

LAWRENCE ERLBAUM ASSOCIATES, PUBLISHERS
2004   MAHWAH, NEW JERSEY   LONDON

Lawrence Erlbaum Associates, Inc., Publishers
10 Industrial Avenue
Mahwah, New Jersey 07430

Cover design by Kathryn Houghtaling Lacey

Library of Congress Cataloging-in-Publication Data

Brachter, Suzanne.
   Evaluating children's writing : a handbook of grading choices for classroom
   teachers / Suzanne Brachter with Linda Ryan. —2nd ed.
      p. cm.
   Includes bibliographical references and index.
   ISBN 0-8058-4454-6 (pbk. : alk. paper)
   1. English language—Composition and exercises—Ability testing.
      2. Children—Writing.   I. Ryan, Linda, 1952–   . II. Title.
   LB1576.B594   2003
   372.62'3—dc21   20020192789
                                                                        CIP

Books published by Lawrence Erlbaum Associates are printed on acid-free paper,
and their bindings are chosen for strength and durability.

Printed in the United States of America
10 9 8 7 6 5 4 3 2 1

Dedicated to
the teachers of
the Northern Arizona Writing Project,
who kept asking until I answered.

CONTENTS

Preface   xi

| PART I | *The Objectives of Evaluation* | 1 |

CHAPTER 1   **In the Background:** *How We Feel about Grading*   3

Chapter Summary   6
EXERCISES   6
References   6

CHAPTER 2   **Specific Situations:** *Putting Evaluation into a Context*   9

Student Audience Considerations   10
Instructional Purposes of Grading   12
Teacher Stance toward Grading   15
Chapter Summary   17
EXERCISES   17
References   18

CHAPTER 3   **The Pieces of the Grading Puzzle**   19

Context   20
  Definition   20
  Grade-level Applications and Examples   21
Content   21
  Definition   21
  Grade-level Applications and Examples   23
Structure   24
  Definition   24
  Grade-level Applications and Examples   26
Mechanics   26
  Definition   26
  Grade-level Applications and Examples   27
Process   28
  Definition   28
  Applications and Examples   29

Chapter Summary   *37*

EXERCISES   *37*

References   *37*

PART II   *Evaluation Options*   **39**

CHAPTER 4   **Approaches to Grading   43**

Analytic Approaches   *43*
   Criterion-referenced Evaluation   44
   Assignment-generated Evaluation   44

Blended Approaches   *52*
   Primary-trait Evaluation   52
   Questions for Grading   61

Holistic Approaches   *63*
   Cluster Grading   66
   Anchor Evaluation   67
   Impressionistic Grading   70

Chapter Summary   *71*

EXERCISES   *71*

References   *74*

CHAPTER 5   **Response Strategies   75**

Oral Responses   *75*
   Writing Conferences   75
   Tape-recorded Responses   79

Written Responses   *80*
   Using the Computer   80
   Handwritten Notes   80
   Grading Sheets   80

Grades without Comments   *81*

Chapter Summary   *81*

EXERCISES   *82*

References   *82*

CHAPTER 6   **Management Systems   83**

Grade Averaging   *83*
   Common Value Systems   83
   Variations of Grade Averaging   84

Cumulative Records   *85*
   Checklists   86
   Anecdotal Records   89
   Cumulative Writing Folders   89

Contracts   *90*

Portfolios   *92*

Chapter Summary   *96*

EXERCISES   *96*

References   *97*

CHAPTER 7   **Evaluation Styles   99**

Teacher-centered Evaluation   *99*

Self-evaluation   *100*

Peer-centered Evaluation   *101*

Teacher/Student Partnerships   *101*

Outside the Classroom   *102*

Chapter Summary   *103*

EXERCISES   *103*

CHAPTER 8   **State Standards and Assessments   105**

State Writing Standards   *105*

State Writing Assessment   *106*

Teaching with State Standards and Assessments   *106*

Grading with State Scoring Guides   *107*

Designing Writing Prompts based on State
    Scoring Guides   *108*

Weighting the Traits   *115*

Sharing the Language of State Standards and
    Scoring Guides with Students   *115*

Thinking about State Standards and Assessments   *116*

Chapter Summary   *117*

EXERCISES   *118*

References   *118*

PART III   *Using Grading as a Teaching Tool*   **119**

CHAPTER 9   **Tools of the Trade:** *Choosing Evaluation*
    Options in a Communication Setting   **121**

Using the Communication Triangle   *121*

    Scenario #1   122

    Scenario #2   123

    Scenario #3   124

Tools of the Trade   *126*

Chapter Summary   *127*

EXERCISES   *128*

CHAPTER 10   **Transcending the Red Ink *or Making Grading Serve Teaching*   129**

Making Grading Serve Teaching   *129*
Working with Revisions   130
Adding Criteria over Time   130
Progressive Weighting of Grades   131

Beyond Evaluation: Alternative Purposes of Grading   *131*

Questions of Power   *132*

A World without Grades   *133*

Chapter Summary   *134*

EXERCISES   *134*

Reference   *134*

CHAPTER 11   **Teach Yourself to Grade *or the Grading Process in Action*   135**

Learning the Grading Process   *135*

Ways of Beginning   *138*
Scenario #1   139
Scenario #2   139
Scenario #3   139

Creating a Personal Grading System   *140*

Chapter Summary   *141*

EXERCISES   *141*

References   *141*

APPENDIX A   Sample Papers   143

APPENDIX B   Annotated Bibliography   187

APPENDIX C   State Scoring Guides   201

Author Index   213

Subject Index   215

PREFACE

What This Book Is

When the subject of evaluating children's writing comes up, teachers sometimes bristle, and when the word "grading" is introduced, some simply leave the room. *Evaluating Children's Writing* addresses this threatening—even painful—topic. It is about judging children's progress in writing, and it is about arriving at numbers or letters, checks and minuses, or smiling and frowning faces, whatever icons teachers use to communicate degrees of success (or failure) to students. *Evaluating Children's Writing* introduces and explains a wide range of evaluation strategies used by classroom teachers to arrive at grades. Samples of student writing accompany the instructions to illustrate the techniques. An appendix of additional student writing is provided for readers who wish to practice particular evaluation strategies.

But *Evaluating Children's Writing* is more than just a catalog of grading options; it is a handbook with a point of view. At the same time that it offers recipes for grading techniques, it also offers a philosophy of evaluating student writing that encourages teachers to put grading into a communication context and to analyze their own individual communication situations. It suggests making choices among the many options for evaluation by determining the instructional purpose of the assignment and considering the advantages and disadvantages of the particular strategy.

Who This Book Is For

This book is for teachers interested in exploring options for evaluating writing. It is for teachers who know how to grade one way but want to experiment with other methods. It is for teachers who are uncomfortable with the way they currently grade writing and for student teachers just learning to grade. It is for teachers who want to add writing to their repertoire of teaching tools but have been hesitant because they have wondered how to evaluate their students' work. While this handbook is primarily aimed at elementary teachers, the principles it lays out are appropriate to the evaluation of writing at any level; therefore, some secondary teachers may find it helpful as well.

The Purpose of This Book

This book is about evaluation—the process which individual teachers use to arrive at marks for their students. It is not about school-wide assessment of writing or about state or national writing assessment. While most elementary teachers are charged with teaching writing, very few teacher education programs include explicit instruction in grading writing. But evaluation is an important skill. Most schools require teachers to give grades, and society emphasizes fairness in grades. Instinctively, teachers know that writing is a complex process, a process that requires mastery of context, content, form, and language. However, evaluation is not instinctive.

Like most teachers of writing, I agree with Stephen and Susan Tchudi (1991), "In our ideal world, student writing and other composing would always be 'graded' pass/fail, successful/unsuccessful, or credit/no credit" (p. 155). Unfortunately, however, most of us do not inhabit "ideal world" schools. However much we might wish to evaluate our students' writing as "successful/unsuccessful," we are literally forced to grade writing. Without explicit instruction in how to evaluate, most of us have taught ourselves to grade, haphazardly, often simply duplicating the way we were graded as students. As with many self-taught skills, learned by necessity rather than by design, evaluation is often a frustrating process for both teachers and students.

The purpose of this book is to offer specific grading strategies and explicit instructions for using them, to offer options so that we may be intentional about our grading rather than haphazard. *Evaluating Children's Writing* is meant to be used with a group—in an in-service or in a class—but it can also be used as a self-help, self-teaching handbook. It is meant to be used as a reference for step-by-step procedures of grading techniques that can be used at different times during the year. *Evaluating Children's Writing* offers suggestions about the craft of evaluation—guidelines for instructional objectives, for student audience analysis, and for teacher self-analysis that help define communication contexts. It also offers a catalog of techniques, options appropriate for a variety of classroom environments. The art of grading—the ability to address the nuances of particular situations by designing innovative hybrids—remains for the individual teacher to master with years of experience.

The Design of the Book

Evaluating Children's Writing is divided into three parts:

   I. The Objectives of Evaluation
   II. Evaluation Options
   III. Using Evaluation as a Teaching Tool

Part I is designed to help teachers identify teaching objectives for the writing assignments they make. Part II enumerates evaluation options (approaches to grading, response strategies, management systems, evaluation styles) and provides specific instructions for implementing these options. Part III puts evaluation into a context larger than a single writing assignment. It raises questions about choosing from among the options and about using evaluation as a teaching tool. It suggests methods by which teachers may teach themselves to grade. Exercises throughout the book offer opportunities for practicing the different techniques, and the appendix provides samples of real student writing that may be used for practice.

Where This Book Came From

For many years I directed a site of the National Writing Project at my university. During the school year I worked with student teachers in a class we called "Writing to Learn." During the summers I worked with public school teachers who came to campus for a five-week Summer Institute. Both groups of teachers were enthusiastic about teaching writing, but at the end of our time together, they invariably said, "O.K. Now—how do I grade my students' writing?"

The first edition of this handbook resulted from my work to answer that question. I discovered that there are many answers, and that each answer depends (as does writing itself) on the context. In revising the book for the second edition, I enlisted the help of Linda Ryan, a third-grade teacher I have worked with for many years. Linda is known nationally for her workshops sponsored by the Bureau of Education and Research and is currently Curriculum and Testing Coordinator for the Prescott Unified School District in Prescott, Arizona. Her help in bringing the text up-to-date, particularly the new chapter on state standards and assessments, was invaluable.

What's New in This Edition

Many of the issues we face when we evaluate student writing are constant from year to year, as are many of the principles on which we design our practice. So, much of what I wrote about grading student papers ten years ago is still applicable. However, the larger context in which we work to teach writing has changed substantially with the advent of state standards and assessments. In addition, my own thinking has continued to evolve as I have received input from teachers and students who have used this book. And, of course, much has been written in the last ten years about evaluating student writing. If you have used this book in the past, you will discover new material in the second edition:

- A new chapter on state standards and assessments
- Updated references throughout the text

- A reorganization of the chapter on approaches to grading
- Additions to the chapter on management systems
- Additions to the chapter on teaching yourself to grade
- Additions to the annotated bibliography

The Stance of This Book

I have taught writing at many levels (sixth grade through graduate school), in many contexts for over thirty years; for fifteen or so of those years I was uncomfortable with grading. So every time a new "answer" to evaluation came down the pike, I jumped on the bandwagon, searching for the perfect grading technique. Like Stephen Tchudi and the NCTE Committee on Alternatives to Grading Student Writing (1997), I never found the perfect grading system, but the search has taught me a lot about writing, about evaluating writing, about my students, and about myself.

I believe that each of the evaluation methods included in this book has a place in teaching writing: they are all different; they all work; none of them is perfect. What we need as teachers of writing is intentionality in grading: we need a smorgasbord of grading strategies from which to choose. We need the ability to match grading techniques to teaching purposes. Grading is communication, and the "proper" grading strategy depends not on fads in the profession, but on the particular teaching purpose of the lesson or the unit or the course itself. Successful grading resides not in the particular grading strategy, but in the teacher's decision making, not in the requirements of the grading form, but in teaching purpose.

While I now teach writing from a strong process bias, I began teaching in 1971—before the paradigm shift occurred that Hairston described in 1982. Therefore, I retain a certain tolerance for a product bias. I believe that neither a process orientation nor a product orientation is sufficient by itself. Balance is required. (Indeed, the profession is leaning this way: "process toward product" is what we now hear.) Throughout this book, I refer to the "writing process," assuming that the reader knows this almost-jargon term. But in case this orientation toward writing is unfamiliar to some, let me explain what I mean by it. Very briefly, I mean the method that writers use to go from a blank sheet of paper to a finished written product. The writing process is recursive and messy, but when we pull out the themes that run through it for most writers, we find *prewriting* (gathering ideas, thinking, organizing), *drafting* (putting words into sentences and sentences into paragraphs), *revising* (rethinking ideas, adding, deleting), *editing* (correcting mechanics), and *publishing* (sharing the finished work with others).

But no matter the teaching bias, in order to evaluate writing with any degree of satisfaction, first we have to ask ourselves, "What is my instructional purpose for this assignment?" And then we have to ask not only which activity will accomplish the purpose, but also which grading strategy will best accomplish the purpose. By putting grading into a communication context, we can make it an extension of our teaching. After all, we came into this profession to be teachers, not to be graders.

Cautions to the Reader

Perhaps the biggest danger of writing a book about evaluation is that the very existence of the book will put too much emphasis on grading writing. John Harmon, in an article entitled "The Myth of Measurable Improvement," advises teachers not to evaluate on day-to-day growth. He asserts that growth in writing is slow and that evaluation is meaningless unless sufficient time has elapsed to allow for growth. He compares young writers to young plants: if we check their growth every day, we will surely be discouraged! I agree with Harmon. I intend the strategies in this book to be used after enough time has passed to allow for growth and *only when grades are necessary*. Not every piece of writing needs to be graded. In fact, when writing is used as a learning tool, it should probably not be graded. And even when students write for the purpose of learning to write, I do not believe that their efforts should be graded on every characteristic presented here. For example, not every piece of writing will be taken through all the stages of the writing process; many will stop after a first draft or even after prewriting. So, not every piece of writing should be graded as if it were a finished product. Further, I believe very strongly that emergent writers should not be graded at all; instead they should be encouraged to write more, to take ever-increasing risks in an environment safe from grades. I hope this book will be a tool for teachers to use in situations in which they find grades either useful or necessary. I hope it will not be used to justify constant evaluation of children as they practice and learn the complex mode of communication we call "writing."

Acknowledgments

A second edition, while not as ambitious a project as a brand new book, can still be a daunting task. As with the first edition, I could never have accomplished this task without the help and input of other people. In particular, I want to thank Naomi Silverman, my editor at Lawrence Erlbaum Associates, for her belief in this project and for making the second edition possible. I also want to thank her staff for the practical support they gave me. I also want to extend special thanks to the reviewers who helped me find the gaps and glitches in the first edition: Jená Burges, Longwood College, and Wendy Bishop, Florida State University. In addition I want to thank Mary Johnson, my friend and colleague, for sharing her students' reactions to the book with me.

References   Hairston, Maxine. "Thomas Kuhn and the Winds of Change," *College Composition and Communication, 33,* (1982), pp. 76–88.

Harmon, John. "The Myth of Measurable Improvement." *English Journal,* 77:5 (September, 1988), pp. 78–80.

Tchudi, Stephen, ed. "Introduction: Degrees of Freedom in Assessment, Evaluation, and Grading" in *Alternatives to Grading Student Writing*. (Urbana, IL: NCTE, 1997), p. ix.

Tchudi, Stephen and Susan Tchudi. *The English/Language Arts Handbook: Classroom Strategies for Teachers*. Portsmouth, NH: Heinemann, 1991.

PART I

The Objectives of Evaluation

Part I explores grading as an act of communication between teacher and students. First, our feelings about grading set the stage for this instructional communication. Second, the many different instructional settings in which we find ourselves drive the decisions we make about how to teach our students. Third, the pieces of the grading puzzle (context, content, structure, mechanics, and process) provide a wide variety of purposes for the writing assignments we make. The theme of this part is that evaluation should serve instruction, not vice versa.

CHAPTER 1   **In the Background:** *How We Feel about Grading*

CHAPTER 2   **Specific Situations:** *Putting Evaluation into a Context*
Student Audience Considerations
Instructional Purposes of Grading
Teacher Stance toward Grading

CHAPTER 3   **The Pieces of the Grading Puzzle**

Context
   Definition
   Grade-level Applications and Examples
Content
   Definition
   Grade-level Applications and Examples
Structure
   Definition
   Grade-level Applications and Examples

1

Mechanics
Definition
Grade-level Applications and Examples

Process
Definition
Applications and Examples

CHAPTER 1

In the Background
How We Feel about Grading

Just after Christmas I was walking down the hall in a K–6 elementary school. On the stairway I encountered a friend, a fourth grade teacher.

I said, "Hi, Ellen [not her real name, of course]. How are you today?"

She groaned. "It's almost report card time! Do you really need to ask?"

I shrugged with what I hoped was the appropriate amount of sympathy.

"You know," she went on in an agonized voice, "I don't know why I leave grading papers till the last minute." She looked at me as if I might be able to enlighten her.

I shrugged sympathetically again.

"It's just that I feel so guilty about grading," she rushed on. "I know grades are important," she added defensively. "I know parents and kids need to know how they're doing, but. . . ." Her voice trailed off.

"Yes, . . ." I began.

"It's just that I work so hard to build a relationship of encouragement and trust with my children in their writing." Her tone was plaintive, the grieving tone of an adult when a favorite dog has died. "And then suddenly I have to become judge and jury." She looked off down the empty hall and spoke more to herself than to me. "Almost every one of my kids tries hard at writing. I just hate to discourage the late bloomers, the slow little turtles who will likely win the race one day."

She turned and looked at me, as if suddenly remembering my presence. "You know what I mean?" she asked.

I nodded. "Yes, . . ." I said, ready to offer my heartfelt condolences. But she had turned down the hall toward her room.

I stood watching her go, her question echoing in my ears: "Why do I leave my grading to the last minute?" Why indeed?

As teachers of writing, we all know exactly how Ellen was feeling that day. We struggle with the dichotomy of teacher versus grader whenever we take up student writing, not just when report cards are due to go home. In fact, we often wind up feeling positively schizophrenic. As Ellen said, we work hard to earn our students' trust as we try to help them improve their writing. We instinctively know the truth of Lynn Holaday's (1997) assertion that writing students need coaches, not judges (p. 35).

But we must grade student writing.

A review of recent books on the subject of teaching writing emphasizes the schizophrenia we feel when we stare at a stack of papers, grade book open. Most of the literature rejects even the word "grading." Instead writers use words like "assessing," "evaluating," "responding." We read the books, and we agree. But most schools still demand grades. Stephen Tchudi (1997) summed up the conflict in an introduction to the report of the NCTE Committee on Alternatives to Grading Student Writing: "The committee is convinced by the research . . . that grading writing doesn't contribute much to learning to write and is in conflict with the new paradigms for writing instruction. As a committee we would unanimously love to see grades disappear from education altogether so that teachers and students can focus on authentic assessment, but we realize in the current educational climate, that's not likely to happen" (p. xii).

No wonder Ellen puts off grading her students' writing. She enjoys reading what they have written. It's easy to respond, to reply to what her students have said, even to make suggestions for future writing. It's not so easy to put a grade on the paper, to reduce the comments she has made to a "B," to a "+," or to an "S." She, like the NCTE Committee, would love to see grades disappear. She feels like Lucy Calkins' (1994) colleague Shirley McPhillips, ". . . you stare at the report card and it looks so foreign and you think, 'How can I convert all that we're doing into those little squares?' You try but you feel like a traitor, like you are betraying something . . . and the whole thing becomes so distasteful" (p. 312). Furthermore, when Ellen turns to educational theory for help, she finds a variety of terms used in discussions of evaluating children's writing—*assessment, grading, evaluating, responding.* Sometimes the terms seem interchangeable; at other times they seem to mean something individual. In an attempt to clear up this confusion, Tchudi (1997) arranges these terms according to the amount of freedom each provides teachers. *Response* to student writing, he explains, offers teachers the most freedom because it grows directly out of the teacher's reaction as a reader and is often based on an emotional reaction to the text. *Assessment* offers less freedom for the teacher because it focuses on practical concerns about how a piece of writing is succeeding (p. xiv). *Evaluation* is even more focused because it compares a piece of writing to some sort of benchmark or criterion. *Grading,* says Tchudi, provides teachers with very little freedom because it condenses so much information into a single symbol that communication about writing is virtually lost (p. xv).

So, we understand Ellen's frustration. She wants more freedom to respond to her students' writing. She wants to deemphasize grading. She talks to her students about writing as a process, a process of getting better. She has explained that the individual grade is not important; progress is the important thing. She has told parents the same things on Back-to-School Night. Still, she watches Billy wad up his paper angrily and throw it in the trash can after she returns it. She knows it's the "C" he resents, possibly because his classmates have told him that a "C" is "terrible," possibly because his father does not pay him for "Cs." In any case, he is responding to the grade, not to her written comment—"I wish I could visit your grandma's farm"—at the end of the paper. And she knows that Sally, a little girl who sits next to Billy, never takes her papers home at all. Ellen realizes that these students would respond differently if she'd put only the comments on the papers. Anna, the best writer in the class, the student who always receives "As," writes at the end of the year exactly like she did the first week of school. So Ellen finds herself putting off grading until the last minute. She reads her students' writing eagerly and enjoys writing responses to what they've written, but she is reluctant to put grades on the papers. She enjoys telling Billy she likes his descriptions of his dog and wants to know more about the day he got it, but she finds herself avoiding the label of a grade. She wants to help Billy feel good about his writing; she doesn't want to discourage him with a grade. Ellen's distress over grading has become so severe that sometimes she takes her students' papers home and leaves them there until she is forced to put grades on them—when she faces a stack of new papers to grade or a blank report card that must be filled in.

Many of us feel as Ellen does. In the struggle to change teaching practices over the last twenty years, we have begun to see writing differently, to see our students differently. We have lived through and been part of the paradigm shift Maxine Hairston (1982) described. We no longer emphasize the products of writing to the exclusion of the process. We no longer assign writing in isolation.

We take students through prewriting activities to build background and to help them learn to think through what they know and what they need to find out in order to write thoughtful prose. We help them visualize different audiences and different purposes. We take our students through drafting to help them separate composing from editing, ideas from surface considerations. We walk students through revising to help them understand that writing is fluid, not fixed, that it can always be improved, that other people participate in writing with us. We work with students on editing to help them become proficient at the conventions of writing. We suggest strategies for helping each other with the surface correctness requirements of written language. We provide publishing opportunities. We celebrate the product of all the hard work that has gone before. We take up the papers. We read them and feel good about the writing our students have done.

And then we must grade those papers.

Parents, principals, school boards, school psychologists—all demand that we grade student writing. The grades we give communicate to these outside audiences in a wide assortment of contexts, some of which we never imagine until we're faced with unexpected conflict. Parents, for example, sometimes interpret the grades we give our students in the context of the instruction they received as children, principals in the context of grading patterns that emerge from year to year, school psychologists in the context of an individual student's accumulating record, school boards in the context of entire districts. . . . On and on it goes: different audiences with different purposes for the grades we are required to put on our students' papers.

We sit, then, with the stack of papers in front of us, aware of this startling variety of audiences and purposes, but most keenly aware of our primary audience—our students—and our primary purpose—teaching.

Most of our students have taken us at our word. They have participated in prewriting, in drafting, in revising, in editing: they have followed the process. And yet there are differences in what they have been able to produce. As teachers we know that writing is not exact, that we are not striving for perfection either in our own writing or in our students' writing. As graders "A+" represents the perfect paper—the one that is error free. Teacher/grader schizophrenia settles upon us.

Because we know we must, we take pen in hand and grade, feeling like the student teacher who said to me one day, "I feel so bad putting all those red marks on my students' hard work. It really does look like I bled all over their papers." Trying to avoid this unfortunate metaphor, we have sometimes graded in blue, bleeding like an aristocrat, or in green, like a snake.

There is hope, however. Teacher/grader schizophrenia can be overcome. If we choose a grading option that matches our teaching purpose, we do not need to bleed at all. And neither do our students.

Chapter Summary

Most of us suffer from "teacher/grader schizophrenia." On the one hand, we are committed to teaching writing as a process. We have read the research on learning to write and understand the rationale for being positive in our response to our students' writing. On the other hand, we are locked into school situations that require us to translate our response to our students' writing into letter grades or even numbers. But there is hope: teacher/grader schizophrenia can be overcome by choosing grading options that match our teaching purposes.

EXERCISES

1. Remember when you were an elementary student. Who was your favorite teacher? Why? How did he or she grade your work? Who was your least favorite teacher? How did he or she grade your work?

2. Write a brief "writing autobiography." Write about when you first started to write and how you developed through school as a writer. What were your feelings about yourself as a writer at different stages in your "writing life"? Were these feelings related to the grades you got in school? Why or why not?

3. Plot yourself on the following "feelings about grading" continuum. Explain why you placed yourself where you did.

|---------------------------------|---------------------------------|---------------------------------|

I think about
quitting my job
when I have to
grade papers.

I have no feelings
about grading—I
don't care one way
or the other.

I look forward
to grading.

References   Calkins, Lucy McCormick. *The Art of Teaching Writing*, new edition. Portsmouth, NH: Heinemann, 1994.

Hairston, Maxine. "Thomas Kuhn and the Winds of Change," *College Composition and Communication, 33* (1982), pp. 76–88.

Holaday, Lynn. "Writing Students Need Coaches, Not Judges" in *Alternatives to Grading Student Writing*, ed. Tchudi, Stephen. (Urbana, ILL: NCTE, 1997), p. 35.

Tchudi, Stephen. "Introduction: Degrees of Freedom in Assessment, Evaluation, and Grading" in *Alternatives to Grading Student Writing*, ed. Tchudi, Stephen. (Urbana, ILL: NCTE, 1997), p. ix.

CHAPTER 2

Specific Situations
Putting Evaluation into a Context

Definition: Grading—Communication between teachers and student that is designed to enhance the student's writing.

Using the above definition of grading to discuss the context of grading—specific evaluation situations—leads us to a familiar schematic called "the communication triangle." This triangle can help us articulate the various contexts in which we grade. Often the teacher/grader schizophrenia we suffer results from our having unconsciously created grading contexts that are at odds with our carefully constructed teaching contexts. Let's look at the communication triangle as it can be applied to evaluation.

The communication triangle has three equally important considerations: the audience intended to receive the communication, the purpose of the communication, and the stance (or chosen attitude) of the communicator. Adapting this triangle to our purposes, we label the three corners "student," "teacher," and "instructional purpose," as illustrated in Figure 2.1.

FIGURE 2.1.   Communication Triangle

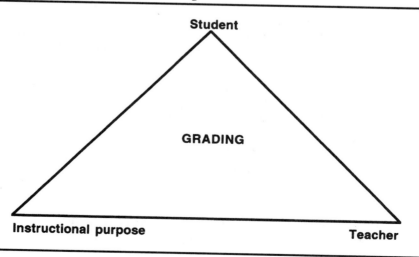

Moving around the triangle as we usually encounter it, we find the following corners: the official purpose of evaluation is to collect data over time that will allow us to justify nine-week grades for the report card; the teacher stance is that of judge, trying to fairly and accurately determine quality of student work; student needs and expectations are implicit at best and often never really thought through at all. (Students who do the best job inferring the criteria the teacher considers important for the report card are the ones who receive "As.")

In this traditional grading situation, the communication triangle has one very important corner—the purpose corner. That corner dictates a second corner—the teacher corner—and the third corner, the student corner, is almost nonexistent. Grading communication winds up looking more like a line than a triangle:

Purpose   Teacher (Student)

The end product of this lopsided triangle is very poor communication at grading time and lots of unhappy feelings for both teachers and students. To control the context in which our grading takes place, we must make that context explicit—for ourselves and for our students. We need to analyze each corner of the grading/communication triangle carefully.

Student Audience Considerations

When we write, we picture the readers to whom we are writing—we analyze the audience and attempt to communicate with them. When we evaluate or grade, we should do the same thing. Perhaps the central challenge of teaching is getting to know a particular set of students, finding out what they already know, and determining how to bridge the gap between where they are and where we want them to arrive. This challenge becomes most obvious when we try to grade a piece of writing (or a nine-week pattern of writing).

The question of how to interpret a particular effort from an individual student can be answered in an intentional way if student (audience) analysis is formally carried out by the teacher. The questions that follow (as well as others) can be used to inform grading and make it an extension of, rather than something separate from, teaching.

Sample Student Audience Analysis
a. What do my students already know about writing?
b. What do they like about writing?
c. What do they dislike about writing?
d. What do I think they need to learn next?

Let's take an example of a fourth grade class in a small town. The teacher, Mrs. Johnson, hands out a writing inventory at the beginning of the year to discover the attitudes her students have toward writing. As she plans her writing instruction, she wants to establish comfort with writing first, before moving on to confidence and finally competence. She asks five questions:

Do you like to write? (Students check either "I love to write," "I like to write sometimes," "I only write when I have to," or "I hate to write.")

Do you think you are a good writer?

What have you written recently?

What kinds of things do you like to write about?

How do you think learning to write better will help you?

Then she has them complete the sentence "I think that writing is . . ." (adapted from Bratcher & Larson, 1992).

From this questionnaire, Mrs. Johnson discovers several things about her student audience:

First, she discovers that almost 75 percent of her students like to write, at least some of the time. The other 25 percent, however, strongly dislike writing. And, she discovers an interesting match between how the students feel about writing and whether or not they consider themselves good writers: in her class there is an 88 percent correlation between students liking to write and considering themselves good writers!

Second, she discovers that the vast majority of the writing her students do is school-related. The few students who write on their own outside of school seem to write stories, poems, and letters.

Third, she discovers that for almost 75 percent of her students there is a large discrepancy between what they are actually writing in school and what they like to write about. The most popular topics among her class are animals, family, and friends. The most popular form is fiction.

Fourth, Mrs. Johnson discovers that almost half of her students view learning to write better as a tool for school and later work. Almost a third of her students do not see learning to write better as something that will help them at all.

Finally, from the sentence completion, Mrs. Johnson learns that about half of her class views writing as fun sometimes.

Mrs. Johnson now has a pretty good picture of her students' attitudes about writing. From her analysis she has learned that she is fortunate because a large number of the children in her class have good feelings about themselves as writers. But she has also learned that she needs to work with some of her students on how they view themselves as writers. Beyond that, she has learned some topics on which her students might like to write. Further, she has learned that the class as a whole needs to expand its understanding of why writing well will help them in their lives.

She can now begin designing her writing instruction for this class. A large number of the students are comfortable, even confident, about their writing and can be challenged toward greater and greater competence. But some of the students are not yet comfortable with writing; they don't even see its importance. Mrs. Johnson decides to begin with cooperative groups, groups that contain confident students as well as uncomfortable students, hoping to use the confident students as encouragers and leaders for the others.

Later in the year, Mrs. Johnson will do more specific audience analyses on specific criteria. For example, when she first teaches editing, she will locate the expert spellers as well as the terrible spellers. She can then offer peer support as well as specialized instruction to the poor spellers.

Instructional Purposes of Grading

Most of us become frustrated with evaluation because we resent what it does to our teaching. Cleary says: "Most teachers see grading as a stumbling block to what they wish they could do differently" (p. 156). Students focus (very pragmatically) on the grades we assign to their writing and seem to ignore our efforts to help them improve. This attitude is especially obvious among students at the extreme ends of the grading scale—the "E" students and the "N" students. How often do we see progress or change in these two populations? They seem to come to us as "E" writers or "N" writers and stay that way as long as they are in our classrooms: the "E" writers are as static and unchanging, as unlearning, as are the "N" writers. Even among the middle population, though, the change is often slight. When was the last time an "S" writer in one of your classes became an "E" writer by the end of the year?

But all of that can change in a classroom where evaluation is seen as a communication tool rather than as a record-keeping function. When grading criteria are made to serve instruction (and therefore change as the teaching emphasis changes), students must focus on the objectives of the writing instruction to get the grades they want.

On a theoretical level it sounds easy, but on a practical level this approach changes writing instruction as well as evaluation. If student grades are to reflect levels of accomplishment of instructional purpose(s), we must first have a clear grasp of the teaching purpose of any given assignment. Evaluation criteria then grow naturally from the instructional purpose(s) of the assignment. So, grading purpose(s) begins with assignment creation.

The list of possible teaching purposes for writing assignments is infinite. But perhaps a list of a few with possible assignments that accompany them will illustrate:

Demonstrate the Writing Process
Sample assignment: Turn in every scrap of paper that went into writing your personal narrative. Be sure to turn in your mind map, your rough draft, your response sheet from your writing group, your editing workshop checklist, and your final draft.

Communicate with a Specific Audience

Sample assignment: Write a Valentine's Day story for Mr. Cook's first-grade class using the vocabulary words he supplied.

Demonstrate Mastery of Specific Content

Sample assignment: Write a report on the growth rate of your bean plants.

Discover New Content

Sample assignment: Write a biography of your favorite author (Shel Silverstein, Dr. Seuss, Louisa May Alcott, etc.).

Of course any one writing assignment may (and probably will) have more than one teaching objective, but it is important that the teacher clearly delineate both the primary and secondary objectives. Thus, the purpose of evaluation changes from a record-keeping function to a teaching function: evaluating how well the piece of writing accomplishes its stated purpose(s). Specific criteria and explanations of the grade point out to the student how the writing could more effectively accomplish its purpose. Coupled with an opportunity for revision or with a follow-up assignment, the graded writing becomes not an ending point but a starting point for the student. Learning becomes more effective because it is focused and goal-driven. To illustrate, let's look at a second-grade class late in the year.

Miss Wells asks her students to write a personal narrative, a story about something that happened to them that they want to remember. She has four possible teaching purposes for this assignment. She wants her students to:

1. choose a topic that interests their readers (the class).
2. tell a story using themselves as narrators.
3. use details in their writing.
4. edit for capitalization, complete sentences, and spelling.

Miss Wells then identifies her primary teaching purpose(s) as well as her secondary purposes. She proceeds to tailor instruction appropriate to her emphasis at the moment. Following instruction, a student in her class, John, turns in the following personal narrative shown in Figure 2.2.

Miss Wells must grade his paper. In her school, primary students are given the following grades: (+) = beyond teacher expectations; (✓) = meets expectations; and (−) = below teacher expectations. Occasionally Miss Wells uses a (✓+) to indicate writing that is beyond her expectations in some areas, but at her expectation level in others.

Depending on the emphasis Miss Wells has made on the teaching purposes—which ones she has identified for herself and the class as primary teaching purpose(s) and secondary teaching purpose(s)—this same student paper may receive different grades.

For example, if Miss Wells has made this personal narrative assignment primarily a learning-to-write assignment, she may have identified teaching

FIGURE 2.2.   John's Personal Narrative

My First Horse Ride

I went to Smoke Tree Ranch in Palm Springs, California. There I learned to ride a horse. It was a lot of fun.

One day my cousins and I even went on a Breakfast Ride.

My favorite horse to ride was Sarly.

The End

purposes number 1 (choose a topic that interests the readers) and number 3 (use details) as her primary teaching purposes. Her audience analysis may have shown that the class has had little practice in considering readers when they write. She has spent time with the class discussing what the other children might like to read and how to pick a topic from their journals.

In this context, John's paper will likely receive a "+." Very few of the children in the class have ever ridden a horse, and all of them would like to. John has included lots of details for a second-grader: he has told where he rode the horse, the name of his favorite horse, and a particular ride he went on. The personal narrative exceeds Miss Wells' expectations for audience awareness and details.

If, on the other hand, Miss Wells has made this writing assignment a concluding activity for a language/mechanics lesson, she may have identified teaching purpose number 4 (edit for capitalization, complete sentences, and spelling) as her primary purpose for this writing assignment. In this situation, her audience analysis has indicated that capitalization is the major new material; these rules are the ones that have been targeted in instruction.

In this context, John's paper will likely receive a (✓+). John's sentences are complete and his spelling is good, but he has misused capital letters in "a Breakfast Ride." His writing is beyond her expectations in spelling and complete sentences, but not at her expectations in use of capital letters.

Teacher Stance toward Grading

But what about the third corner of the triangle, the teacher corner? Sometimes (perhaps often) teachers feel at odds with evaluation. As mentioned before, this teacher/grader schizophrenia often results when we adopt a grading stance or persona that is at odds with our teaching persona. For example, as teachers we know that positive reinforcement has more power than negative, and we adopt a cheerleading persona. But as graders we often think we should be perfectionists, sticklers for detail, focused on the quality of the product offered for evaluation, and we adopt a judge-and-jury persona. In short, having given up hitting students with rulers generations ago, we are uncomfortable striking them with grading pens.

But with purpose-driven evaluation, we can grade with the same persona with which we teach. Students can be encouraged by knowing which criteria they met successfully and by having concrete suggestions about how to improve the criteria that were not met so successfully. The teacher can encourage and praise what is done well, separating it from what needs more work. As Donald Graves (1994) explains, we can move "from extensive correcting of children's work to showing them how to handle the very problems [we] might have red-lined in the past" (p. 169).

Further, with a match between teaching emphasis and evaluation criteria, the teacher can adjust later revisions and assignments to meet student needs illustrated by criteria not met by large numbers of students in the class. After a particular assignment has been graded, class discussions can focus on the same emphases instruction has focused on, serving as review and further challenge for students who need to relearn. Grading criteria can be tailored to assignments as students move to more complex writing.

To return to the example of Miss Wells. As a writing teacher, she has adopted the instructional stance of encourager. She wants her students to take risks with their writing, to stretch beyond what they can already do and move into new territory. Consequently, as a grader she wants to maintain this encouraging stance. In the first instance (the assignment was used as an audience-awareness task) Miss Wells will follow the "+" grade with an encouraging note to John. She may say something like this: "John, the class really enjoyed your personal narrative. What a good topic choice you made! I'd like to go to Smoke Tree Ranch and meet Sarly myself." She may comment to John orally about the capitalization error or she may let it go entirely.

As a language/mechanics teacher, Miss Wells has adopted a rather matter-of-fact, be-sure-to-brush-your-teeth, stance. As a grader of mechanical assignments, then, her stance will follow suit. In the second instance (the assignment was a follow-up to a language/mechanics lesson), her comments that follow the (✓+) may be like this: "John, you did a great job making all of your sentences complete. Your spelling is perfect in this paper as well—good job! In the second paragraph "a Breakfast Ride" does not need to be capitalized. Can you find the rule about that on our chart and point it out to me?"

In short, depending on her audience analysis, her instructional goals, and the stance she has taken as a teacher, Miss Wells' grade and response to a particular piece of writing may differ. In this context, there is no such thing as the perfect "+" paper. The grade a paper receives is determined by how well it meets the instructional goals Miss Wells has set for that particular assignment.

Let's examine another example: a TV news report. It is turned in by a sixth-grader, Karl, in Mr. Thayer's class (see Figure 2.3).

Context 1: The assignment is part of a careers' unit. Following a field trip to the local TV station, Mr. Thayer asks each student to write a portion of a newscast for a class videotape. Karl is assigned to do a news' report on safety issues for children. Mr. Thayer's primary purpose (stated to his students) is to illustrate what news people do.

FIGURE 2.3.   Karl's Writing

Jimmy Jet

   This is News Channel 3 with Heidi Fogalson, Heidi thanks Bob. Today a 9 year old child in New Jersey was said to be turned into a t.v. set. Yes I did say t.v. He watched to much t.v., so he finally turned into one. He watched it night and day. He watched the news, t.v. shows, soap operas, and cartoons. He cherished the t.v. The first word he said was "t.v." The first sentence was "change the channel mom!" He walked at five months old, so he could turn the t.v. knob. So children, unless you want to be run on electricity, don't watch to much t.v. There's an old saying you are what you eat, well this boy turned into what he watched. That's all the news right now, thanks for watching five "o" clock news. Good-night.

In this context, Karl would likely receive an excellent grade on the assignment. The writing shows a clear understanding of how a news report would sound. The mechanical errors are unimportant because this piece is meant to be read aloud by Karl to the video camera, and Karl knows what his own punctuation means.

Context 2: The assignment is a book report. Mr. Thayer has encouraged students to use creative formats, like a TV news' report or a journal entry or a letter between characters in the book, but the primary (stated) purpose of the assignment is to illustrate knowledge of the book. The book reports will be assembled in a class collection and kept for students to browse through when they are choosing their next book. A secondary purpose is to illustrate editing skills—in particular compound sentences and homophones.

In this context, Karl would likely receive an unsatisfactory grade. First, "Jimmy Jet and his TV Set" is only one poem in a large collection of Shel Silverstein's, so the piece does not illustrate knowledge of the book's entirety. Second, the editing is extremely weak: the paper contains three run-on sentences (incorrectly handled compounds) and two misspellings of the homophone "too." Karl needs to rewrite, attending to the purposes of the assignment and the instruction he has received.

Chapter Summary

Although we do not generally think of it this way, grading is first and foremost communication between teacher and student. It is communication aimed at learning: it is a teaching tool. Evaluation can be far more effective communication if we explicitly respond to the considerations delineated by the communication triangle—the particular student audience we are working with, the purpose(s) of writing assignments, and our stance as teachers when we grade.

When evaluation is looked at in this way (as communication), it becomes clear that there are no hard-and-fast "correct" answers to grading. Rather, there are objectives to be articulated and options from which to choose. Consideration of the communication triangle makes choices explicit and gives us the control to match our grading personae with our teaching personae.

EXERCISES

1. For a class you currently teach (or, for student teachers, one you can spend some time observing), do a grading analysis based on the communication triangle for one writing assignment:

   Writing Assignment (Report the instructions the student received here):

   Student Audience (What background do the students have for this assignment?)

Purpose(s) of the Assignment:
Primary:
Secondary:

Teacher Stance:
a. What kind of teaching persona do I (or the teacher) use in this class?
b. How can the teaching stance be translated into a grading persona for this assignment?

Grading Criteria:
After considering the three corners of the communication triangle, generate three grading criteria for this assignment. Weight them by percentage of the grade.

2. Choose a sample student paper from the appendix. Grade it twice—according to the two scenarios set for either Miss Wells' class or Mr. Thayer's class. If possible, grade the paper a third time according to the context you invented in Exercise 1.

References

Bratcher, Suzanne and Jan Larson. "Teaching the Personal Narrative: A Case Study in the Fourth Grade." Flagstaff, AZ: Unpublished essay, Spring 1992.

Cleary, Linda Miller. *From the Other Side of the Desk: Students Speak Out about Writing.* Portsmouth, NH: Heinemann, 1991.

Graves, Donald. *A Fresh Look at Writing.* Portsmouth, NH: Heinemann, 1994.

CHAPTER 3

The Pieces of the Grading Puzzle

To escape teaching/grading schizophrenia, we must delineate for ourselves the objectives we have for student writing. This task is daunting, to say the least, for (in a language arts context) we must take into account context, content, structure, and mechanics, as well as process. (In a social studies context, we may focus only on content.) Perhaps our writing puzzle, then, might look something like Figure 3.1. But how to grade for all the pieces of the writing puzzle?

When I sit down to work a puzzle, the first thing I do is sort the pieces by color. Next I study the picture on the box and decide where the blue pieces will go, where the green ones, and so on. As I begin to piece the puzzle together, I look closely at shades of color and shapes, differentiating a blue piece that is part of the sky from a blue piece that is part of the lake. In this chapter, grading is a picture puzzle; objectives of grading are the pieces. Hence, this chapter discusses each objective as if it were a truly discrete entity, but only for purposes of analysis and definition. It is important to remember, however, that in real writing the objectives discussed here impact one another and do not function as discrete entities. (For example, purpose often determines audience and audience often determines grammatical, or mechanical, choices.)

When you begin a puzzle, any order you bring to the task is arbitrary. So let's pick up the pieces one at a time and examine them. And just as we sometimes pick up a puzzle piece and examine it quickly, or indeed, leave it on the table and not look at it at all, readers should pick and choose among the definitions that follow, studying those that are unfamiliar and skipping others. The order I have chosen is: context, content, structure, mechanics, process.

This chapter is provided primarily as a reference to commonly used terms; like a dictionary, it is not intended to be read paragraph by paragraph from beginning to end. Each section begins with a definition. The definition is followed by specific applications appropriate for particular grade-levels and examples of student writing.

Note: Particular grade-appropriate behaviors overlap from year to year and cannot be isolated as appropriate for a single grade level. Readers should examine the listing provided by their state departments of education or individual school district curriculum guides and adapt the principles in this chapter accordingly.

FIGURE 3.1.   The Pieces of the Writing Puzzle

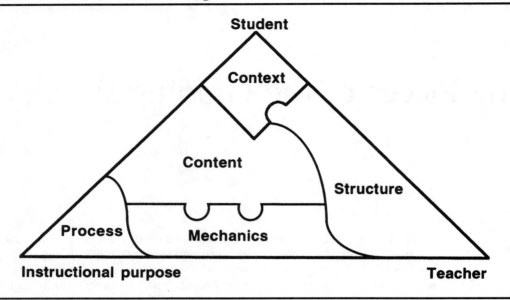

Context

Definition

    Context is the situation that creates and controls writing: reader, purpose, and writer's stance.

    The *reader* for a student's writing may be a parent, a teacher, a friend, or simply the student himself or herself. Sometimes, of course, there may be more than one reader: the stated reader may be a class speaker (a thank-you letter, for example), but the teacher may be a reader as well if the letter will be evaluated before it is sent.

    In any case, who the reader will be makes a tremendous difference to how the writing will be handled. A note to a friend, for example, can be written on scratch paper in pencil or crayon; spelling does not matter. A story the same student enters in a contest must conform to the requirements of the contest: it will need to be neat, and grammar will need to be accurate. It may even have to be written on special paper in ink, or perhaps it will need to be typed.

    Likewise, the *purpose* for which the writer is writing will dictate certain decisions about the writing. A letter from a student to a parent asking for money to take on a field trip will need to be more complete in its explanation than a letter thanking the parent for the money after the trip is over. By the same token, a book report intended to prove that the student has read the entire book will require more detail than a book talk intended to entice another student to read the book.

    The third part of the context of the writing that controls decision making is the *stance* of the writer, his or her voice in relationship to the audience and/or the content of the writing. In the first example discussed earlier, if the child who is writing the request for money to take on the field trip has a parent who has plenty of money and is free with it, the letter may be cursory—an informative note. However, if the child has a parent who is either seriously short of money at the time or who is tightfisted, the letter may be petitionary—exhaustive in its defense of the need for the money.

In the book report example used earlier, if the student liked the book, the book report will be enthusiastic, even expansive in tone; it may even be longer than required by the teacher. If, however, the student disliked the book, the book report will be detached in tone and very likely as brief as possible.

Grade-level Applications and Examples

For students in grades K–3, the important components of context are the ability to identify the purpose of the writing and the student's personal satisfaction with his or her writing. The piece in Figure 3.2 (written by a third-grader) illustrates the ability to identify the purpose of writing. First the class read a story about an injured owl. This piece was then written in response to the assignment: "Would you be glad to be free if you were Little Red? Why or why not?"

Clearly, this student understands the purpose of this writing. The first sentence answers the question, even using some of the same words used in the prompt. (This sentence does, however, make it clear that the student does not consider the question to be as straightforward as perhaps the teacher does.) The next sentence goes on to answer the "Why?" by telling what the writer would do first upon gaining freedom.

In grades 4–6, it is important that students go further with context. They should learn to identify the reader(s) for their writing, as well as the purpose. At this level they can also begin to articulate their stance as writer to both the reader(s) and the topic. The piece in Figure 3.3 (written by a fourth-grader) illustrates what happens when no reader has been identified for writing.

The writing in this piece is vague in the extreme. No names are included; no examples are cited. Had this writer been writing to a real audience, say to her mother, she would have felt safe to tell the story of what happened with "Jan" on the playground that afternoon. As it stands, the writer seems to have had no one at all in mind when she composed this piece.

Content

Definition

Content consists of the factual information, interpretations, and ideas a writer uses. It takes in main idea articulation, use of details, and completeness of communication about ideas and/or events being discussed in the writing.

Content concerns cannot be taken for granted with elementary students. *Main idea* is a high-level thinking skill calling for synthesis of details. Because finding the main idea may seem intuitive to us as adults, teaching students to

FIGURE 3.2.   Purpose

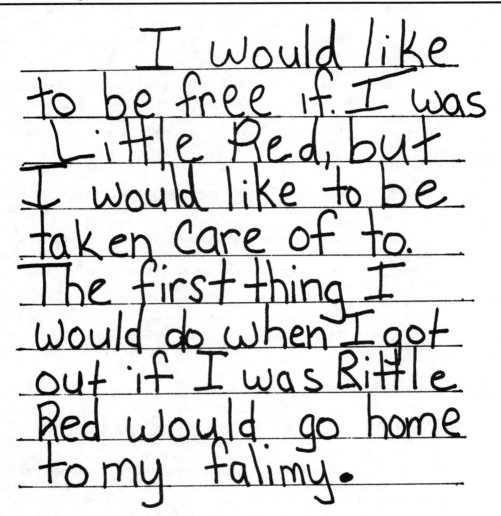

I would like to be free if. I was Little Red, but I would like to be taken care of to. The first thing I would do when I got out if I was Rittle Red would go home to my falimy.

articulate the purpose or theme of what they are writing is sometimes difficult. Students often need lots of practice finding and expressing main ideas. Fred, reporting on a nature walk, may list every stop along the way, even describe the stops in great detail, but may never write that the purpose of the walk was to find frogs.

Adding *details* can be difficult for students as well. Leah may write a letter to the judges of the science fair arguing that her favorite entry should win because it was the "best." She may consider this assertion sufficient and overlook the need for persuasive details like the colored string on the globe that traced the flight path of hummingbirds from South to North America.

Students also frequently need help in making their writing *complete:* kids often believe that other people (especially adults) can read their minds, thus

FIGURE 3.3.   No Reader

When you meet a new friend they are nice and kind. And then after you have played with her alot then she may get mean but they may stay nice and kind to you. They may start to be mean and angey at you then you get in a fight with her. You may not talk to each other but after a while you and her may be nice and say your sorry. Then you will be friends and she and you will probably meet new friends you and her will still stay friends but you may not. Then you and your new friend will be nice and kind to each other .

eliminating the necessity for explanation. Randy, telling a funny story of trying to give a bird a bath, may overlook the need to explain why he was attempting this task at all. At the same time, kids sometimes don't realize that their readers have not had the same background experiences that they have had. If Julio is telling the story of his trip to New York City to his class in Billings, Montana, he may not realize he needs to explain what a subway is.

Grade-level Applications and Examples

In grades K–3, content concerns usually include completion of ideas and elimination of gaps or omissions that may be confusing to a reader without the same level of understanding about the topic as the student writer. Furthermore, teachers often begin to challenge students at this level to include details that support and explain the main idea of the writing. Figure 3.4 (written by a third-

FIGURE 3.4.   Completion of Ideas

Yes I think it was rell becasue i

grader) illustrates what happens when a student does not complete the idea. The assignment was "Do you think this story really happened or do you think it's make-believe? Why?"

The student clearly understands the purpose of the writing. He answers the first question, "Yes, I think it was real." He also knows he is supposed to tell why: he says "because," but he does not complete his thought. A reader will never know what the "because" meant to the writer, what his reasons were for coming to the conclusion that the story was not make-believe.

In grades 4–6, students are ready to learn to narrow a topic or a subject, to delineate the boundaries of the discussion or of the story. Juanita, for example, can choose to write only about what her family saw at the zoo, leaving out exhaustive descriptions of the 150-mile car trip that took them to the zoo and the explanation of her aunt's wedding that took them to Phoenix in the first place.

Beyond simply avoiding assumptions about a reader's knowledge, or gaps or omissions that interfere with a reader's understanding, students can begin to develop ideas with details tailored to the main idea of the piece of writing on which they are working. The piece in Figure 3.5 (written by a fourth-grader) illustrates how students can include details.

Notice the name of the horse, the description of the tracks, the description of the watch, the explanation of the parents' absence. This student has written a detailed piece that allows the reader to "see" his story. The details make the piece interesting to a reader.

Structure

Definition

The term *structure* refers to the organization of a piece of writing: how the sentences/paragraphs/chapters communicate meaning by their order. Writing offers many different structures: none of them inherently "better" than others. Chronological order, order of importance, comparison and contrast, haiku, and newspaper editorial are all examples of common structures. Genres also offer structures to writers. Short fiction and personal narratives generally make use of chronological structures or beginning–middle–end structures. Poetry often follows particular patterns based on rhyme or shape or word structures. Essays

FIGURE 3.5.   Details

Crystal Quartz Cave

One day, I needed a little space to just sit around, relax, and get away from it all, so I went outside and jumped on my horse named Scarlett. I explored the hills, the road, and so on. I came upon some snow, and in the snow I followed some small Jack Rabbit tracks to a deep cave completely made of Quartz Crystal. It was the most beautiful thing I ever saw in my entire life. It wasn't made by nature, it was man made. When I said "Hello" to see if anyone was there, my voice echoed through the cave. I looked at my gold trimmed, white watch it was seven thirty. I jumped on Scarlett and rode home. Mom & dad weren't home. I hoped they did not go out looking for me. Well, Mom & dad got home after 3 hours. They said they had to gone for dinner and a play.

usually follow a main idea-supporting information structure, with informative essays depending more heavily on logical arguments and persuasive essays depending more heavily on emotional arguments. At the elementary-school level, writers begin to learn that organization is important to help readers understand their content. As they work, these young writers begin to learn to use some of the more common structures found in writing. These structures make writing easier for them: story maps, Venn diagrams, and genre guidelines help them focus what they want to say.

Grade-level Applications and Examples

In grades K–3, structure concerns focus primarily on sequence of ideas (beginning, middle, end). Personal experience narratives, imaginative stories, reports based on personal observation as well as letters and poems are common organizational structures for writing at this level. The personal narrative piece written by John in Miss Wells' class (Chapter 2, Figure 2.2) illustrates the personal experience narrative structure: it is the story of the writer's first horse ride.

This student sequenced the ideas appropriately. The writing begins with the trip to the ranch, the first thing that happened in chronological order. The next two sentences discuss learning to ride, something that happened after arrival. The next paragraph tells about a particular trip the writer went on after learning to ride. The last sentence sums up the whole experience by telling which horse the writer favored among all those he rode on this trip.

In grades 4–6, students are ready to work with paragraph structure. They can begin to write paragraphs that state main ideas as a topic sentence, and they can organize paragraphs according to specialized structures such as cause and effect, comparison and contrast, time order, and so forth. Students at this level are ready to write expository papers (description, directions, explanation, cause and effect, comparison and contrast, summary, etc.) along with the personal-writing structures they began in earlier grades.

The piece of writing turned in to Mr. Thayer (Chapter 2, Figure 2.3) by Karl illustrates a specialized kind of explanation structure—the TV news report.

The writer has "explained" the central event in Shel Silverstein's poem "Jimmy Jet and the TV Set" as if it were a news item, following the demands of that structure. Notice the station and personnel identifications in the first sentence. Further, notice how the writer speaks directly to the audience, complete with a conclusion for the children ("So children, unless you want to . . ."). Notice as well how the piece concludes in the expected way ("That's all the news . . ."). This student has demonstrated a good understanding of this particular structure.

Mechanics

Definition

Mechanics is the term I prefer for grammatical correctness in writing. Other terms often used are "conventions," "surface structure," "usage," and "editing concerns." Mechanics can refer to simple accuracy (Are the periods placed properly?) or they can refer to sophistication of grammatical stylistic choices (Does the writer use compound–complex sentences?). Mechanics are important, for done clumsily they can confuse a reader and even change intended meaning. Sometimes, however, mechanics are overemphasized, literally sweeping away a writer's competence in context, content, and structure. Because research has shown that grammar rules taught in isolation do not carry over to writing fluency, most teachers of writing address mechanical errors at the cleanup stage of writing after context, content, and structure have been controlled. Grammar mini-lessons focus on specific rules writers need to follow.

Research into the connections between grammar instruction and writing improvement has given us a new perspective on mechanical errors. Constance Weaver (1996) has shown that errors are a natural part of learning language and that as children become more sophisticated users of their native language, old errors disappear only to be replaced by more sophisticated errors. In fact, she asserts that even though children are growing in language use, the "overall rate of errors may not lessen much over the years" (p. 72). Other research (Zemelman, Daniels, & Hyde, 1998) has shown that focusing on one or two kinds of errors is more effective than marking every error we see. If we take this research seriously, we will recognize that mechanical errors are a part of language learning and make sure that students have enough time to edit their work. And because proofreading is a specialized skill separate from simple rereading (Bratcher, 1994), we will encourage students to think of correctness as community responsibility: Gina, who is good at capitalization rules, chooses to help Joey and Esther by looking for capitalization errors in their writing. Joey, the best speller in their pod, helps Gina and Esther by looking for spelling errors in their writing. Esther, who never writes incomplete sentences, chooses to help Gina and Joey by looking for the correct placement of periods (and so on). Because the students have chosen their editing tasks based on their own skills, they begin to take ownership of the accuracy of their own and other students' writing.

Grade-level Applications and Examples

In grades K–3, appropriate mechanical concerns include completion of thoughts as sentences, use of transitions and conjunctions to connect ideas, conventional word endings, personal pronouns, contractions, singular possessives, verb tenses, subject–verb agreement, conventional spelling, punctuation, and capitalization.

It is important to note here, that out of this list, punctuation, spelling, and capitalization relate only to writing and need to be taught to every child. The rest of the list springs from spoken usage: particular children, especially students whose first language is not English, will need to work on particular items, but all students will not need instruction in all the items on the list. As teachers, we may choose to guide our students' spoken usage toward standard English or we may choose not to. As teachers of writing we need to make a clear distinction between spoken and written language, guiding our students toward standard written usage. (Register, or the context of the communication, is of course an important consideration, but that discussion is beyond the scope of this book.)

FIGURE 3.6.   Transitions

THE FIGHT

```
            One day while my
    cousin, friend and I were walking home
  we saw a boxer at the store when my dog
  Dinkey a male redheeler came running
  toward the boxer.The boxer grabbed
  Dinkey's hind leg we were screaming
  when my friend Bob who lived across us
  got his gun, and followed the boxer when
  he shot the boxer.Later we took him
  to the vet.
```

"My First Horse Ride" (Chapter 2, Figure 2.2) illustrates the proper use of the period by a young writer. Each sentence is a complete thought.

In grades 4–6, the list of mechanical concerns remains the same with several additions: sentence variety (simple, compound, and complex), use of homophones, and use of comparisons.

The essay about friends (the fourth-grade example of "context" discussed earlier) illustrates the improper use of homophones: "your" is spelled the same way twice, although the first time it means "you are" and the second time it is second-person possessive. Furthermore, this essay illustrates the incorrect usage of a compound sentence (the next to last sentence).

The piece in Figure 3.6, "The Fight," illustrates the problems that sometimes surface for students working in a second language. This piece was written by a sixth-grader whose first language is Navajo. Notice the use of "when" in the next to the last sentence: *when* he shot the boxer. This phrasing might represent a confusion between *when* and *then*, or it might represent a missing piece of action in the story (the fact that the boxer didn't die and Bob kept following it). As teachers of children working in a second language, we need to take the time to discuss writing we consider confusing with individual students before "correcting" the language.

Process

Definition

A fifth component of writing is the process used by the writer to produce the product. While the sophistication of the activities writers carry out at each point in the process varies as students get older and more experienced, the components of the process remain the same.

Prewriting happens before a rough draft ever occurs. It includes brainstorming, discussions, drawing, dramatization, listening, reading, observing, researching, selecting a topic, and identifying the context of the writing. Most theorists agree that well over 50 percent of writing time is devoted to some form of prewriting.

Drafting begins when pencil hits paper and sentences begin to be composed. It includes freewriting, reading what has been written, and deciding what to do next.

Revising occurs when a writer rereads a draft for ideas. Content and structure concerns are addressed in the revising stage, most often with the help of peer readers.

Editing focuses on sentence structure, word choice, and usage and mechanics. Most often it includes both attempts at self-editing and the help of an outside editor. Once editing is complete, the student generally rewrites and proofreads the final draft for mistakes in copying.

Publishing results in sharing the final draft. Teachers provide many different ways to publish student work: by displaying it on a bulletin board, by binding it into a class book, by printing it in a newsletter, by entering it in a contest, by sending it home to parents, by giving it as a gift, by sharing it in ad hoc groups, by reading it to the whole class from an author's chair, and so forth.

Applications and Examples

The following checklist (Bratcher & Larson, 1992) illustrates the writing process as one teacher used it for an instructional sequence in writing a personal narrative:

cluster map

partner checklist for topic, audience, and purpose

rough draft

revising worksheet

editing workshop

final copy submitted for class book

Students stapled the list on the front of their writing folders and then checked off each item as they completed it.

Figures 3.7 through 3.12 illustrate the aforementioned process as used by one fourth-grader. The cluster (Figure 3.7) shows how this student planned for writing about her trip to Havasupai Canyon (a tributary of the Grand Canyon). Notice that the cluster includes information on setting, time, and characters involved in the trip.

Figure 3.8, "partner checklist," illustrates how another student helped this writer add more details to her personal narrative.

The rough draft (Figure 3.9) and revising worksheet (Figure 3.10) illustrate how this student's partner made suggestions for a final draft. Notice the suggestions for more details.

The editing workshop sheet in Figure 3.11 illustrates how this pod of students divided up the mechanical checking for each other.

The final copy (Figure 3.12) illustrates the quality of work that was accepted for the class book. (The student's mother typed the personal narrative.) The final class book was bound and placed in the school library for other students to read.

FIGURE 3.7.   Cluster

Cluster Map

FIGURE 3.8.   Partner Checklist

PARTNER CHECKLIST

My partner is Jane

His/Her topic is Havasupi

This topic is about himself/herself (yes or no) yes
It is interesting to the class (yes or no) yes
He/she wants to write about it (yes or no) yes

The purpose is ~~is~~ Fun

The cluster contains (check off if it is there; circle if it is missing)
    place ✓
    (time)
    people ✓
    interesting details ✓

The cluster has the items numbered in order for telling the story Yes

Veronica
SIGNATURE

FIGURE 3.9.   Rough Draft

Going to Hava Supi

When I was 9 years old I went to Havasupi. I went with my friend Katie, my dad, my dad's friend, my dad's friends son Eric, and Eric's friend Rubbin. We all went down to the South Rim of the Grand Canyon~~and~~ and ate lunch. After lunch we got our back packs and went down the trail. On the trail, at ~~the~~ first it was switch backs for about a mile. Then it was straight. We had our own groups. Eric and Rubbin who stayed ahead. Katie and I who stayed in the middle. My Dad and his friend who stayed behind.

FIGURE 3.10. Revising Worksheet

REVISING WORKSHEET

1. My partner is JAne

2. His/Her topic is Going to Havasupi

3. His/Her personal narrative uses "I" to tell the story. (yes or no)
yes

4. It is interesting to the class because ~~was~~ It is About
friends

5. I can tell he/she wanted to write about it because She had ~~pictu~~
pictures for it.

6. The purpose of this personal narrative is An adventure
(happy, sad, an adventure, a surprise, funny, or something else)

7. In the personal narrative,
   (a) the setting is Havasupi .
   It is fine like it is ✓ or It needs more detail _____

   (b) the time is Summer .
   It is fine like it is ✓ or It needs more detail _____

   (c) the characters are Katie, Her Dad, A friend, Eric, and Rubbin
   They are fine like they are ✓ or They need more detail _____

8. The thing I like the best about my partner's personal narrative is
All the adventures in it

9. One thing I'd like to know more about in this personal narrative is
What her horse's name was.
Veronica
SIGNATURE

FIGURE 3.11.   Editing Workshop

EDITING WORKSHOP

Your pod is going to help each other clear up grammar and spelling mistakes in your personal narratives. In this workshop there will be four jobs: checking for complete sentences
              checking for good use of capital letters
              checking for spelling
              checking for punctuation.

Each person in the pod will have one job. He/She will then look for that error in everyone's paper (including his/her own), so each pod member will have four papers to look for one thing in. There are three steps to this workshop.

1. Please choose jobs and then list which person has which job below:

checking for complete sentences *Veronica*

checking for good use of capital letters *Paul and Felix*

checking for spelling *Jane*

checking for punctuation *Paul and Felix*

2. If you find what you think is a mistake, circle it. The writer can then check to make sure what he/she has written is correct.

3. When you finish checking a paper, at the bottom of the last page write your job and initials to indicate that you are finished. (It might look like this—capitals/ SJB.)

FIGURE 3.12.   Final Draft

GOING TO HAVASUPI

When I was nine years old I went to Havasupi. My dad said that I could invite one friend, so I invited my best friend Katie. My Dad invited Tom, his best friend. Tom has one son. His name is Aaron and Aaron came. Aaron got to invite a friend. He invited his best friend Rubbin.

We all went down to the South Rim of the Grand Canyon and ate lunch. After lunch we got our backpacks on and went down the trail. At first the trail was switchbacks for about a mile. Then it was straight. We all stayed in groups: Eric and Rubbin who stayed in front, Katie and I who stayed in the middle, and Tom and Dad, who stayed behind. As I said, we had our own groups, but once we all go together to eat lunch.

Katie and I stopped twice. Once we saw a sign that said four more miles. After a while Katie and I heard some running water, but we could not find what was making the sound until... SPLASH! We both fell into a creek. The reason why we fell was because we could not see the stream. It was covered by bright green bushes. After we fell we decided to soak our feet. While we were soaking our feet, we saw a little village. We were glad to see Havasupi was we were tired of walking; we did walk nine miles!

When we got to the motel and went into the lounge, we saw Aaron and Rubbin. I guess they planned to say, "Where were you guys?" because at the same time they said, "Where were you guys?"

Together Katie and I said, "Walking."

Then I had an idea to say "Where were you guys?" to Tom and Dad. I told Katie, Aaron, and Rubbin my plan. They all agreed, so when Tom and Dad got to the lounge Katie, Aaron, Rubbin, and I all said, "Where were you guys?"

Tom and Dad said, "Walking and looking at rocks."

We all went to the hotel room and got our bathing suits on. We went to a little river up a ways from the hotel. While Tom, Dad, Aaron, and Rubbin swam, Katie and I looked at rocks. We stayed there for about 30 minutes.

When we got back to the room, Aaron and Rubbin took a shower. That's when Katie and I discovered the light switch to the bathroom

FIGURE 3.12.   Final Draft (continued)

was in the other room. So Katie and I just happily turned off the light. But when Tom and Dad heard the boys falling and yelling, they turned the light back on. The only problem with turning off the light was when we were taking our shower, off went the light!

In Havasupi there is only one place to eat, and it closes at 6 o'clock p.m., so after Aaron, Rubbin, Katie, and I had taken half of our shower in the dark, we went to eat. After we ate, we went back to the hotel room. We all did our own thing. Tom and Dad looked at the stars, Aaron and Rubbin played Nintendo, and Katie and I talked.

In the morning we walked to Havasu Falls, which is two miles away from the hotel. When we got to Havasu Falls, my dad told us about a rope swing. At Havasu Falls there are circles of rock, and in those circles of rock is water. I call them pools. Down away from the pools is a place to river raft. Aaron and Rubbin played on the rope swing, Katie and I played in the pools, and Tom and Dad went river rafting. Havasu Falls is 75 feet tall.

After about two hours, we started toward Mooney Falls. When we got to Mooney, we went down a trail and through two tunnels and we got to a chain that hangs down about 30 feet. By the time we got to the bottom of the chain, we were soaked from the sprays of Mooney. When we got down we had to hide behind a rock so we didn't get wetter. We stayed down there for about 15 minutes. Then we went back to the top. Mooney Falls is 200 feet tall.

On the way back from Mooney, Katie and I, Tom and Dad stopped at a mine. The boys were too far ahead, so they didn't get to come. Katie and I filled our pockets with pretty rocks. That night, Aaron and Rubbin, Katie and I, all took our showers in the dark.

That morning Tom, Aaron, and Rubbin left on foot. Later Dad, Katie, and I left on horses. Katie's horse was Shadow. My dad's was named Cinnamon. My horse's name was Taffy. The hike down is nine hours, but with horses it is only seven. I think it was more fun to ride up on horses than walk, but I'm not sure because since I couldn't reach the stirrups, it was a bouncy ride. The funny part about riding up was that Katie and I had horses because we were light, but my dad had a mule because he was heavier.

When we got back to the top, we met Aaron, Rubbin, and Tom. We all drove home. One thing for sure was Katie and I were glad to get those rocks out of our backpacks!

Chapter Summary

Healing teacher/grader schizophrenia depends on setting teaching objectives for writing assignments and then grading according to those objectives. To set objectives, we must examine the various pieces of the writing puzzle: context, content, structure, mechanics, and process. We must determine the grade-appropriate writing behaviors in each of these areas so that we may design instruction (and grades) accordingly.

EXERCISES

1. Find a copy of your state's guidelines for writing or your district's curriculum guide. For the grade you teach, classify the writing expectations according to the categories provided in this chapter.

2. Analyze your own writing according to the categories provided in this chapter. In what areas are you strong? In what areas are you weak? Might these strengths and weaknesses affect how you teach writing?

3. Choose a paper from those in the appendix and analyze it according to the categories provided in this chapter.

References

Arizona Department of Education, *Arizona Academic Standards: Standard 2–Writing*. 3rd Grade Student Guide to AIMS: Arizona's Instrument to Measure Standards 2002. Revised 11/2001.

Bratcher, Suzanne. "Understanding Proofreading (or Frank Smith Meets the Surface Error)," *Visions and Revisions: Research for Writing Teachers*, v. 4 Spring, 1994, pp. 61–68.

Bratcher, Suzanne and Jan Larson. "Writing with fourth-graders: a personal narrative experience." Unpublished study. Flagstaff, AZ: DeMiguel Elementary School, 1992.

Weaver, Constance. *Teaching Grammar in Context*. Portsmouth, NH: Heinemann, 1996.

Zemelman, Steven, Harvey Daniels, and Arthur Hyde. *Best Practice: New Standards for Teaching and Learning in America's Schools*, 2nd edition. Portsmouth, NH: Heinemann, 1998.

PART II

Evaluation Options

If we accept the premises that evaluation is communication and that instructional contexts and purposes differ, it follows that we need a repertoire of different evaluation strategies to match different teaching situations. This part classifies twenty grading techniques into four large categories and provides step-by-step instructions for using these techniques. Samples of student papers illustrate the grading techniques.

CHAPTER 4   **Approaches to Grading**

Analytic Approaches
   Criterion-referenced Evaluation
   Assignment-generated Evaluation

Blended Approaches
   Primary-trait Evaluation
   Questions for Grading

Holistic Approaches
   Cluster Grading
   Anchor Evaluation
   Impressionistic Grading

CHAPTER 5   **Response Strategies**

Oral Responses
   Writing Conferences
   Tape-recorded Responses

Written Responses
   Using the Computer
   Handwritten Notes
   Grading Sheets

Grades without Comments

CHAPTER 6   Management Systems

Grade Averaging
Common Value Systems
Variations of Grade Averaging

Cumulative Records
Checklists
Anecdotal Records
Cumulative Writing Folders

Contracts

Portfolios

CHAPTER 7   Evaluation Styles

Teacher-centered Evaluation

Self-evaluation

Peer-centered Evaluation

Teacher/Student Partnerships

Outside the Classroom

CHAPTER 8   State Standards and Assessments

State Writing Standards

State Writing Assessment

Teaching with State Standards and Assessments

Grading with State Scoring Guides

Designing Writing Prompts Based on State Scoring Guides

Weighting the Traits

Sharing the Language of State Standards and Scoring Guides with Students

Thinking about State Standards and Assessments

The four categories I have used here to classify the techniques are important to any discussion of evaluation. Sometimes I have heard teachers talk about management systems as if they were grading approaches, suggesting that portfolios were an alternative to criterion-referenced grading, for example. But a portfolio is a management system: it falls in a separate category from criterion-referenced grading. There are lots of different types of portfolios—analytic as well as holistic. So it is entirely possible to create a criterion-referenced portfolio!

The categories, then, are critical to an understanding of how grading works. Grading approaches, response strategies, management systems, and evaluation styles work together—they are not isolated techniques. (Any grading system will contain all the categories.) By "grading approaches," I mean options teachers have for determining letter or number grades. By "response strategies," I mean options teachers have for communicating the grades they have determined to their students. By "management systems," I mean options for determining longer-term grades (grades for a nine-week session or for a year). By "evaluation styles" I mean power options—will the decision making lie in the hands of the teacher, the student, or both? By state standards and assessments, I mean the criteria for instruction and assessment required by our state departments of education.

CHAPTER 4

Approaches to Grading

Like almost any behavior we might name, grading approaches can be conceptualized as occurring along several different continua. The continuum I find most helpful for thinking about grading approaches looks like the one below, with analytic grading at one end of the spectrum and holistic grading at the other end:

Analytic Scales   Holistic Measures

Analytic approaches to grading compare a piece of student writing to a list of criteria that describe an ideal piece of writing; holistic approaches compare a piece of student writing to other pieces of student writing from the same assignment. Blended approaches compare a piece of student writing both to a list of criteria and to other pieces of student writing.

In this chapter I discuss six options within "grading approaches." They are present on the holistic–analytic continuum below:

Analytic Scales   Holistic Measures

| Criterion-referenced | Assignment-generated | Primary-trait | Questions | Cluster | Anchor |

I have used all of these approaches in my own teaching, and I have seen them all used by other teachers. All of them can be useful (just as all of them can be useless), depending on the particular writing assignment and its instructional purpose. I begin the explanations with analytic approaches simply because they are easier to explain, not because they are somehow superior to holistic approaches. The order of presentation, then, is arbitrary—no hierarchy is intended.

Analytic Approaches

Analytic approaches attempt to break a piece of writing into its component parts. Analytic strategies of grading are based on the assumption that the quality of a piece of writing is the sum of the quality of each component of the writing. Sometimes the characteristics of good writing that form the parts to be evaluated are identified by the individual grader and sometimes by an outside agency (like the writers of curriculum guides or specialists in a state department of education). Once the parts have been identified and described, individual student writing is compared against a scale that has been created from the chosen characteristics. Some teachers do this identification in their heads; others make use of written rubrics (grading guides). The biggest advantage of rubrics is that they communicate the teacher's grading guidelines to the student. Rubrics often avoid the common complaint that a grade was "subjective" (usually meaning unfair). They also communicate a clear message to the writer about what the evaluator thinks is successful and what he or she thinks needs more work.

Two analytic options appear on the extreme end of the continuum: criterion-referenced evaluation and assignment-generated evaluation. We next turn to these options.

Criterion-referenced Evaluation

The most atomistic analytic approach is criterion-referenced evaluation, which attempts to take into account every possible criterion of good writing at any level. A criterion-referenced evaluation system would look at Chapter 3 of this book (or a similar source) and make a list of all the items in context, content, structure, mechanics, and process that are appropriate to the grade-level being taught. Items in the list would then be weighted by points, and a grade could be determined. For example, a criterion-referenced scoring sheet for a fourth-grade expository writing (based on the Arizona Essential Skills document in Chapter 3) might look like Figure 4.1. Henry, a fourth-grade student in Mrs. Spiro's class, has turned in the essay in Figure 4.2. Mrs. Spiro grades Henry's essay using the criterion-referenced scoring sheet. Her completed scoring sheet looks like Figure 4.3.

Some Advantages of Criterion-referenced Evaluation
a. It evaluates each of the identified skills of the good writer.
b. It lists for the student everything the evaluator wants him or her to work on.

Some Disadvantages of Criterion-referenced Evaluation
a. It assumes that the quality of a piece of writing is the sum of its parts.
b. It evaluates a product without reference to current instruction.
c. It can overwhelm both students and teachers.

Assignment-generated Evaluation

A second type of analytic evaluation is based on criteria generated by a particular assignment. In this approach, someone—the teacher, the students, or everyone together—generates a grading guide based on the particular assignment. Sometimes these rubrics look like criterion-referenced grading sheets tailored for a particular type of writing (expository or personal narrative, for

FIGURE 4.1.   Criterion-referenced Grading Sheet

TOTAL POINTS POSSIBLE: 100

TOTAL POINTS EARNED: _____

CONTEXT (20 pts.)
   purpose of the writing identified
   reader identified
   writer's stance identified

Points Earned: _____

CONTENT (20 pts.)
   topic is narrowed
   ideas are complete
   main idea is clear
   details are tailored to the main idea

Points Earned: _____

STRUCTURE (20 pts.)
   sequence of ideas (beginning, middle, end)
   follows assigned structure (expository form)
   paragraphs contain topic sentences

Points Earned: _____

MECHANICS (20 pts.)
   completion of thoughts as sentences
   use of transitions and conjunctions to connect ideas
   conventional word endings
   personal pronouns
   contractions
   singular possessives
   verb tenses
   subject–verb agreement
   conventional spelling
   punctuation
   capitalization
   sentence variety (simple, compound, and complex)
   use of homophones
   use of comparisons

Points Earned: _____

PROCESS (20 pts.)
   prewriting turned in
   partner checklist for topic, audience, and purpose
   rough draft
   revising worksheet
   editing workshop
   final copy submitted for class book

Points Earned: _____

FIGURE 4.2.   Henry's Essay

By Henry

The San Francisco Peaks
The San Francisco Peaks
are north of Flagstaff, AZ. They
erupted about 1.8 million years
ago and built up over a long
period to form what they are
now. They're about 12,600
feet high and are made up of
five main peaks.

The San Francisco Peaks
have an interresting history. The Peaks
erupted from 1.8 million years ago
to 400,000 years ago. The Peaks
where named by a group called the

FIGURE 4.2.   Henry's Essay (continued)

Franciscans. When the Franciscans went to convert the Hopi, they gave the Peaks their name.

The Peaks have many kinds of trees on them. Going up the Peaks is like going north to the artic circle. It gets colder and less humid. This is the order the tree grow up the Peaks: Juniper-Pinyon woodland, Ponderosa Pine forest, Mixed conifer and Spruce-Fir forest.

There are also plants and animals on the Peaks. There are

FIGURE 4.2.   Henry's Essay (continued)

animals like dwarf shrews, lincoln
sparrows, hawks, hummingbirds,
chickadees, steel jays, marrian elk
and mule deer living on the Peaks.
There are 80 kinds of plants on
the Peaks like lupine, wild strawberrys,
wild tuft, groundsel and buttercups.

Bibliography
Pewe, T. L, and Updike, R. G, San
    Francisco Peaks, A Guide to
    the geogly Flagstaff, Arizona,
    Northern Azizona Society
    of Science and Art, Inc, 1976

Aitchison, S. W, and Breed W. J,
    San Francisco Peaks Flagstaff,
    Arizona, Museum of
    Northern Arizona, 1989

FIGURE 4.3.   Criterion-referenced Grading Sheet for "San Francisco Peaks"

TOTAL POINTS POSSIBLE: 100   TOTAL POINTS EARNED: ___74___

CONTEXT (20 pts.)   *about 7 points per category*   Earned: ___6___
    purpose   *partially—the last paragraph omits animal and plant life*
    reader identified   *no*
    writer's stance identified   *no*

CONTENT (20 pts.)   *5 points per category*   Earned: ___20___
    topic is narrowed   *yes—the San Francisco Peaks*
    ideas are complete   *yes*
    main idea is clear   *yes*
    details are tailored to the main idea   *yes*

STRUCTURE (20 pts.)   *about 7 points per category*   Earned: ___18___
    sequence of ideas   *yes—past to present*
    follows assigned structure (expository form)   *yes*
    paragraphs contain topic sentences   *partially—paragraph 3 wanders from trees to climate
       and back to trees again; trees should be part paragraph 4—plants and animals*

MECHANICS (20 pts.)   *1.5 points per category*   Earned: ___16___
    completion of thoughts as sentences   *yes*
    use of transitions and conjunctions to connect ideas   *yes*
    conventional word endings   *yes*
    personal pronouns   *none needed*
    contractions   *yes—paragraph 1*
    singular possessives   *none needed*
    verb tenses   *yes—past and present*
    subject–verb agreement   *yes*
    conventional spelling   *six errors—paragraph 2 "interresting", "where" for "were"; paragraph 3
       "artic"; paragraph 4 "duarf", "strawberrys"*
    punctuation   *yes*
    capitalization   *two errors—"lincoln" and "marrian"*
    sentence variety   *partial—one complex sentence in paragraph 2 "When the Franciscans"—
       the rest are simple*
    use of homophones   *yes*
    use of comparisons   *yes*

PROCESS (20 pts.)   *about 3 points per category*   Earned: ___14___
    process evidence not supplied here: turned in
    prewriting turned in   *yes*
    partner checklist for topic, audience, and purpose   *no*
    rough draft   *yes*
    revising worksheet   *yes*
    editing workshop   *no*
    final copy submitted for class book   *yes*

example); most, however, have fewer criteria—six to ten. An example of an assignment-generated rubric for primary students (grades 1–3) writing friendly letters to a character from a reading assignment might look like this:

> Letter is to someone in the story we read (+, −)
> Letter mentions something from the story (+, ✓, −)
> Letter tells something about the writer (+, ✓, −)
> Letter form is followed (+, ✓, −)
>> date
>> Dear _____ ,
>> paragraphs are indented properly
>> Love or Your friend,
>> signature
> Periods are in the right places (+, ✓, −)
> Pod partners have made suggestions (+, ✓, −)
> Final copy is neat and ready to mail (+, ✓, −)
> Grade (+, ✓, −).

Miriam turns in the letter illustrated in Figure 4.4.

We can evaluate Miriam's letter using the rubric. The letter is addressed to Koko, the main character in the story. It mentions that Miriam is glad Koko got a new cat and tells several things about her pets. The letter form is good (the date, opening and closing, her signature—the P.S. is something she added herself!), but the paragraphs are not indented properly. The periods are correct, Miriam has participated in her pod-revision group, and the final copy is neat. Mr. Avery, her teacher, gives Miriam a "+" on her letter, but suggests that she make one more copy, correcting her paragraphing before she mails it.

The best time to design an assignment-generated rubric is when you design the assignment. Rubrics can be shared with children in words or in pictures. One good way to create an assignment-generated rubric is to use the following process:

1. Set instructional goals for the assignment.
2. Prioritize the goals.
3. Set points or percentages for each of the instructional goals according to its priority. (This is the rubric or grading guide.)
4. Share the rubric with your students when you make the assignment.
5. Spend class time teaching the goals on the rubric as they apply to this assignment.
6. Have students revise their drafts following the rubric.

(For a more thorough discussion of matching rubrics to instructional purposes, see Bratcher, *The Learning-to-Write Process in Elementary Classrooms*, pp. 162–174.)

FIGURE 4.4.   Miriam's Letter

March 10

Dear Koko,

I am Miriam. I am glad you got a new cat. I am getting a new cat today. He is going to be black and white. I am going to be so glad. I love animals especially gorillas. I love you. Last year my dog got ran over and I cried too, but I got another dog. I got a hamster and he is gray and white. His name is Sqeekers.

your Friend,
Miriam

P.S. write back soon.

Some Advantages of Assignment-generated Evaluation

a. It communicates to students the goals of the particular assignment.
b. It changes as instruction changes.

Some Disadvantages of Assignment-generated Evaluation

a. It may not be sensitive to a particular strength or weakness in an individual student's writing.
b. It may emphasize the differences in writing tasks rather than the similarities.

Blended Approaches

Blended approaches to grading writing usually include a list of criteria for the assignment and sample papers that illustrate acceptable and unacceptable responses. Primary-trait evaluation and questions for grading are both blended approaches.

Primary-trait Evaluation

Primary-trait evaluation is similar to assignment-generated evaluation in that writing is evaluated against a list of criteria, but in this approach, the list is much shorter. Primary-trait evaluation is generally used to highlight foundational matters by selectively focusing students' attention on very few issues.

A primary-trait rubric designed to evaluate expository writing (how to play a game) by second-graders early in the year might look something like this:

1. The piece is focused on one game.
2. The writing describes the game.
3. The piece is presented in direction format.

The teacher's primary instructional purpose is to help students learn to focus on a single topic in their writing. Therefore, the three traits Mrs. Garcia chooses are all designed to direct her students' attention to that instructional purpose. While other writing skills are inherent in this assignment (sequencing, spelling, clarity, etc.), she decides not to grade on these other proficiencies for this assignment. She uses a "+," "✓," and "–" to grade with. Floyd turns in the paper in Figure 4.5. Using her primary-trait rubric and sample papers from the year before, Mrs. Garcia arrives at a "+" for Floyd's paper. The writing is focused on one game (Scrabble); it describes the game by including information about the object of the game, the number of players needed, and how to win; it is presented like game directions as a numbered list.

Natelle, another student in Mrs. Garcia's class, turns in the paper in Figure 4.6. Using the primary trait guide, Mrs. Garcia gives Natelle's paper a "–": the paper is not set up in direction format, rather it is written like an essay; the description of the game does not include the object of the game (a form of chase)

FIGURE 4.5.   Floyd's Paper

This is how to play

Scrabble.

1. You make a word and

get so more letters   then

you   put them down and

Let the other play

go.   2. you need to have

one, two, three or four

player's to play 3. you need

the game   and some

players. 4. and the first

player to run out of and

no words in the bag wins

5. if you don't play the game

right. you get Kicked out of

the gume.   Floyd

FIGURE 4.6.   Natelle's Paper

Do you Know how to play
not it. I know how to
play not it it is fun.
This how you play not it
you have to put your
hand in the ather people
hand then Who ever the
last one to take out there
hand they are it. It is fun
game to play out side. We
play lot of fun.game. We
fell so tired. We biut a
snowman out side can
you biut one. ~~~~~~ We

FIGURE 4.6.   Natelle's Paper (continued)

know   are   rules. Do   you

know   your   rules.   Do   you

know   how   to   play   baseball

we   have   lot   of   people.

Do   you   know   how   to   play

bubble   gum.   We   play   like

this   you   have   to   put

all   our   hand   in   the

ather   hand   they   you   have

to   say   bubble   gum

bubble   gum.

Natelle

or the fact that there is not really a winner and loser; the writing wanders off into other games (building a snowman, baseball, and bubblegum). Mrs. Garcia suggests that Natelle read some of her classmates' stories and then talks to her about her own. She suggests that Natelle do a revision to raise her grade.

A specific type of primary-trait evaluation called "Six-Traits" is important to mention here because it has come into such wide use. This evaluation tool, developed over a fifteen-year period by Oregon teachers, the Northwest Regional Educational Laboratory, and Vicki Spandel (2000), delineates six characteristics of good writing: idea development, organization, voice, word choice, sentence fluency, and conventions. Figures 4.7–4.10 illustrate sample papers and six-trait criteria (Arizona's Instrument to Measure Standards, 1999). These papers were written by third-graders in Arizona responding to the prompt: "Most people have at least one thing that means a lot to them. Think of something you have that you would like to keep forever. Tell about it so that your readers can picture it in their minds and understand why it is special."

While the six traits unquestionably appear in good writing at all levels, it remains for the classroom teacher to prioritize the traits according to instructional goals. As with assignment-generated rubrics, teachers can focus evaluation of student writing based on what instruction has actually taken place in the classroom rather than feeling obligated to evaluate every student paper on every trait. One useful way of looking at the six traits (or any other primary-trait inventory, for that matter) is by superimposing the writing process on the traits and asking where in the process of writing writers usually address the particular trait. As Figure 4.11 illustrates, concern about particular traits appear, reappear, and finally disappear as writers come closer to finishing their task, so no magic formula exists to determine when to teach a particular trait. Nevertheless, the notion that different traits are more or less important at different points in the process of developing a piece of writing is useful.

Some Advantages of Primary-trait Evaluation
a. It focuses the student on a small number of instructional items.
b. It is highly responsive to instruction.

Some Disadvantages of Primary-trait Evaluation
a. It may allow students to de-emphasize past instruction.
b. It may overlook some important criteria.

FIGURE 4.7.

STUDENT WRITING SAMPLE 1
Title: My Porclain Doll

Write the final copy of your paper here.

My Porclain doll

When it was my birthday and I was turning eight. I got a porcelain doll from by Grandma. I hope I get to keep it for my hole life. That is how special it is to me. It is a ballet dancer. Her hair is braded. She has roseis in her head band.

Her skirt is pink. She has a rose on her white blaws. Her ballet shoes are pink. She has blue eyes. Her hair is blondish brown. Her lips are rosie pink. her skin is whiteish peachish. She has beautifull pink bow on the edge of her sleeves. She makes beautifull music when you wind her up. She is the most beatifull thing I've ever had.

FIGURE 4.8.

SCORE SHEET FOR WRITING SAMPLE 1
Title: "My Porclain Doll"

This sample is an ACCEPTABLE response.

Ideas and Content	Organization	Voice
6 5 ④ 3 2 1	6 5 ④ 3 2 1	6 5 ④ 3 2 1

Word Choice	Sentence Fluency	Conventions
6 5 ④ 3 2 1	6 5 ④ 3 2 1	6 5 4 ③ 2 1

NOTE: The underlined sentences are taken directly from the student scoring guide in Appendix B.

Ideas and Content: This paper scores a 4 in ideas. <u>The writing is clear and sticks to the topic</u> <u>The writer has chosen details that help explain the main idea.</u> The writer explains what the dol looks like, but does not tell much about why it is special.

Organization: This paper scores a 4 in organization. <u>The writing has a clear beginning, middle</u> <u>and end. Details fit where placed and help the reader understand the message.</u>

Voice: This paper scores a 4 in voice. <u>The writer speaks to the reader and the paper shows</u> <u>honesty and sincerity.</u> *I hope I get to keep it for my hole life. She is the most beautiful thing I've ever had.*

Word Choice: This paper scores a 4 in word choice. The word choices work <u>to make the</u> <u>message clear</u>, but there is not much variety; the writer uses mostly color words. *Her skirt is pink...her white blows....her shoes are pink....her hair is blondish brown...her lips are rosie pink...she has blue eyes.*

Sentence Fluency: This paper scores a 4 in fluency. <u>Sentences make sense and flow from one</u> <u>to the other.</u> Although the writer does repeat the same sentence patterns, (*her hair...her lips...her shoes...her skirt...*) there is control of simple sentences and some control of more complex sentences.

Conventions: This paper scores a 3 in conventions. There are a variety of errors in <u>spelling,</u> <u>capitalization, end punctuation.</u>

FIGURE 4.9.

STUDENT WRITING SAMPLE 3
Title: "Grila Alien"

Write the final copy of your paper here.

Grila Alien

I have a toy that is a grila
Alien. He is pritty cool Alien but
sum times he can be annon.
but hes pritty cool. My friend's
really like to play with the Alien a
lot I gave him a pretty cool name it
is grilue Alien He has softue pointy
elboes and neas

FIGURE 4.10.

SCORE SHEET FOR WRITING SAMPLE 3
Title: "Grila Alien"

This is NOT an acceptable response.

Ideas and Content	Organization	Voice
6 5 4 ③ 2 1	6 5 4 3 ② 1	6 5 4 ③ 2 1

Word Choice	Sentence Fluency	Conventions
6 5 4 3 ② 1	6 5 4 3 ② 1	6 5 4 3 ② 1

NOTE: The underlined sentences are taken directly from the student scoring guide in Appendix B.

Ideas and Content: This paper scores a 3 in ideas. <u>The reader can understand what the writer is trying to say, but the writing does not have enough details; details are somewhat general.</u>

Organization: This paper scores a 2 in organization. <u>The writing is too short to show any organization.</u> The writer moves from one idea (sentence) to the next without a clear plan. It needs an ending.

Voice: This paper scores a 3 in voice. The writer is not always involved with the topic. Voice appears but then disappears. *He is a pritty cool Alien but sum times he can be annuon but he's pritty cool.*

Word Choice: This paper scores a 2 in word choice. Some words are used over and over for such a short piece. Words are not specific and do not create clear pictures for the reader.

Sentence Fluency: This paper scores a 2 in fluency. Most sentences are understandable but not very smooth. The writer shows limited control of simple sentences. For a short paper, there are quite a few run-on sentences. *He is pritty cool but sum times he can be annuon but he's pritty cool. My friend's really like to play with him alot I gave him a really cool name it is grilue Alien He has soft pointy elboes and neas*

Conventions: This paper scores a 2 in conventions. <u>Frequent errors make the paper difficult to read.</u> A variety of errors include spelling, punctuation, capitalization, and usage.

FIGURE 4.11. Traits and the Writing Process

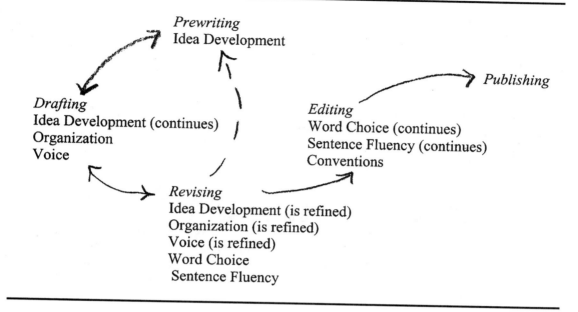

Prewriting
Idea Development

Drafting
Idea Development (continues)
Organization
Voice

Editing
Word Choice (continues)
Sentence Fluency (continues)
Conventions

Publishing

Revising
Idea Development (is refined)
Organization (is refined)
Voice (is refined)
Word Choice
Sentence Fluency

Questions for Grading

Another approach to grading is based on a set of questions. Sometimes these questions may be preset, like the journalist's questions; sometimes they may be generated for the particular assignment. Questions have analytical characteristics because they focus the evaluator on a set of specific items; they have holistic characteristics because they take into account the whole of the piece for the answer to any particular question. An example of this approach, appropriate for intermediate students writing a story, might be the "W" questions. The evaluation guide might look something like this:
The story answers the following questions:

Who? (20%)

What? (20%)

When? (20%)

Where? (20%)

Why? (20%).

Kassandra, a student in Mr. Ruggles' class, turns in the story in Figure 4.12. Using the questions to guide his grading, Mr. Ruggles gives Kassandra's story 90%. Her story does a good job with "who" (full credit—20%). Chica is a clearly described, whimsical character. Her story also does a good job with "what" (full credit—20%). Chili peppers are described (how they grow, their hot characteristics, how they can be neutralized, that they are canned, etc.). The "when" of the story is there, but less clear (partial credit—15%). We know

FIGURE 4.12.   Kassandra's Story

CHICA: THE WALKING TALKING CHILI PEPPER

by Kassandra

I was asleep in bed when I heard a sound. I got up and shined my flashlight around the room. Then I went downstairs to see what was the matter. Still looking around with my flashlight, I opened the door and there it was: Chica, the walking, talking Chili Pepper!

Chica was bright red as many chili peppers tend to be. She wore a bright pink visor around her stem. Her earrings were orange hoops and her eyes were bright yellow. She came up to me and tried to touch me in greeting. I touched her back and accidentally - I'd like to think - she burned me a bit since she was a hot pepper! I asked her if she wanted to have a glass of milk but since milk neutralizes the stinging burn that a pepper can give. But she said the milk would make her less hot so when I suggested it she ran and hid.

I looked everywhere with my flashlight and just when I was ready to give up I found Chica in my cellar staring up at all the jars of pickled peppers I had canned She spoke enough English to ask me, pointing up toward the jars of peppers, "Chica's friends up there?" She stared at me and her face had a confused look upon it. She trembled in fear until I said, "No, they are not your friends so don't worry." She calmed down. Then said, "Chica very hungry. Prepare a nice feast for one hungry chili pepper girl. By the way, you boy or girl?" I told her I was a boy and then she asked if I spoke the language of the Chili Pepper. I told her no. She gazed up at me with her big yellow eyes.

During our awkward conversation in the kitchen Chica told me she had popped down off my chili plant in the garden then realized she could walk and talk.

Chica asked me if perhaps she could sleep in a pot with flowers in them. Then, she said, she'd feel at home. So I put her gently in a flowerpot of Colorado daisies. I read her a story, Hansel and Gretel. She got a bit scared from it but I told her I was not the witch.

After Chica had gone to sleep in the flowerpot, I laid down in my own bed when I heard a noise outside...who knows? Maybe...it could be Tom the walking talking Tomato!

it happens at night, but that is all. We don't know (although we might guess) what time of year it is or how old the narrator is at the time of the story. Likewise, the "where" is a bit fuzzy (partial credit—15%). We know the story takes place in the kitchen, but it is not described. The why of the story is clear (full credit—20%). A noise has awakened the narrator. The ending of the story—another noise—suggests another story!

Here is an example of assignment-generated questions for grading. Mrs. Washington teaches second grade. Her students have just finished studying the body. She asks each student to choose an organ and write an acrostic poem about that organ. She creates these questions for grading:

> Does your poem use all of the letters of the organ's name?
>
> Does your poem tell at least three things about the organ?

Georgia, a student in Mrs. Washington's class, turns in the poem in Figure 4.13. Using sun, cloud, and rain stickers for her "grades," Mrs. Washington puts a sun sticker on Georgia's poem because the answer to both questions is "yes": Georgia's poem uses all the letters in "liver," and it tells three things about the liver (that it cleans the blood, that people die without a liver, and that mammals other than humans have livers, too).

Andrew turns in the poem in Figure 4.14. Mrs. Washington puts a cloud sticker on Andrew's poem because the answer to one of the questions is a "yes" and the answer to the second question is "no": Andrew's poem uses all the letters in "kidney," but tells only one correct thing about kidneys (that they fight germs). Mrs. Washington asks Andrew to redo the kidney center and rewrite his poem.

Some Advantages of Questions for Grading

a. They can offer a new way of looking at writing.

b. They can be tailored to the particular assignment.

Some Disadvantages of Questions for Grading

a. They may be prejudicial to one aspect of a piece of writing, overlooking other important features.

b. If overused, they may be ignored by students.

Holistic Approaches

Holistic approaches to measuring writing quality evaluate the success (or lack of it) of a whole piece of writing. Evaluation, by its very nature, compares a piece of writing to something outside itself; holistic grading depends on comparisons with other pieces of writing rather than on comparisons against a predetermined scale of criteria. Two different types of holistic measures are discussed here: "cluster" grading (within-group comparison grading) and "anchor" grading (sometimes called "benchmark," "prototype," or "touchstone"). "Impressionistic" grading, a sort of pseudo-holistic grading, which is often referred to as "holistic grading," causing confusion, is also discussed.

FIGURE 4.13.   Georgia's Poem

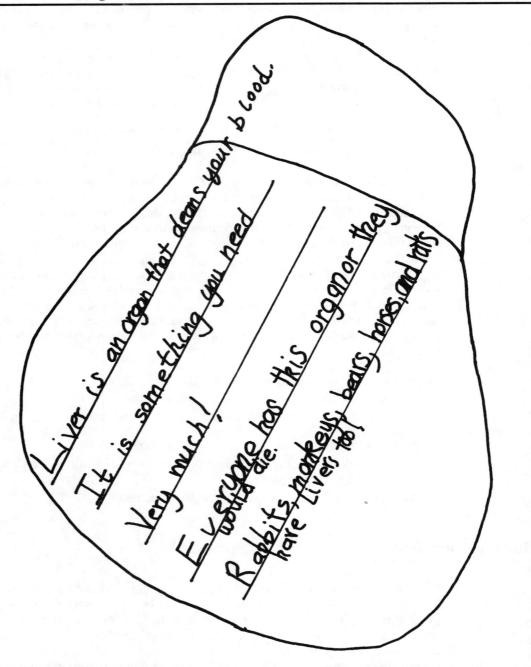

FIGURE 4.14.   Andrew's Poem

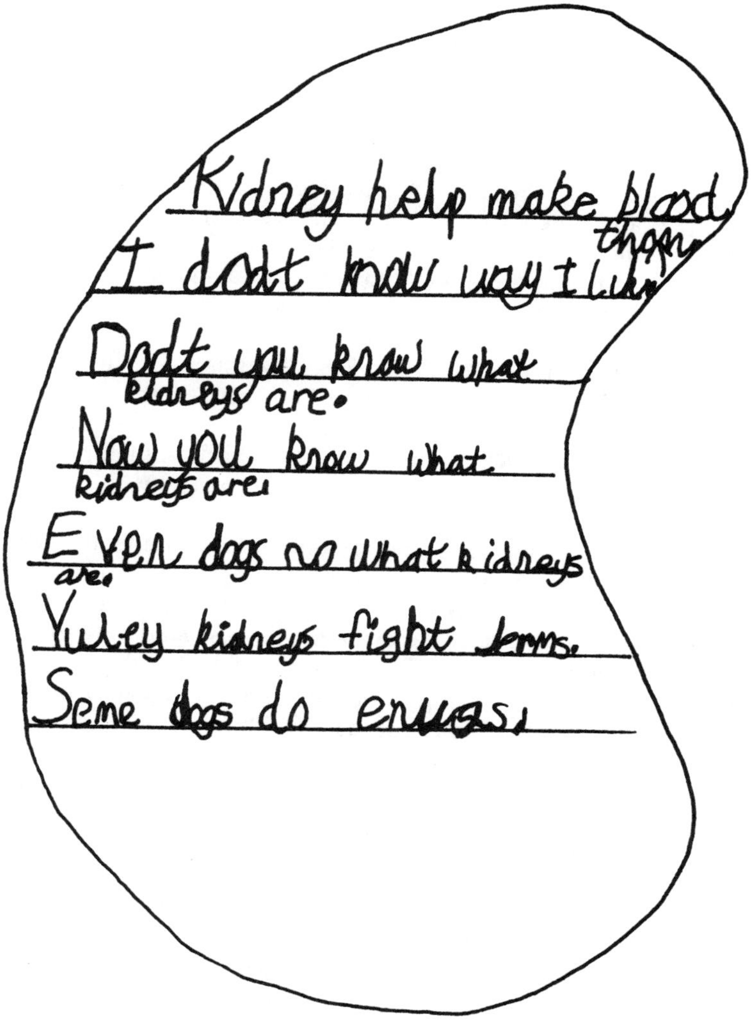

Cluster Grading

In this approach papers are compared not against criteria, but against papers within the class group. Here's how it works. An entire set of papers from a single class on a single assignment is read more than once. (For cluster grading to work, the pieces of writing must have something in common. Most teachers who use cluster grading design assignments that have a common structure—say poetry or exposition or imaginative stories—but that allow for individual topic choice.) On the first reading, the evaluator makes three stacks of papers as he or she reads. One stack represents "good" papers. A second stack represents papers that clearly "need improvement." A third stack represents papers that are somewhere "in between." A second reading of the papers validates the first impression: some papers may be moved from one stack to another. At this point papers in the "good" stack may be assigned a grade of "+," papers in the "needs improvement" stack may be assigned a "−," and so on. If, however, a five-point scale ("1–5" or "+, ✓+, ✓, ✓−, −," or "A–F") is used, a third reading is required. At this point the three stacks become five. The "good" stack is divided into an "A" stack and a "B" stack. The "needs improvement stack" is divided into an "F" stack and a "D" stack. The "in between" stack is divided among the "B" stack, the "C" stack, and the "D" stack. A final rapid reading of each stack validates the evaluator's decisions.

Let's look at an example. Mr. Martinez teaches fourth grade. He has just finished teaching a poetry unit, and his students have handed in their poems to be graded. On a quick first reading some of the poems stand out as carefully constructed—as "good" poems he can be enthusiastic about. He puts these poems in one stack. A few of the poems stand out as having been carelessly tossed together—as "weak" poems in which he is disappointed. He puts them in a second stack. The rest of the poems are somewhere in between—they have characteristics that he is enthusiastic about as well as characteristics that disappoint him. He puts them in a third stack. Since he does not wish to make finer distinctions than "+," "✓," and "−," he simply rereads his stacks, validating his grouping. He switches a few poems here and there—Suzy's poem (one of the first he read) doesn't seem as strong as the rest of the poems in the "+" pile, so he moves it to the "✓" pile. Isaac's poem, on the other hand, seems stronger on a second reading than he first thought. He moves it from the "✓" pile to the "+" pile. Once this second reading is complete, he places the grades on the poems, according to stack. He then makes a rapid survey of each stack, making sure he still agrees with his grades.

Some Advantages of Cluster Grading

a. It compares writers to their immediate peers, to students who have had the same instruction as well as the same assignment.

b. Once the evaluator is familiar with this system, it is a relatively fast method.

Some Disadvantages of Cluster Grading

a. It provides only a grade to a student. There is no systematic feedback provided on what the student has done well or what he or she needs to keep working on.

b. It can create rivalry among student writers in a class.

c. It depends on the intuitional evaluation of a single grader.

Anchor Evaluation

Anchor evaluation is an approach that is used for large-scale writing assessments. While an individual teacher would not use anchor evaluation, grade-level teams might use it in a particular district. In this approach evaluators read representative responses to a prompt and sort the responses into groups as in cluster evaluation. In a norming (scoring) session, they discuss their choices with each other to arrive at a common understanding of what a very successful response looks like, what an unsuccessful response looks like, and what average responses look like. (Most often anchor holistic scoring works with a 4-point scale with 4 being high and 1 being low.)

The group then chooses anchor papers (sometimes called benchmark papers) to keep individual scores from drifting from the norms. Once the evaluation process begins, each student paper is read by two evaluators and given two independent scores. If the two scores agree, the paper is scored as a pure number (a 4, 3, 2, or 1). If the two scores do not agree, but are within 1 point of each other, the paper is scored as a half-point score (3.5, 2.5, 1.5). If the two scores are more than a single point apart, the paper is read by a third evaluator before it is scored. The poems in Figure 4.15 illustrate anchor evaluation. The writing prompt asked third-graders in the state of Arizona to write a 6-line poem about a toy that used descriptive words and told how they felt about their toy (Arizona Student Assessment Program, 1995). The explanations that follow each anchor describe the common scores and rationale arrived at in the norming sessions.

The poem in Figure 4.16 was written to the same assignment that the anchors were written to. This poem, "Fuzzy Bear," is more like the "4-point" anchor. The relationship between the writer and the toy is well described. The setting in which the toy is kept is also well described. The emotional attachment is well established. Furthermore, the poem contains physical description of the toy as well as some rhyme. "Fuzzy Bear," then, would be scored "4."

Some Advantages of Anchor Evaluation

a. More than one person is involved in determining what quality of writing constitutes a particular level of work or grade.

b. Once the evaluator is familiar with the anchors, this is probably the fastest way to determine a grade.

Some Disadvantages of Anchor Evaluation

a. It is isolated from instruction and does not allow for different emphases in grading over time.

b. It provides only a grade to a student. There is no systematic feedback provided on what the student has done well or what he or she needs to keep working on.

FIGURE 4.15.   Anchors

TITLE: *My Cat*

My cat looks pretty and she's got a laddybug.
On her pawse She looks so cute every night,
I turn on my light and look at her.
I take care of her very much.
I let nobody to nuch her or drop her.
I leav it on my night stun by the light.
And it is important to me because my,
Mom guve it to me and I take care of it
very much and good.

SCORE POINT: 4   Though this paper is not strong on physical
description, the relationship between writer and toy is well
described, as well as the setting in which the toy is kept.   The
emotional attachment between writer and toy is well established.

TITLE: My bike

My Bike is red and black
I ride it quite alot
The seat on it is cushined
And Sometimes it is hot
And when I ride it I feel great
And when I ride some ware I'm never late

SCORE POINT: 3   Though short, this poem does describe the toy
through various sense images, and the writer is able to
successfully incorporate both rhyme and meter.   The creativity of
this paper raises it above the 2/3 line.

FIGURE 4.15.   Anchors (continued)

TITLE: _My Car_

A car is yellow
It tastes like sour grapes.
It smells like a car,
It looks like a flash of lighting
It feels like metal
It makes me to drive it.

SCORE POINT: 2   This typical 2 is merely a list of sensory
impressions, some inappropriate ("tastes like sour grapes") plus
a reaction to the toy, per the checklist.   It has no creativity
and does nothing to enliven the object it describes.

SCORE POINT:1   This is not a poem describing a toy, but a
narrative about the adventures of "Sir Hiss;" clearly the writer
has misunderstood the requirements of the assigned task.

TITLE: _Sir had to walk 3,560 milse_

Sir Hiss, Missed The train,
He was slithering to slow   so   he had
to Slither to New York, He lived in
Washington   It was 3,560 miles, but
he was tired on the 500th mile
So, He had to stop in hotsprings
North Dokota, He had 460 milesto
go, He started out early in the
morning   very   early, He had
to, Jump offa cliff 300feet high
and he was there and he
met his freinds. THE END

FIGURE 4.16.   Sample Poem

TITLE: Fuzzy Bear

Cute and cutley,
And very soft!
I love her,
She is my own.
She is very furry,
But I still love her.
She stays on my bed,
And waits tell I get home.
She came from Santa,
At the north pole
Smells like a baby,
Day and night,
Very soundless,
And she sleeps with me at night.

Impressionistic Grading

Impressionistic grading is sometimes referred to as holistic grading, but it is really the "subjective" grading most of us objected to when we were students. All grading is subjective (that is, based on the evaluator's value system), but impressionistic grading has the added drawback that nowhere are the values made explicit, even by pointing to writing that illustrates the values being sought. Impressionistic grading is therefore less defensible and less useful as a method of communication. As a quick method of categorizing papers it is probably reliable—if the teacher has had lots of experience grading and if he or she does not have any clues as to the identity of the writer. But even if the teacher is relatively inexperienced, impressionistic evaluation can be a useful tool in the interim stages of writing. For example, when Anna comes to Ms. Lehmann's desk with a first draft and asks "How's my story?"—she reads it through rapidly and answers on her impressions—"I really like the excitement when you found your puppy, but I want to know more about what he looks like."

Some Advantages of Impressionistic Grading
a. It is very fast.
b. Since it is traditional, it is often accepted by parents.

Some Disadvantages of Impressionistic Grading
a. It is personally based, subject to the enthusiasms and irritations of the moment.
b. It can be attacked as "subjective."

Chapter Summary

Grading approaches can be classified along a continuum with analytic approaches at one end and holistic approaches at the other. Analytic approaches (criterion-referenced evaluation and assignment-generated evaluation) are based on the assumption that a piece of writing is equal to the sum of its parts. They, therefore, attempt to identify and list the parts of the writing being targeted for instruction. Student work is graded by reference to the list.

Primary-trait scoring and questions for grading fall somewhere on the middle of the continuum, between analytic and holistic approaches. They examine a piece of writing as a whole, but they do so against a list of a small number of traits and a sample paper.

Holistic approaches look at a piece of writing as a whole. They ask the question, "How does this piece of writing work?" They do not examine each puzzle piece separately. So, for example, mechanics are not noticed unless they call attention to themselves—if there are so many errors that the piece is unintelligible or noticeably flawed. (The same is true for context, structure, and content.) There are two common holistic approaches: anchor evaluation and cluster grading.

EXERCISES

For Analytic Approaches

1. From a school curriculum guide or from your state's guidelines, make a criterion-referenced rubric for poetry written by intermediate writers (grades 4–6).

2. Using the same tools as in Exercise 1, make a criterion-referenced rubric for another kind of writing at a primary level.

3. Choose a piece of writing from the Appendix. First, design an assignment that the writing might be responding to. Next, using your school or state guidelines (or the guidelines provided in Chapter 3), design an assignment-generated rubric. Grade the paper accordingly.

For Holistic Approaches

4. Using the anchors reproduced in the text (Arizona's Instrument to Measure Standards, 1999), score the samples in Figures 4.17–4.18.

5. As a group, locate one complete set of papers from a classroom. Take turns grading the set using a "+," "✓," "–" system of cluster grading. Compare the final grades. On how many papers did you agree? Discuss the papers on which you disagreed.

6. Using the same set of papers in Exercise 5, as a group choose an anchor for the "+," "✓," "–" groups. (This exercise is only a simulation, anchors would never be chosen from one set of papers!)

For Blended Approaches

7. From the criterion-referenced rubric you created in Exercise 2, make a primary-trait rubric to use early in the year and a second one to use late in the year.

FIGURE 4.17.

STUDENT WRITING SAMPLE 4
Title: "My Friend"

Write the final copy of your paper here.

My Friend

My Friend is Nicece to me
and I am Nicece to him
and his name is jereme
jereme is Nicece to me
and I am Nicece to
him and he is Nicece
to me and I lick him.

FIGURE 4.18.

STUDENT WRITING SAMPLE 2
Title: "My Kitten"

Write the final copy of your paper here.

My Kitten

I own a kitten. She is black and white. She some times curles up in my lap and falls a sleep. some times when shes a sleep and I'm petting her she has a bad dream. She stats squrming.and squrming. She wakes up and runs under my bed. She some times acts weird but she is usully very camb. When I pet her she purrs very very loud. She is usully nice but some times she bites. and starts kicking me. She can get very skaird I usully sit by her in front of the heter. She atacs my dog. its very funny! I like her very much!

8. Find a paper in the Appendix that is appropriate to the rubrics you created in Exercise 7. Using your rubrics, grade it twice. How do the grades compare?

9. Choose a second paper from the Appendix. Design (or choose) a set of questions for grading that is appropriate to the topic. Evaluate the paper using your questions. Trade papers with someone else in your group. Using his or her questions, grade his or her paper. Have him or her grade yours. Compare your grades.

References

Arizona's Instrument to Measure Standards, *3rd Grade Student Guide to AIMS*. Phoenix, AZ: Arizona Department of Education, 1999.

Arizona Student Assessment Program. Riverside, CA: Riverside Publishing Company, 1995.

Bratcher, Suzanne. *The Learning-to-Write Process in Elementary Classrooms*. Mahwah, NJ: Lawrence Erlbaum Associates, Inc. 1997, pp. 162–174.

Spandel, Vicki. *Creating Writers*, 3rd edition. New York: Addison-Wesley/Longman, 2000.

CHAPTER 5

Response Strategies

Response strategies are techniques that teachers use to communicate the grades they have arrived at by using one of the approaches in Chapter 4. There is no hard-and-fast pairing of particular response strategies with particular grading approaches: a student conference may be centered around a primary-trait assessment of the piece of writing, an assignment-generated rubric, or a holistic anchor paper, for example. Three common ways of responding to student writing are with oral responses, with written responses, and with grades without comments. While these ways of responding are very different in how they communicate, all of them can be useful at one time or another.

Oral Responses

Writing Conferences

Using this response method, teachers sit down with students one-on-one and orally discuss the evaluation. Usually a rubric, an anchor paper from outside the class, or a checklist forms the basis for the discussion. A few guidelines will get you started on student conferences:

Let the student talk first.
Ask leading questions:

Which part of this piece are you happiest with? Why?

Which parts don't sound right? Can you explain that part to me in another way?

What things gave you trouble in this piece of writing?

How can I help you?

When you talk . . .
Keep it positive—"I like this part a lot." And be concrete—"I like the name you chose for the dog in your story."

Make suggestions, not criticisms. Suggestions focus on the positive—what can be done better—and they are just suggestions (that is, your point of view); they are not demands or orders. Suggestions leave the ownership of the next action with the writer, not with the teacher. Criticisms focus on what's wrong without giving any feedback about how the "mistake" can be corrected. When discussing a weak point in the writing, it is always a good idea to point to a place where the writer has done a good job. So, for example, a teacher might say, "I think your story would be more interesting if you described the trail more. Remember your last story—the one about the first time you made brownies? In that story I knew that your kitchen had coffeepots on the wallpaper. Can you tell me things like that about the trail so I can see it in my head like I could see the kitchen in my head?" This kind of suggestion is concrete—and it draws on something the writer has done well before.

Talk about the piece of writing, not about the writer. Say "Your story does a good job when it . . ." or "Your story would be stronger if it . . ." not "You did a good job," or "You need to improve . . ."

Stick to the things you're teaching at the moment (evaluating on) unless the student brings up something else.

Keep it short. Make suggestions; don't rewrite the student's work orally.

If the conference is being used to put a grade on a piece . . .

First, ask the student what grade he or she would give the piece, and why. Next, state what grade you think the piece should have and why. Finally, negotiate between your two positions if there is a difference.

Let's look at an example. In this situation Ms. O'Neil has asked her intermediate-level students to write a descriptive piece about an animal they like. Her instruction has focused on descriptive language and punctuation. She is using a primary-trait approach to evaluate the writing on those two items. Crystal brings the piece in Figure 5.1 to her conference with Ms. O'Neil. The conference goes like this:

Ms. O'Neil (M):   Hi, Crystal. Are you ready to evaluate your descriptive piece?

Crystal (C):   It's a poem.

M: O.K. Let's take a look at it. Tell me what you wrote about.

C: Tigers.

M: Great. You like cats, don't you?

C: [Nods.]

M: O.K. This time we're working on descriptions and punctuation, right? Tell me what you think works well in your poem.

C: I like my descriptions. I think I told a lot about the tiger.

M: [Reads.] Yes. I agree. I especially like this description of the tiger being so quiet. What else?

C: My handwriting is smaller. I got more on the page.

M: That's right. Good. You've been working on your handwriting haven't you?

C: Yes. It doesn't look so babyish now.

M: Good. Anything you're not happy with about this poem?

C: I'm worried about punctuation. I think I wrote some run-on sentences.

M: What is a run-on sentence?

C: It's just I keep going and going. There should be a period, but I don't put it.

M: How do you find one?

C: I have to read back through it and when I run out of breath, I say, "Should there be a period? Yeah." I can't keep going. Because usually I just put a comma right after the subject. Like 'The beach was pretty, the seagulls flew,' no period between those, so I have to put one.

M: O.K. That's good. So show me a run-on sentence in your poem. I see a couple. Can you find them?

C: Maybe a period after "quiet."

M: Right. Do you see the next one?

C: After "food."

M: Good! There are two more. See if you can find them.

C: "The tiger runs to catch its food."

M: Did you learn about semicolons last year?

C: Yes. A comma with a dot over it.

M: Do you know what a semicolon means?

C: There's either a comma there or a period there or something.

M: [Nods.] It means a period ought to go here—that's what the dot is—but I want a comma to go here—that's what the comma is. And so it's strong enough to stand in the place of a period, but it still keeps it one sentence like a comma would. Like the first—a semicolon would be re-

FIGURE 5.1. Crystal's Poem

The Tiger

The Tiger is so quiet, its like a tree swaying in the wind

The tiger stalks its food, he is as quiet as a mouse.

The tiger sees the long tall grass sway as the creature walks through it

the tiger knows its prey is there

The tiger runs to catch its food, he's as fast as a race car.

The tiger pounces on its prey, its prey was a mouse.

ally good between "the tiger is so quiet" and "it's like a tree swaying in the wind." Can you tell me why?

C: Because it's all the same subject.

M: Exactly. The tiger is quiet and the tiger is like a tree.

C: Yeah.

M: Now tell me about the next one.

C: Well, "quiet as a mouse" tells how he stalks his food.

M: Exactly. And what about the last one. Would you put a period or a semicolon?

C: Well, I'd put a period.

M: I would too. How come?

C: Because the tiger pounces is one idea and the prey was a mouse is another idea.

M: Right. The tiger is the worker in this sentence. The mouse is the worker in the other one, so a period separates them into two sentences. That's good. Why don't you take your poem and fix all the run-ons?

C: O.K.

M: How do you think you'll feel about this poem once you're done with it?

C: I think it's pretty good. Maybe I'll put it in my portfolio.

M: Good idea.

Sometimes teachers use group conferences. If she had read the writing ahead of time and realized that several students were ready to learn about semicolons, Ms. O'Neil might have chosen to group three or four writers together for this conference rather than dealing only with Crystal. In situations where grades would be determined by the conference, however, group conferences are not a good idea.

If the conference stalls . . .

Occasionally writing conferences don't work as we imagine they're going to or even as they have in the past. If we take a few minutes to analyze our interactions in a particular conference, we can often identify specific problems. Sometimes problems stem from our misunderstanding what the child is trying to do and inadvertently making suggestions that make the writing more ours than the child's. Other times, problems arise because children aren't far enough along in their writing to be ready to talk about their work. The reverse situation can stall conferences just as easily: if children are finished with a particular piece and have no unresolved issues, there may not be very much to say in a conference. When a writing conference seems to be stalling, then, the best remedy is to return the focus of the conference to the child and listen carefully. As Lois Bridges reminds us in *Writing as a Way of Knowing*, we should always listen first as a caring, compassionate human being and second as a writing teacher (p. 77). (For a research-based look at why writing conferences sometimes don't work and recommendations for getting them back on track, see Jodi Nickel's article, "When Writing Conferences Don't Work," in the November 2001 issue of *Language Arts*.)

Some Advantages of Writing Conferences

a. Students have a chance to explain what they did and give input into the evaluation.

b. Students get immediate explanations of the evaluation; these explanations offer on-the-spot teaching opportunities.

c. The teacher receives immediate feedback regarding his or her assessment of the student's writing; negotiation is possible.

Some Disadvantages of Writing Conferences

a. Conferences are time-consuming.

b. Negative confrontations sometimes occur. (Students can become emotional.)

Tape-recorded Responses

Tape-recorded responses are one-way "conferences" with students; teachers who use this method simply speak their responses into a tape recorder and provide an opportunity (and the equipment) for students to listen to the tape-recorded message. The guidelines are the same as for two-way conferences: be positive, be concrete, offer suggestions rather than criticisms, talk about the piece of writing rather than the writer, keep it short, and stick to what is being evaluated.

Some Advantages of Tape-recorded Responses

a. Students get an explanation of the grade with some revision tips.

b. Tape-recordings do not take as much time as face-to-face conferences.

Some Disadvantages of Tape-recorded Responses

a. They require a tape recorder, tapes, and a listening station.

b. The teacher does not get feedback from the student.

Now let's look at a scenario for using oral responses. Ms. Ratliff teaches sixth grade. For the most part, her students are enthusiastic writers. In the spring she teaches a unit on state history. She requires all of them to do a piece of writing, but she allows them to make choices about what kinds of things they want to write. Some of her students are working on research reports; some are writing tall tales; a few are writing letters to state legislators. The grading approach Ms. Ratliff is using is an analytic approach, assignment-generated rubrics (she has designed a rubric for the research report, another for a tall tale, a third for a letter). She decides to have conferences to grade the writing because the pieces are so highly individualized.

She schedules ten minutes for each conference. The first student she sees, Maureen, has written a research report about the wildflowers of the state. Ms. Ratliff gets out the research report rubric (which Ms. Ratliff had given to Maureen when she chose her topic). She asks Maureen to tell her about her report by referring to the rubric. Maureen points out the strong points and the things that gave her trouble. Ms. Ratliff agrees with Maureen's analysis of her report. She makes a few suggestions for revision and they agree on a grade of

"B." Ms. Ratliff suggests that Maureen revise her report according to their discussion and the rubric if she would like to have an "A."

Written Responses

Using the Computer

Teachers who work in a computer lab often compose written responses to their students at the end of the computer file containing the piece of writing being evaluated. Other teachers who have computers at home compose letters to students on their own word processors and print them out for distribution. The guidelines for these letters are similar to the guidelines for writing conferences and tape-recorded responses.

Handwritten Notes

Handwritten notes usually appear in three forms: Post-it notes positioned throughout the piece of writing, a code system of editor's marks throughout the piece, and comments at the end. Post-it notes have the advantage of leaving the writer's work intact. They can literally be removed and followed or ignored. The student writer retains ownership of the writing. Systems of editor's marks throughout the paper, while common in practice, rob students of ownership, are often confusing, and tend to focus on the negative. Comments at the end often get overlooked. Written notes should also follow the guidelines for writing conferences.

Grading Sheets

A grading sheet is usually a teacher-made form (often simply a copy of a rubric) designed to provide standardized responses to an entire class of writers. Grading sheets have the advantage of superimposing an appearance of standardization on grading. This is also their disadvantage.

Some Advantages of Written Responses
a. They provide a permanent record of teacher response.
b. They can be brief or lengthy, depending on need.
c. They can be made without the student being physically present.

Some Disadvantages of Written Responses
a. Traditionally they have focused on the negative.
b. They are often ignored or overlooked by students.

Now let's look at a scenario for using written responses for grading. Remember Mr. Martinez and his poems from cluster grading? Because he is pressed for class time (achievement testing is underway), he decides to respond to his fourth graders in writing. For example, he writes Tina a note on his home computer commenting on what he likes about her poem—the imagery. (Tina's poem was in the "✔" group.) He suggests that she read several poems by class-mates (from the "+" group) if she wants to revise her poem.

A Word of Caution

Some teachers believe that written comments on student work shifts own-ership of the writing from the student to the teacher. While I believe that a shift in ownership can happen with any response style, we most often write com-ments to students when they are not present, thereby increasing the possibility of losing sight of individual students' purposes. In their book *Exploring and Teaching the English Language Arts*, Stephen Tchudi and Diana Mitchell recom-mend varying response strategies rather than depending too heavily on written comments (pp. 284–285). I concur.

Grades without Comments

Grades without comments communicate very little to students. However, in situations where students will not have their papers returned or where they will not revise, grades without comments get the job done very quickly. At other times during the year, however, they can be disappointing to students who have worked hard on their writing. Sometimes teachers choose to provide voluntary opportunities for students who would like in-depth responses to ac-company their grades. These students sign up for conferences to discuss their grades, but students who are happy with simply a grade are accommodated as well. The disadvantage to this approach is that often only a few students ap-proach the teacher for comments.

Here is a possible scenario. Mr. Foster teaches third grade. In his school, students must write an end-of-the-year writing sample to pass along to their next year's teacher. Because the students do not get their papers back and they have no opportunity to revise, Mr. Foster simply puts grades on the papers (with no response) and includes them in the last nine weeks' writing grade.

Chapter Summary

Teacher responses can be delivered orally by face-to-face conferences or by tape-recorded messages. They can also be delivered in written form by com-puter, Post-it notes, a system of editor's marks, or comments at the end of the piece. Using any of these strategies, teacher responses should be positive and concrete, should focus on the piece of writing rather than on the writer, and should offer suggestions rather than criticisms.

EXERCISES

1. Think back to when you were an elementary school student. What method(s) did your teachers use to respond to your writing? List them. How did you feel about the teachers' responses to your writing? How much did you learn from your teachers' responses.

2. Think about the writing you do now. What kind of response is the most helpful to you? What kind is the least helpful?

3. Write brief anecdotes of the most helpful and least helpful responses you remember getting from a teacher about your writing. Share them with your group.

4. Imagine a scenario in which you, as a teacher, might use in a positive manner each of the response strategies described in this chapter. Imagine a scenario for other response strategies with which you are familiar. Discuss these scenarios with your group.

References

Bridges, Lois. *Writing as a Way of Knowing*. York, Maine: Stenhouse Publishers, 1997.

Nickel, Jodi. "When Writing Conferences Don't Work: Students' Retreat from Teacher Agenda." *Language Arts* 79, 2 (November 2001): 136–147.

Tchudi, Steven and Diana Mitchell. *Exploring and Teaching the English Language Arts*, 4th edition. New York: Longman, 1999.

CHAPTER 6

Management Systems

Management systems are options that teachers have for arriving at cumulative grades—grades for a nine-week grading period or for a year. This chapter discusses four management systems: traditional grade averaging and three less-traditional methods—checklists, contracts, and portfolios. Management systems are not grading approaches, nor are they response strategies, so both a grading approach and a response strategy will have to be superimposed upon a management system. For example, grades arrived at by some holistic measure can still be averaged in a traditional way or they can be grouped into a portfolio. They can be reported to students in conferences, on tapes, in notes, and so forth. Some grading approaches work better with some management systems than others, and some response strategies seem to "fit" better, but there are no hard-and-fast rules for matching a management system with grading approaches and response strategies—always there are choices, options. The context of the individual classroom is what drives the decisions. (This issue is discussed in depth in Part III.)

Grade Averaging

This traditional system assigns a mathematical value to a particular grade and computes an average mathematical score. The mathematical value is then reconverted to the appropriate grade. The process is often referred to as a common value system. Grade averaging works well with approaches that yield numerical grades to begin with. Problems arise, however, when a grading approach yields something other than a number (a letter or a ✓, for example).

Common Value Systems

Common Value System #1

E (excellent) = above 85%

S (satisfactory) = between 85% and 70%

I (improving) = between 70% and 60%

N (needs to improve) = below 60%

For example, Mr. Johnson has decided on the following system: E = 95; E– = 87; S+ = 82; S = 78; S– = 72; I+ = 68; I = 65; I– = 62. If Teresa, a student in his class, has written four graded pieces with the grades of "E," "E," "S+," and "S–," her nine-week grade might be calculated as follows:

```
 95
 95
 82
+72
───          344 divided by 4 = 86
344
```

Teresa would receive an "E" for the nine weeks.

Common Value System #2

"+" = 80% or better

"✓" = between 80% and 50%

"–" = less than 50%

If, for example, Tony had done five pieces of writing on which he had received three grades of "+" and two grades of "✓," Ms. Brewer might average his grade like this: 90 + 90 + 90 + 70 + 70 = 410. Since 410 divided by 5 is 82, Tony would receive a "+" for the nine weeks.

Common Value System #3

A = 90%

B = 89%–80%

C = 79%–70%

D = 69%–60%

F = 59%–

If Angela had done seven pieces of graded writing in the nine weeks, and had received grades of "C–," "D+," "C+," "B–," "C," "C–," and "C," Mrs. Avery might average her grade like this: 72 + 68 + 78 + 82 + 75 + 72 + 75 = 522. Since 522 divided by 7 is 74.6, Angela would receive a grade of "C" for the nine weeks.

Variations of Grade Averaging

Point systems.   Rather than using a letter grade at all, a teacher may assign points to a piece of writing in the first place. So, for example, a "+" may be assigned a "3," a "✓" may be assigned a "2," and a "–" may be assigned a "1." In this variation, Tony's grade (common value system #2 discussed earlier) would look like this: 3 + 3 + 3 + 2 + 2 = 13. Thirteen divided by 5 = 2.6, so Tony would receive a "+" for the nine weeks.

Grade weighting.   Rather than weighting each assignment equally, a teacher may assign different point values to various pieces of writing. So, for example, the first piece of writing might be worth 50 points, the second two might be worth 75 points, and the last worth 100 points, even though the assignments were of about the same length. This variation assumes growth on the part of students as time goes by. In this variation, Teresa's grade (common value system #1 discussed earlier) might look like this:

```
E  (.95 × 50)   48
E  (.95 × 75)   71
S+ (.82 × 75)   62
S− (.72 × 100)  72
                253
```

Since there are 300 points possible, her nine-week grade would be 253 divided by 300, or 84. She would receive an "S."

In all three of the sample value systems, the teachers will still impose a grading approach. For example, Mr. Johnson grades Teresa's writing holistically against anchor papers provided by his district. Ms. Brewer grades Tony's writing with questions for grading, and Mrs. Avery creates rubrics for each individual assignment. Likewise, they all use different response strategies. Mr. Johnson tapes his responses to Angela, Ms. Brewer gives Tony a grading sheet based on the questions, and Mrs. Avery attaches Post-it-note comments throughout Andrea's writing.

Some Advantages of Grade Averaging

a. This is a traditional method of arriving at grades, used in most subject areas. It is familiar.

b. Final grades are easy to "defend" using this system. The math involved provides a sense of objectivity to a long-term grade.

Some Disadvantages of Grade Averaging

a. Converting letter grades to numbers and back again is a statistically unsound procedure. Letter grades divide student work into three to five categories. Percentages assume 100 categories. Arbitrarily assigning a percentage to a letter so that the letters can be "added up" leads to relatively meaningless final grades.

b. As the example of Teresa shows, final grades can vary depending on how points are assigned by the teacher.

Cumulative Records

Cumulative records provide a collected history of student achievement. They allow a teacher to track the progress of individual students and see at a glance which parts of the writing puzzle have been mastered and which parts need more work. Final grades can be determined based on cumulative perform-ance rather than on the success of any single piece of writing.

Checklists

Checklists provide teachers with an at-a-glance overview of student prog-ress. Cumulative checklists that catalog all the instructional goals for writing in a given year can track when a particular student meets a particular goal. At any time, then, the teacher can tell at a glance what focus an individual child might need. Figure 6.1 is an example of a cumulative checklist for second-grade writ-ing. This type of checklist is often developed from district curriculum guides or lists of state standards.

Mr. Starner is a second-grade teacher who uses the checklist in Figure 6.1. Andrea is a student in his class. As Andrea turns in her pieces of writing, Mr. Starner records her successes on the checklist. A "✓" in a box lets him know that Andrea has successfully used the item identified. The first two sections of Andrea's checklist are illustrated in Figure 6.2.

At the end of the nine weeks, Mr. Starner knows that Andrea has success-fully completed five out of the six items on these first two sections of the check-list. Her writing still contains content gaps, and she has only recently demon-strated a grasp of purpose in her writing, but she has enjoyed her own writing from the first, and it is filled with details. Mr. Starner examines the rest of the checklist in the same way. To arrive at a grade, however, he must impose a grading approach on his management system. Because a checklist is analytic in nature he will probably choose an analytic approach. This particular checklist is based on an exhaustive list of criteria, so Mr. Starner will probably choose a criterion-referenced approach and simply assign points to each category on his checklist and add up Andrea's grade.

But checklists can be used with other approaches as well. A primary-trait checklist can be created, for example. Or the checklists from a whole class may be graded using a cluster holistic method (one stack of the best checklists, a second of the weakest, a third of those in between, etc.). Or a grade-level com-mittee might choose anchor checklists for various grades, and teachers might compare individual student checklists with the anchor profile. Checklists can also be designed to be used by children. For primary children, these checklists often use pictures as well as words. Figure 6.3 shows one way the sample checklist in Figure 6.2 could be designed for Andrea to use herself. For a look at some other examples of checklists designed to be used by children, see Bird, Goodman, and Goodman, *The Whole Language Catalog.*

Mr. Starner will also need to choose a response strategy. For example, he may schedule a conference with Andrea to discuss her checklist with her and to suggest things she might like to focus on for the next nine weeks, or he may give Andrea her checklist with its grade at the top (grade with no response), or he may write her a note, and so forth.

FIGURE 6.1.   Sample Checklist

Student's Name _____   Beginning Date _____

                                                       Ending Date _____

Writing Assignment   1   2   3   4   5   6

I. CONTEXT CONCEPTS

___ identifies purpose of the writing

___ expresses personal satisfaction with own writing

II. CONTENT CONCEPTS

___ main idea is clear

___ completes ideas

___ eliminates content gaps

___ includes details to support the main idea

III. STRUCTURE CONCEPTS

___ writing contains a beginning, a middle, and an end

___ details are sequenced logically

___ personal experience narrative successfully completed

___ imaginative story successfully completed

___ report based on personal observation successfully completed

___ letter successfully completed

IV. MECHANICS—The final draft illustrates:

___ sentences containing a complete thought

___ transitions and conjunctions to connect ideas

___ conventional word endings

___ personal pronouns used correctly

___ contractions used correctly

___ singular possessives used correctly

___ verb tenses used correctly

___ subject–verb agreement

___ conventional spelling

___ proper punctuation

___ correct use of capital letters

FIGURE 6.1.   Sample Checklist (continued)

Writing Assignment	1	2	3	4	5	6
V. PROCESS CONCEPTS						
successfully prewrites						
writes a rough draft						
participates in revising						
participates in editing						
writes a final draft						
shares writing with an audience						

Some Advantages of Checklists

a. They provide a cumulative record of particular skills students have mastered.
b. They show clearly which skills a student needs to continue to work on.

Some Disadvantages of Checklists

a. They assume that if a student can master a particular list of skills, his or her writing will be good.
b. They superimpose an assumption that each item on the checklist is of equal value, while in reality understanding the context of a piece of writing may be far more important to its success than having every word spelled correctly.

FIGURE 6.2.   Partial Checklist Filled Out

	Writing Assignment					
	1	2	3	4	5	6
I. CONTEXT CONCEPTS						
identifies purpose of the writing						✓
expresses personal satisfaction with own writing		✓				
II. CONTENT CONCEPTS						
main idea is clear					✓	
completes ideas		✓				
eliminates content gaps						
includes details to support the main idea		✓				

FIGURE 6.3.

I know why I'm writing
__Yes __Sometimes __Not yet

I like my own writing
__Yes __Sometimes __Not yet

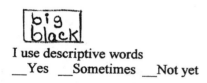

I write what I want to say
__Yes __Sometimes __Not yet

I finish my ideas
__Yes __Sometimes __Not yet

I use descriptive words
__Yes __Sometimes __Not yet

Anecdotal Records

Some teachers keep anecdotal records of observations of students over the course of the year. Teachers who use writing workshop techniques often do formal observations, noting how each student is performing in a specific area. They then collect the notes from the observations in a file. As the year progresses, a picture of how the child is growing in writing skill emerges.

Some Advantages of Anecdotal Records

a. They provide a holistic view of student work.

b. They provide insight into aspects of student work that do not appear in other kinds of records.

Some Disadvantages of Anecdotal Records

a. They are subjective, dependent on the teacher's perception of what a child is thinking or doing at a particular time.

b. They are sometimes incomplete.

Cumulative Writing Folders or District Portfolios

Because they do not result in grades per se, cumulative writing folders are not technically a classroom management system. However, many school districts maintain writing folders that follow elementary students from year to year, and so it seems appropriate to comment on them in this chapter. In this system each teacher places one or more representative pieces of writing from each child in his or her folder at the end of the year. The folders are then made available for the next year's teacher to examine when school starts, often before the children return. Cumulative writing folders are intended to give an overview of each student's development in writing throughout his or her elementary experience. Some districts or states connect cumulative folders with standards and mandate specific samples of writing at specific grade levels: personal experience narrative at second-grade, for example. Sometimes districts require teachers to include checklists or anecdotal records in cumulative writing folders. In recent years these multiyear collections of student writing have sometimes been called portfolios.

Some Advantages of Cumulative Writing Folders

a. They provide an overview of writing development over a long span of time.

b. They provide insight into aspects of student work that do not appear in other kinds of records.

Some Disadvantages of Cumulative Writing Folders

a. Because cumulative folders sometimes have no instructional purpose, teachers may not use them, reducing the folders to just another collection of paper to maintain.

b. If a child has had a difficult year previously, the folder may give an inaccurate picture of the child's writing skill.

Contracts

This management system allows students to choose how much (and sometimes what type of) work they wish to do. Grades are attached to work that is completed at a specified level of acceptability. Individual pieces of writing are evaluated simply by the words "accepted," "needs to be redone," or "not done." While at first glance this management system may appear to be an exception to the grade-approach rule, in reality a grade approach will still be superimposed on a contract. A contract may be analytic or holistic: it may be based on completion of primary-trait criteria, for example, or on successful illustration of different forms of writing ("successful" being judged holistically). In this management system, however, individual grades are not accumulated. The long-term grade is determined by the fulfillment (or lack of fulfillment) of the contract.

A sample will illustrate. The contract in Figure 6.4 might be used by Mr. Adler in an intermediate classroom for a unit on expository writing.

This contract is an example of a primary-trait contract. For "N" the trait is simply completion of the assignments. For "I" the traits are completion, organization, and general surface-level accuracy. For "S" the traits are completion, organization, accuracy, and process participation. For "E" the traits are the same as for "S" but there is one more piece of writing required. If Mr. Adler grades his

FIGURE 6.4. Sample Contract

STUDENT'S NAME _____ Beginning Date _____

Ending Date _____

For a grade of "N" (needs improvement), the student will write

1. directions for completing a process (working a jigsaw puzzle, changing a bicycle tire, giving a home permanent, etc.)
2. an explanation of a point of view (why Christmas is your favorite time of year, why you hate baseball, why gerbils make good pets, etc.)
3. a summary (of a book you've read, of three encyclopedia articles on the same topic, of December's newspaper reports on the drought, etc.)

For a grade of "I" (improving), the student will complete the requirements for "N," but essays will be

a. clearly organized with main idea statements and paragraph topic sentences
b. be largely free of mechanical errors

For a grade of "S" (satisfactory), the student will complete the requirements for "I" and show evidence of the writing process:

a. turn in prewriting and at least two different drafts
b. participate in peer revision and editing groups
c. share the final drafts with an audience

For a grade of "E" (excellent), the student will complete the requirements for "S" as well as write one more essay:

a comparison/contrast essay (how sixth grade is different and how it is the same as fifth grade, how pet dogs are different and how they are the same as pet cats, how the movie is the same as the book *Old Yeller*, etc.)

---

students using this contract, he will still have to choose a response strategy. Will he have conferences? Will he write a letter to each student? Or will he choose not to comment at all?

Some Advantages of Contracts

a. They reduce the decision making (and therefore the pressure) of final grades.
b. Students know exactly what kind of and how much work is required for a particular grade.
c. They allow students to make choices about what grade they wish to work for, providing students who are not particularly interested in writing an opportunity to focus their energy in channels of their own choosing.

Some Disadvantages of Contracts

a. Not all students fall neatly into contract packages. Teachers are left to negotiate grades with those students who fulfill the requirements of a particular grade but do so with marginal quality.

b. Students with low self-images may opt to work for a lower grade than they are actually capable of achieving, simply out of a lack of self-confidence.

Portfolios

The term *portfolio* has come to have almost as many meanings as it has teachers who use this system. In *A Fresh Look at Writing*, Donald Graves (1994) says, "Students usually have two collections: a folder containing all their writing from the beginning of the school year, and a portfolio containing work they have carefully selected from their folder." By contrast, in *The Art of Teaching Writing*, Lucy Calkins (1994) says, "A portfolio should not be confused with a collection of Best Work. It is meant, instead, as a record of the writer's journey." To further confuse matters, some districts call cumulative writing folders "portfolios." Basically, then, the term *portfolio* means whatever it means to the speaker. As teachers, we simply have to listen and ask questions to clarify what the speaker is thinking of when he or she says "portfolio." There is no "right" way to put together a portfolio, but there are different purposes behind portfolios. Figure 6.5 illustrates four common purposes (Ryan, 1997).

When portfolios are used as a management system for grading, students choose pieces of writing to be graded. As students finish assignments and projects, they collect all of their writing in a writing folder. When it is time for writing to be graded, students (and sometimes their parents) look back through their folders and choose the pieces they consider to be their best writing. Figure 6.6 illustrates this (Ryan, 1997).

Once students have chosen their best work, they explain to the teacher why they have chosen particular pieces and how they view their progress with

FIGURE 6.5.

✍ Growth over time

Samples of specific tasks collected early in the school year to compare with samples of similar tasks performed at the end of the year. Both student and teacher participate in the selection process.

✍ Showcase or Treasury

"Best" pieces, final drafts, and finished projects are largely selected by the student to show their best efforts and most treasured pieces.

✍ Show the learning process

Prewriting, drafts with evidence of revision and editing, and final drafts are saved for one or more genres of writing. In math - calculations, drawings, and reflections on problem solving may be included. Teachers generally set the criteria and students make the selections.

✍ Evaluation/competence

District assessment plans may dictate the types of student samples required. Teachers select pieces which show a student's highest level of competence on the required tasks.

FIGURE 6.6.

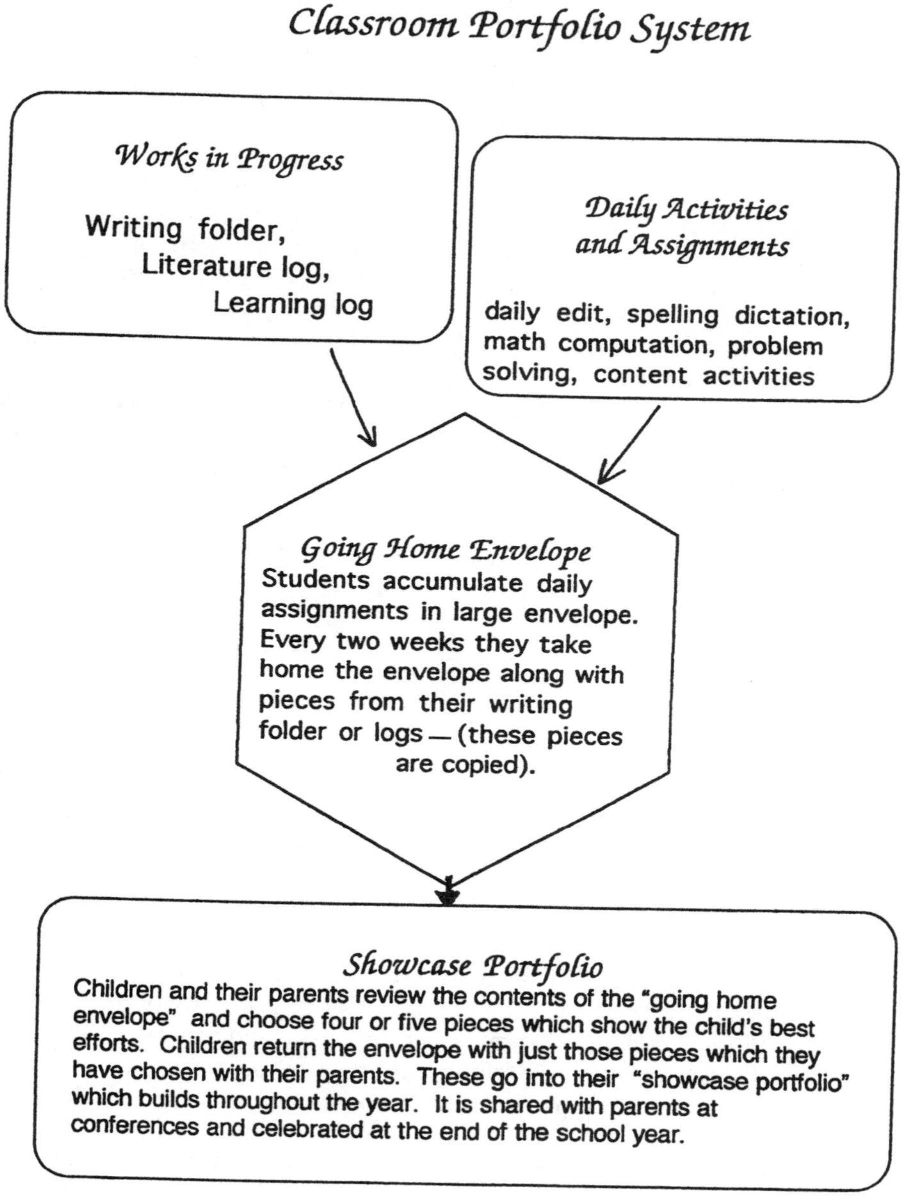

Classroom Portfolio System

Works in Progress

Writing folder,
Literature log,
Learning log

Daily Activities and Assignments

daily edit, spelling dictation, math computation, problem solving, content activities

Going Home Envelope
Students accumulate daily assignments in large envelope. Every two weeks they take home the envelope along with pieces from their writing folder or logs — (these pieces are copied).

Showcase Portfolio
Children and their parents review the contents of the "going home envelope" and choose four or five pieces which show the child's best efforts. Children return the envelope with just those pieces which they have chosen with their parents. These go into their "showcase portfolio" which builds throughout the year. It is shared with parents at conferences and celebrated at the end of the school year.

writing. Figure 6.7 shows a prompt one third-grade teacher developed for this purpose (Ryan, 1997). The teacher then evaluates the portfolios in light of students' self-evaluation. He or she may talk with other teachers about trends in students' portfolios, and teachers may trade portfolios to establish school-wide grading norms. Once the teacher has arrived at grades, he or she conferences with students and their parents about the portfolio.

Sometimes teachers use portfolios like a classroom cumulative writing folder, grading each piece as it is completed and then giving a separate portfolio grade for the student's self-evaluation and overall presentation. Because portfolios are a management system, teachers must still choose a grading approach (analytic, primary-trait, holistic, etc.).

Portfolios that are graded with reference to a list of skills demonstrated might be thought of as "criterion-referenced portfolios." Portfolios that are graded with reference to anchors or with reference to the other portfolios developed in the classroom might be thought of as "holistic portfolios." It is possible to create a set of questions to use as a grading approach with portfolios, or a short list of primary-traits. In fact, portfolios can be developed using any of the grading approaches.

An example will illustrate. Mrs. Ford has organized her fifth-graders' writing into a portfolio system. Her curriculum guide requires her to teach the following types of writing over the course of the year:

personal narrative
friendly letter
business letter
description
directions
explanation
summary
comparison and contrast
persuasive writing
the short story
poetry

She divides these types of writing into four units: self-expressive writing (personal narrative and friendly letter); expository writing (business letter, directions, explanation, summary, comparison and contrast); persuasive writing; and literary writing (description, short story, and poetry). Within each unit she makes three or four writing assignments, all of which go into the students' writing folders. At the end of each unit, she instructs her students to select the one assignment they consider shows their best writing from that unit. These pieces are then revised and edited with peer help and placed in their portfolios. At the end of the year, each student has a portfolio containing four pieces of excellent writing—one for each unit. If Mrs. Ford wishes to grade the pieces of writing as the year goes along, she must determine whether she will use an analytic or a holistic approach. If she wishes to look at the portfolios as entities, she must

FIGURE 6.7.

Portfolio Picks
from my writing folder

Name _____

*Date*_____

I consider these my best pieces of writing:

I like them because . . .

Some of the things I have learned about writing are . . .

I think I need to work on . . .

spelling	capital letters
periods and question marks	expressing my ideas better
working with others	handwriting

In the future I would like to write about . . .

decide whether she wishes to look at them holistically (clusters of portfolios or anchor portfolios), or if she wishes to look at them analytically (primary traits of "E" portfolios, for example, or a list of criteria that "A" portfolios must meet).

As with the other management systems, Mrs. Ford will choose a response strategy. Conferences seem a natural companion for portfolios, but certain factors in the instructional context may make other choices appropriate as well.

Some Advantages of Portfolios

a. They can dramatically decrease the pressure of grades on students, thus providing an environment conducive to risk-taking and real learning.
b. They can allow students to participate in the grading process by choosing which pieces they wish to have graded.
c. They can decrease the pressure of grades on the teacher as well because grading occurs much less frequently.
d. They can make an excellent focus for both student and parent conferences.
e. They can make an excellent focus for school and district discussions of writing instruction.

Some Disadvantages of Portfolios

a. Some students are uneasy receiving grades only periodically. They continually ask for reassurance—"How am I doing, teacher?"
b. The paper load may increase at grading time. The teacher may be faced with evaluating four or five papers per student at one time rather than seeing one paper at a time over a term.

Chapter Summary

Management systems provide options for teachers in determining long-range grades. While grade averaging is the traditional management system, checklists, contracts, and portfolios offer alternative methods of arriving at nine-week or year-end grades. Each management system will be accompanied by a grading approach—analytic or holistic—and a response strategy—oral, written, or no comment.

EXERCISES

1. Create a holistic contract.
2. Create a rubric for grading a primary portfolio.
3. Which of the management systems described in this chapter have you experienced as a student? As a teacher? Add to the lists of advantages and disadvantages for those systems.

4. Which of these management systems is new to you? Describe a situation in which you think that system might be useful.

5. What local political ramifications of these management systems might you have to cope with? (How are they viewed by power groups in your school district?)

References   Bird, Lois Bridges, Kenneth S. Goodman, and Yetta M. Goodman. *The Whole Language Catalog: Forms for Authentic Assessment.* SRA: McMillan/McGraw-Hill, 1994.

Calkins, Lucy McCormick. *The Art of Teaching Writing,* new edition. Portsmouth, NH: Heinemann, 1994.

Graves, Donald. *A Fresh Look at Writing.* Portsmouth, NH: Heinemann, 1994.

Ryan, Linda. *Strengthening Your Third-Grade Students' Skills Achievement.* Bellevue, WA: Bureau of Education and Research, 1997.

CHAPTER 7

Evaluation Styles

Evaluation styles are options teachers have for centering the power of the decisions. The power for the decisions may reside with the teacher (the traditional approach); it may reside with the student (self-evaluation) or with peers (student-centered); it may reside with all three (teacher/student partnerships); or it may reside outside the classroom (school or district guidelines).

Teacher-centered Evaluation

Teacher-centered grading is the traditional evaluation style. In this style, teachers set grading standards, evaluate student work against those standards, and assign grades. Teacher-centered evaluation can occur not only with traditional grading techniques such as analytic grading, comments at the end of a paper, and grade averaging, but also with less traditional approaches, responses, and management systems.

For example, following a teacher-centered evaluation style, using an assignment-generated criteria approach, Mr. Thomas would design a rubric for a personal narrative assignment and share that rubric with his students, explaining to them what he thinks makes a strong piece of personal writing. The students would write their papers and turn them in to him; Mr. Thomas would compare each paper to his rubric and assign a grade. He might tape-record his responses to his students and provide a listening station for them. He might average their grades at the end of the nine weeks, or he might collect their best work in a portfolio to send home to parents.

Some Advantages of Teacher-centered Evaluation
a. As the most knowledgeable person in the class, the teacher retains control of the evaluation criteria (and thus the instructional goals).
b. Because this is the traditional evaluation style, most parents and students are comfortable with it.

Some Disadvantages of Teacher-centered Evaluation

a. Classrooms often become autocratic when this evaluation style is used exclusively.

b. Most students, especially as they get older, are not as concerned about the teacher's criteria for evaluation as they are about their peers'.

Self-evaluation

Self-evaluation of work is implicit in the choices for portfolios, but self-evaluation can be used with other grading techniques as well. In self-evaluation the student writer makes evaluation decisions. The student writer may choose the form of the piece of writing, research it, and draw up a rubric against which he or she plans to evaluate the final draft. Or the student writer may compare the piece of writing against a checklist of criteria. The student writer may state an appropriate grade for the portfolio and write a letter defending that decision.

Let's look at an example. Miss Benjamin teaches second grade. Above all she wants her students to become independent workers. She decides to have her students use a self-evaluation style. She chooses a primary-trait grading approach, a written response strategy, and a checklist management system.

First, Miss Benjamin teaches personal writing to her students. She creates a checklist of the different types of personal writing her students must complete before the end of the unit. She reads them letters and stories written in the first person; she has them tell personal stories to small groups; and she shares pieces of her own personal writing with the class. Next, she asks each of her students to choose one type of writing from the checklist. Once they have chosen, they each make a list of the three things they like best in that type of writing. They then write a piece using that form.

After her students have completed the final drafts of their personal pieces, Miss Benjamin asks them to compare their own writing against their lists of things they liked. She asks them to write her a letter telling her how they think their own writing compared to their lists and check the piece off on the checklist.

Self-evaluation occurs whenever student writers set their own goals and compare their work against these goals. It may also play a part in other grading techniques such as writing conferences. For example, students may be asked open-ended questions that call for evaluative decisions: what was hardest about this piece? What did you do better today? Writers' journals may include self-evaluation: after each assignment the student may be asked to write a journal entry answering open-ended, evaluative questions.

Some Advantages of Self-evaluation

a. Students internalize criteria when they generate them.

b. Competition is against the self only.

c. Students take charge of their own progress.

Some Disadvantages of Self-evaluation

a. Students may overlook some important pieces of the writing puzzle, resulting in "practicing their oversights."

b. Students who are not self-starters may be uncomfortable with self-evaluation.

c. Administrators may need to be educated about how this evaluation style works.

d. Parents may need to be educated about the advantages of this evaluation style.

Peer-centered Evaluation

Peer-centered grading depends on the class for criteria, evaluation, and grades. In this style, students cooperatively set the standards for writing assignments; they evaluate one another's work; and they assign grades to each other. For example, in the same class cited in Mr. Thomas's class (in the teacher-centered evaluation discussed earlier), instead of working from Mr. Thomas's definition of good personal writing, the class would discuss the criteria of good personal writing, based on their experiences. They would then create a class rubric and write their papers. Then teams of students (perhaps peer revision groups) would read the papers, compare them to the class-generated rubric, and assign grades to each other.

Some Advantages of Peer-centered Evaluation

a. Students internalize criteria when they generate them.

b. Students learn from each other's work when they evaluate their peers' writing.

Some Disadvantages of Peer-centered Evaluation

a. Students do not possess the training and experience teachers have for setting criteria.

b. Students are sometimes unreasonably hard on each other.

c. Administrators may need to be educated about how this evaluation style works.

d. Parents may need to be educated about the advantages of this evaluation style.

Teacher/Student Partnerships

This evaluation style depends on student input as well as teacher guidance. A teacher may lead a discussion in which the class adds input to grading criteria or creates a rubric or a checklist. In a conference, the teacher may work with an individual student to set personal writing goals for the next assignment. Individual or group contracts might be designed with both teacher and student input. The variation is endless. The common theme is input from both sides of the teacher's desk.

For example, Mr. Thomas might discuss the characteristics of good personal writing with his class. On the board they might together design a rubric that contained some characteristics of good personal writing suggested by the students and some suggested by Mr. Thomas. Together they would negotiate the final form of the evaluation rubric. The students would write their papers, help one another revise according to the rubric, and turn in their papers. At that point Mr. Thomas might evaluate the papers against the class rubric and assign grades; he might have students do self-evaluations based on the rubric; he might have peer groups evaluate each other's papers; or he might do something else in a teacher/student combination.

Some Advantages of Teacher/Student Partnerships

a. Students invest in grades in which they feel they have had input.
b. Students learn to think critically about writing by being involved in the evaluation process.
c. Teachers become sensitive to what their students consider good writing.

Some Disadvantages of Teacher/Student Partnerships

a. Administrators may need to be educated about how this evaluation style works.
b. Parents may need to be educated about the advantages of this evaluation style.

Outside the Classroom

This evaluation style depends on an outside authority to set evaluation criteria and standards. Most often the outside authority is represented by a set of guidelines, a rubric, or an anchor provided by a grade-level committee, a school, or a district. In this style, teachers are expected to conform with standards created by someone else or agreed on by a majority vote. Approaches, response strategies, and management systems may be dictated as well, or they may be left up to the individual teacher's choice.

In this system, new teachers are trained in the agreed-on criteria and expected to follow the guidelines used by everyone else. Sometimes evaluation is conducted by teams of teachers grading the writing of each other's students, rather than being left to the classroom teacher. In this way, then, instruction and evaluation may become divergent, or evaluation criteria may drive instruction.

Some Advantages of Outside Authority

a. Teamwork among writing teachers develops, often leading to frequent interchange about goals of instruction and criteria for particular grades.
b. Students (and parents) who remain in this school soon learn "what is expected."

Some Disadvantages of Outside Authority

a. Guidelines imposed from outside make it virtually impossible for a classroom teacher to match his or her instructional purposes to a particular student audience, unless the teacher chooses to ignore evaluation criteria when designing lessons.

b. Outside authority is often out of step with current practice—either outstripping it in an effort to force change or lagging behind it and not allowing change.

Chapter Summary

Evaluation styles determine where the power for the decision-making in grading resides. If the power resides with the teacher, we call the evaluation style "teacher-centered." If the power resides with the student writer, we call the evaluation style "self-evaluation." If the class makes grading decisions, the style is "peer-centered." A combination of any of these styles results in a "teacher/student partnership." Occasionally the power may reside in an outside authority.

EXERCISES

1. Discuss the power issues of evaluation styles.
2. Where on this continuum have you encountered grades—as a student? As a teacher?

|---------------------------|---------------------------|---------------------------|
| Teacher | Partners | Students |

3. In what kind of evaluation style are you most comfortable as a student? Why?
4. As a teacher? Why?

CHAPTER 8

State Standards and Assessments

Most often, teachers choose from among the evaluation options and design their own systems using a combination of techniques. For example, it is possible to begin with primary-trait grading and gradually add traits until, by the end of the year, the teacher has arrived at a criterion-referenced approach. Or it is possible to use student-generated rubrics from which the teacher grades or teacher-generated rubrics from which the students evaluate each other's work. Or a contract may specify particular inclusions in an end-of-the-year portfolio. A rubric may be created from anchor papers. A group of portfolios may be graded using a "cluster" holistic method (one stack of excellent portfolios, a second stack of weak portfolios, a third stack of in-between portfolios, and so forth). Anchor portfolios can be created at a particular grade level, or a checklist may dictate the entries in a portfolio. The evaluation choices teachers have seem infinite, just as instructional contexts seem infinite. An important exception to instructional and evaluative choices is state-mandated writing standards and assessments.

State Writing Standards

According to H.R. 1-20, section 1111. State Plans, the "No Child Left Behind Act" (2001), all states must articulate academic standards for Language Arts. An important source used by state departments for writing their standards was the *Standards for the English Language Arts* (1996) by the National Council of Teachers of English and the International Reading Association. The following standards taken from this publication are found in many state writing standards documents:

- Students employ a wide range of strategies as they write and use different writing process elements appropriately to communicate with different audiences for a variety of purposes.

- Students apply knowledge of language structure, language conventions (e.g., spelling and punctuation), media techniques, figurative language, and genre to create, critique, and discuss print and non-print texts.
- Students conduct research on issues and interests. . . . They gather, evaluate, and synthesize data from a variety of sources to communicate their discoveries in ways that suit the purpose and audience.
- Students use spoken, written, and visual language to accomplish their own purposes (e.g., for learning, enjoyment, persuasion, and the exchange of information).

State Writing Assessment

Through H.R. 1-450, section 6112 grant money, the United States Congress (2001) has encouraged states to develop assessment instruments that "measure student academic achievement using multiple measures of student academic achievement from multiple sources." The United States Department of Education interprets the "multiple measures" phrase in the resolution to mean multiple item types, such as short answer and extended writing prompts. According to Kelly Powell (2002), former Director of Testing and Accountability for the Arizona Department of Education, "No state with a strictly multiple-choice test was deemed wholly acceptable" (p. 1) by a United States Department of Education peer review panel reviewing state testing systems in 2001. As a result, most states have developed assessments that include a performance-based writing component to measure Language Arts Standards.

Because state writing assessments are designed by state departments of education rather than by individual teachers and because of high-stakes testing that has become standard practice in many states, some teachers may believe that their evaluation choices are limited. They may limit writing instruction to the form of writing they believe will be tested at their grade level and use only their state department's assessment/scoring guide for grading in their classrooms. However, while as classroom teachers we must be informed of our state's academic standards and assessments, we do not have to lose control of either instructional decisions or choices in evaluating students' writing.

Teaching with State Standards and Assessments

In this chapter we explore how we can make state standards a priority in our own classroom contexts yet still use a variety of instructional strategies and discuss how to use a state scoring guide selectively, relative to instructional purposes. As teachers all over the United States have begun to work to balance state standards with classroom context, they have discovered that much of what is required for state standards and assessments is already an integral part of their teaching and grading practice. Applying common concepts and language between classroom practices and state tests can help students perform well without directly "teaching to the test." In an article titled "Teaching True and To the Test in Writing," authors Shelby and Kenneth Wolf (2002) discuss in detail how exemplar teachers in Kentucky and Washington balanced their state assessments with what they believed about writing pedagogy. In the same way, we can balance a variety of evaluation options with the specific options targeted by our state assessments.

The first step in this balancing process is to analyze our state's standards and assessments and ask ourselves how those standards and assessments relate to the instructional context in which we are working: how the purposes of the state assessment compare with or diverge from our instructional purposes, how our students feel about the state assessment, and how the state standards compare with or diverge from our own goals as teachers.

The next step is to compare the state standards and assessments with the grading puzzle as we conceptualize it. The writing process, for example, is a foundational requirement in most lists of state standards and in many state assessments. Asking students to generate their own topics, draft, revise, and edit is the premise on which students develop the ability to complete a variety of writing tasks. Because the writing process is one of the pieces of the grading puzzle, this standard already supports most writing curricula. State standards also ask that students develop proficiency in various forms of writing such as personal experience narrative, creative story, expository report, essay, persuasive pieces, and poetry. Again, because structure is part of the grading puzzle, these standards often coincide with instructional purposes already present in the writing curriculum, although teachers and school districts may need to consider at which grade levels it is most appropriate to introduce, develop, and expect certain levels of proficiency for the various forms of writing. For example, a second grader can be expected to develop the ability to write simple personal experience narratives and expository reports, but not be expected to become proficient with persuasive writing pieces.

Grading with State Scoring Guides

Another consideration for teachers is balancing state standards and assessment evaluation in the classroom with state scoring guides used to measure the state standards. The first step in this process is to determine where on the grading approach continuum the state assessment falls. Most states use a four-point holistic or six-trait analytic rubric for scoring student writing on state assessments. Florida and Kentucky, for example, both use a four-point holistic scoring guide, while Oregon, Washington, and Arizona use a six-trait analytic system. (The Florida and Arizona state scoring guides appear in Appendix C.)

Once we have an understanding of how our state's assessment scoring guide compares or conflicts with our own goals for instruction and evaluation, we can begin using it in our classrooms. We then face questions of evaluation style. Will we interpret the traits to the students ourselves (teacher-centered)? Will we ask students to interpret the traits for each other (peer-centered)? Will we ask students to evaluate their own writing against the traits (self-evaluation)? Or will we use some combination of interpretations?

Designing Writing Prompts Based on State Scoring Guides

As we begin to personalize state standards and prioritize the concepts and objectives we know are important to teach, we can feel more in control of instructional and evaluation decisions for students. We can select objectives from state standards and traits from scoring guides as we determine the specifics of the grading puzzle in our own instructional contexts and as we develop writing prompts and rubrics to share with students. In the example that follows, the teaching purpose chosen from the state standards is *writing an observational report* and the traits of *ideas/content development, organization,* and *conventions* are selected from the state's six-trait scoring guide. Another important factor in this lesson is its integration with science concepts. The standards-based science objective chosen from the district's curriculum guide follows: *Students will be able to make observations and gather data associated with energy, movement and change.* The writing concept and objectives selected for this lesson are stated as follows in the Arizona Academic Standards (1997) document for Language Arts and expected of students in grades 1–3:

> Students will be able to gather, organize and accurately, clearly and sequentially report information gained from personal observations and experiences such as science experiments, field trips and classroom visitors.

Objectives:

1. Record observations (e.g., logs, lists, graphs, charts, tables, illustrations)
2. Write an introductory statement
3. Report events sequentially
4. Write a concluding statement

Ms. Dell, the third-grade teacher designing this lesson, decides to demonstrate a science experiment for children to observe. Her students already use learning logs (suggested in objective #1) to take notes and make entries based on their learning. As she begins the experiment, she asks students to record the procedure, make a prediction, and summarize the results of the experiment in their learning logs. She considers this a valuable prewriting exercise. Ms. Dell also wrote the words "styrofoam" and "insulation" on the board for students. The following example illustrates this:

Procedure	*Prediction*	*Results and Conclusions*
Put hot water in a plastic baggie, a nurse's glove, and a styrofoam cup. Put all these in a bowl of cold water for about two minutes. You need a thermos for the hot water.	I think the nurse's glove will keep the water warmest because it is made of real thick material and it won't leak.	The styrofoam cup kept the water warmest because it has better insulation. These cups keep hot drinks warm longer. It's like whale blubber keeps a whale warm in cold water.

After students have finished writing in their learning logs and discussed the experiment, Ms. Dell reads the following writing prompt and gives them each a copy:

Write a report about what happened in our science experiment (based on state standard).

> ➤ Describe the experiment.
> ➤ Explain the results.
> ➤ Explain why this happened.
> ➤ Explain how this science principle works in our world.

I will look for the following when grading your paper (based on state scoring guide):

> ❑ Ideas are clear and information is accurate.
> ❑ Information is organized in the order it happened.
> ❑ Spelling, punctuation, and grammar are correct.

Hint: Your first sentence should introduce the topic and your last sentence makes a conclusion.

The prompt is written using language from the state's writing standards and scoring guide, yet is still understandable to third graders. Ms. Dell has chosen only three of the state's six traits to be used as grading expectations for this assignment: *ideas, organization*, and the *conventions*. Children are given more than one day to draft, revise, and edit their papers. Because the teacher uses this assignment as a practice for the state assessment, she expects students to revise and edit their papers individually, without help from peers. They are encouraged to use a dictionary and thesaurus, also allowed on their state assessment. Two examples of students' final drafts appear in Figures 8.1 and 8.2.

The analytic rubric used to score these examples has a range of 1, lowest, to 6, highest possible level of proficiency (see Figures 8.3, 8.4, and 8.5.) Because this school district requires traditional grades, Ms. Dell assigns a numerical value for use in determining percentages to each of the six points on the rubric as follows:

1 = 20 points   2 = 40 points   3 = 60 points   4 = 80 points   5 = 100 points   6 = 20 points extra credit

Because there are three traits being assessed, the total point value expected is 300 points; however, scoring a 6 on any trait provides 20 points extra credit, which can offset weaker trait scores.

If we analyze the first paper (Figure 8.1) for *ideas and content* development following the guidelines provided by the state (Figure 8.3), the description of a 4 seems to fit best. "The writing is characterized by an easily identifiable purpose . . . a topic that is explored/explained, although developmental details may occasionally be out of balance with the main idea(s)." The paper, therefore, receives 80 points for *ideas and content*.

FIGURE 8.1.

Report on Science Experiment

Are class did a experiment. Are teacher bought to school a

baggie, strofoam cup and a glove. Are teachr put some hot water

in each thing. Then she put each of the things in a cold bowl of

water. Then after a while she took the things out and then she

had Amanda and David put their hand in each thin. They all said

that the Styrofoam cup keep the water the warmenst and the

second was the glove. I thought the glove because it looked

thicker then the cup. Then the baggie.

Moving on to the trait of *organization*, the teacher recognizes that the conclusion is missing and the introduction is weak. She decides to compare the descriptions of a 3 paper and a 2 paper. Using Figure 8.4, the paper seems stronger than a 2; "the writing lacks a clear organizational structure." She agrees with the statement under 3, "an attempt has been made to organize the writing; however overall structure is skeletal," but the bullet under the description of a 2 paper, "a missing or extremely undeveloped beginning, body, and/or ending" definitely fits this piece of writing. Ms. Dell decides this paper is between a 2 and a 3 and gives it a 2.5 for *organization*, which translates to 50 points.

The errors in *conventions* on this paper stand out, on a first reading, especially the use of "are" for "our." As we look deeper, however, we may agree that "the writing demonstrates control of standard writing conventions" (see Figure 8.5) under a 4, rather than the characteristics of "limited control . . . errors begin to impede readability" for a 3. The paper receives the teacher's correlation of 80 points for a 4 in *conventions*.

After averaging the three scores, 80 points for *ideas*, 50 points for *organization*, and 80 points for *conventions*, the writer receives a grade of 70%, which translates into a C in this classroom's grading system. The teacher gives the writer feedback with comments as well as listing the scores and points for each trait. She indicates that an introduction and conclusion were an important part of the assignment and suggests that the writer listen carefully to examples of the introductory statements and concluding sentences when some of the other writers in the class read their papers aloud.

The second example in Figure 8.2 appears to be a stronger paper. As we consider the prompt, we have to ask if the writer really describes the experiment.

FIGURE 8.2.

Report on a Science Experiment

Our class experiment was which object can keep hot water the

hottest. Our objects were a surgeons glove, a styrofoam cup and

a plastic bag. All of these objects are like a whale because a

whale has insulation and so do these objects. The results of our

experiment were astonishing. The stryofoam cup kept the water

hotteset because of it's insulation and thickness.

Example: A whale. A whale has insulation. The blubber acts like

a heater and keeps the whale warm.

He begins to describe it by listing the objects, and he clearly tells about the "astonishing" results, but details of the procedure are missing. As we begin to score for *ideas and content* following scoring guide in Figure 8.3, the first statement under 5, "the writing is clear, focused and interesting," describes the paper better than simply ". . . clear and focused" under 4. The writing does not have ". . . strong support and rich details . . ." as required for a 6. Since the writing shows some of the characteristics listed under the score of 4, and did not address the purpose of describing the experiment accurately, Ms. Dell awards the paper a 4.5, giving it 90 points for *ideas and content*.

Using the scoring guide in Figure 8.4, Ms. Dell evaluates the *organization* of the piece with a score of 5, or 100 points. Moving on to Figure 8.5, Ms. Dell finds that the paper shows sophisticated control of *conventions*. The description of a 5—"The writing demonstrates exceptionally strong control of standard writing conventions . . . manipulation of conventions may occur for stylistic effect"—is evident, especially with the use of a colon, a skill most third graders have not yet mastered. The writer also used the term "surgeons" glove, which was spelled correctly without being part of the word bank and never discussed during the prewriting learning log or discussion. The concept of a plural possessive was never taught to these third graders, so we can't expect to see it used correctly by this writer. Therefore, the paper receives 100 points for *conventions*, plus 20 extra credit points for the 6, bringing the average of all three trait scores to 96 + 20 extra credit points, for an A+. This paper will be read aloud to the class for its strong organization and interest.

FIGURE 8.3.

Official Scoring Guide: Arizona's Instrument to Measure Standards

IDEAS and CONTENT

6
The writing is exceptionally clear, focused and interesting. It holds the reader's attention throughout. Main ideas stand out and are developed by strong support and rich details suitable to audience and purpose. The writing is characterized by
- clarity, focus, and control.
- main idea(s) that stand out.
- supporting, relevant, carefully selected details; when appropriate, use of resources provides strong, accurate, credible support.
- a thorough, balanced, in-depth explanation/ exploration of the topic; the writing makes connections and shares insights.
- content and selected details that are well suited to audience and purpose.

5
The writing is clear, focused and interesting. It holds the reader's attention. Main ideas stand out and are developed by supporting details suitable to audience and purpose. The writing is characterized by
- clarity, focus, and control.
- main idea(s) that stand out.
- supporting, relevant, carefully selected details; when appropriate, use of resources provides strong, accurate, credible support.
- a thorough, balanced explanation/ exploration of the topic; the writing makes connections and shares insights.
- content and selected details that are well-suited to audience and purpose.

4
The writing is clear and focused. The reader can easily understand the main ideas. Support is present, although it may be limited or rather general. The writing is characterized by
- an easily identifiable purpose.
- clear main idea(s)
- supporting details that are relevant, but may be overly general or limited in places; when appropriate, resources are used to provide accurate support.
- a topic that is explored/explained, although developmental details may occasionally be out of balance with the main idea(s); some connections and insights may be present.
- content and selected details that are relevant, but perhaps not consistently well chosen for audience and purpose.

3
The reader can understand the main ideas, although they may be overly broad or simplistic, and the results may not be effective. Supporting detail is often limited, insubstantial, overly general, or occasionally slightly off-topic. The writing is characterized by
- an easily identifiable purpose and main idea(s).
- predictable or overly-obvious main ideas or plot; conclusions or main points seem to echo observations heard elsewhere.
- support that is attempted; but developmental details that are often limited in score, uneven, somewhat off-topic, predictable, or overly general.
- details that may not be well-grounded in credible resources; they may be based on clichés, stereotypes or questionable sources of information.
- difficulties when moving from general observations to specifics.

2
Main ideas and purpose are somewhat unclear or development is attempted but minimal. The writing is characterized by
- a purpose and main idea(s) that may require extensive inferences by the reader.
- minimal development; insufficient details.
- irrelevant details that clutter the text.
- extensive repetition of detail.

1
The writing lacks a central idea or purpose. The writing is characterized by
- ideas that are extremely limited or simply unclear.
- attempts at development that are minimal or non-existent; the paper is too short to demonstrate the development of an idea.

FIGURE 8.4.

Official Scoring Guide: Arizona's Instrument to Measure Standards

ORGANIZATION

6

The organization enhances the central idea(s) and its development. The order and structure are compelling and move the reader through the text easily. The writing is characterized by

- effective, perhaps creative, sequencing; the organizational structure fits the topic, and the writing is easy to follow.
- a strong, inviting beginning that draws the reader in and a strong satisfying sense of resolution or closure.
- smooth, effective transitions among all elements (sentences, paragraphs, ideas).
- details that fit where placed.

5

The organization enhances the central idea(s) and development. The order and structure are strong and move the reader through the text. The writing is characterized by

- effective sequencing; the organizational structure fits the topic, and the writing is easy to follow.
- an inviting beginning that draws the reader in and a satisfying sense of resolution or closure.
- smooth, effective transitions among all elements (sentences, paragraphs, ideas).
- details that fit where placed.

4

Organization is clear and coherent. Order and structure are present, but may seem formulaic. The writing is characterized by

- clear sequencing.
- an organization that may be predictable.
- a recognizable, developed beginning that may not be particularly inviting; a developed conclusion that may lack subtlety.
- a body that is easy to follow with details that fit where placed.
- transitions that may be stilted or formulaic.
- organization which helps the reader, despite some weaknesses.

3

An attempt has been made to organize the writing; however, the overall structure is inconsistent or skeletal. The writing is characterized by

- attempts at sequencing, but the order or the relationship among ideas may occasionally be unclear.
- a beginning and an ending which, although present, are either undeveloped or too obvious (e.g. "My topic is...", "These are all the reasons that...")
- transitions that sometimes work. The same few transitional devices (e.g., coordinating conjunctions, numbering, etc.) may be overused.
- a structure that is skeletal or too rigid.
- placement of details that my not always be effective.
- organization which lapses in some places, but helps the reader in others.

2

The writing lacks a clear organizational structure. An occasional organizational device is discernible; however, the writing is either difficult to follow and the reader has to reread substantial portions, or the piece is simply too short to demonstrate organizational skills. The writing is characterized by

- some attempts at sequencing, but the order or the relationship among ideas is frequently unclear.
- a missing or extremely undeveloped beginning, body, and/or ending.
- a lack of transitions, or when present, ineffective or overused.
- a lack of an effective organizational structure.
- details that seem to be randomly placed, leaving the reader frequently confused.

1

The writing lacks coherence; organization seems haphazard and disjointed. Even after rereading, the reader remains confused. The writing is characterized by

- a lack of effective sequencing.
- a failure to provide an identifiable beginning, body and/or ending.
- a lack of transitions.
- pacing that is consistently awkward; the reader feels either mired down in trivia or rushed along too rapidly.
- a lack of organization which ultimately obscures or distorts the main point.

FIGURE 8.5.

Official Scoring Guide: Arizona's Instrument to Measure Standards

CONVENTIONS

6

The writing demonstrates exceptionally strong control of standard writing conventions (e.g., punctuation, spelling, capitalization, paragraph breaks, grammar and usage) and uses them effectively to enhance communication. Errors are so few and so minor that the reader can easily skim right over them unless specifically searching for them. The writing is characterized by

- strong control of conventions; manipulation of conventions may occur for stylistic effect.
- strong, effective use of punctuation that guides the reader through the text.
- correct spelling, even of more difficult words.
- paragraph breaks that reinforce the organizational structure.
- correct grammar and usage that contribute to clarity and style.
- skill in using a wide range of conventions in a sufficiently long and complex piece.
- little or no need for editing.

5

The writing demonstrates strong control of standard writing conventions (e.g., punctuation, spelling, capitalization, paragraph breaks, grammar and usage) and uses them effectively to enhance communication. Errors are so few and so minor that they do not impede readability. The writing is characterized by

- strong control of conventions.
- effective use of punctuation that guides the reader through the text.
- correct spelling, even of more difficult words.
- paragraph breaks that reinforce the organizational structure.
- correct capitalization; errors, if any, are minor.
- correct grammar and usage that contribute to clarity and style.
- skill in using a wide range of conventions in a sufficiently long and complex piece.
- little need for editing.

4

The writing demonstrates control of standard writing conventions (e.g., punctuation, spelling, capitalization, paragraph breaks, grammar and usage). Minor errors, while perhaps noticeable, do not impede readability. The writing is characterized by

- control over conventions used, although a wide range is not demonstrated.
- correct end-of-sentence punctuation; internal punctuation may sometimes be incorrect.
- spelling that is usually correct, especially on common words.
- basically sound paragraph breaks that reinforce the organizational structure.
- correct capitalization; errors, if any, are minor.
- occasional lapses in correct grammar and usage; problems are not severe enough to distort meaning or confuse the reader.
- moderate need for editing.

3

The writing demonstrates limited control of standard writing conventions (e.g., punctuation, spelling, capitalization, paragraph breaks, grammar and usage). Errors begin to impede readability. The writing is characterized by

- some control over basic conventions; the text may be too simple to reveal mastery.
- end-of-sentence punctuation that is usually correct; however, internal punctuation contains frequent errors.
- spelling errors that distract the reader; misspelling of common words occurs.
- paragraphs that sometimes run together or begin at ineffective places.
- capitalization errors.
- errors in grammar and usage that do not block meaning but do distract the reader.
- significant need for editing.

2

The writing demonstrates little control of standard writing conventions. Frequent, significant errors impede readability. The writing is characterized by

- little control over basic conventions.
- many end-of-sentence punctuation errors; internal punctuation contains frequent errors.
- spelling errors that frequently distract the reader; misspelling of common words often occurs.
- paragraphs that often run together or begin in ineffective places.
- capitalization that is inconsistent or often incorrect.
- errors in grammar and usage that interfere with readability and meaning.
- substantial need for editing.

1

Numerous errors in usage, spelling, capitalization, and punctuation repeatedly distract the reader and make the text difficult to read. In fact, the severity and frequency of errors are so overwhelming that the reader finds it difficult to focus on the message and must reread for meaning. The writing is characterized by

- very limited skill in using conventions.
- basic punctuation (including end-of-sentence punctuation) that tends to be omitted, haphazard, or incorrect.
- frequent spelling errors that significantly impair readability.
- paragraph breaks that may be highly irregular or so frequent (every sentence) that they bear no relation to the organization of the text.
- capitalization that appears to be random.
- a need for extensive editing.

Weighting the Traits

State assessment scoring practices tend to give equal value to each of the traits. For instructional purposes, however, teachers may decide to "weight the traits" by giving more value to the traits reflecting the primary teaching objectives. For example, using the same standards-based objectives given for the observational report, a teacher may decide to give *ideas and content* and *organization* more weight than *conventions*. In this case, the teacher may decide to grade as follows:

Ideas and Content = 60 possible points (pts; 1 = 10 pts, 2 = 20 pts, 3 = 30 pts, 4 = 40 pts, 5 = 50 pts, 6 = 60 pts)

Organization = 60 possible points (same as Ideas and Content)

Conventions = 30 possible points (pts; 1 = 5 pts, 2 = 10 pts, 3 = 15 pts, 4 = 20 pts, 5 = 25 pts, 6 = 30 pts)

Total = 150 possible points.

Well-developed ideas and organization are given more value since they are primary teaching objectives in this assignment. A teacher then applies standard percentage ranges: 90–100% (135–150 points) receives an A, 80–89% (120–134 points) for a B, 70–79% (105–119 points) for a C, and so forth. By weighting the traits with different score values, a teacher can select and emphasize specific traits based on her instructional purposes and evaluative style.

Sharing the Language of State Standards and Scoring Guides with Students

One of the strongest bridges we can build between classroom practices and state assessments is to share the language of standards and scoring guides with students in simplified form, depending on their age. Posters of the six traits or key words from statewide scoring guides appear in classrooms across the country. We can use phrases from the concepts and objectives from state standards in our writing prompts. Words and phrases from state scoring guides can be used when we lead revision lessons and conferences, and in responses to children about their writing. An excellent example of this kind of bridging is an illustrated, "kid friendly" rubric that teachers at Atkinson Elementary School in Louisville, Kentucky developed so their younger students could understand the Kentucky state assessment (Figure 8.6).

We can share many traits of effective writing, such as ideas, organization, voice and word choice, with very young children long before they can produce conventional written work. We can help children recognize characteristics of effective writing by discussing the great ideas, descriptive details, and wonderful words an author uses in a picture book. One method for introducing standards-based concepts is by modeling the writing process on chart paper in front of children using a variety of genres and purposes for writing. As young children dictate their own personal narratives, fictional stories, reports, and poems, teachers can pose questions and give feedback using the language of the traits. As Ruth Culham (1998) explains in her book, *Picture Books*, "When students really understand what makes writing—any kind of writing—work effectively, that's when they really take ownership of the writing process. They learn from

FIGURE 8.6.

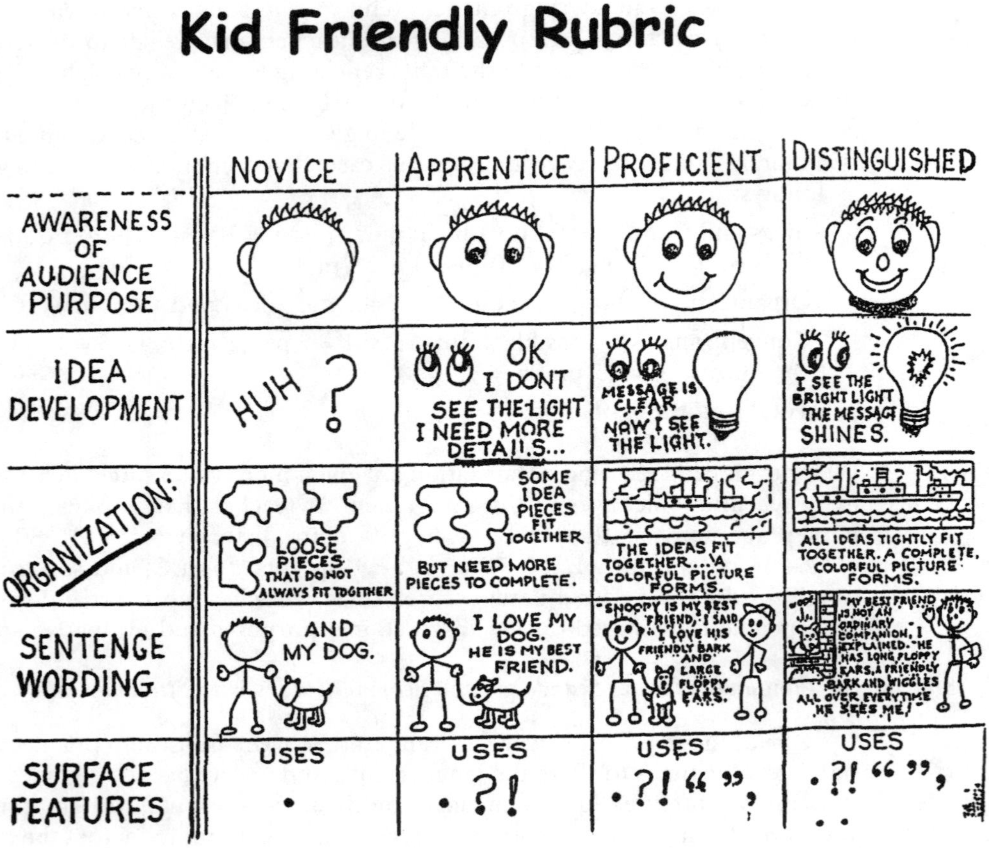

Kid Friendly Rubric

	NOVICE	APPRENTICE	PROFICIENT	DISTINGUISHED
AWARENESS OF AUDIENCE PURPOSE				
IDEA DEVELOPMENT	HUH ?	OK I DONT SEE THE LIGHT I NEED MORE DETAILS...	MESSAGE IS CLEAR NOW I SEE THE LIGHT.	I SEE THE BRIGHT LIGHT THE MESSAGE SHINES.
ORGANIZATION:	LOOSE PIECES THAT DO NOT ALWAYS FIT TOGETHER	SOME IDEA PIECES FIT TOGETHER BUT NEED MORE PIECES TO COMPLETE.	THE IDEAS FIT TOGETHER...A COLORFUL PICTURE FORMS.	ALL IDEAS TIGHTLY FIT TOGETHER. A COMPLETE, COLORFUL PICTURE FORMS.
SENTENGE WORDING	AND MY DOG.	I LOVE MY DOG. HE IS MY BEST FRIEND.	"SNOOPY IS MY BEST FRIEND, I SAID. "I LOVE HIS FRIENDLY BARK AND LARGE FLOPPY EARS."	"MY BEST FRIEND IS NOT AN ORDINARY COMPANION, I EXPLAINED. "HE HAS LONG FLOPPY EARS, A FRIENDLY BARK AND WIGGLES ALL OVER EVERYTIME HE SEES ME."
SURFACE FEATURES	USES .	USES . ?!	USES . ?! " ",	USES . ?! " ", ..

the [six trait] criteria and internalize them so that the language of the traits be-comes a powerful revision tool" (p. 3).

Thinking about State Standards and Assessments

While all states are now required to articulate standards for writing and while most states currently have some sort of assessment of writing standards, the state assessment movement has not been without its opponents. Issues in-clude the amount of instructional time given over to testing, the disadvantaging of minority students, the amount of money spent on assessments, and the use of the results of the tests. High-stakes testing, which determines whether stu-dents are promoted or even graduate from high school, has been particularly controversial. As we weigh how much emphasis to place on state standards in our own classrooms, we need to remember that the choices we make communicate to children about writing. As we think about state standards and assessments and evaluating children's writing, we need to think intentionally about what we want children to hear about their writing. As teachers, we need to remember our primary instructional purposes and the importance of giving positive evaluative feedback to students rather than just preparing them for a test. There is an old saying, "weighing the pig more often doesn't make it fatter." Likewise, testing a child more often doesn't make him or her smarter.

Some Advantages of Using State Standards for Evaluation

- They may provide students with writing goals for which they know they'll be held accountable.
- They may provide students with a common language for discussing the elements of good writing and revising their own work.
- They may provide models for students to evaluate their own beliefs about what makes a good piece of writing.

Some Disadvantages of Using State Standards for Evaluation

- They may not be appropriate for a particular instructional context.
- They may not include all the writing goals a teacher has for his or her students, or provide too many writing goals for a particular group of students.
- They may overemphasize the role of assessment in the classroom.

Chapter Summary

It is important for teachers to understand their state's academic standards in writing and apply the concepts and objectives expected in those standards to their instructional and evaluative practices. Teachers also need to understand how their state assessment and scoring guide are both used to measure writing proficiency. After selecting the appropriate standards-based objectives for their primary teaching purposes, classroom teachers can use a variety of instructional strategies. They can choose from their state's scoring guide only the traits they wish to address in a particular assignment. To teach with state standards and assessment, teachers do the following:

Compare state standards and assessment to the following:

- Classroom instructional context: purpose, student response, teacher goals.
- Grading puzzle.
- Analytic/holistic continuum.

Determine the following:

- Which evaluation style to use with standards: teacher, student, or cooperative choice.
- The priority of the state standards based on instructional purposes.

Using the language of both the state standards and scoring guides can help teachers communicate clear writing prompts and help children communicate about the characteristics of effective writing. Many educators believe that state standards and assessments have become overemphasized.

EXERCISES

- Design a writing assignment based on an objective from your state's writing standards and an objective from one of your state's content standards.
- Go to your state department's website and download the writing assessment scoring guide and any sample student papers with explanations about the scores they received.
- Go to appendix A and select a sample of student writing to score with your state's scoring guide.
- Find a picture book and analyze it according to the traits your state utilizes in its scoring guide for writing assessments.

References

Arizona Department of Education. *Arizona Academic Standards*. Standard 2—Writing, Foundations Level, Concept 4, Performance Objectives 1–4, August 1997.

Arizona Department of Education. *Official Scoring Guide: Arizona's Instrument to Measure Standards*, August, 1997.

Culham, Ruth. *Picture Books—An Annotated Bibliography with Activities for Teaching Writing.* Northwest Regional Educational Laboratory, 1998.

International Reading Association and National Council of Teachers of English. Standards for the English Language Arts, IRA & NCTE, 1996.

Powell, Kelly. Email to Linda Ryan. March 8, 2002.

United States Congress, H.R.1-20, section 1111. State Plans, January, 2001.

United States Congress, H.R.1-450, section 6112. Grants for enhanced Assessment Instruments, January, 2001.

Wolf, Shelby Anne and Kenneth Paul Wolf. "Teaching True and to the Test in Writing." Language Arts 79, 3 (January 2002): 229–240.

PART III

Using Grading as a Teaching Tool

The first two parts of this book offer objectives and options for evaluating children's writing. But there remain questions larger than merely what tools are available for what purposes. These larger questions are as follows: How to match a particular option with a particular purpose? How to learn to grade? How to use grading for more than arriving at "fair marks"? This part addresses these questions.

CHAPTER 9   Tools of the Trade: *Choosing Evaluation Options in a Communication Setting*

Using the Communication Triangle
   Scenario #1
   Scenario #2
   Scenario #3
Tools of the Trade

CHAPTER 10   Transcending the Red Ink, *or Making Grading Serve Teaching*

Making Grading Serve Teaching
   Working with Revisions
   Adding Criteria over Time
   Progressive Weighting of Grades
Beyond Evaluation: Alternative Purposes of Grading
Questions of Power
A World without Grades

CHAPTER 11   Teach Yourself to Grade, *or the Grading Process in Action*

Learning the Grading Process

Ways of Beginning
  Scenario #1
  Scenario #2
  Scenario #3

Creating a Personal Grading System

CHAPTER 9

Tools of the Trade
Choosing Evaluation Options in a Communication Setting

Using the Communication Triangle

As you think about how to choose from among the many evaluation options, you may want to review the communication triangle introduced in Chapter 2. For convenience, it is repeated here as Figure 9.1.

Next, let's review the grading options presented in this book: approaches, response strategies, management systems, and evaluation styles.

Any grading system we create will employ some choice in each of these categories. But too often we confuse the categories or overlook a category. When that happens, we lose our intentionality and often fall back on grading systems that our teachers used to grade us. (The traditional system, as most of us experienced it, consisted of teacher-centered analytic grading with no response, or brief—usually negative—comments written at the end of the paper. Grade averaging was the management system.) If we give up our intentionality, it is possible to find ourselves using a self-contradictory system of grading. The consequences of this self-contradiction can even affect instruction since grading often drives instruction and student learning.

An example will illustrate. Ms. McMillan attends a workshop on portfolios. She leaves the workshop enthusiastic about promoting student ownership of writing in her class, so she implements a portfolio management system. However, without thinking, she retains her traditional teacher-centered evaluation style: she dictates to the students what will go in their portfolios and the criteria upon which she will grade them. Without realizing it, Ms. McMillan has created a self-contradictory system: the evaluation style undercuts the instructional purpose of her management system. By dictating to her students what will go in their portfolios and what will make a good portfolio, she has actually retained ownership of her students' writing herself.

In order to avoid the trap of self-contradictory grading and instructional systems, we must always keep the communication triangle in mind. For it is in the interaction of the three corners of the triangle that we can make sensible, intentional decisions. Which corner we begin with cannot be prescribed—it is driven by the moment, by the context in which we find ourselves. The three scenarios that follow illustrate.

FIGURE 9.1.   Communication Triangle

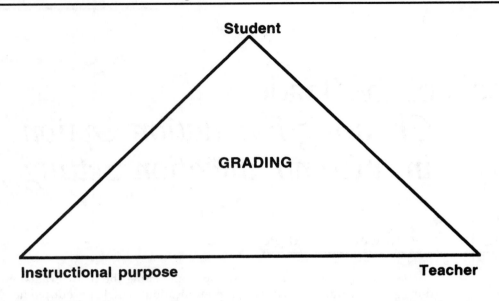

Scenario #1

Mr. Jaramillio's second-grade class is large and boisterous. By the end of the first week of school he knows he has a challenge on his hands. Some of his students are enthusiastic about writing, but some are fearful (they seem especially tense about spelling). Since he is a new second-grade teacher whose student teaching experience was in a fifth-grade classroom in another state, he is a bit unsure of what primary writers can do. He likes to write himself and wants to protect the enthusiasm for writing that some of his students possess as well as help the fearful students to feel more comfortable with writing. He wants to challenge them to develop as writers, and he wants to give them ownership of their writing. He thinks the best way to do this is to focus on writing for an audience, an unfamiliar concept to most of his students. Because his students are natural-born performers he counts on channeling this energy into writing.

Let's analyze Mr. Jaramillio's situation beginning at the "student" corner of the communication triangle:

> *Students:* large, hard-to-control class; some enthusiastic writers, some fearful writers
>
> *Teacher:* new at his job; likes to write
>
> *Instructional purpose(s):* engender enthusiasm for and ownership of writing; focus on audience-awareness.

Mr. Jaramillio makes the following choices:

Grading approach: primary-trait

Evaluation style: teacher-based

Response strategy: written (sticky pads)

Management system: contracts.

Why did he make these decisions?

He has chosen a primary-trait approach because his two instructional goals look at pieces of writing as wholes—how kids feel about writing and how audiences respond to their writing.

He has chosen a teacher-based style for two reasons—because his students are largely unaware of what it means to write for someone other than themselves or their teachers and because of the control problems he is experiencing. He feels that until he achieves more decorum he needs to simply tell his students what he expects from their writing.

Because of his desire to develop student ownership of writing, he wants his response to be as unobtrusive as possible. He has decided to use brief written notes positioned on sticky paper at places in the writing where he wants to praise or make a suggestion. Using this method, students will see graphically that the writing is still their own, in spite of his comments.

He is enthusiastic about writing and he wants his students to feel the same way. He wants to avoid grades as much as possible. He has chosen a contract system to emphasize for his students that they can all get "+s." The contract spells out exactly how they can do this.

Scenario #2

Mrs. Begay has been teaching fourth grade for twenty years. She has always felt that writing was important and has had high standards for her students' work. She has taught from a traditional curriculum guide in traditional units: grammar, spelling, paragraphs, and so forth. But now she is ready for a change. She has been attending workshops and reading about holistic grading and is interested in trying it. Her students know her by reputation from their older brothers and sisters and expect a traditional approach, but some of them are familiar with portfolios because two of the third-grade teachers in the school use a portfolio system. In one of the workshops she attended, Mrs. Begay started keeping a personal journal. She has been surprised at how much she has enjoyed starting to write again after so many years of teaching writing but not writing herself. In fact, she is thinking about writing a collection of stories for her students. This year she wants to get away from the constant pressure of grades, both for herself and for her students. She wants her students to discover writing for themselves as she so recently has. She wants them to look at writing as a whole and as a process.

Let's analyze Mrs. Begay's situations beginning at the "teacher" corner of the communication triangle:

Teacher: highly experienced but making a change in her philosophy of teaching writing; wants to get away from the constant pressure of grades

Students: expect a traditional approach, but some of them have experience with portfolios

Instructional purpose(s): help students relax with writing and discover the fun of it; help them view writing as a whole and as a process.

Mrs. Begay makes the following choices:

Management system: portfolios

Evaluation style: partnership

Response strategy: combination of oral and written

Grading approach: holistic cluster.

Let's look at why she made these decisions.

Since Mrs. Begay wants to avoid the constant pressure of grades for herself and for her students, she has chosen to use portfolios to determine nine-week grades. The portfolios will allow her to focus with her students on their progress, rather than on pieces of the puzzle isolated from each other as she has in the past. Because she wants her students to view writing as a whole rather than as the sum of its parts, Mrs. Begay has chosen a holistic method. She is comfortable with a cluster approach because of her years of experience with fourth-grade writing.

But, because Mrs. Begay will only assign grades at the end of each nine weeks, she has chosen a combination response strategy based on a partnership evaluation style. She plans to have conferences with her students about each one of their writing assignments and then provide them with evaluation guidelines to help them choose which of these assignments they will put in their portfolios. She will also have her students do a written evaluation of their portfolios after assembling them. Her evaluation of the portfolios will also be written, but she will schedule conferences with students who wish to discuss their portfolios with her. She hopes all of them will take advantage of this opportunity, but she does not wish to require these conferences because she will require assignment conferences.

Scenario #3

Ms. Paxton is an experienced teacher who has been teaching third grade for four years in a K–6 school. She has asked for and has been given a transfer to sixth grade. Because her students will be going to a junior high next year, she has spent several hours talking to the three seventh-grade English teachers. As a result of these conversations, she wants her students to get a conscious knowledge of all of the pieces of the writing puzzle. She also wants them to be able to articulate clearly what parts of their writing are well under control and what parts they need to continue to work on. However, since she is making a switch in level of student, she is a bit unsure of reasonable criteria for sixth-graders. She already knows some of her students from three years before, but many of the others are completely unknown to her. She wants to avoid making her "new" students feel less welcome than her "old" students.

Let's analyze Ms. Paxton's situation:

Instructional purpose(s): raise the pieces of the writing puzzle to a conscious level for the students; enable students to articulate what they do well in writing and what they need to work more on

Teacher: experienced but in a new setting; unsure of her expectations for this group of students

Students: sixth graders who are preparing for junior high, a new level of their education; a mix of kids she knows and kids she doesn't.

To begin the year Ms. Paxton makes the following choices:

Grading approach: analytic

Evaluation style: peer-centered

Response strategy: oral

Management system: checklist.

Let's look at why she made these decisions.

Because her instructional purposes call for students to be able to articulate the pieces of the writing puzzle, both in general and personal terms, she has chosen an analytic approach. A holistic approach would group students into "strong writers" and "weak writers," but it would not focus on the pieces of the puzzle. The checklist management system will support the analytic approach she has decided on as well as her second instructional purpose—to help her students get to know their strengths and weaknesses as writers.

She has chosen a partnership evaluation style because of the situation in which she finds herself: she is unsure of reasonable expectations for sixth-graders. Because she wants to get to know her "new" students quickly and because she wants to renew her acquaintance with her "old" students, she has chosen to respond to their writing orally, face-to-face, in conferences.

But let's follow Ms. Paxton through the year. She makes different choices as her situation changes. This is how the year progresses:

Ms. Paxton decides to begin her students' writing using a personal experience narrative. It is required by the curriculum guide and she is familiar with it from teaching her third-graders. In a class discussion, she asks the students what they think makes a good personal narrative. Based on what they have said, she creates a primary-trait rubric for the personal narrative. The students write their papers following their rubrics, and she reads them. In individual conferences she discusses with the students how they assess the quality of their writing based on the class rubric. In the conferences, she arrives at a grade.

By January, Ms. Paxton begins to get some confidence. She moves from the student-based style to a partnership style. In this setting, she begins to add criteria to the class-generated rubrics. Because she feels comfortable with her students and confident that they will all approach her if they need to, she begins to tape-record her responses. As she reads a student's paper, she tapes her own evaluation of the quality of the writing based on the rubric. She creates a checklist in order to begin a cumulative record of how each student is progressing on the criteria she and the class have chosen up to this point.

By spring, Ms. Paxton has developed a criterion-referenced grading sheet from the checklist. She discusses junior high English classes with her students and moves into written responses based on her criterion-referenced grading sheet. She reinstitutes conferences: using the grading sheets, she discusses with her students which parts of their writing they feel are working well and which parts they think need more work. She calculates the last nine-week grades from the criterion-referenced checklist she has created.

In this scenario Ms. Paxton has used her grading system to support her instructional goals and to support herself as she gets to know a new teaching situation. She has balanced her students' perceived needs as writers with the needs she perceives them to have for the next level of their education. She has developed a flexible system that has allowed her instructional goals to develop.

Tools of the Trade

My suggested approach to evaluation—as decision making based on a communication context—views grading options as tools designed to serve instruction. It has been my experience that none of these options for grading is inherently "good" or "bad," just as a hammer or a pair of scissors is not inherently "good" or "bad." The "goodness" or "badness" depends on how the tool is used. A hammer that is used to build a church is a "good" hammer, while a hammer that is used to destroy an art object is a "bad" hammer. Therefore, I suggest that we use the metaphor of a toolbox as we think about matching grading strategy with instructional purpose. We have a toolbox full of tools: it is up to us to determine the shape of the job before us and choose appropriate tools. If I need to shorten a piece of molding, I need a saw, not a screwdriver. But if I need to tighten the leg on a couch, a screwdriver is exactly what I need.

And so it is for instructional jobs. Analytic grading is a useful tool for isolating problem areas and working to improve them. Anchor holistic grading is a useful tool for arriving at quick, accurate categories for large numbers of writers. Cluster holistic scoring is a tool that is useful for arriving at a quick, accurate profile of one class of student writers. Teacher-generated rubrics are useful for challenging students who need a better understanding of writing. Student-generated rubrics are useful for engendering student ownership of writing. Conferencing is a useful tool for building a writing-mentor relationship between a teacher and a student. Grades without comments are useful for final papers that will never be handed back or revised. A contract is a good tool for relieving the pressure of grades. A cumulative record is a good tool for diagnosing patterns of surface errors. A portfolio is a good tool for showing growth in writing. And on it goes.

So far this all sounds like common sense, right? But I have arrived at this toolbox metaphor after twenty years of abandoning old "wrong" grading techniques and adopting new "right" techniques. (I've done this a dozen times, perhaps.) Looking back on those abandoned techniques—the first ones and then the next ones and the later ones—I see that all of them had strong points.

By the same token, all of them had weak points as well. The context made the difference!

However, as a profession, it seems to me that we are moving farther away from acknowledging context in instruction rather than closer to it. In fact, in recent years we have begun to ignore context and have adopted political (and sometimes religious) metaphors for particular instructional strategies (my grading options). I sometimes hear my colleagues referring to one teacher we know as "right-wing" because she does direct instruction of grammar. Another teacher I know has been called "leftist" because he grades his students' papers holistically. Whole language proponents are sometimes called "missionaries." Many of the teachers I know have begun to label one another, using these religious and political metaphors. (These same teachers fight heroically to avoid labeling students.) And sometimes the labels have led to antagonism. ("I can't believe she's so conservative that she's still teaching spelling! I thought she knew about the writing process. I just don't even feel like I can get through to her.")

Somehow we have created an implicit continuum for teaching and grading strategies. As best as I can construct it from the innuendos that surround it, it looks something like this:

"Liberal"	"Conservative"
holistic scoring	analytic scoring
student-centered approach	teacher-centered approach
peer response	teacher response
portfolios	grade-averaging
portfolios	cumulative records

(Grading strategies like primary-trait scoring; rubrics, teacher–student partnerships, and contracts are viewed as falling somewhere in the middle of this political continuum—they are "middle-of-the-road.")

But as I wrote the text for this book I kept constantly vigilant to avoid politically-charged categorizations like the one described earlier. I believe that the political metaphor has left us in the position of sometimes throwing out, if not the baby with the bathwater, at least a perfectly good bar of soap. And so I argue for my toolbox metaphor. As teachers we need to analyze the communication context in which we find ourselves at any given moment in any given year and choose appropriately from among the many grading options that are open to us.

Chapter Summary

In order to choose among options and remain consistent to our teaching contexts, we must consider each corner of the communication triangle. Whether we begin with our own corner—the teacher corner—or whether we begin somewhere else, it is crucial that we take into account instructional purpose and student needs as well as our own point of view. At the same time, it is not helpful for us to label someone else (or ourselves) with a political label—"conservative" or "liberal"—based on evaluation (or, for that matter, teaching) choices. The important thing is to make sure our own choices are consistent with our teaching context.

EXERCISES

1. Design a grading system for the scenario that follows. Explain the choices you made.

   Scenario

       Mr. Lincoln teaches sixth grade in a big city school. Many of his students come from low-income families who speak a variety of "nonstandard" dialects of English. Some of his students want to go to college and are already focused on "doing well" in school. They perceive a need to learn "standard" English, and want to know the academic terms for what they are writing. Others are bored and want to quit school like their older brothers and sisters have done. Mr. Lincoln has been teaching for five years in this school, and he has a good grasp of the situation. He wants to support the students who want to concentrate on their academics, but he also wants to change the attitudes of some of the other students. Grades motivate the academically oriented students but threaten the others.

2. Write your own scenario, including information about the teacher, the students, and the instructional purposes. Design a grading system to fit your scenario. Write a letter to the parents of your students explaining what you will be doing and why.

3. In your mind, superimpose politics onto the scenarios presented in this chapter. Imagine that Mr. Jaramillio, Ms. Paxton, and Mrs. Begay all teach in the same school district. What political attacks might Mr. Jaramillio and Ms. Paxton make on each other? What might Mrs. Begay say to them both? Write a skit of a polarized faculty meeting using these characters. Share your skit with the other members of your group.

4. State your own ideas about how you wish to grade. Defend your ideas in nonaccusatory language without making reference to the shortcomings of other systems of grading.

CHAPTER 10

Transcending the Red Ink
or Making Grading Serve Teaching

Making Grading Serve Teaching

When I first approached a publisher with the idea for this book, I was asked, "But why don't you write a book about *teaching* writing?"

My spoken answer was "Because that book has already been written, and written very well—several times." But my unspoken answer was "This book *is* about teaching writing."

One of the corners of the communication triangle as I have applied it to grading is "instructional purpose"—the teaching objective of the writing assignment. Throughout this book, in as many ways as I can think of, I have said, "Think about what you're trying to teach and evaluate on that. Make your evaluation serve your instruction."

This is harder than it sounds. How many times have I sat in the back of a classroom and watched an enthusiastic student teacher direct a fun writing activity that was so out of context that it had become meaningless? The student teacher had developed a lesson plan, but had no idea why a particular activity was being used, beyond the fact that the kids would like it. There was no instructional intentionality driving the lesson. Just as later no intentionality drove the evaluation of the piece of writing the students handed in (the product of the assignment).

And so this book is about teaching writing. It is about assessing student need, drawing on teacher expertise, identifying appropriate instructional objectives, and then choosing a grading tool that supports the teaching purpose of the writing assignment.

For the most part, communication-based grading is a matter of objectives and options, but now we come to the three *rules* of this kind of grading:

1. Analyze your grading/communication context and choose your evaluation tools when you *design* the writing assignment.
2. Tell your students how you will grade their papers *before* they begin to write.
3. Never grade on something you haven't taught.

When we are clear ourselves on where our students are, on what we think is important about writing, and on what we want to teach them to do next, we can make meaningful use of the fun writing activities that are as close as *Idea Exchange* (National Council of Teachers of English) and the teacher next door. But if we don't think ahead, or if we keep this information to ourselves and make our students guess at what it is we want them to learn from the activity, or if we refuse to teach them something because "they should have learned it last year" or "they're not ready for it," we cloud the issues monumentally.

Imagine for a moment an expert chef trying to teach a child to cook without first deciding on a recipe or teaching the child to use a measuring cup (or at least reviewing the process). Throughout the lesson the child would be anxious and guessing. "Are we making brownies?" "Or will we end up with oatmeal?" "I wish I could remember how much a teaspoon was!"

If the chef had not decided what they were trying to make, they might wind up with a concoction such as chocolate oatmeal or brownie mix with milk on it that no one would eat! And yet that is exactly what we do when we don't plan our criteria, tell our students ahead of time what our instructional goals are, and teach them what we expect them to know.

By deciding ourselves, telling our students what we plan to evaluate before they write, and teaching to our goals, we make evaluation serve an individual assignment. But how do we make evaluation serve our teaching of writing over the entire course of instruction? There are three techniques I have found useful for accomplishing this purpose: working with revisions of student writing, adding grading criteria over time, and progressive weighting of grades. Let's look at them one at a time.

Working with Revisions

If we look at writing and grading as processes, it makes sense to allow students to revise even after a piece has been evaluated. The grade is no more an end point than is sharing or publishing. If we are using grades to communicate, then it stands to reason that we want our students to respond to the communication: we want them to revise. And then we can revise the grade. The only proviso I would make on student revisions is that they should be strictly voluntary. Sometimes a piece of writing is finished, whether it is "good" or not. And students know this best about their own work. If a student wishes to leave a piece as it is and go on to the next one, we should respect his or her wishes.

Adding Criteria over Time

The best way to reach any goal is to break the process of reaching that goal down into its component steps. If I want to write a book on evaluation, for example, I must first decide on my audience. Next I must sketch out an annotated map of the book I intend to write. Then I will approach a publisher. Next I will revise my ideas based on what the publisher knows about books. And so on, until I have finished my book. But if I say "I am going to write a book" and stop there, I will surely become paralyzed at the audacity of my thought!

The same is true for students. If we break down the process they must go through to move from where they are as writers to where we want them to be and then inform them of the steps one at a time, we keep them from the paralysis of the magnitude of the task before them. We grade first on one portion, then on a second, and so forth, until something has been learned. For example, Mr. Ashley, a fifth-grade teacher, begins the year by teaching the writing process. He evaluates the first two writing assignments solely on the process: evidence of prewriting, participation in peer revision groups, actual changes between drafts, and participation in the author's chair (class sharing of writing). Next he adds context. He teaches audience, purpose, and writer's stance. He evaluates assignments two and three on process and on context—the appropriateness of subject matter and language for a chosen audience, the accomplishment of the purpose of the writing, and the writer's voice. Next he adds structure. The class writes expository papers. He grades them on process, context, and structure. And so on until the end of the year Mr. Ashley is grading his students on a list of specified criteria.

Progressive Weighting of Grades

A third way to make evaluation serve instruction over time is to weight grades differently. As teachers we want growth and progress in our students' work. Why then is the first piece of writing they do weighted as heavily as the last? Why not make the first few pieces worth three points, the next few five, and the last ten? This technique allows students time to write and develop as writers with increasing pressure to keep pace with increasing skill.

Beyond Evaluation: Alternative Purposes of Grading

Grading can be a useful tool beyond even its instructional purposes. It can give us important information about instructional design and teaching success. As we map out a long-term plan of evaluation goals, we are actually mapping out long-term instructional goals. And if we are certain that we have taught to our goals, we have followed our plan. This system of planning, teaching, and rechecking serves the same purpose as does course design. If I ask myself "On what do I want to grade primary writers?", I have asked myself "What do second-graders need to learn about writing this year?"

By the same token, thoughtful reflection at the end of the year about how well my students have met my evaluation criteria provides feedback about instructional success. If I have planned to teach (and evaluate) audience awareness with my third-graders and they are successful at writing differently to a class speaker and to the kindergartners down the hall, then my instruction has been successful. But if they do not alter vocabulary and topics to the different audiences—if, in fact, the majority of the class is getting low grades on audience awareness—my instruction needs improvement.

With this orientation toward the larger communication that grades can provide to us about our own work, grading becomes not only student-evaluation, but self-evaluation as well. Too many low grades among our students, then, result in a low mark for our instruction as well.

Questions of Power

How early do grades become synonymous with success and failure? How soon do they cause our stomachs to churn? Too early. The week before my daughter was to begin kindergarten, she told me with deep anxiety that she was afraid she was going to "flunk" because she couldn't yet hop on one foot in a straight line. (I have no idea where she got the information about hopping on one foot or about flunking; certainly I had never discussed either with her.) Last night (she is now a fifth-grader), after she finished decorating the folder her Halloween story was going into, she looked up at me and said wistfully, "I hope I get a good grade on my story." She did not say, "I'm proud of this story" or "I had fun working on this story" or even "I worked hard on this story and did what the teacher asked. I know I'm going to get a good grade." She said, "I hope" in the same tone I use when it's been raining for a week and I say, "I hope the sun will come out this afternoon." And yet she did have fun working on the story and she had done a good job. So why the wistful tone?

Too often grades do cause kids to feel wistful (or angry, or frightened, or ashamed). In an ideal world where every child (or even most of them) came to school with an internalized self-esteem that had no reference to success or failure in school, grades would not have this power. But in the world in which we teach, grades have very great power, and no discussion of evaluation would be complete without some mention of that power. As graders, then, we hold great power over our students. We have all experienced teachers who have used that power for their own ends rather than for instructional ends (and perhaps sometimes we too have been guilty). And so I say that evaluation should be a tool made to serve instruction. It is not an end in itself; it is a means to an end.

How to keep the tool in its place? How to make it serve the teacher and the students rather than the other way around?

First, focus the grade on the writing product, not on the student. Say, "This is a great paper!" not "You did a great job." Jane may have done a great job in simply turning something in. Don's paper, on the other hand, may have been written by his grandmother. Assess the work, not the kid. If Jane's paper is not so great, she probably knows it, and she probably knows why. It is important to affirm for her that the paper needs more work. But it is not O.K. to say, "You're a better writer than this Jane—I expect better work from you." By the same token, Don knows if he didn't write his paper, whether the teacher ever finds out or not. By praising the paper (his grandmother, after all, did a lot of work on it!) but not him, the evaluation—and Don—are kept at least minimally honest.

But Jane and Don are extreme cases. Kids who have done their own work and done it to the best of their ability deserve an honest appraisal of the work. The teacher's opinion of their ability level is only that—an opinion. And mistaken opinions about abilities cause untold heartache.

After an in-service I recently conducted, an anxious teacher came up to me. He was middle-aged and very intense. "You know," he said, "I've always worked hard at my grading. I think it's so important for kids to be good writers. When I was in elementary school I was labeled learning disabled because I couldn't spell. I've spent the better part of thirty years overcoming that label. I don't want my students to experience what I did."

We all know stories like this one. In the last few years we've made a conscious effort to mainstream kids who are different to avoid labeling them one thing or another. But sometimes we forget that grades are labels too. How many times have you heard someone say to you, "I was a 'C'-student in school"? How different would it be if that same person said, "I wrote several 'C' papers in school." So label the work, not the kid!

But there is a second power concern. Earlier in this chapter I argued for telling students ahead of time what we want them to learn from a particular writing assignment and then evaluating them on only those announced goals. This procedure, which looks so simple at first glance, is really a power issue. When we keep our grading criteria to ourselves (or even worse—when we fail to articulate them, even to ourselves) we corner the power market for ourselves (or for our subconscious!). If our students are working to guess at what is important to us, they are focused on us rather than on their work. But when we share the goals, perhaps even formulating the goals in a partnership, we share the power of the grade as well. It is one thing if Maria knows clearly what are the criteria for a particular writing assignment and yet fails to meet them. It is something entirely different if she fails to meet criteria she knows nothing about. In the first case, if her grade is lower than she would like, she knows why and has a route open to her to correct the situation, a route that is much clearer than "I just have to work harder."

And, of course, there are the power issues related to the other adults in our students' lives. A third-grade teacher I know told me about a student in her class whose parents grounded him every time he brought home a grade lower than an "A." Principals have been known to place students (or refuse to place them) in enrichment programs of various titles (gifted, talented, etc.) based on a pattern of grades. Counselors have been known to refer students to special programs of all types based on grades. Beyond doing our best to educate people around us about what we are trying to communicate with our grades, there is very little we can do to change some of these larger issues. But, we must always take grades seriously. Often they have more power than we intend for them.

A World without Grades

In my ideal educational world, grading would not exist at all. (Lots of other things would be different too, but they are beyond the scope of this book.) Some progressive schools are attempting alternative approaches to evaluation. For example, I know of a district in which students are not given grades at all until they reach the fourth grade. I know of another school that is developing a system of portfolios of student work accompanied only by anecdotal records. As we move into a new millennium, educators worldwide envision new ways of assessing writing. In an article that appeared in *Reading Research Quarterly*, Robert Tierney (2000) articulated seven goals for evaluating writing that would not result in grades at all. Instead, his process of evaluation would raise more questions about student learning than it would answer. The push toward standardization of writing evaluation that we're seeing in many states stands in stark contrast to this vision. Most of the schools I work in use grades and require teachers to provide grades to parents and students at regular intervals (sometimes every week, sometimes every nine weeks) and teachers are faced with the realities of grades and power and politics. While we work toward a better educational system, it becomes important to find ways of transcending the sea of red ink we sometimes find ourselves awash in so that we can use evaluation to communicate about instruction with our students.

Chapter Summary

Sometimes we feel ourselves awash in a sea of red ink. Some schools are experimenting with systems without grades, but for most of us there is no escape from grades. Therefore, we must make sure our evaluation is not separate from our instruction: we must make our evaluation serve our teaching.

EXERCISES

1. Design a year's evaluation plan to go with the beginning you made in Chapter 9, Exercise 2. Explain how you could use evaluation to support the development of instructional purposes.

2. Explain how you could use the grading plan you designed in Exercise 1 to evaluate your own teaching for the year and revise your teaching for the following year.

Reference

Tierney, Robert J. "How Will Literacy be Assessed in the Next Millenium?" *Reading Research Quarterly* 35, 2 (April/May/June 2000): 244–246.

CHAPTER 11

Teach Yourself to Grade
or the Grading Process
in Action

Learning the Grading Process

Grading is a craft, just as calligraphy is a craft. To do calligraphy we must learn about oddly shaped pens, india ink, and textures of papers. We must study and practice the shapes of the alphabet, maybe even attempting gold illumination of tall letters on crackling onionskin.

But calligraphy can be an art as well. An artist-calligrapher who lived in my town died recently. As a coincidence, there happened to be a show of his work at the university art museum at the same time. (The show became a tribute show.) As I wandered up and down the rows, I was filled with excitement. This man (Dick Beasley was his name) had succeeded in making art from calligraphy. I had never seen calligraphy art before—pictures of energy, pictures of thanksgiving, pictures of ancient elegance—all made from the alphabet. The walls of the exhibit were punctuated with quotations from Dick about his work. One quotation spoke to the tension he felt between art and craft:

> The process, or medium, for me, is simply a means to an end, not an end in itself. The end product must stimulate visually my own eyes quite apart from the means I employ to execute the image. I claim no mastery over any process, but expect of myself enough technical competence not to be apologetic for the quality of any work produced by my own hands and mind. Art and craft, you realize, can in no way be separate from each other. Art is the concept, or mental image of the artist, craft is the making of that concept or image. This applies to any process or medium where an artist is imposing ideas upon materials for a given end.

Dr. Beasley's work displayed in the room included abstract designs, weavings, pottery, illuminated lettering, even certificates. All of the pieces testified to the fact that he had managed to take the stylized letters of his craft and make them his own, draw them so that they spoke what he, Dick Beasley, felt inside his soul. He had made his craft into an art.

And so it is with evaluation. To grade students' papers competently, we must learn what options we have and how to choose from among them. To

135

grade them humanely and touch the art of teaching with our evaluation, we must become sensitive to the nuances in our instructional situations. To become the best teachers of students, we must adapt the tools to make them our own, to make them serve our instructional purposes.

But this is a how-to book. How, then, to . . . ?

First, no one but you can teach yourself to grade. A book or a workshop or a presenter can give you ideas, hints, and suggestions, but you must be in charge of your own learning. The learning of a craft or an art is as individual as every person who has ever become an artist or a craftsman. Usually, however, we learn crafts and arts by some combination of observation, learning of principles, and practice. As students ourselves we have had years of observing certain kinds of evaluation. As with any observation, however, our personal record is spotty, incomplete. The purpose of this book is to lay out the principles of evaluation—grading options. Grading cannot be learned from reading a book any more than calligraphy can be learned from a book. The real learning takes place once the beginning artist or beginning grader begins to experiment and practice.

The writing process itself can point the way: Prewriting—Drafting—Rewriting—Sharing. Or is it Prewriting—Rewriting—Prewriting—Drafting—Sharing—Drafting—Rewriting—Sharing—Prewriting?

But then, like the writing process, perhaps the grading process can be untangled into primary activities: Pregrading—Guessing—Regrading—Grading. To me, "pregrading" means studying the communication situation and matching our options—this entire book, in fact. As with "prewriting," "pregrading" should occupy a lot of our time and thought. As you do brainstorming and legwork necessary before you begin to grade, consider the following questions and the possible answers. Make your choices in the light of your classroom context.

Consider your classroom context

Question: What are my strengths and challenges as a writing teacher?

Question: What are my students' needs and attitudes toward writing?

Question: What are the goals of the writing instruction my students will receive?

Consider possible grading approaches

Question: How do I plan to determine the letter or number grade on this assignment?

Possible Answers: Analytic, blended, or holistic approach.

Consider possible response strategies

Question: How do I plan to communicate the grade on this assignment?

Possible Answers: Conferences, taped responses, computer-written responses, handwritten notes, grading sheets, grades without comments.

Consider possible management systems

Question: How do I plan to arrive at a six-weeks' or year grade?

Possible Answers: Grade-averaging; cumulative records such as checklists, anecdotal records, or cumulative writing folders; contracts; or portfolios.

Consider possible evaluation styles

Question: Who will have the decision-making power in my classroom?

Possible Answers: Teacher, student, peers, student/teacher partnership, someone outside the classroom.

Once you've answered the questions and have chosen your grading tools, you're ready to move on in the process of grading. "Guessing" comes first, putting the first tentative grade on the first student papers. Then comes "re-grading," going back and making sure the grades we gave the first and last papers agree. "Grading" is the moment when we commit ourselves and hand back the papers or send home the report cards. And maybe the grading process is just as recursive as the writing process. Maybe it looks like the schematics of the writing process we have begun to draw, messy and recursive, bending back infinitely on itself until we finally just stop. In his book *Write to Learn*, Donald Murray offers a model of the writing process that illustrates the messy, recursive nature of writing, the jumble that happens in our heads (p. 6). His model is presented in Figure 11.1. Perhaps a graphic of the grading process (see Figure 11.2) would look much the same.

And as with writing, experimenting with grading is O.K.; in fact, it is mandatory if we are to truly match our evaluation to our instruction, if we are to develop the individual grading system each of us as "teacher" needs, and if we are to find our own voices as graders.

FIGURE 11.1.   The Writing Process

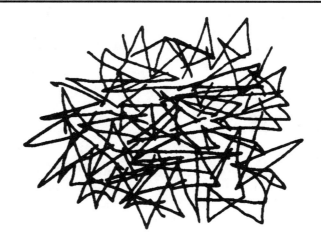

From *Write to Learn* 2E 2nd edition by Donald Murray © 1987. Reprinted with permission of Heinle, a division of Thomson Learning: www.thomsonrights.com. Fax 800-730-2215.

FIGURE 11.2.   The Grading Process

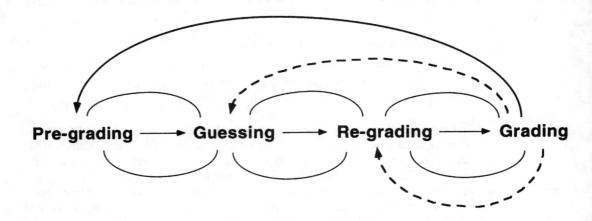

In recent years I have had the pleasure of getting to know several fiction writers on a personal basis. One of the questions I love to ask is, "How do you write?" The answers are fascinating and varied. One writer I know writes in longhand on a yellow legal pad in the library. Another writer I know writes on a word processor in a study at home. In her book *The Writing Life*, Annie Dillard tells about a writer who does errands and then rushes into his house to retype everything he's written up to that point and add a sentence or two. Another writer I know of needs solitude so intensely that she moves to a new city whenever she is beginning a new book. Some writers drink, some listen to music, some eat popcorn. Oddly, perhaps, all of these writers are good writers. But how did these people develop these systems for writing? The answer is, of course, by writing, by practicing, by seeing what fit their personal work styles and what did not. Learning to grade is much the same.

Ways of Beginning

But lest I leave you where my teachers left me—"you have to work it out yourself"—I will lay out for you three scenarios of possible ways to begin teaching yourself to grade. Please remember, though, that these are only three of an almost infinite number of scenarios. If none of these works for you, strike out across the desert on your own. Do errands madly and then rush into your house to grade a paper or two.

Scenario #1

Begin from an analytic base. Find your district's curriculum guide or state's standards. Make a list of all of the writing skills someone else has compiled that are labeled as "appropriate" for the grade level you teach. Divide them into the five categories I have suggested in Chapter 3 (context, content, structure, mechanics, process). Read the paper once for context and content, a second time for structure, a third time for mechanics. Examine the process the student used. Pick up another student's work. Read that student's work in the same way as you did the first one's. Do this a hundred times or until the pieces begin to blur before your eyes and you can move toward primary-trait scoring and, finally, holistic scoring.

Scenario #2

Begin from a primary-trait base. If the pieces of the grading puzzle are new concepts for you, teach yourself to grade as you teach your students to write. You may begin with any piece of the puzzle you choose (I would recommend beginning with process). Using your state scoring guide or the list in Chapter 3, make yourself a rubric that covers only that piece of the puzzle (the writing process—prewriting, drafting, revising, editing, publishing). Teach process to your students. Grade their papers only on process.

Now move to another piece of the puzzle—context, perhaps. Make yourself a rubric about audience, purpose, and author's stance. Teach context concerns to your students. Evaluate their papers on process and context. Move to content, and so on. Begin with the six traits. Select one trait and evaluate your students' writing only on that one trait. Add another trait and another until you are evaluating on all six traits.

Do this a hundred times or until you begin to get a feel for the pieces.

Scenario #3

Begin from a holistic base. Read a set of papers straight through. Without thinking too much, sort them into three piles—"Good," "O.K.," and "Weak." Read your "Good" stack a second time and divide it into "Excellent" and "Good" and "Not Quite as Good as I Thought." Read your "O.K." stack a second time and divide it into "Pretty Good Really," "O.K.," and "Just Barely O.K." Read your "Weak" stack a second time and divide it into "Almost O.K.," "Weak," and "Needs Another Try." Sift through your stacks (you'll remember the papers this time) and double check that you've been fair. Move a paper or two around. If in doubt, move the paper to a higher stack (both you and the student will feel better and no harm will be done). Collapse your stacks ("Excellent" is stack one. "Good," "Not Quite as Good as I Thought," and "Pretty Good Really" is stack two. "O.K.," "Just Barely O.K.," and "Almost O.K." become stack three. "Weak" is a fourth stack.) Put grades on your stacks ("A" for stack one, "B" for stack two, "C" for stack three, "D" for stack four—or use the "+," "✓+," "✓," or "✓−"). Give back the "Needs Another Try" stack, have conferences with those students, and ask them to redo the assignment.

Do cluster grading a hundred times or until the stacks begin to have specific characteristics for you. Write down those characteristics. Make a rubric from your lists. Grade from your rubric until you are ready to examine the state's curriculum guide for more characteristics.

Creating a Personal Grading System

Why teach yourself to grade using all the different approaches? You don't have to, of course. No one is going to come to your classroom with a five-year checklist and see if you've tried all of the approaches. But no grading strategy tells the whole story. Writing is an exceedingly complex behavior, and the different approaches to evaluating it offer us different bits of information about the process of becoming an articulate writer. From holistic grading we learn that writing is more than the sum of its parts. We acknowledge that a piece of writing can be heavily flawed (like Flannery O'Connor's drafts) and still be powerful and wonderful. We also acknowledge that writing can be flawless in design and still say absolutely nothing worth saying (a high school senior's five-paragraph essay on "the future"). From analytic grading we learn that writing can be taught, that we can oftentimes define for a writer what it is that he or she needs to work on to improve. I believe that it is important for any teacher who grades writing to understand all the approaches to grading. Only then can meaningful choices be made that match grading strategies to instructional goals.

Learning to grade is like learning any other craft. It is not easy to learn to grade, just as it is not easy to learn to ride a bicycle, fly an airplane, crochet an afghan, or create art from calligraphy. It takes a long time and a lot of practice to get good at evaluation. But because most of us teach ten, twenty, or even forty years, an investment of two or three years teaching ourselves to grade writing will pay off in the long run. The more intentional each of us becomes about evaluation, the more we each pick a system and practice with it, the quicker and more consistent we become. After several years of teaching and grading writing you may find that you grade very differently from the teacher next door. And guess what? That's O.K.

We teach and grade from our values. All of us value different things about different kinds of writing. (My husband likes to read travelogues that offer philosophical comments along the trail; I enjoy murder mysteries about characters who fool the world but not the detective.) As long as students understand clearly what we value about writing—what it is that we are trying to teach them—and as long as our evaluation reflects our instruction, our grades are "fair." Students stay in school for twelve to sixteen to twenty-two years. They have different teachers who teach them different things about writing. Thank goodness, right? So clarify for yourself what you value most about writing, match your instructional goals to those values, match your grading system to those instructional goals, inform your students of your system, and grade their papers with conviction!

Chapter Summary

Learning to grade involves both art and craft. The craft is knowing which tools to use in which situation. The art is in knowing what you want your grades to do. While learning to grade it is important to understand both analytic and holistic grading, so it is unimportant where on the continuum a teacher begins to learn to grade.

EXERCISES

1. Answer the "pregrading" questions listed in the beginning of this chapter. Check to make sure that none of your choices undercuts the purpose of the other choices you've made. Write a statement describing and defending your grading scheme in light of the classroom context in which you're working. Explain and defend your grading scheme to a small group of other teachers.

2. Decide where on the grading approach continuum you want to begin learning to grade. Grade five papers from Appendix A according to the approach you have chosen.

3. Find someone in your group who began at a different point on the continuum. Swap papers (with the grades kept secret from each other). Grade the other teacher's papers using your approach. Ask the other teacher to grade yours using his or her approach. Compare the grades of all ten papers. Discuss any grades that are radically different. Is the difference a result of the method, or of your values as teachers, or of something else?

References   Beasley, Richard. *Tribute Show*. Flagstaff, AZ: Northern Arizona University Art Gallery, October–November, 1992.

Dillard, Annie. *The Writing Life*. New York: Harper and Row, 1990.

Murray, Donald. *Write to Learn*, 2nd ed. New York: Holt, Rinehart and Winston, 1987.

APPENDIX A
Sample Papers

Appendix A contains thirty samples of writing done by children in first through sixth grades. Wherever I could gather more than one sample from an assignment, I did so, attempting to provide samples that illustrated the range of work turned in to the teacher for evaluation. The samples illustrate a variety of instructional purpose and student audience, drawn as they were from different classrooms in schools sometimes over 100 miles apart. I have intentionally omitted the original context of the piece of writing: invent your own contexts for it. In the context of a primary classroom, Figure A.14 (for example) may represent excellent work; however, in the context of a sixth-grade classroom, it may represent work that needs to be redone. Experiment with instructional purpose as well. See what happens to the grade on the piece as the context changes. Trade papers with another teacher and see what happens to the grade. Discuss what you each did and why.

But beyond providing practice for grading and points of departure for discussion, this appendix illustrates the range and richness of children's writing. So use your own imagination, and enjoy the imaginations of the kids who so kindly allowed me to use their work.

FIGURE A.1a.   Fortunately/Unfortunately

FIGURE A.1b.   Fortunately/Unfortunately (continued)

FIGURE A.1c.   Fortunately/Unfortunately (continued)

FIGURE A.1d.   Fortunately/Unfortunately (continued)

Unfortunately,
My house was a
mess.

FIGURE A.1e. Fortunately/Unfortunately (continued)

Fortunately,
I had enough room to
fit the presents in and
I got so a SuperSoaker

FIGURE A.1f.   Fortunately/Unfortunately (continued)

FIGURE A.2a.   Unfortunately/Fortunately

Fortunately my mom was going to buy me a monkey!

FIGURE A.2b.   Unfortunately/Fortunately (continued)

Unfortunately my mom didn't have enough money excpt for a dollar.

FIGURE A.2c.   Unfortunately/Fortunately (continued)

FIGURE A.2d.   Unfortunately/Fortunately (continued)

Unfortunately we couldn't find a place where people buy monkeys.

FIGURE A.2e.   Unfortunately/Fortunately (continued)

Fortunately we went to the Zoo and the zookeeper said that we could keep his monkey.

FIGURE A.2f.   Unfortunately/Fortunately (continued)

Unfortunately it was not house trained.

FIGURE A.2g.   Unfortunately/Fortunately (continued)

Fortunately We trained her
we named her Lily.

FIGURE A.3a.   Spring Break

Spring Break

He came from the earth, a great mass of writhing darkness, darker than the blackest night. The master of darkness, the world from which he came knew no light. Great sharp talons that reached out, long and bony, were it's only real features and he came to destroy them, to catch them sleeping safe and sound in their warm little beds and do away with them all.

The smoke rose in dark puffs, visible against the pale winter sky. Inside the cottage, the awful stench of rot and decay was strong. The children's cheeks were hollow with hunger and the mother sat silently staring into the fire from her chair. The harsh winter winds blew fiercely outside, shaking the small shack and making the bare, finger like branches of the trees dance wildly about. To add to all of that, there came a strange mournful wail that threaded it's way through the forest and came dwindling to mere wisps at the door. Everyone was aware of it. The smallest children shuddered violently against the fierce cold and the eerie sound. The older children tried to ignore the steadily growing moan but soon they too were gathered around their mother, all eyes begging for reassurance and comfort. The mother did her best to dry their tears and build up the dying fire but she could not offer an explanation for this strange and frightening noise. Just as the sound was beginning to grow beyond bearing, everything stood still, the wind stopped and the moaning sound ceased to surround them.
The silence was like an explosion, it seemed to enclose them in an envelope of darkness and in that awful stillness, a blood curdling scream split the air and the dying fire sputtered and went out. The family stood frozen until the piercing sound of another scream aroused them into an intense terror that none had ever known before. It was so strong that everyone seemed to be out of breath from the weight of it. Then the rumbling sound began, It was similar to the sound of distant thunder rolling gently along the hills but at the same time, the earth began to shake, gently at first but then violently, sending everyone and everything shattering to the floor.
The children screamed, terrified, as the ground beneath them heaved upward and then began to tilt. There were several deffening explosions that sent earth, rock, tree and many splintered cottages tumbling through the air. Cries for help from other women and children could be heard everywhere and with the last lights of day disappearing over the horizon, the night set in. No moon rose and no twinkling starlight gave even the slightest hint of light and in the utter blackness, raging fires could be seen burning like brilliant flowers in a land of rubble and dust. The strong voice of a man cut through the darkness like a ray of light, "Do not despair," he said and paused. Many cries of protest went up and he went on, "Do you remember the legend of the underworld and how it's king would one day rise up and take our land, destroying us? This legend has been passed down for many generations and now, this very second he sets forth from the

FIGURE A.3b.   Spring Break (continued)

place where he erupted from the earth to conquer us. The strange
sounds you just heard were the sounds of the earth and the trees
and all living things announcing his coming. All the men of this
village and many others have gone to meet this evil creature they
call king of the underworld and hold him back until more help is
sent." Who shall protect us?" a weak voice cried out from
somewhere in the darkness.

"All the men from this land will come together to fight this
evil creature. Until it has been destroyed you will have to fend
for yourselves, I am sorry." His voice was strained and sad as he
said these last words as if it hurt him to say them. Then he was
gone and the people of the village began picking through the
wreck of smashed houses and gathering together for warmth. In the
morning it was still pitch black and throughout all that day and
the next the sun did not shine and no word came from the north
where the great battle was being fought. Sometimes small groups
of men carrying pitchforks and torches could be seen marching
northward. At first these men were always cheered on by the women
and children but after a while everyone was so tired and weak
that they could barely speak to each other without collapsing
with the effort. Sometimes they gathered around in a circle and
told what little they could remember from the legend of the
underworld.

Seven days passed in complete darkness and on the seventh
night the stars shone bright in the sky and a beautiful moon rose
full over the troubled land. At dawn the sky grew pink and the
sun rose with a blinding fierceness. Along with the restoring of
the sun there came a runner from the north bearing a message. He
reported that the battle had been fought and won by the villagers
and that the king of the underworld had been killed and flung off
the edge of the world, never to haunt the land again. The men of
the village were cleaning up the mess and working their way back
toward the home.

With this relieving news, the women and children were filled
with a surprising new strength and began to clean up the awful
wreck in the village. By the time the mess had been totally
cleared away and the men came marching over the hill and down
into the valley there was much celebrating and feasting that
lasted far into the warm days of spring, Spring brought a promise
of a new beginning. The trees that had slept for so long during
those dark winter months awakened with a joyful explosion of
delicate green leaves. The grass grew soft where nothing but
crunching leaves had blown silently across barren ground and the
crops grew plentifully. No one was hungry and everyone was in
good health.

They lived in peace forever and always remembered the seven
days of darkness in which the great battle was fought. In fact
they decided to take a seven day vacation from work and school in
memory of those seven days of darkness and the people that fought
through them. This vacation is now commonly refered to as spring
break and not a single person remembers the reason we have it.

FIGURE A.4.   Dear Penny . . .

Dear Penny,
I think it would be
hard to train a gorilla. I have
always wanted a gorilla like Koko.
I wont to know is it fun playing
with Koko?

Your friend,
Miriam

FIGURE A.5.   The Anasazis

WHY THE ANASAZI'S DISAPPEARED?

One hot summer night, in a beautiful desert place named Red Canyon, some Indians were sitting around a fire telling stories about how the white men came and took their land and killed their people. All of a sudden they heard some sticks crackling behind them in the bushes. One of the Indians grabbed his bow and arrow and said to the noise in the bushes, "Come out of there and show your face to us Indians." Then a white man stepped out from behind the bushes. The Indian said, "Get off my land!" The white man said, "No, this is not your land this land is the governments land." "You barbarians are ruining the land." "And those marking (petroglyphs) you wrote all over the mountains, what do they mean?" The Indian said. "Those are our special prayers." "We do not want you white men carving your names and dates all over them and ruining our messages." "Now leave our land before you ruin anything else." Then the Indian pointed his bow and arrow at the white man and said, "Go and leave me and my people alone." The white man said, "Okay, I will leave, but I will be back for you and your people."

After the white man left, one of the Indian kids said, "What will happen to us when the white men come back?" The Indian man said, "We won't be here when the white men come back for us." Everyone said, "What do you mean we won't be here when the white men come back?" The Indian man said, "We are going to move to a new home." So all of the Indians packed their things and left. The next day a whole army of white men came to the Indian village. they looked all over but couldn't find the Indians. And to this day no one knows what happened to those Indian people.

FIGURE A.6.   China

I know three
things about China
They use Chopstiks
To eat They bilt a
grato wol to Keep the
enomes out ay ther
viligs They eat rise.

FIGURE A.7.   My mom is . . .

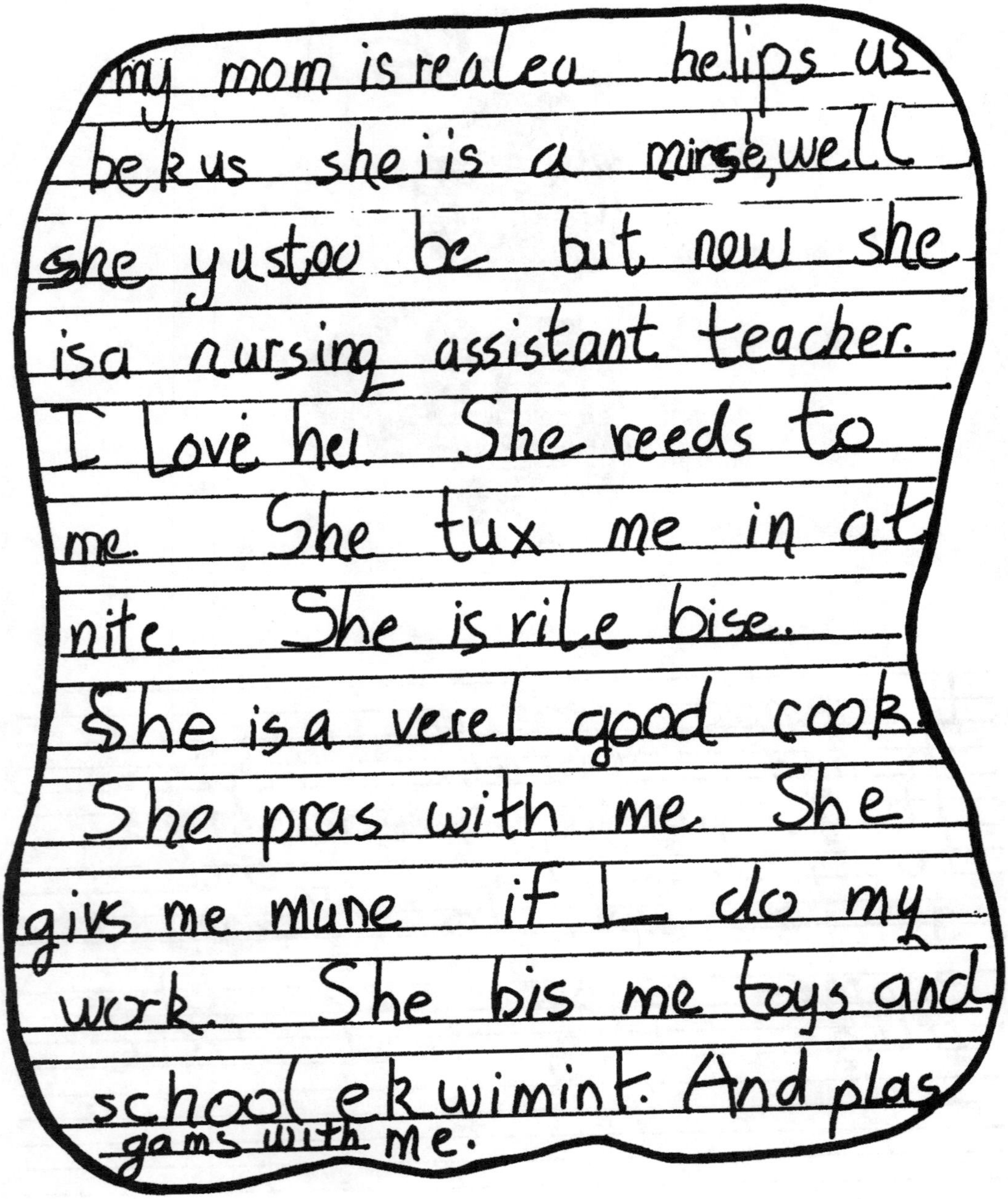

my mom is realea helips us
bekus she iis a mirse, well
she yustoo be but now she
isa nursing assistant teacher.
I love her. She reeds to
me. She tux me in at
nite. She is rile bise.
She is a verel good cook.
She pras with me. She
givs me mune if I do my
work. She bis me toys and
school ekwimint. And plas
gams with me.

FIGURE A.8.   A Ship

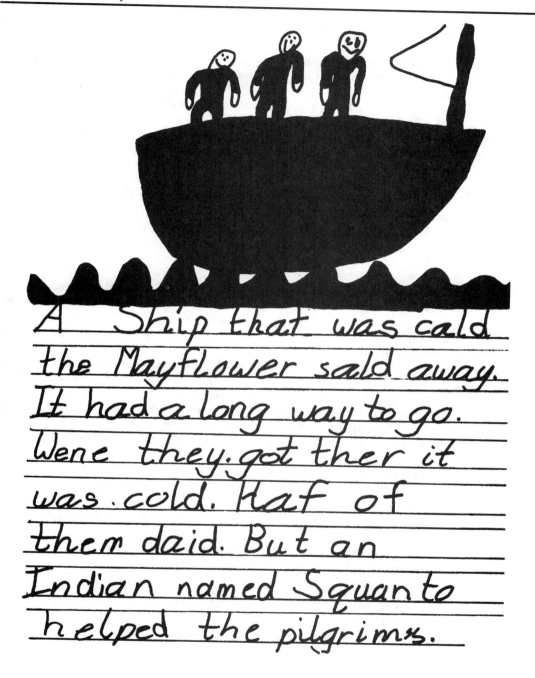

A Ship that was cald
the Mayflower sald away.
It had a long way to go.
Wene they got ther it
was cold. Haf of
them daid. But an
Indian named Squanto
helped the pilgrims.

FIGURE A.9.   A Sequel to Tom Sawyer

___

(A sequel to a chapter from Tom Sawyer)

Tom was so sad after Becky had said those words to him. He felt sick again. Actually Becky liked him too, but didn't admit it. Tom went home sad as ever, so did Peter.

Aunt Polly said, "Tom, what's a matter with you? You look like your stomach fell out."

"Well," said Tom. "Becky Thatcher has been out of school for a long time and I missed her a lot. She just came back today and well, Aunt Polly, I'm tired, I'm gonna rest."

"OK Tom," answered Aunt Polly.

Tom thought and thought about what to say to Becky. Finally he said, "I'll just be me for awhile."

As they were eating supper, Aunt Polly thought about what was wrong with Tom.

Tom said, "What's a matter with Peter?"

"Why, I don't know, Tom," answered Aunt Polly.

"I was just wondering because he sleeps all the time." explained Tom.

What was wrong with Peter was that he liked Becky too. He went to his bed thinking about how in the world he could get Becky to like him. Tom didn't know that Peter liked Becky because he was too busy thinking about how to get to sleep. Finally both of them fell asleep.

When Tom woke he ate breakfast quickly and ran to school as fast as he could.

There was Becky standing in the schoolyard talking to her friends. Tom walked into the schoolyard whistling a happy tune.

Becky noticed and said, "There's Tom Sawyer, isn't he cute!" They all giggled. Little did Tom know that he was in for a big surprise.

After school Becky said to Tom, "My birthday party is tomorrow, could you come?"

Tom was so overjoyed that he said, "Yes, I can come!"

"Great," said Becky. "See you tomorrow."

"Bye," said Tom.

Tom ran home. He burst through the door and yelled, "Aunt Polly!"

"Yes, I'm in the kitchen," answered Aunt Polly. "What is it?"

"I'm going to Becky's birthday party tomorrow, ok?" asked Tom.

"That's fine Tom, but be careful," decided Aunt Polly.

"I will, I promise," said Tom.

The next morning Tom dressed himself in his Sunday best. "Bye, Aunt Polly," waved Tom.

"Bye Tom, have a good day at school," said Aunt Polly.

FIGURE A.9. A Sequel to Tom Sawyer (continued)

Tom had an excellent day at school. He got good grades on all of his tests. Then it came, it was time for Becky's birthday party. All the kids rushed to Becky's house.

They played games, and then it was time for cake and ice cream. Becky's mom gave the first piece to Becky, then some to Tom and the rest of the kids. Tom said, "This is a really fun birthday, I've had a really great time."

"Thanks," said Becky and she kissed him on the cheek.

Tom had finally won Becky's heart, but he still had not figured out what was wrong with Peter.

FIGURE A.10. Mr. Ed

Mr. Ed was at the laundromat at noontime. He was feeling angry and bad. He had lost his job at J.B.'s restaurant a few hours ago. He had been a waiter there.

Earlier in the morning he and his wife had gotten in an argument. His wife had shouted at him "Fine" and stormed out of the house. He tried to call her back, "Ellen, come back." But she didn't respond or turn around. So he went to work upset. He thought during lunch, "I'll bring some flowers and we'll have a great brunch. Everything will be fine." But as it turned out he was wrong. The customers accused him of shouting at them. Then shortly afterwards he was yelling at his boss. Mr. Hogan, his boss, said, "Don't bother coming over tomorrow for work, you're fired!"

So he got in his car and he drove to his wife's office. They both apologized to each other. But after he told her how he got fired, she again stormed out and went home. When he got home she had his clothes on the porch. She started screaming words that he never heard her say before. All of a sudden before he knew what was happening the door slammed. He was just about to get in his car when he heard her come out and say, "Don't come back!" Questions were running through his head. Where am I going to stay? How will I get food? What if I die! HELP me somebody.

FIGURE A.11.   Monkey Bars

Monkey Bars

Slippery, hard and cold
My hands go across the bars and cross back.
It makes my arms tired,
But I like it.

Béésh ndaaz' ahígíí

Bídéelto', ntłiz, dóó sik'az
     (

Shila' béésh ndaaz' ahígíí bee tsé'
     naa ałnáhaná shchał dóó nat' áá
                         ((

Shigaan ninadalna, ndi shił yá á tééh.

FIGURE A.12.   My Favorite Author

My Favorite Author: H.G. Wells

H.G. Wells was born in 1886. He was a great author in his time. He wrote "romantic fiction," which was what they called science-fiction at that time. He earned a scholarship to the Normal School of Science in London. He wrote science articles for some magazines. He then wrote THE TIME MACHINE, which many consider his most well-written work. The success of that book started a career in which he in his "great period" wrote THE ISLAND OF DR. MOREOU (1896), THE INVISIBLE MAN (1897), THE WAR OF THE WORLDS (1898), WHEN THE SLEEPER WAKES (1899) and THE FIRST MEN IN THE MOON (1901). He wrote these books about a century ago, and they are still popular today because he wrote so well. After the turn of the century, Wells began writing social issue books. When he became less successful, he started to write short stories; these had normal success.

My favorite book written by Wells is THE INVISIBLE MAN. It is about a man who found a way to become invisible. He found out that he didn't have an antidote. He wanted to use his invisibility to his advantage. He started a "reign of terror" in which those who did not obey his commands would be murdered. At the end, the people catch the invisible man.

Two interesting things happened with Wells' stories. Winston Churchill liked the story THE LAND IRONCLADS and later designed tanks after the ones of which Wells had written. Another thing that happened was that one Halloween night in the 30's a radio station was doing THE WAR OF THE WORLDS, which is about Martians taking over our world. It sounded so real to people who tuned in at the middle that they panicked, thinking that the Martians were really taking over the world.

I like Wells' books because they have good dialect and dialogue. I also like his characters. He always has a "bad guy" or "bad guys," but there really isn't a hero because everybody seems so dimwitted. The settings aren't very important in the books he wrote; the story is really interesting by itself, but the setting doesn't help you understand it more. I like his science-fiction ideas because they are things that everybody dreams about. He really likes to do that kind of thing. This is why I like his books.

FIGURE A.13.   The Plane

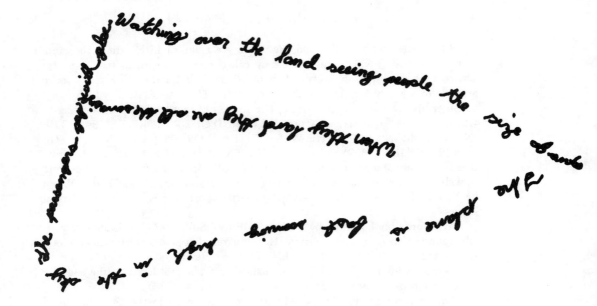

FIGURE A.14.   The Important Thing about Whales . . .

The important thing about whales is that they are almost gone. Killer whales are members of the dolphin family. Whales are nice. Whales are very big. Whales are mammals. Killer whales live in the cold waters. But the important thing about whales is that they are almost gone.

FIGURE A.15.   The Important Thing about My Dog . . .

The important thing about my dog is she is a Golden Retriever. She is special to my family. She is my best friend. She plays with me. She loves me. But the important thing about my dog is that she is a Golden Retriever.

FIGURE A.16.   Stomach

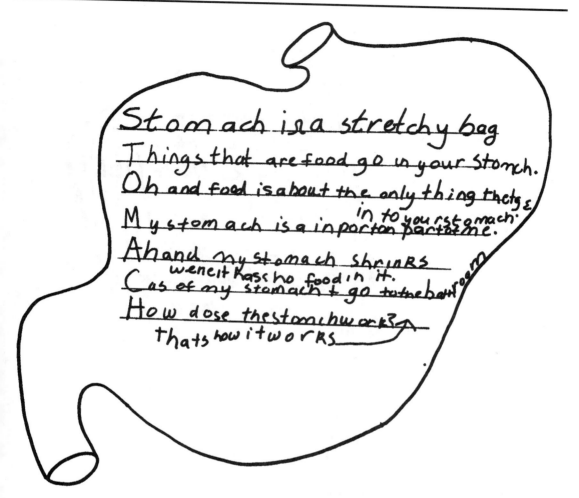

Stomach is a stretchy bag
Things that are food go in your Stomch.
Oh and food is about the only thing thatg
     in to your rstomach.
My stomach is a inportan part of me.
Ahand my stomach shrinks
     weneit hass no food in it.
Cas of my stomach t go to the bathroom
How dose the stomich work?
     thats how it works

FIGURE A.17.   Muscles

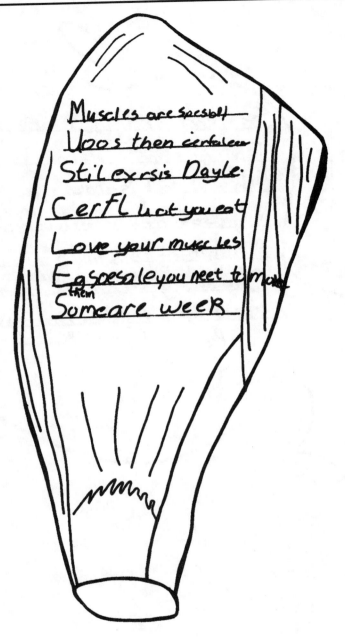

FIGURE A.18.   Excited

SYNESTHETIC POETRY

Excited

LOOKS LIKE a scared cat

TASTES LIKE a juicy cherry

SMELLS LIKE cotton candy

SOUNDS LIKE yelling for joy

FEELS LIKE a rough stone

FIGURE A.19.   Excited (second example)

SYNESTHETIC POETRY

excited

LOOKS LIKE Fire worcks

TASTES LIKE bubbles

SMELLS LIKE Fire

SOUNDS LIKE explosion

FEELS LIKE earthquake

FIGURE A.20.   A Persian Kitten

A Persian Kitten

A Persian Kitten is white and fluffy, like a cloud

This Persian kitten plays with string, like a dog trying to catch a snake

Soon the kitten gets tired, but soon after her nap she will play agin.

This Pesian kitten likes to stay inside were it is warm and cosy.

This kitten will grow up end wan't be as playful but I will shil rember when she was a kitten.

FIGURE A.21.   A Great Person

A Great Person
Born in 1706
He published a newspaper,
He was Philadqias Postmaster,
He was the father of the Govenor of New Jersey,
He wrote the Almanac, and
He flew a kite. These are not all of the wonderful things He did.
Do you know hoo this Person was?
This great person was... Benjaman Franklin.

FIGURE A.22.   I Like to Play . . .

I like to play hideing go seek. This is how you play hideing go seek. It Like if someone is goingto count number and wine the othern pirsin will triy to find you and if he or she find you have to cant if you find he or she and then she or he find you you just need to be doing the same thing I told you on the papen you gust nid tu fulo the ruls at I git you I pirsin ride tu cont in tapyou can hiem

FIGURE A.23.   How You Play . . .

This How you play hockey
you get to get a hockey stick
. But there are rules
I do not fight. 2 do not hit.
that are all the rules.
Now you got to drop the puck
in the middle then you
hit the puck into the
goal if you make 20 ponlts
you winner the game.

FIGURE A.24.   Dear Matt . . .

Dear Matt,

Thank you for the letter I enjoyed reading it, you said you liked the Phoenix Suns I went to see them January 30th. They played Dallas Mavericks. The Suns won by 15 points.

I don't really care for football but I watch it occasionally and played in 1st grade. Have you played other sports?

I'm going to Lake Havasu this month. I've never been there before, is it a nice town.

Yes I do go cross contry skiing and I've been down hill once. My family goes skiing about once a weekend. You should come up here and try it some time. You'll probably like it. I have one brother named Joshua who is 4. I also have a ginea pig named Colorfull, a dog named Spot, four salamaders and a toad. Do you have any pets, brothers or sisters? Hope write you'll soon.

Sincerely,
Tom

FIGURE A.25.   Dear William . . .

Dear William,
    l am 10 yeas old
also l would like to
know why your called
Brett when your name
is William?
    l was born in
flagstaff and lived in
the same house all my
live. l really don't
have a favorite pet
because l like them
all the same. My sister
is 7. How old is

FIGURE A.25.   Dear William . . . (continued)

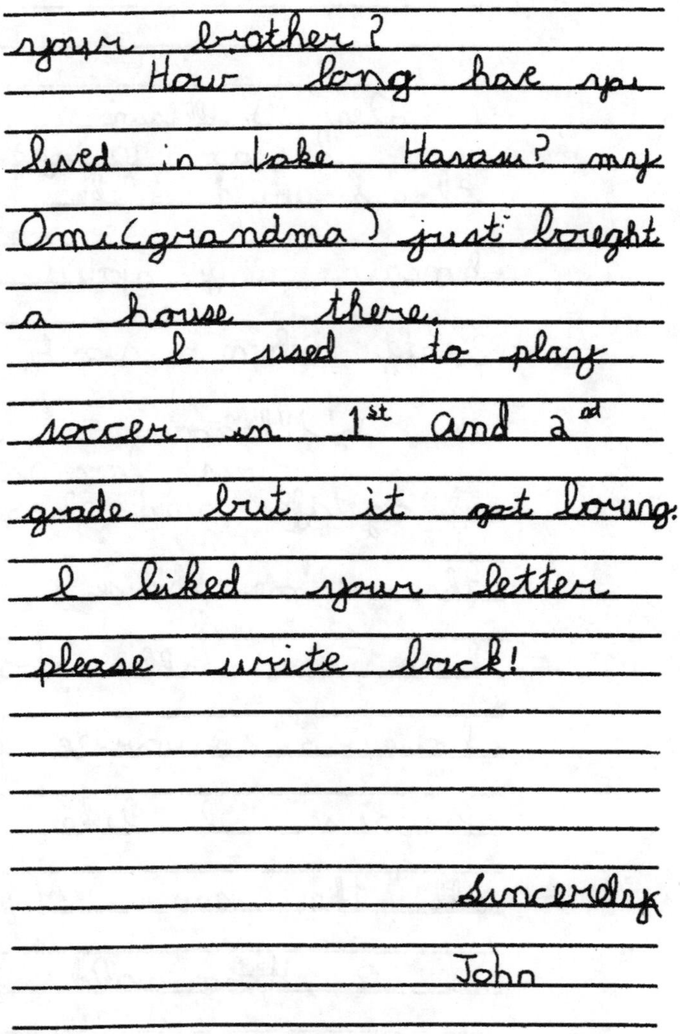

your brother?
    How long hae you
lived in lake Havasu? my
Omi (grandma) just bought
a house there.
        I used to play
soccer in 1st and 2nd
grade but it got boring.
I liked your letter
please write back!

                Sincerely
                John

FIGURE A.26.   The Beaver

THE BEAVER
THE BEAER

The beaver is a very diffrent and interesting animal. When beaver are born they are called kits, they weigh 8 to 24 ounces, are 15 inches long, and their tail is 3½ inches long. By their third summer ready to mate. A female beaver first breeds when its 2½ years old. The young stay with their mother till their second year. When the young are gone, the mother has another litter.

Beavers are builders, by cutting down trees with their teeth, they build dams, lodges, and canals. Some wood they sink in the water near their lodge (dam or canal). This will form an under-water storehouse, for keeping their winter food. Beavers live most of their life in or near water. Have you learned more about beavers than you use to know?

MY source is Comtons Encyclopedia

FIGURE A.27.   Bald Eagles

Bald   Eagles   are intereresting birds. They are called the bald eagle because if you are far away they look bald. They lay too two eggs each year, The bald eagles have white on their heads; They eat fish and snatch it out of the water with there talons. They have big talons for big fish. The bald eagles build there nests to last for 12 months.

FIGURE A.28.   Iguanas

IGUANAS

THE IGUANA IS A WEIRD SPECIE. THEY LIKE HOT PLACES. IF YOUR SHOULDER IS HOT AND THE IGUANA IS COLD IT WILL LAY ON YOUR SHOULDER. THEY LIKE TO EAT BANANAS, APPLES, AND ROMAIN LETTUCE. THEY LIVE IN THE DESERT. THEY LIVE 10 TO 12 YEARS IN CAPTIVITY.

IGUANAS ARE A COMMON REPTILE IN ARIZONA. THEY GROW TO BE 5 FEET LONG. THEY HAVE NO TEETH. THEY HAVE TWO ROUND BLACK MARDS AND THOSE ARE PRESENT IN THE IGUANAS CHEEKS.

SOURCE: ALL ABOUT IGUANAS
            BY MERVIN F. ROBERT AND
            MARTHA D. ROBERT

FIGURE A.29.   My Earliest Memory

My Earliest Mememory

When I was about four or five I went to the carnival with my brother, my stepdad. We also had a boy mambed Tom. We babysit him. His mom is my moms freind. We lived in the same hause we live in right know.

As lots of kids love to do I love to go on rides. You know, rides that are like at the festival in the pines or the carnival that they have once a year. When I get really dizzy I seem get kind of sick.

That day we went to the carnival that my family was really excited about. My parents play in a band, so they like to watch other bands so we watched the band for a while. When their was good songs Wayne and Tom and I were jumping up and down so excited because watching the band was getting kind of boring. Wayne and Tom and I wanted to go an more rides and play games. You know, the games that you throw the arrows and pop balloons. Finally mom let us go on rides. Wayne and I saw this ride we had to on It. It looked so fun. Then my mom let us go on it. When we got on, it went so fast it was great. Then it started going faster. I was practically turning blue. I felt like I was going to throw up. I was so sick. I felt like I. I remember that feeling really well. When the ride stopped Wayne and Tom wouldn't get off. They wanted to go again. Finally they got of, and my stepdad picked me up.

FIGURE A.30. My Earliest Memory (second example)

My Earliest Memory

When I was about three or four, I lived in Maine. I remember the house we lived almost perfectly. Well, I remember the outside perfectly. It was a white house with red shutters and a red back porch.

There were some kids across the street from us named Jaimie and Nicole. Jaimie was a boy, and, Nicole was a girl. They were friends of ours. They were fun to play with, too.

One day the older kids (which were my brother, Jaime and Nicole) decided go to a street called Garfield (Garfield Street was named after the president). I rode on the back of Nicole's bike. We went to a path in the trees that leads to Garfield Street.

As we were entering the path I screamed, I thought we were going to see Garfield the cat. And that's where my memory ends. Nothing more, nothing less.

APPENDIX B
Annotated Bibliography

Research and Theory

Ackerman, John. *Students' Self-Analysis and Judges' Perceptions: Where Do They Agree?* Technical Report #23. University of California, Berkeley: Center for the Study of Writing, May 1989.

> This study argues that giving and responding to a writing assignment is an act of negotiation that depends on at least seven variables. The writing task was divided into source, format, and plan; student perceptions and judges' perceptions of these categories were compared.

Anson, Chris M., ed. *Writing and Response: Theory, Practice, and Research.* Urbana, IL: National Council of Teachers of English, 1989.

> This collection of sixteen essays addresses a wide range of theoretical issues grouped into three large categories: toward a theory of response in the classroom community, new perspective for responding to writing, and studies of response in the instructional context.

Applebee, Arthur N., et al. *Learning to Write in Our Nation's Schools: Instruction and Achievement in 1988 at Grades 4, 8, and 12.* The National Assessment of Educational Progress, prepared by Educational Testing Service, June 1990.

> Of particular interest is the discrepancy between student perceptions and teacher perceptions of feedback on completed work (pp. 53–56).

Cooper, Charles R. and Lee Odell, eds. *Evaluating Writing: Describing, Measuring, Judging.* Urbana, IL: National Council of Teachers of English, 1977.

> This collection of six essays summarizes methods of describing writing and measuring its growth. Essays cover holistic evaluation, primary-trait scoring, computer-aided description of mature word choices in writing, early blooming and late blooming syntactic structures, measuring changes in intellectual processes as one dimension of growth in writing, individualized goal setting, self-evaluation, and peer evaluation.

Dyson, Anne Haas and Sarah Warshauer Freedman. *On Teaching Writing: A Review of the Literature.* Occasional Paper #20. University of California, Berkeley, Center for the Study of Writing, July 1990.

This bibliography is an invaluable tool for a survey of the literature. A section on the evaluation of writing (pp. 7–9) cites sources that discuss classroom issues, local issues, and national issues.

Freedman, Sarah Warshauer. *Evaluating Writing: Linking Large-Scale Testing and Classroom Assessment*. Occasional Paper #27. University of California, Berkeley, Center for the Study of Writing, May 1991.

This paper focuses on large-scale testing and classroom assessment in an attempt to bridge the gap between teachers of writing and the testing and measurement community. A lengthy (and useful) reference list is appended.

Harmon, John. "The Myth of Measurable Improvement." *English Journal* 77 (9/1988): 79–80.

This essay argues that because writing skill develops over a long period of time, a portfolio grading system makes the most sense.

Horvath, Brooke K. "The Components of Written Response: A Practical Synthesis of Current Views." In *The Writing Teacher's Sourcebook*, New York: Oxford University Press, 1988.

This essay summarizes and synthesizes some of the guidelines, based on a study of the literature, for making effective written comments on student papers. The basic concern of the essay is with formative rather than summative evaluation.

Hyslop, Nancy B. "Evaluating Student Writing: Methods and Measurements," ERIC Clearinghouse on Reading and Communication Skills, March 1990.

This page and a half digest synthesizes nine major contributions between 1977 and 1988 to the field of evaluating student writing.

Krest, Margie. "Time on My Hands: Handling the Paper Load." *English Journal* 76 (12/1987): 37–42.

This essay redefines the role of "teacher" as it redefines the role of evaluation of student writing. It provides an overview of timesaving techniques as well.

Lees, Elaine O. "Evaluating Student Writing." In *The Writing Teacher's Sourcebook*, 2nd ed., edited by Gary Tate and Edward P. J. Corbett, pp. 263–267. New York: Oxford University Press, 1988.

This essay looks at writing evaluation from a communication perspective: What do I as evaluator have to say to my student as an audience? The author discusses seven kinds of responding: correcting, emoting, describing, suggesting, questioning, reminding, and assigning.

Lindemann, Erika. *A Rhetoric for Writing Teachers*. New York: Oxford University Press, 1987.

Chapter 13 of this book (pp. 191–223) is titled "Making and Evaluating Writing Assignments." In this chapter, the author discusses the relationship between grading and making writing assignments. She also discusses the various reasons for grading and some of the options available to teachers.

Schriver, Karen A. *Evaluating Text Quality: The Continuum from Text-Focused to Reader-Focused Methods*. Technical Report #41. University of California, Berkeley, Center for the Study of Writing, March 1990.

This report focuses on methods available to writers for evaluating the effectiveness of the texts they produce. It begins by isolating persistent questions raised by readers and then reviews typical methods of writer evaluation in three classes: text-focused, expert-judgment focused, and reader-focused approaches.

Shaugnessy, Mina. *Errors and Expectations: A Guide for the Teacher of Basic Writing*. New York: Oxford University Press, 1977.

> While the population with which Shaugnessy worked was college freshmen, this book is a classic in the field of evaluation. Its basic premise is that student writing errors are not simply careless or random, that, in fact, they are consistent within the writing of any single student, and can be analyzed for patterns to determine what relearning must take place to achieve correct written language.

Sperling, Melanie. *I Want to Talk to Each of You: Collaboration and the Teacher–Student Writing Conference*. Technical Report #37. University of California, Berkeley, Center for the Study of Writing, October 1989.

> This study examines interactive teacher–student writing conferences. Using ethnographic procedures, the study examines conferences over a six-week period for six case study ninth-graders.

Tchudi, Stephen, ed. *Alternatives to Grading Student Writing*. Urbana, IL: NCTE, 1997.

> This book reports the findings of the National Council of Teachers of English Committee on Alternatives to Grading Student Writing. The collection of nineteen essays is broken into three sections: background and theory, responding to student writing, and classroom strategies and alternatives to grading student writing. It also offers six outlines for faculty workshops on alternatives to grading writing.

Tiedt, Iris McClellan. *Writing: From Topic to Evaluation*. Boston: Allyn & Bacon, 1989.

> This book contains explanations of contemporary theories about teaching writing and sample applications designed to illustrate how to put the theory into practice. Methods of evaluation that are discussed include analytic, holistic, and primary-trait. Self-evaluation and peer evaluation strategies are also included.

Weaver, Constance. *Teaching Grammar in Context*. Portsmouth, NH: Heinemann, 1996.

> Working from research, the author discusses how children develop grammatical competence. She offers suggestions for sound instructional strategies and sample lessons on selected aspects of grammar.

White, Edward M. "Post-structural Literary Criticism and the Response to Student Writing." In *The Writing Teacher's Sourcebook*, 2nd ed., edited by Gary Tate and Edward P. J. Corbett, pp. 285–293. New York: Oxford University Press, 1988.

> In this essay, the author draws parallels between post-structuralist literary criticism and the practice of process-oriented writing teachers in reading and responding to student papers.

Yancey, Kathleen Blake. *Reflection in the Writing Classroom*. Logan, Utah: University of Utah Press, 1998.

> This book applies Donald Schon's work on reflection to the writing classroom and suggests ways reflection can impact both how teachers teach writing and how students learn to write. Of particular interest is Chapter 5, "Reflective Reading, Reflective Responding," which suggests ways of developing a philosophy of reading, responding to, and evaluating student writing.

Classroom Practice

Beaver, Teri. *The Author's Profile: Assessing Writing in Context*. York, Maine: Stenhouse, 1998.

> This book offers a method of continuous assessment of student writing, suggesting criteria for "nonassessable, emerging, and developing through advanced" writing in both fiction and nonfiction.

Belanoff, Pat and Marcia Dickson, eds. *Portfolios: Process and Product*. Portsmouth, NH: Boynton/Cook (Heinemann), 1991.

> This collection of essays addresses questions of evaluation of portfolios in different contexts. Of particular interest are the essays collected in Section III—Classroom Portfolios, pp. 151–228.

Bird, Lois Bridges, Kenneth S. Goodman, and Yetta M. Goodman. *The Whole Language Catalog: Forms for Authentic Assessment*. SRA: McMillan/McGraw-Hill, 1994.

> This book is filled with forms teachers can use for monitoring, observing, interacting with, and reporting student learning. Occasional explanatory sections put the forms into a context.

Block, Cathy Collins. *Teaching the Language Arts: Expanding Thinking through Student-Centered Education*, 3rd edition. Boston: Allyn & Bacon, 2001.

> This book covers all aspects of language arts, addressing each issue from three angles: theoretical foundations, putting theory into practice, and teachers as continual learners.

Bratcher, Suzanne. *The Learning-to-Write Process in Elementary Classrooms*. Mahwah, NJ: Lawrence Erlbaum Associates, Inc., 1997.

> This book takes an in-depth look at strategies teachers can use to establish their students' comfort with writing, build their confidence, and develop their competence. It examines the four major modes or genres of writing—personal writing, informative writing, persuasive writing, and literary writing—and discusses how writing can be used in a variety of content areas. In addition, it offers suggestions for teachers just learning to teach writing.

Bridges, Lois. *Assessment: Continuous Learning*. York, Maine: Stenhouse Publishers, 1995.

> This book defines "authentic assessment" and offers strategies teachers can use to assess not only student learning but teaching as well. An excellent chapter on portfolios and a useful professional bibliography are included as well.

Bridges, Lois. *Writing as a Way of Knowing*. York, Maine: Stenhouse Publishers, 1997.

> This book offers strategies for teachers who want to begin teaching writing to elementary-age students. It includes suggestions for various classroom activities like designing and running a writing workshop or conferencing with students. It also takes a look at the conventions of writing, writing to learn, and genres.

Bunce-Crim, Mana. "New Tools for New Tasks." *Instructor* 101, 7 (March, 1992): 23–26.

> This article offers tips and techniques for ongoing evaluation of primary and elementary age students. It details a system that includes observation, conferencing, and student self-assessment.

Calkins, Lucy McCormick. *The Art of Teaching Writing*, new edition. Portsmouth, NH: Heinemann, 1994.

> This new edition of what is now a classic work on teaching writing focuses throughout on how children teach us how they learn to write and how we can help them in that venture. The author emphasizes teaching writing using workshop methods.

Cleary, Linda Miller. *From the Other Side of the Desk: Students Speak Out about Writing.* Portsmouth, NH: Boynton/Cook (Heinemann), 1991.

> Of particular interest in this fascinating case-study book is the section entitled "Problems with Writing Curricula" (pp. 150–161). In addition, reflections on evaluation of writing are imbedded throughout the student stories.

Goodman, Kenneth, Yetta M. Goodman, and Wendy J. Hood, eds. *The Whole Language Evaluation Book*. Portsmouth, NH: Heinemann, 1989.

> The essays collected in this book center around particular stories of individual classrooms. The book is rich in student writing examples and evaluation forms created by teachers for various purposes.

Graves, Donald H. *Writing: Teachers and Children at Work*. Portsmouth, NH: Heinemann, 1983.

> Chapters 28 and 29, "Record Each Child's Development" and "Share the Children's Development with Parents and Administrators," give practical step-by-step directions for record keeping and communication. Eleven different kinds of records are discussed.

Graves, Donald. *A Fresh Look at Writing*. Portsmouth, NH: Heinemann, 1994.

> This follow-up to the classic *Writing: Teachers and Children at Work* focuses on actions teachers can take to teach more. It stresses teaching experiments and teachers learning right along with children. The book is wide-ranging, offering strategies to help teachers rethink why we teach writing, what responsibilities children can take for their own learning, what the fundamentals of writing are, what kinds of writing we want children to learn to do, and how to learn in an educational community.

Haley-James, Shirley. "Twentieth-Century Perspectives on Writing in Grades One through Eight." In *Perspectives on Writing in Grades 1–8*, edited by Shirley Haley-James. Urbana, IL: National Council of Teachers of English, 1981.

> A portion of this essay (pp. 14–16) offers an interesting historical summary of methods of evaluation from 1900 to 1979.

Linck, Wayne M. "Grading and Evaluation Techniques for Whole Language Teachers." *Language Arts* 68, 2 (February, 1991): 125–132.

> This article explains three systems for grading: individual comparison techniques, group comparison techniques, and criteria comparison techniques.

McCarrier, Andrea, Gay Su Pinnell, and Irene C. Fountas. *Interactive Writing: How Language and Literacy Come Together, K–2*. Portsmouth, NH: Heinemann, 2000.

> This book engages the issues of very early writing. It discusses the characteristics of a quality literacy program, both in theory and in practice. Two sections are of particular interest: Section 2, "Sharing the Pen with Young Writers," and Section 5, "The Foundations of Effective Writing Practice." Appendices 3 and 4 are also applicable: "Self-Assessment Rubric for Interactive Writing" and "Analysis of Writing."

Mayher, John S., Nancy Lester, and Gordon M. Pradl. *Learning to Write, Writing to Learn*. Portsmouth, NH: Boynton/Cook (Heinemann), 1983.

> Chapter 7 of this book, "Responding and Evaluating," offers examples of teacher response to reprinted student texts. Categories include teacher response, collaborative peer response, conferencing, and editing. Content-area writing is an added dimension of this text.

Moffett, James and Betty Jane Wagner. *Student-Centered Language Arts, K–12*. Portsmouth, NH: Boynton/Cook (Heinemann), 1992.

> Chapter 10, "Evaluation," discusses five functions of evaluation and offers strategies for inside-the-classroom evaluation as well as for outside-the-classroom evaluation. Classroom strategies include observation, charting, portfolios, and conferences.

Ruddell, Robert B. *Teaching Children to Read and Write*, 2nd edition. Boston: Allyn & Bacon, 1999.

> This book focuses on how reading and writing instruction support one another. It offers "How to Do" instructions throughout to help teachers learn to use recommended instructional strategies. It delineates the teacher's role in student learning and suggests ways teachers can become influential for parents and children.

Smitherman, Geneva. *Talkin that Talk: Language, Culture and Education in African America*. New York: Routledge, 2000.

> This collection of essays brings together Smitherman's most important writings on Ebonics, or Black English. Of particular interest is "English Teacher, Why You Be Doing the Thangs You Don't Do?" In this essay Smitherman proposes a Five-point Program for teaching English in the inner-city. While the essay was first written thirty years ago in the context of junior-high education, its main points are as important today in elementary classrooms as they were in 1972.

Spandel, Vicki. *Classroom Applications of Writing Assessment: A Teacher's Handbook*. Clearinghouse for Applied Performance Testing, May 1981. In ERIC ED214995.

> This handbook was written to meet the needs of the classroom teacher who is teaching writing and who wishes to use performance-based assessment strategies: holistic, analytic, and primary-trait.

Spandel, Vicki and Richard Stiggins. *Creating Writers: Linking Assessment and Writing Instruction*. New York: Longman, 1990.

> Chapter 5, "Grading: What It Will and Will Not Do," discusses what grades are, what to grade, and when to grade. Special emphasis is given to analytical grading.

Tchudi, Steven and Diana Mitchell. *Exploring and Teaching the English Language Arts*, 4th edition. New York: Longman, 1999.

> This book surveys strategies for teaching all of the language arts to elementary-age students. The two chapters on writing, "Teaching Writing" and "Writing for the Here and Now," offer strategies for teaching writing that range from journals to preparing students for college and suggest ways teachers can become writing coaches.

Tchudi, Stephen N. and Susan J. Tchudi. *The English/Language Arts Handbook*. Portsmouth, NH: Boynton/Cook (Heinemann), 1991.

> Chapter 4, "Assessment, Evaluation, and Grading," distinguishes between assessment, which describes and documents what is happening; evaluation, which imposes judgment standards on assessment; and grading, which condenses assessment and evaluation into a symbol.

Tompkins, Gail E. *Teaching Writing: Balancing Process and Product*. Columbus, OH: Merrill Publishing Co., 1990.

> Chapter 10, "Assessing Students' Writing," focuses on three types of assessment for elementary age students: informal monitoring, process assessment, and product assessment. Samples of questions to ask in conferences, checklists, anecdotal records, and self-assessment questionnaires are included. Communication with parents is also discussed.

Zemelman, Steven, Harvey Daniels, and Arthur Hyde. *Best Practice: New Standards for Teaching and Learning in America's Schools*, 2nd edition. Portsmouth, NH: Heinemann, 1998.

> Chapter 3 of this book, "Best Practice in Writing," describes exemplary programs in writing in public schools, focusing on practices teachers should consider increasing or decreasing. Of particular interest is the description of a third-grade writing classroom in Chicago.

Specific Strategies

Analytic Scoring

Stoneberg, Bert, Jr. "Analytic Trait Writing Assessment." A report of the Greater Albany Public Schools District Assessment of Writing of Students in Grades 5, 7, 9, and 11. Greater Albany, Oregon, 1988. In ERIC, ED299567.

> This report describes analytic assessment of student writing based on six areas: ideas and content; organization and development; voice; word choice; sentence structure; and the conventions of writing. Writing samples and scores for each grade level are included.

Anecdotal Records

Rhodes, Lynn K. and Sally Natenson-Mejia. "Anecdotal Records: A Powerful Tool for Ongoing Literacy Assessment." *The Reading Teacher* 45, 7 (September 1990): 44–48.

> The authors discuss anecdotal notes: how to collect and analyze them. Teachers reported that they saw and heard with greater clarity when using anecdotal records.

Checklists

"Evaluation Checklist for Student Writing in Grades K–3, Ottawa County." Ottawa City, Ohio, Office of Education, 1988. In ERIC, ED299583.

> This checklist was the primary record-keeping tool for a competency-based education program in Ohio. Guidelines for the development of the checklist are included.

Conferences

Bloom, Diane. "Conferencing: Assessing Growth and Change in Student Writing." New Jersey State Department of Education, June 1986. In ERIC, ED308513.

> This booklet presents three practical procedures for conferencing to help upper elementary level teachers evaluate the language development of students as they teach the writing process.

Goldstein, Lynn M. and Susan Conrad. "Student Input and Negotiation of Meaning in ESL Writing Conferences." *TESOL Quarterly* 24, 3 (Fall 1990): 443–460.

This article examines the degree of student control in writing conferences when English is the second language of the student. It focuses particularly on how students dealt with revision.

Nickel, Jodi. "When Writing Conferences Don't Work: Students' Retreat from Teacher Agenda." *Language Arts* 79, 2 (November 2001): 136–147.

This article describes situations this teacher encountered when students resisted writing conferences. Through extensive reflection and data analysis, the author arrives at five reasons conferences sometimes don't work and eight recommendations to help teachers design effective conferences.

Turbill, Jan, ed. *No Better Way to Teach Writing.* Rozelle, New S. Wales, Australia, 1982.

This book describes the conference approach to teaching writing as it is practiced in an Australian Writing Project. It is divided into grade-level sections (K–2; primary) and contains a chapter on evaluation.

Valcourt, Gladys. "Inviting Rewriting: How to Respond to a First Draft." *Canadian Journal of English Language Arts* 12, 1–2: 29–36.

This article examines teachers' responses to students' first drafts. It suggests three ways to encourage rewriting: dialog feedback, student conferences, and reader-reaction summaries.

Vukelich, Carol and LuAnn Laverson. "Text Revisions by Two Young Writers Following Teacher/Student Conferences." *Journal of Research in Childhood Education* 3, 1 (Spring–Summer 1988): 46–54.

This article describes ways in which two second-grade writers used questions and comments made by their teacher during revising conferences.

Contracts

Beale, Walter and Don King. "A Grading Contract that Works." *Exercise Exchange* 26, 1 (Fall 1981): 17–20.

This article describes a contract the authors developed for freshman English. It could be adapted, however.

Holistic Measures

Gearhart, Maryl, et al. "Writing Portfolios at the Elementary Level: A Study of Methods for Writing Assessment." In ERIC, ED344900 (1992).

This study investigated the utility and meaningfulness of using holistic and analytic scoring rubrics for portfolios.

Herron, Jeannine. "Computer Writing Labs: A New Vision for Elementary Writing." *Writing Notebook: Creative Word Processing in the Classroom* 9, 3 (January 1992): 31–33.

This article asserts that writing must have as honored a place as reading in first grade instruction. It discusses the need for computers, cooperative learning, and holistic assessment. It reports on implementation in a Los Altos, CA, school.

Myers, Miles. *A Procedure for Writing Assessment and Holistic Scoring*. Urbana, IL: National Council of Teachers of English, 1980.

> This explanation for holistic scoring has been used by many school districts for district-wide writing assessments, such as writing proficiency tests, for over ten years. It is considered a classic in the field.

Vaac, Nancy Nesbitt. "Writing Evaluation: Examining Four Teachers' Holistic and Analytic Scores." *Elementary School Journal* 90, 1 (September 1989): 87–95.

> This study examines the concurrent validity of holistic scores and analytic ratings of the same writing samples.

Portfolios

Cooper, Winfield. "What is a Portfolio?" *Portfolio News*, Spring 1991.

> This essay offers a collection of twelve definitions of what portfolios are, drawn from a variety of teachers and schools.

Fu, Danling and Linda L. Lamme. "Assessment through Conversation." *Language Arts* 79, 3 (January 2002): 241–250.

> This article discusses why teachers should use portfolio assessment in conjunction with state assessments. The authors suggest that the best way to get a complete picture of student improvement in writing is through conversations among parents, teachers, and children around writing portfolios.

Galley, Sharon Martens. "Portfolio as Mirror: Student and Teacher Learning Reflected through the Standards." *Language Arts* 78, 2 (November 2000): 121–127.

> This article recounts the process one teacher invented to use student portfolios to think about state standards, student learning, and her own teaching. The process helped her reflect on what her classroom had been during the year as well as look forward to what she wanted her classroom to become the next year.

Grady, Emily. "The Portfolio Approach to Assessment." *Fastback 341*. Bloomington, Indiana: Phi Delta Kappa Educational Foundation, 1992.

> This overview of portfolios covers the basics: purposes and standards for portfolios, what goes into a portfolio, personal professional portfolios, and implementation and management strategies.

Hanson, Jane. "Literacy Portfolios." *The Reading Teacher* 45, 8 (April 1992): 604.

> This article discusses New Hampshire's reevaluation of its literacy portfolio system. Researchers found that students are better able to determine their own abilities and progress.

"Picture of a Portfolio." *Instructor* 101, 7 (March 1992): 26–28.

> This article summarizes the Vermont Department of Education's portfolio system for grades 4, 8, and 12. It offers examples from a fourth-grade portfolio.

Portfolio News. A quarterly published by the Portfolio Assessment Clearinghouse. Winfield Cooper and Jon Davies, co-directors. c/o San Dieguito Union High School District, 710 Encinitas Boulevard, Encintas, CA 92024.

> This quarterly is published fall, winter, spring, and summer. It includes brief articles on the uses of portfolios in different content areas as well as in different parts of the country.

Vermont Department of Education. "A Different Way of Looking at Math: Explaining Portfolios to Students." *Portfolio News*, Winter 1991.

> This article explains how portfolios were used in math for fourth and eighth graders. A definition and rationale are given.

Vermont Department of Education. "Explaining Portfolios to Students in Vermont, Part II: Writing 'Your History as a Writer.' " *Portfolio News*, Winter 1992.

> This article discusses the what, why, and how of portfolio keeping as it is used in Vermont.

"Writing and Reading Portfolios in Primary Grades." *Portfolio News*, Winter 1992.

> This article reviews Donald Graves' book, *Build a Literate Classroom*, from a portfolio perspective. It includes details of creating portfolios from work folders by selection, replacement, and addition.

Primary-Trait Scoring

Bebermeyer, Ruth, et al. "Sample Exercises and Scoring Guides." ERIC, November 30, 1982 (ED224036).

> This paper presents forty writing assignments and sixteen primary-trait scoring guides used by elementary and secondary teachers who participated in a writing research project.

Holdzkom, David, et al. "Purpose and Audience in Writing: A Study of Uses of the Primary-Trait System in Writing Instruction." Paper presented at the annual conference of the American Educational Research Association, Montreal, April 1983. In ERIC, ED236687.

> This study investigated instructional uses of primary-trait scoring techniques devised by the National Assessment of Educational Progress. Eleven elementary and secondary teachers participated in the study. The scoring techniques were used for five specified purposes.

Student-Centered Strategies

Collins, Jeffrey. "Establishing Peer Evaluation of Writing: Students Need an Informed Teacher Model." In ERIC, ED243122 (1983): 11 pages.

> The author of this essay argues that peer evaluation promotes ownership of writing and that the key to the success of peer evaluation is teacher modeling in conferences. The teacher encourages the students to respond to each other as real readers would.

Jochum, Julie. "Whole-Language Writing: The Critical Response." *Highlights* (the Journal of the Minnesota Reading Association) 11, 2 (May 1989): 5–7.

> This article discusses peer response to writing. Writers' circles, writers' conferences, and the writer as informant to open-ended questions are discussed.

Lewis, Melva and Arnold Lindaman. "How Do We Evaluate Student Writing? One District's Answer." *Educational Leadership* 46, 7 (April 1989): 70.

> The district reported on in this article has the entire school write about one topic in the fall and then another in the spring. Students evaluate their own writing; parents and teachers offer comments.

Writing Process Strategies

Hillerich, Robert. *Teaching Children to Write K–8: A Complete Guide to Developing Writing Skills*. Englewood Cliffs, NJ: Prentice Hall, 1985.

> This book has as its cornerstone the notion that children learn to write by writing in an enjoyable atmosphere. The last chapter deals with evaluating the writing process.

Proett, Jackie and Kent Gill. *The Writing Process in Action: A Handbook for Teachers*. Urbana, IL: National Council of Teachers of English, 1986.

> This brief but excellent handbook outlines the writing process and illustrates it with classroom activities. Evaluation strategies reviewed include traditional methods and holistic scoring methods.

Written Comments

Coleman, Mary. "Individualizing Instruction through Written Teacher Comments." *Language Arts* 57, 3 (March 1980): 294–298.

> This article suggests four ways of using written comments to communicate with individual students: reaction, encouragement, correction, and evaluation.

Corley, Donna. "Thoughts from Students of Language Arts at the Elementary, High School, and College Level on Teacher Written Comments." Paper presented at the annual meeting of the Southern Educational Research Association, Austin, Texas, January 25–27, 1990. In ERIC, ED316876.

> This study was conducted to determine how written teacher comments affected students who received them. At the elementary level, all of the students read the comments. Sixty-six percent of the elementary students read the comments to see what they did wrong; the rest read them to see what they had done right.

Olson, Mary and Paul Raffeld. "Effects of Written Comments on the Quality of Student Composition and the Learning of Content." *Reading Psychology* 8, 4 (1987): 273–293.

> This study investigated the effect of written teacher comments on students. The findings support the idea that content comments are helpful to students.

Straub, Richard. *The Practice of Response: Strategies for Commenting on Student Writing*. Cresskill, NJ: Hampton Press, Inc., 2000.

> This book follows up on previous research by Straub and Lunsford (*Twelve Readers Reading: Responding to College Student Writing, 1995*). While it is written in the context of college writing, the principles that Straub identifies cut across grade-level boundaries. Of particular interest is chapter 2, "A Way to Analyze Comments." In this chapter Straub categorizes the modes of comments available to us as responders to student writing: corrections, criticism, qualified criticism, praise, commands, advice, closed questions, open questions, and reflective statements.

State Assessments

Arizona Department of Education, *Academic Standards and Accountability*, 2001, http://www.ade.state..az.us/standards/ (30 March 2002)

> Arizona's Writing Standards can be found at this web address.

Arizona Department of Education, *Official Scoring Guide to Arizona's Instrument to Measure the Standards*, 2001, http://www.ade.az.gov/standards/download/6traits.pdf (30 March 2002)

> Information about Arizona's Instrument to Measure the Standards in Writing are found at this web address.

Culham, Ruth. *Picture Books—An Annotated Bibliography with Activities for Teaching Writing*, Northwest Regional Educational Laboratory, 1998

> This is a resource book for teachers full of creative lessons for presenting and using the concepts of the Six Traits researched and developed by the Northwest Regional Educational Laboratory. Lesson plans are available for use with students K–12.

Florida Department of Education, *Florida Writes! Home Page*, 2000, http://www.firn. edu.doe/sas/flwrites.htm, (30 March 2002)

> Florida's Holistic Scoring Guide and rubric can be found and explained at this web address.

Kentucky Department of Education, *Kentucky Writing Assessment*, 2000, http:// www.ael.org/rel/state/ky/kyasesmet.htm, (30 March 2002)

> Information about Kentucky's holistic scoring method and writing portfolio system is explained at this web address.

Murphy, Sharon and Curt Dudley-Marling. "Editors' Pages." *Language Arts* 78, 2 (November 2000): 108–110.

> This editorial suggests that equating state standards with success in writing results in the psychological abandonment of students. The authors suggest that we think about standards not as excellence but as adequacy, not only for children's educational progress but also for school buildings and playgrounds, curricular materials, food, shelter, and medical care.

Murphy, Sharon and Curt Dudley-Marling. "Editors' Pages." *Language Arts* 78, 5 (May, 2001): 412–413.

> This editorial stresses the power of writing to effect social change and suggests that as teachers we need to continually reconsider our understanding of the writing process so that we can teach in ways that address both the power of writing and high-stakes tests.

National Council of Teachers of English, *On Urging Reconsideration of High Stakes Testing*, http://www.ncte.org/resolutions/highstakes002000.shtml (Business Meeting in Milwaukee, WI, 2000)

> This website includes the full text of a National Council of Teachers of English resolution addressing high-stakes testing. In part the resolution reads, ". . . high stakes tests often fail to assess accurately students' knowledge, understanding, and capability. . . ."

Northwest Regional Education Laboratory, *Seeing with New Eyes*, NWREL, 1999

> The guidebook provides ideas for teaching and assessing beginning writers. It is designed to help primary teachers build awareness of the Six Traits through reading children's literature and developmentally appropriate writing activities. A continuum of writing skills from kindergarten–second grade and a rubric that spells out criteria for evaluating young writers help teachers observe and document growth.

Oregon Department of Education, *Write Score Guides*, 2001, http://www.ode. state.or.us/asmt/resource/scorguides/writesg.htm, (4 April 2002)

> Download Oregon's six-trait scoring guide for use on its state writing assessment at this web address.

Spandel, Vicki. *Books, Lessons, Ideas for Teaching the Six Traits*, Great Source Education Group, 2001.

> This annotated bibliography lists books that can be used to teach the Six Traits in elementary and middle grades. It is divided into seven sections: one for each trait

and a Teacher Resource section. The books labeled "Vic's Picks" are must-have titles according to the author.

Tierney, Robert J. "How Will Literacy be Assessed in the Next Millenium?" *Reading Research Quarterly* 35, 2 (April/May/June 2000): 244–246.

This article stresses the social inequity emphasized by high-stakes testing. The author surveys organized resistance to high-stakes testing across the United States and internationally. He suggest six goals for positive evaluation in the future.

Wolf, Shelby Anne and Kenneth Paul Wolf. "Teaching *True* and *to* the Test in Writing." *Language Arts* 79, 3 (January 2002): 229–240.

This article describes the methods that six teachers in Kentucky and Washington have devised to enable them to help their students prepare for annual state assessments on standards and remain true to the writing pedagogy in which they believe. The authors categorize their strategies into five classroom activities: understanding the criteria, analyzing various models, responding to others' writing, reflecting on one's own writing, and rehearsing the performance.

APPENDIX C
State Scoring Guides

Appendix C includes two state scoring guides that represent two different scoring methods. Arizona's scoring guide is an analytic guide based on the six traits developed by the Oregon Department of Education. The Florida scoring guide is a holistic guide.

Official Scoring Guide: Arizona's Instrument to Measure Standards
http://www.ade.state.az.us/standards/

IDEAS and CONTENT

6

The writing is exceptionally clear, focused and interesting. It holds the reader's attention throughout. Main ideas stand out and are developed by strong support and rich details suitable to audience and purpose. The writing is characterized by

- clarity, focus, and control.
- main idea(s) that stand out.
- supporting, relevant, carefully selected details; when appropriate, use of resources provides strong, accurate, credible support.
- a thorough, balanced, in-depth explanation/exploration of the topic; the writing makes connections and shares insights.
- content and selected details that are well suited to audience and purpose.

5

The writing is clear, focused and interesting. It holds the reader's attention. Main ideas stand out and are developed by supporting details suitable to audience and purpose. The writing is characterized by

- clarity, focus, and control.
- main idea(s) that stand out.
- supporting, relevant, carefully selected details; when appropriate, use of resources provides strong, accurate, credible support.
- a thorough, balanced explanation/exploration of the topic; the writing makes connections and shares insights.
- content and selected details that are well-suited to audience and purpose.

4

The writing is clear and focused. T reader can easily understand the ma ideas. Support is present, although may be limited or rather general. T writing is characterized by

- an easily identifiable purpose.
- clear main idea(s).
- supporting details that are relevan but may be overly general or limited in places; when appropriate, resources are used to provide accu rate support.
- a topic that is explored/explained, although developmental details m occasionally be out of balance wit the main ideas(s); some connections and insights may be present
- content and selected details that a relevant, but perhaps not consistently well chosen for audience an purpose.

3

The reader can understand the main ideas, although they may be overly broad or simplistic, and the results may not be effective. Supporting detail is often limited, insubstantial, overly general, or occasionally slightly off-topic. The writing is characterized by

- an easily identifiable purpose and main ideas(s).
- predictable or overly-obvious main ideas or plot; conclusions or main points seem to echo observations heard elsewhere.
- support that is attempted; but developmental details that are often limited in score, uneven, somewhat off-topic, predictable, or overly general.
- details that may not be well-grounded in credible resources; they may be based on clichés, stereotypes or questionable sources of information.
- difficulties when moving from general observations to specifics.

2

Main ideas and purpose are somewhat unclear or development is attempted but minimal. The writing is characterized by

- a purpose and main idea(s) that may require extensive inferences by the reader.
- minimal development; insufficient details.
- irrelevant details that clutter the text.
- extensive repetition of detail.

1

The writing lacks a central idea or purpose. The writing is characterize by

- ideas that are extremely limited o simply unclear.
- attempts at development that are minimal or nonexistent; the paper is too short to demonstrate the de velopment of an idea.

Official Scoring Guide: Arizona's Instrument to Measure Standards

ORGANIZATION

6

The organization enhances the central idea(s) and its development. The order and structure are compelling and move the reader through the text easily. The writing is characterized by

- effective, perhaps creative, sequencing; the organizational structure fits the topic, and the writing is easy to follow.
- a strong, inviting beginning that draws the reader in and a strong satisfying sense of resolution or closure.
- smooth, effective transitions among all elements (sentences, paragraphs, ideas).
- details that fit where placed.

5

The organization enhances the central idea(s) and its development. The order and structure are strong and move the reader through the text. The writing is characterized by

- effective sequencing; the organizational structure fits the topic, and the writing is easy to follow.
- an inviting beginning that draws the reader in and a satisfying sense of resolution or closure.
- smooth, effective transitions among all elements (sentences, paragraphs, ideas).
- details that fit where placed.

4

Organization is clear and coherent. Order and structure are present, but may seem formulaic. The writing is characterized by

- clear sequencing.
- an organization that may be predictable.
- a recognizable, developed beginning that may not be particularly inviting; a developed conclusion that may lack subtlety.
- a body that is easy to follow with details that fit where placed.
- transitions that may be stilted or formulaic.
- organization which helps the reader, despite some weaknesses.

3

An attempt has been made to organize the writing; however, the overall structure is inconsistent or skeletal. The writing is characterized by

- attempts at sequencing, but the order or the relationship among ideas may occasionally be unclear.
- a beginning and an ending which, although present, are either undeveloped or too obvious (e.g., "My topic is . . .", "These are all the reasons that . . .").
- transitions that sometimes work. The same few transitional devices (e.g., coordinating conjunctions, numbering, etc.) may be overused.
- a structure that is skeletal or too rigid.
- placement of details that may not always be effective.
- organization which lapses in some places, but helps the reader in others.

2

The writing lacks a clear organizational structure. An occasional organizational device is discernible; however, the writing is either difficult to follow and the reader has to reread substantial portions, or the piece is simply too short to demonstrate organizational skills. The writing is characterized by

- some attempts at sequencing, but the order or the relationship among ideas is frequently unclear.
- a missing or extremely undeveloped beginning, body, and/or ending.
- a lack of transitions, or when present, ineffective or overused.
- a lack of an effective organizational structure.
- details that seem to be randomly placed, leaving the reader frequently confused.

1

The writing lacks coherence; organization seems haphazard and disjointed. Even after rereading, the reader remains confused. The writing is characterized by

- a lack of effective sequencing.
- a failure to provide an identifiable beginning, body and/or ending.
- a lack of transitions.
- pacing that is consistently awkward; the reader feels either mired down in trivia or rushed along too rapidly.
- a lack of organization which ultimately obscures or distorts the main point.

Official Scoring Guide: Arizona's Instrument to Measure Standards

VOICE

6

The writer has chosen a voice appropriate for the topic, purpose and audience. The writer seems deeply committed to the topic, and there is an exceptional sense of "writing to be read." The writing is expressive, engaging, or sincere. The writing is characterized by

- an effective level of closeness to or distance from the audience (e.g., a narrative should have a strong personal voice, while an expository piece may require extensive use of outside resources and a more academic voice; nevertheless, both should be engaging, lively, or interesting. Technical writing may require greater distance.).
- an exceptionally strong sense of audience; the writer seems to be aware of the reader and of how to communicate the message most effectively. The reader may discern the writer behind the words and feel a sense of interaction.
- a sense that the topic has come to life; when appropriate, the writing may show originality, liveliness, honesty, conviction, excitement, humor, or suspense.

5

The writer has chosen a voice appropriate for the topic, purpose, and audience. The writer seems committed to the topic, and there is a sense of "writing to be read." The writing is expressive, engaging or sincere. The writing is characterized by

- an appropriate level of closeness to or distance from the audience (e.g., a narrative should have a strong personal voice while an expository piece may require extensive use of outside resources and a more academic voice; nevertheless, both should be engaging, lively or interesting. Technical writing may require greater distance.).
- a strong sense of audience; the writer seems to be aware of the reader and of how to communicate the message most effectively. The reader may discern the writer behind the words and feel a sense of interaction.
- a sense that the topic has come to life; when appropriate, the writing may show originality, liveliness, honesty, conviction, excitement, humor, or suspense.

4

A voice is present. The writer demonstrates commitment to the topic, and there may be a sense of "writing to be read." In places, the writing is expressive, engaging, or sincere. The writing is characterized by

- a questionable or inconsistent level of closeness to or distance from the audience.
- a sense of audience; the writer seems to be aware of the reader but has not consistently employed an appropriate voice. The reader may glimpse the writer behind the words and feel a sense of interaction in places.
- liveliness, sincerity, or humor when appropriate; however, at times the writing may be either inappropriately casual or personal, or inappropriately formal and stiff.

3

The writer's commitment to the topic seems inconsistent. A sense of the writer may emerge at times; however, the voice is either inappropriately personal or inappropriately impersonal. The writing is characterized by

- a limited sense of audience; the writer's awareness of the reader is unclear.
- an occasional sense of the writer behind the words; however, the voice may shift or disappear a line or two later and the writing become somewhat mechanical.
- a limited ability to shift to a more objective voice when necessary.

2

The writing provides little sense of involvement or commitment. There is no evidence that the writer has chosen a suitable voice. The writing is characterized by

- little engagement of the writer; the writing tends to be largely flat, lifeless, stiff, or mechanical.
- a voice that is likely to be overly informal and personal.
- a lack of audience awareness; there is little sense of "writing to be read."
- little or no hint of the writer behind the words. There is rarely a sense of interaction between reader and writer.

1

The writing seems to lack a sense of involvement or commitment. The writing is characterized by

- no engagement of the writer; the writing is flat and lifeless.
- a lack of audience awareness; there is no sense of "writing to be read."
- no hint of the writer behind the words. There is no sense of interaction between writer and reader; the writing does not involve or engage the reader.

Official Scoring Guide: Arizona's Instrument to Measure Standards

WORD CHOICE

6

Words convey the intended message in an exceptionally interesting, precise, and natural way appropriate to audience and purpose. The writer employs a rich, broad range of words which have been carefully chosen and thoughtfully placed for impact. The writing is characterized by

- accurate, strong, specific words; powerful words energize the writing.
- fresh, original expression; slang, if used seems purposeful and is effective.
- vocabulary that is striking and varied, but that is natural and not overdone.
- ordinary words used in an unusual way.
- words that evoke strong images; figurative language may be used.

5

Words convey the intended message in an interesting, precise, and natural way appropriate to audience and purpose. The writer employs a broad range of words which have been carefully chosen and thoughtfully placed for impact. The writing is characterized by

- accurate, specific words; word choices energize the writing.
- fresh, vivid expression; slang, if used, seems purposeful and is effective.
- vocabulary that may be striking and varied, but that is natural and not overdone.
- ordinary words used in an unusual way.
- words that evoke clear images; figurative language may be used.

4

Words effectively convey the intended message. The writer employs a variety of words that are functional and appropriate to audience and purpose. The writing is characterized by

- words that work but do not particularly energize the writing.
- expression that is functional; however, slang, if used, does not seem purposeful and is not particularly effective.
- attempts at colorful language that may occasionally seem overdone.
- occasional overuse of technical language or jargon.
- rare experiments with language; however, the writing may have some fine moments and generally avoids clichés.

3

Language is quite ordinary, lacking interest, precision and variety, or may be inappropriate to audience and purpose in places. The writer does not employ a variety of words, producing a sort of "generic" paper filled with familiar words and phrases. The writing is characterized by

- words that work, but that rarely capture the reader's interest.
- expression that seems mundane and general; slang, if used, does not seem purposeful and is not effective.
- attempts at colorful language that seem overdone or forced.
- words that are accurate for the most part, although misused words may occasionally appear, technical language or jargon may be overused or inappropriately used.
- reliance on clichés and overused expressions.

2

Language is monotonous and/or misused, detracting from the meaning and impact. The writing is characterized by

- words that are colorless, flat or imprecise.
- monotonous repetition or overwhelming reliance on worn expressions that repeatedly distract from the message.
- images that are fuzzy or absent altogether.

1

The writing shows an extremely limited vocabulary or is so filled with misuses of words that the meaning is obscured. Only the most general kind of message is communicated because of vague or imprecise language. The writing is characterized by

- general, vague words that fail to communicate.
- an extremely limited range of words.
- words that simply do not fit the text; they seem imprecise, inadequate, or just plain wrong.

Official Scoring Guide: Arizona's Instrument to Measure Standards

SENTENCE FLUENCY

6

The writing has an effective flow and rhythm. Sentences show a high degree of craftsmanship, with consistently strong and varied structure that makes expressive oral reading easy and enjoyable. The writing is characterized by

- a natural, fluent sound; it glides along with one sentence flowing effortlessly into the next.
- extensive variation in sentence structure, length, and beginnings that add interest to the text.
- sentence structure that enhances meaning by drawing attention to key ideas or reinforcing relationships among ideas.
- varied sentence patterns that create an effective combination of power and grace.
- strong control over sentence structure; fragments, if used at all, work well.
- stylistic control; dialogue, if used, sounds natural.

5

The writing has an easy flow and rhythm. Sentences are carefully crafted, with strong and varied structure that makes expressive oral reading easy and enjoyable. The writing is characterized by

- a natural, fluent sound; it glides along with one sentence flowing into the next.
- variation in sentence structure, length, and beginnings that add interest to the text.
- sentence structure that enhances meaning.
- control over sentence structure; fragments, if used at all, work well.
- stylistic control; dialogue, if used sounds natural.

4

The writing flows; however, connections between phrases or sentences may be less than fluid. Sentence patterns are somewhat varied, contributing to ease in oral reading. The writing is characterized by

- a natural sound; the reader can move easily through the piece, although it may lack a certain rhythm and grace.
- some repeated patterns of sentence structure, length, and beginnings that may detract somewhat from overall impact.
- strong control over simple sentence structures, but variable control over more complex sentences; fragments, if present, are usually effective.
- occasional lapses in stylistic control; dialogue, if used, sounds natural for the most part, but may at times sound stilted or unnatural.

3

The writing tends to be mechanical rather than fluid. Occasional awkward constructions may force the reader to slow down or reread. The writing is characterized by

- some passages that invite fluid oral reading; however, others do not.
- some variety in sentences structure, length, and beginnings, although the writer falls into repetitive sentence patterns.
- good control over simple sentence structures, but little control over more complex sentences; fragments, if present, may not be effective.
- sentences which, although functional, lack energy.
- lapses in stylistic control; dialogue, if used, may sound stilted or unnatural.

2

The writing tends to be either choppy or rambling. Awkward constructions often force the reader to slow down or reread. The writing is characterized by

- significant portions of the text that are difficult to follow or read aloud.
- sentence patterns that are monotonous (e.g., subject–verb or subject–verb–object).
- a significant number of awkward, choppy, or rambling constructions.

1

The writing is difficult to follow or to read aloud. Sentences tend to be incomplete, rambling, or very awkward. The writing is characterized by

- text that does not invite—and may not even permit—smooth oral reading.
- confusing word order that is often jarring and irregular.
- sentence structure that frequently obscures meaning.
- sentences that are disjointed, confusing, or rambling.

Official Scoring Guide: Arizona's Instrument to Measure Standards

CONVENTIONS

6

The writing demonstrates exceptionally strong control of standard writing conventions (e.g., punctuation, spelling, capitalization, paragraph breaks, grammar and usage) and uses them effectively to enhance communication. Errors are so few and so minor that the reader can easily skim right over them unless specifically searching for them. The writing is characterized by

- strong control of conventions; manipulation of conventions may occur for stylistic effect.
- strong, effective use of punctuation that guides the reader through the text.
- correct spelling, even of more difficult words.
- paragraph breaks that reinforce the organizational structure.
- correct grammar and usage that contribute to clarity and style.
- skill in using a wide range of conventions in a sufficiently long and complex piece.
- little or no need for editing.

5

The writing demonstrates strong control of standard writing conventions (e.g., punctuation, spelling, capitalization, paragraph breaks, grammar and usage) and uses them effectively to enhance communication. Errors are so few and so minor that they do not impede readability. The writing is characterized by

- strong control of conventions.
- effective use of punctuation that guides the reader through the text.
- correct spelling, even of more difficult words.
- paragraph breaks that reinforce the organizational structure.
- correct capitalization; errors, if any, are minor.
- correct grammar and usage that contribute to clarity and style.
- skill in using a wide range of conventions in a sufficiently long and complex piece.
- little need for editing.

4

The writing demonstrates control of standard writing conventions (e.g., punctuation, spelling, capitalization, paragraph breaks, grammar and usage). Minor errors, while perhaps noticeable, do not impede readability. The writing is characterized by

- control over conventions used, although a wide range is not demonstrated.
- correct end-of-sentence punctuation, internal punctuation may sometimes be incorrect.
- spelling that is usually correct, especially on common words.
- basically sound paragraph breaks that reinforce the organizational structure.
- correct capitalization; errors, if any, are minor.
- occasional lapses in correct grammar and usage; problems are not severe enough to distort meaning or confuse the reader.
- moderate need for editing.

3

The writing demonstrates limited control of standard writing conventions (e.g., punctuation, spelling, capitalization, paragraph breaks, grammar and usage). Errors begin to impede readability. The writing is characterized by

- some control over basic conventions; the text may be too simple to reveal mastery.
- end-of-sentence punctuation that is usually correct; however, internal punctuation contains frequent errors.
- spelling errors that distract the reader; misspelling of common words occurs.
- paragraphs that sometimes run together or begin at ineffective places.
- capitalization errors.
- errors in grammar and usage that do not block meaning but do distract the reader.
- significant needs for editing.

2

The writing demonstrates little control of standard writing conventions. Frequent, significant errors impede readability. The writing is characterized by

- little control over basic conventions.
- many end-of-sentence punctuation errors; internal punctuation contains frequent errors.
- spelling errors that frequently distract the reader; misspelling of common words often occurs.
- paragraphs that often run together or begin in ineffective places.
- capitalization that is inconsistent or often incorrect.
- errors in grammar and usage that interfere with readability and meaning.
- substantial need for editing.

1

Numerous errors in usage, spelling, capitalization, and punctuation repeatedly distract the reader and make the text difficult to read. In fact, the severity and frequency of errors are so overwhelming that the reader finds it difficult to focus on the message and must reread for meaning. The writing is characterized by

- very limited skill in using conventions.
- basic punctuation (including end-of-sentence punctuation) that tends to be omitted, haphazard, or incorrect.
- frequent spelling errors that significantly impair readability.
- paragraph breaks that may be highly irregular or so frequent (every sentence) that they bear no relation to the organization of the text.
- capitalization that appears to be random.
- a need for extensive editing.

SITEMAP   KEYWORD SEARCH

Curriculum, Instruction & Assessment
Assessment & Evaluation

Florida Department of Education   Public Schools
http://www.firn.edu/doe/sas/fw/fwaphols.htm

Florida Writing Assessment Program (*FLORIDA WRITES!*)

Holistic Scoring Method

Definition of Holistic Scoring

Holistic scoring is a method by which trained readers evaluate a piece of writing for its overall quality. The holistic scoring used in Florida requires readers to evaluate the work as a whole, while considering four elements: focus, organization, support, and conventions. This method is sometimes called focused holistic scoring. In this type of scoring, readers are trained not to become overly concerned with any one aspect of writing but to look at a response as a whole.

Focus

Focus refers to how clearly the paper presents and maintains a main idea, theme, or unifying point. Papers representing the higher end of the point scale demonstrate a consistent awareness of the topic and do not contain extraneous information.

Organization

Organization refers to the structure or plan of development (beginning, middle, and end) and whether the points logically relate to one another. Organization refers to (1) the use of transitional devices to signal the relationship of the supporting ideas to the main idea, theme, or unifying point and (2) the evidence of a connection between sentences. Papers representing the higher end of the point scale use transitions to signal the plan or text structure and end with summary or concluding statements.

Support

Support refers to the quality of the details used to explain, clarify, or define. The quality of support depends on word choice, specificity, depth, credibility, and thoroughness. Papers representing the higher end of the point scale provide fully developed examples and illustrations in which the relationship between the supporting ideas and the topic is clear.

Conventions

Conventions refer to punctuation, capitalization, spelling, and variation in sentence used in the paper. These conventions are basic writing skills included in Florida's Minimum Student Performance Standards and the Uniform Student Performance Standards for Language Arts. Papers representing the higher end of the scale follow, with few exceptions, the conventions of punctuation, capitalization, and spelling and use a variety of sentence structures to present ideas.

| SITEMAP | KEYWORD SEARCH |

Curriculum, Instruction & Assessment
| Assessment & Evaluation

Florida Department of Education   Public Schools

Florida Writing Assessment Program (*FLORIDA WRITES!*)

Score Points in Rubric

The rubric further interprets the four major areas of consideration into levels of achievement. The rubric used to score papers in spring 1995 is shown below.

6 Points

The writing is focused, purposeful, and reflects insight into the writing situation. The paper conveys a sense of completeness and wholeness with adherence to the main idea, and its organizational pattern provides for a logical progression of ideas. The support is substantial, specific, relevant, concrete, and/or illustrative. The paper demonstrates a commitment to and an involvement with the subject, clarity in presentation of ideas, and may use creative writing strategies appropriate to the purpose of the paper. The writing demonstrates a mature command of language (word choice) with freshness of expression. Sentence structure is varied, and sentences are complete except when fragments are used purposefully. Few, if any, convention errors occur in mechanics, usage, and punctuation.

5 Points

The writing focuses on the topic, and its organizational pattern provides for a progression of ideas, although some lapses may occur. The paper conveys a sense of completeness or wholeness. The support is ample. The writing demonstrates a mature command of language, including precision in word choice. There is variation in sentence structure, and, with rare exceptions, sentences are complete except when fragments are used purposefully. The paper generally follows the conventions of mechanics, usage, and spelling.

4 Points

The writing is generally focused on the topic but may include extraneous or loosely related material. An organizational pattern is apparent, although some lapses may occur. The paper exhibits some sense of completeness or wholeness. The support, including word choice, is adequate, although development may be uneven. There is little variation in sentence structure, and most sentences are complete. The paper generally follows the conventions of mechanics, usage, and spelling.

3 Points

The writing is generally focused on the topic but may include extraneous or loosely related material. An organizational pattern has been attempted, but the paper may lack a sense of completeness or wholeness. Some support is included, but development is erratic. Word choice is adequate but may be limited, predictable, or occasionally vague. There is little, if any, variation in sentence structure. Knowledge of the conventions of mechanics and usage is usually demonstrated, and commonly used words are usually spelled correctly.

2 Points

The writing is related to the topic but include extraneous or loosely related material. Little evidence of an organizational pattern may be demonstrated, and the paper may lack a sense of completeness or wholeness. Development of support is inadequate or illogical. Word choice is limited, inappropriate or vague. There is little, if any, variation in sentence structure, and gross errors in sentence structure may occur. Errors in basic conventions of mechanics and usage may occur, and commonly used words may be misspelled.

1 Point

The writing may only minimally address the topic. The paper is a fragmentary or incoherent listing of related ideas or sentences or both. Little, if any, development of support or an organizational pattern or both is apparent. Limited or inappropriate word choice may obscure meaning. Gross errors in sentence structure and usage may impede communication. Frequent and blatant errors may occur in the basic conventions of mechanics and usage, and commonly used words may be misspelled.

Unscorable

The paper is unscorable because

- the response is not related to what the prompt requested the student to do.

- the response is simply a rewording of the prompt.
- the response is a copy of a published work.
- the student refused to write.
- the response is illegible.
- the response is incomprehensible (words are arranged in such a way that no meaning is conveyed).
- the response contains an insufficient amount of writing to determine if the student was attempting to address the prompt.
- the writing folder is blank.

© Florida Department of Education, 2000.

AUTHOR INDEX

A

Ackerman, John , *187*

B

Beale, Walter, *194*
Beaver, Teri, *190*
Bebermeyer, Ruth, *196*
Bird, Lois Bridges, 86, *97*, 190
Block, Cathy Collins, *190*
Bloom, Diane, *193*
Bratcher, Suzanne, 11, *18*, 27, 29, *37*, 50, *74*, 190
Bridges, Lois, 78, *82*, 190
Bunce-Crim, Mana, *190*

C

Calkins, Lucy McCormick, 4, *6*, 92, *97*, 191
Cleary, Linda Miller, 12, *18*, 191
Coleman, Mary, *197*
Collins, Jeffrey, *196*
Conrad, Susan, *194*
Cooper, Winfield, *195*
Corley, Donna, *197*
Culham, Ruth, 115, *118*, 198

D

Daniels, Harvey, 27, *37*, 193
Dillard, Annie, 138, *144*
Dudley-Marling, Curt, *198*
Dyson, Anne Haas, *187*

F

Fountas, Irene C., *191*

F

Freedman, Sarah Warshauer, *187, 188*
Fu, Danling, *195*

G

Galley, Sharon Martens, *195*
Gearhart, Maryl, *194*
Gill, Kent, *197*
Goldstein, Lynn M., *194*
Goodman, Kenneth, 86, *97*, 190
Goodman, Yetta, 86, *97*, 190
Grady, Emily, *195*
Graves, Donald, 15, *18*, 92, *97*, 191

H

Hairston, Maxine, xv, *xvi*, 5, 7
Haley-James, Shirley, *191*
Hanson, Jane, *195*
Harmon, John, *xv*, 188
Herron, Jeannine, *194*
Hillerich, Robert, *197*
Holaday, Lynn, 3, *7*
Holdzkom, David, *196*
Horvath, Brooke K., *188*
Hyde, Arthur, 27, *37*, 193
Hyslop, Nancy B., *188*

J

Jochum, Julie, *196*

K

King, Don, *194*
Krest, Margie, *188*

L

Lamme, Linda L., *195*
Larson, Jan, 11, *18*, 29, *37*
Laverson, LuAnn, *194*
Lees, Elaine O., *188*
Lester, Nancy, *192*
Lewis, Melva, *196*
Lindaman, Arnold, *196*
Lindemann, Erika, *188*
Linck, Wayne M., *191*

M

Mayher, John S., *192*
McCarrier, Andrea, *191*
Mitchell, Diana, 81, *82*, *192*
Moffett, James, *192*
Murphy, Sharon, *198*
Murray, Donald, 137, *141*
Myers, Miles, *195*

N

Natenson-Mejia, Sally, *193*
Nickel, Jodi, 78, *82*, *194*

O

Olson, Mary, *197*

P

Pinnell, Gay Su, *191*
Pradl, Gordon M., *192*
Proett, Jackie, *197*

R

Raffeld, Paul, *197*
Rhodes, Lynn K., *193*
Ruddell, Robert B., *192*

Ryan, Linda, 92, 94, *97*

S

Schriver, Karen A., *188*
Shaughnessy, Mina, *189*
Smitherman, Geneva, *192*
Spandel, Vicki, 56, *74*, *192*, *198*
Sperling, Melanie, *189*
Stoneberg, Bert, Jr., *193*
Straub, Richard, *197*

T

Tchudi, Stephen, xii, xiv, *xvi*, 4, 7, 81, *82*, *189*, *192*
Tchudi, Susan, xii, *xvi*, *192*
Tiedt, Iris McClellan, *189*
Tierney, Robert, 133, *134*, *199*
Tompkins, Gail, *193*

V

Vaac, Nancy Nesbitt, *195*
Valcourt, Gladys, *194*
Vukelich, Carol, *194*

W

Wagner, Betty Jane, *192*
Weaver, Constance, 27, *37*, *189*
White, Edward M., *189*
Wolf, Kenneth, 107, *118*, *199*
Wolf, Shelby, 107, *118*, *199*

Y

Yancey, Kathleen Blake, *189*

Z

Zemelman, Steven, 27, *37*, *193*

SECOND EDITION

Using Joomla

Ron Severdia and Jennifer Gress

Beijing · Cambridge · Farnham · Köln · Sebastopol · Tokyo

Using Joomla, Second Edition

by Ron Severdia and Jennifer Gress

Copyright © 2014 Ron Severdia and Jennifer Gress. All rights reserved.

Printed in the United States of America.

Published by O'Reilly Media, Inc., 1005 Gravenstein Highway North, Sebastopol, CA 95472.

O'Reilly books may be purchased for educational, business, or sales promotional use. Online editions are also available for most titles (*http://my.safaribooksonline.com*). For more information, contact our corporate/institutional sales department: 800-998-9938 or *corporate@oreilly.com*.

Editors: Meghan Blanchette and Allyson MacDonald	**Indexer:** WordCo Indexing Services
Production Editor: Nicole Shelby	**Cover Designer:** Randy Comer
Copyeditor: Gillian McGarvey	**Interior Designer:** David Futato
Proofreader: Becca Freed	**Illustrator:** Rebecca Demarest

December 2009:   First Edition

June 2014:   Second Edition

Revision History for the Second Edition:

2014-06-10:   First release

See *http://oreilly.com/catalog/errata.csp?isbn=9781449345396* for release details.

Nutshell Handbook, the Nutshell Handbook logo, and the O'Reilly logo are registered trademarks of O'Reilly Media, Inc. *Using Joomla*, the picture of a white stork, and related trade dress are trademarks of O'Reilly Media, Inc.

Many of the designations used by manufacturers and sellers to distinguish their products are claimed as trademarks. Where those designations appear in this book, and O'Reilly Media, Inc. was aware of a trademark claim, the designations have been printed in caps or initial caps.

While every precaution has been taken in the preparation of this book, the publisher and authors assume no responsibility for errors or omissions, or for damages resulting from the use of the information contained herein.

ISBN: 978-1-449-34539-6

[LSI]

Table of Contents

Foreword. xi
Preface. xiii

1. Overview. 1
   A Brief History of Joomla   1
   Joomla Series End-of-Life Dates   3
   Why Open Source and the GPL?   3
   The Advantages and Disadvantages of Using a CMS: Static Versus Dynamic   3
   Joomla Concepts   4

2. Planning Your Website. 7
   Example Website: Joomla Pet Center   7
   Goals of the Website   7
      Hands-On Exercise: Write Your Goals   8
   Planning Menu Items   8
      Hands-On Exercise: Choose Menu Items and Layout   12
   Planning Categories   14
      Hands-On Exercise: Make Your List of Categories   15
   Planning Articles   15
      Hands-On Exercise: Make Your List of Articles   16
   Planning Users   16
      Hands-On Exercise: Write Out Your Users and What They Can See or Do   17
   Choosing Extensions   18
   Choosing a Template   18
   Home Page Layout   20
      Hands-On Exercise: Draw Out Your Home Page   20
   Internal Page Layout   21

Hands-On Exercise: Draw Out Your Internal Page Layout 22

3. A Tour of the Administrator Panel.. 23
   Control Panel 23
   Administrator Menus 25
     System 25
     Users 26
     Menus 27
     Content 28
     Components 29
     Extensions 29
     Help 30
     Personal Information Settings 32
   Administrator Modules 32
   Top Toolbar 33
   Filtering and Display 33
   Footer Menu 34

4. Setting Up the Basics of Your Website... 37
   Content Categories 37
   Creating Categories 38
     Hands-On Exercise: Create Your Categories 38
     Publishing and Unpublishing Categories 40
     Copying Categories 42
     Uncategorized Category 42
   Creating Articles 43
     Hands-On Exercise: Create Your Articles 44
     Article Publishing and Unpublishing 46
   Creating Menu Items 47
   Text Separator Menu Item type 47
     Hands-On Exercise: Create Text Separator Menu Items 47
   Creating Single Article Menu Item Types 49
     Hands-On Exercise: Single Article Menu Item Types 49
   Category Blog Layout 51
     Hands-On Exercise: Category Blog 52
   Category List Menu Item Type 55
   Mastering Backups 56
   Template Parameters 58
     The Style Tab 62
     Template CSS Overrides 67
     Features Tab 69
     Menu Tab 70

Layouts Tab   71
Advanced and Assignments Tabs   72
Creating Modules   72
Placeholder Custom HTML Module   73
Hands-On Exercise: Create Custom HTML Placeholder Modules   74
Ordering Modules   79
Duplicating Modules   79
Deleting Modules   81
Frontend Layout After Building the Structure   82

5. Creating Content **85**
Joomla Pet Center Article Options Hierarchy   85
Hands-On: Setting the Global Article Options   87
Changing Menu Item Options   91
The WYSIWYG Editor   93
Installing JCE   94
Customizing Articles: Recommended Guidelines   97
Copying and Pasting   98
Pasting Lists   100
Heading Tags   102
Text Color and Underline   104
Tables   105
Hyperlinking   105
Internal Links to Content Items   106
Hands-On Exercise: Hyperlinking to Internal Content   106
Hands-On Exercises: External Hyperlinks   109
Hands-On Exercise: Email Address Hyperlinks   110
Adding Embedded HTML Code and Text Filtering   112
Hands-On Exercise: Add a YouTube Video   115
Read More and Pagebreak   117
Meta Description and Keywords   118
Article Management   119
Versioning/Revisions and Editing Articles   119
Check In   121
Ordering Articles   121
Permissions   122
Archiving Articles   123
Trashing Articles   123
Adding Content to Modules   124
Hands-On Exercise: Showing Modules Inside an Article   124

6. Managing Media and Creating Galleries **127**

Media Manager   127
  Navigating Views and Managing Media   128
Uploading and Deleting Media   128
  Hands-On Exercise: Uploading Media   128
  Hands-On Exercise: Deleting Media   129
Using Media in Your Articles   131
  Hands-On Exercise: Adding an Image to an Article   131
  Hands-On Exercise: Adding Folders and Uploading Images from the Editor   132
  Hands-On Exercise: Changing an Image   136
  Hands-On Exercise: Removing an Image   136
  Hands-On Exercise: Hyperlinking an Image   136
  Hands-On Exercise: Linking Documents   137
Organizing Media   137
Resizing, Optimizing, and Naming Image Files   139
Global Media Manager Options   140
Adding an Image Gallery   140
  Hands-On Exercise: Installing sigplus   141
  Hands-On Exercise: Creating a Gallery in a Module   141
  Hands-On Exercise: Embedding a Gallery in an Article   142
Other Gallery Resources   144

7. Making Your Website Speak Multiple Languages. **145**
Offering Your Site Content in Multiple Languages   145
  Hands-On Exercise: Installing Multiple Languages When Joomla is Initially
    Installed   145
  Hands-On Exercise: Installing Additional Site Languages After Joomla is
    Installed   147
Uninstall a Language   149
Translating Your Content   149
Using the Joomla Administrator Interface in Another Language   152
  Hands-On Exercise: Setting the Language Options for Site Administrators   153

8. Starting a Blog. **155**
Joomla Articles as a Blog   155
  Hands-On Exercise: Creating a New Blog Post   156
  Hands-On Exercise: Scheduling an Article to Publish and Unpublish   156
Adding Comments, Tags, and Modules to Your Blog   157
  Hands-On Exercise: Adding Comments Using Komento   157
  Hands-On Exercise: Adding Comments Using the Kunena Forum   159
  Hands-On Exercise: Adding Joomla Tags to Your Blog   160
  Hands-On Exercise: Adding a Popular Tags Module   161

| | Hands-On Exercise: Adding a Latest Posts Module | 162 |

9. Create and Share an Event Calendar **165**
Hands-On Exercise: Installing and Configuring JEvents | 165
Hands-On Exercise: Creating a Calendar | 166
Hands-On Exercise: Creating Event Categories | 167
Hands-On Exercise: Adding JEvents to the Menu | 167
Hands-On Exercise: Adding Events to JEvents | 169
Create One-Time Events | 169
Create Recurring Events | 171
Adding Events from the Frontend by Visitors/Registered Users | 176
Add a Module Showing Latest Events on Other Pages of the Site | 176

10. Creating Forms **179**
Contact Form with Contact Enhanced | 179
Hands-On Exercise: Installing Contact Enhanced | 180
Hands-On Exercise: Creating Beautiful Contact Pages with Forms | 180
Hands-On Exercise: Adding a Contact Form to the Menu | 184
Hands-On Exercise: Configuring Contact Enhanced | 185
Hands-On Exercise: Adding a Contact Form to an Article | 185
Hands-On Exercise: Add a Form Field to the Contact Form | 186
Hands-On Exercise: Adding Captcha to the Form | 188
Testing Your Contact Form | 188
Donation Form with RSForm Pro | 190
Installing RSForm | 190
Configuring RSForm | 190
Installing Plugins and Modules for RSForm Pro | 190
Creating a Donation Form with PayPal Payment Integration | 191
Adding a Form to the Menu | 193

11. Building an Online Store **197**
Hands-On Exercise: Installing HikaShop | 199
Hands-On Exercise: Configuring HikaShop | 200
Hands-On Exercise: Setting Up Payments, Shipping, and Taxes | 200
Payments | 200
Zones | 201
Shipping | 201
Tax | 203
Hands-On Exercise: Adding Categories, Products, and Attributes | 204
Adding the Shop to the Menu | 205
Adding HikaShop-Specific Modules | 208

Notes About Security, SSL, and PCI Compliance 208

12. Engaging and Keeping in Touch with Your Users 211
Getting Social with JomSocial   211
  Hands-On Exercise: Installing and Configuring JomSocial   211
  Hands-On Exercise: Setting Up a Custom User Profile   213
  Hands-On Exercise: Setting Up Groups in JomSocial   216
  Hands-On Exercise: Creating Events in JomSocial   218
Social Media Sharing   222
  Hands-On Exercise: Adding an AddThis Module   222
Creating a Discussion Forum with Kunena   224
  Hands-On Exercise: Creating Forum Categories   225
  Hands-On Exercise: Creating Category Permissions and Moderating Users   228
  Preventing Spam in Your Forum   229
  Customizing the Look of Kunena   231
Getting the Word Out with a Newsletter   231
  Hands-On Exercise: Setting Up and Creating a Mailing List   232
  Hands-On Exercise: Send Your First Newsletter   233
  Hands-On Exercise: Letting Users Manage Their Subscriptions with the
    AcyMailing Module   235
  Troubleshooting AcyMailing   236
Additional Newsletter Options   236

13. Solutions to Common Problems 237
Database Fix Tool   237
SEF URL Settings and SEO Basics   238
  SEF URLs   238
  Search Engine Optimization (SEO) Basics   240
Favicon   241
Language Overrides   241
Users, User Groups, Access Control Lists (ACLs), and Frontend Editing   244
  Hands-On Exercise: Creating Users   244
  User Groups   245
Access Control Lists (ACLs)   246
  Hands-On Exercise: Allowing a User Group to Edit Specific Content   246
  Hands-On Exercise: Control What the User Sees with ACLs   248
  Set the Access Level of Your Content   249
  Hands-On Exercise: Login Module   249
  Setting User Options   250

14. Making Your Website Secure and Optimized 253
Tips and Best Practices   254

Using Security Tools and Performing Health Checks   254
   Additional Resources   256
Enable Two-Factor Authentication   257
I Was Hacked!   259

A. How to Install Joomla. 261

B. Updating and Migrating Joomla. 289

C. Choosing the Right Extensions. 311

D. Developing for Joomla. 321

E. Tips and Tricks. 325

Index. 329

Foreword

In 1999, I found myself in the middle of a war zone, embedded with a humanitarian relief organization in Eastern Europe. I was just another recent college graduate looking for ways to serve a higher purpose. During college, I'd paid my way through school by doing database consulting gigs since I had a knack for technology. In the golden era of the dot-com boom, I thought it would be great if there were a way to find affordable, effective, and open source technology that could be used to help those in need. Flash forward a few years to 2003. As I'm preparing to present a website solution to a nongovernmental organization in New York, an engineer on my company's team showed me a content management system (CMS) called Mambo. At the time, trying to manage content on your website either required an engineering degree or was woefully underpowered to run even a simple blog. Mambo was different. It provided just the right balance of ease-of-use and robustness. "Power in simplicity" was the tagline. I was hooked.

Little did I know that 11 years later, more than 3% of the Web would be powered by Mambo's successor, Joomla. Joomla brought a new way of thinking about website management when it evolved from Mambo in 2005. Website creation and management was no longer the domain of software developers, and instead "accidental techies" within organizations could now create content on the Web to share with the world. It also brought with it the powerful ability to make your website more than just a blog or content. Third party extensions could be easily added to allow you to sell merchandise, create an online community, and share your message with the world in a variety of new ways.

While Joomla provided liberation from standard technology for accidental techies, its true success was in the growth of a worldwide community of developers, designers, contributors, and users. Bringing diverse backgrounds and cultures to a software project was not novel when Joomla started, but the way it attracted the nonengineer was certainly unique. Due to this community development, Joomla has continued to grow in two directions at the same time, serving the needs of both the average end user and the software engineer.

One of the most striking differences between Joomla and any other software I've used is its focus on community. From two worldwide conferences each year to more than 40 local conferences spread around the globe, Joomla is truly a community of individuals passionate about harnessing the power of the Internet to improve the world. It's a community that speaks more than 50 languages, is used in more than 190 countries, and which actively promotes and encourages the ideas and contributions of nondevelopers. As the Internet continues to evolve, and as more technology is created to better serve a more global, mobile, and social online world, Joomla continues to change with it.

The book in your hands is a testament to Joomla's progress, as it contains the information you need not only to be successful in building and managing a Joomla website, but also the insight as to where to look for the next generation of technology to help your organization thrive online. Whether you're running a small business or operating a multinational organization, Joomla provides the tools you need to build a successful website. I met Ron at the very first JoomlaDay event on Google's campus in 2007 and we've been great friends ever since. I also met Jenn at a JoomlaDay (in San Francisco) recently and was immediately impressed by her great attitude, organizational skills, and ability to get things done. Jenn and Ron provide you with a simple step-by-step game plan to create your Joomla website—and the encouragement to go beyond the basics and explore all the richness the Joomla community has to offer.

I hope to see you in the Joomla community soon!

—Ryan Ozimek
Board Member, Open Source Matters (OSM)

Preface

Welcome to Joomla!®. If you're new to content management systems (CMSs) or even new to building websites, this book will help you get up and running in no time. Whether you're a web designer or an experienced developer, this tome will help you to use Joomla, one of the most popular content management systems available today.

Who Should (and Shouldn't) Read This Book

Have you been asked to build a website in a short period of time? Do you want to convert an existing site to a CMS? Do you have a client who needs a powerful website with lots of functionality? If any of these are true, or you just want to know more about this thing called "Joomla" that people are talking about, this book is for you.

We'd like to think Joomla is for everyone, but if you're a developer looking to create extensions or build on top of Joomla's framework, this book isn't for you. It's also not meant for those who want to build a static site that rarely needs altering, as Joomla comes with management overhead.

How This Book Is Organized

Each chapter of this book breaks down the extensive features of Joomla into easy-to-understand sections, many with hands-on exercises to help you get going quickly:

Chapter 1, Overview
> Get a little background on Joomla and its history, and a tour of the administrator panel.

Chapter 2, Planning Your Website
> Planning is number one in most endeavors. Plan your navigation (menus), categories, articles, modules, templates, and more in this planning chapter.

Chapter 3, A Tour of the Administrator Panel
Learn how to move around the Administrator Control Panel.

Chapter 4, Setting Up the Basics of Your Website
Create categories, articles, menus, and modules for your website. Set up your template in this chapter, too.

Chapter 5, Creating Content
Learn the ins and outs of creating content.

Chapter 6, Managing Media and Creating Galleries
Discover how to manage images, files, and videos in Joomla. Learn how to create image galleries as well.

Chapter 7, Making Your Website Speak Multiple Languages
The Internet makes a very big world small. Make your website serve content in multiple languages.

Chapter 8, Starting a Blog
You, too, can be a writer with your very own blog! Learn how to create a great blog with Joomla.

Chapter 9, Create and Share an Event Calendar
Events are fun for everyone. Keep an events calendar on your site to make your visitors aware of fun events happening in your world.

Chapter 10, Creating Forms
Very few sites exist without forms. Create contact forms or even forms that can accept payments.

Chapter 11, Building an Online Store
Sell your wares in an online store in Joomla.

Chapter 12, Engaging and Keeping in Touch with Your Users
Your website needs people. Chapter 12 helps you engage and stay in touch with your visitors in multiple ways.

Chapter 13, Solutions to Common Problems
Learn about more lengthy solutions that didn't fit into other chapters, such as SEO, User Groups, ACLs, and more.

Chapter 14, Making Your Website Secure and Optimized
Keeping your visitors and your website safe is very important. It takes diligence yet isn't difficult.

Appendix A
Here you'll find step-by-step instructions to install Joomla.

Appendix B

    Keep your Joomla installation up-to-date and learn how to migrate it, which is sometimes necessary to keep it secure.

Appendix C

    So many extensions, so little time. Learn how to choose the right extensions for your site. A list of extensions used in this book can be found here.

Appendix D

    You may want to develop an extension or app with the Joomla Framework. Perhaps you're not a coder and want to get more involved and give back. This is the appendix for you.

Appendix E

    Little snippets and goodies are here.

Conventions Used in This Book

The following typographical conventions are used in this book:

Italic

    Indicates new terms, URLs, email addresses, filenames, and file extensions.

`Constant width`

    Used for program listings, as well as within paragraphs to refer to program elements such as variable or function names, databases, data types, environment variables, statements, and keywords.

`Constant width bold`

    Shows commands or other text that should be typed literally by the user.

`Constant width italic`

    Shows text that should be replaced with user-supplied values or by values determined by context.

    This element signifies a general note.

    This element indicates a warning or caution.

Using Code Examples

This book is here to help you get your job done. In general, if this book includes code examples, you may use the code in this book in your programs and documentation. You do not need to contact us for permission unless you're reproducing a significant portion of the code. For example, writing a program that uses several chunks of code from this book does not require permission. Selling or distributing a CD-ROM of examples from O'Reilly books does require permission. Answering a question by citing this book and quoting example code does not require permission. Incorporating a significant amount of example code from this book into your product's documentation does require permission.

We appreciate, but do not require, attribution. An attribution usually includes the title, author, publisher, and ISBN. For example: "*Using Joomla* by Ron Severdia and Jennifer Gress (O'Reilly). Copyright 2014 Ron Severdia and Jennifer Gress, 978-1-449-34539-6."

If you feel your use of code examples falls outside fair use or the permission given above, feel free to contact us at *permissions@oreilly.com*.

Some Basic Terminology

In dealing with any new technology, becoming familiar with the lingo can be a frustrating process. This section explains some of that lingo in plain English.

Frontend Versus Backend

If you're not familiar with Joomla, you'll quickly learn the difference between the *frontend* and *backend*. It is a very simple concept. The frontend is what visitors see when viewing your website. However, site administrators have access to a control panel they can use to build and manage the website. This is called the backend, which is sometimes referred to as the *Administrator Backend*.

Extensions

Like most modern content management systems, Joomla allows the installation of add-ons to extend the basic functionality. In Joomla, users can extend the functionality to add features like a shopping cart, discussion forum, calendar, and lots more. These add-ons are collectively referred to as *extensions*.

There are seven different types of extensions: components, modules, plugins, templates, languages, libraries, and packages. Each of these types interact with Joomla in a unique way and offer tremendous flexibility in what a user will experience on the frontend of the website. Each extension type is summarized below and will be addressed in more detail throughout this book.

Components

These are typically the most powerful of the seven types of extensions. Located in the main body of the page, a component is an application that runs within your Joomla website. Examples of a component include a discussion forum, calendar, or contact form, or even displaying a simple article of text. Every page on a Joomla website must load at least one component.

Modules

If you think of your web pages broken up into blocks or zones, most of the blocks that live outside the main page area are made up of modules. A module can display a menu, show how many items are in your shopping cart, randomly display an article, or even ask the user for certain information. Modules themselves are managed and created through the *Module Manager*. The location and position modules on the frontend are dictated by module positions in the template. The possibilities are almost endless as to what you can do with a module. Modules are optional but very useful.

Plugins

Plugins are a lot more powerful than they are given credit for. In short, they process web page information as it loads and can do just about anything, from searching content to masking email addresses to protect them from spambots. Plugins are optional extensions on the frontend, but are very powerful.

Templates

Although most people do not think of templates as extensions, they are classified as such. You can think of a template as a theme or a skin. Joomla makes it easy to change the template on your site as a whole or use templates for individual pages. At least one Site template and one Admin template must be installed on every Joomla website.

Languages

Joomla is truly an international CMS and is used by people all over the world. For instance, if you live in the Netherlands, you might prefer to have the Joomla interface in Dutch. Using the Dutch translation, this is done with only a few mouse clicks. Every page on a Joomla website must load at least one language.

Libraries

Libraries are packages of code that provide a related group of functions. Third-party extension developers can use libraries for their extensions.

Packages

Packages are a collection of extensions. For example, a package might contain a template, modules, and plugins used by that template. When a package is uninstalled, it uninstalls all the extensions in the package.

Site Content

As in other content management systems, content is the information contained on your web site. There can be many different types of content on your web site including articles, photos, calendar events, products for sale, and more.

Categories and articles

The most common type of content in a default Joomla installation are called articles. Articles are organized into categories. Categories are used to group related articles.

For many users new to Joomla, the concept of articles and categories is fairly easy to understand. We'll make it even simpler, though, to clear up any confusion. Think of your website like a filing cabinet. The file folders are the categories. The pieces of paper inside the folders are the articles. You can have multiple articles in a single category. You cannot have an article in multiple categories.

Safari® Books Online

 *Safari Books Online* is an on-demand digital library that delivers expert content in both book and video form from the world's leading authors in technology and business.

Technology professionals, software developers, web designers, and business and creative professionals use Safari Books Online as their primary resource for research, problem solving, learning, and certification training.

Safari Books Online offers a range of product mixes and pricing programs for organizations, government agencies, and individuals. Subscribers have access to thousands of books, training videos, and prepublication manuscripts in one fully searchable database from publishers like O'Reilly Media, Prentice Hall Professional, Addison-Wesley Professional, Microsoft Press, Sams, Que, Peachpit Press, Focal Press, Cisco Press, John Wiley & Sons, Syngress, Morgan Kaufmann, IBM Redbooks, Packt, Adobe Press, FT Press, Apress, Manning, New Riders, McGraw-Hill, Jones & Bartlett, Course Technology, and dozens more. For more information about Safari Books Online, please visit us online.

How to Contact Us

Please address comments and questions concerning this book to the publisher:

O'Reilly Media, Inc.
1005 Gravenstein Highway North
Sebastopol, CA 95472
800-998-9938 (in the United States or Canada)
707-829-0515 (international or local)
707-829-0104 (fax)

We have a web page for this book, where we list errata, examples, and any additional information. You can access this page at *http://bit.ly/joomla-2e*.

The authors also have a companion website at *http://www.usingjoomlabook.com*.

To comment or ask technical questions about this book, send email to: *bookques tions@oreilly.com*.

For more information about our books, courses, conferences, and news, see our website at: *http://www.oreilly.com*.

Find us on Facebook: *http://facebook.com/oreilly*

Follow us on Twitter: *http://twitter.com/oreillymedia*

Watch us on YouTube: *http://www.youtube.com/oreillymedia*

About the Technical Reviewers

Matt Simonsen, a systems engineer at Khoza Technology, Inc. (*http:// www.khoza.com*), became interested in Joomla as clients needed solutions to their hosting challenges. As his team has grown and began to take on more development projects, Matt has actively participated in the Bay Area Joomla User Group (*http://www.meet up.com/webdesign-461/*) and is a founding member of the Central Valley Joomla Users Group (*http://bit.ly/cv-usrgrp*).

David Beuving is the CTO of Khoza Technology, Inc. (*http://www.khoza.com*) and leads the company's LAMP development team. He has been using Joomla since version 1.0, has authored a number of extensions, and has contributed code to numerous third-party extensions and even the Joomla core. He lives in Jackson, California, where he enjoys spending time with his family and playing music at church.

Duke Speer is on a campaign to save the world, one nonprofit at a time. He let passion become mission a decade ago when he traded the world of being a CIO at a major Southern California-based broker-dealer for the Park City, Utah, lifestyle. As a contributer to The Joomla Project, Duke is the Manager of the Trademark and Licensing

Team, serves on the Governance Working Group, and contributes articles and art to the Marketing Team and Joomla Community Magazine. He is probably best known in the Joomlaverse as the designer of the Joomla Framework's logo, a popular speaker at many JoomlaDays, and the Host of Joomla!Ignite at the Joomla World Conference.

Acknowledgments

I want to thank the Joomla people who got me involved in the project back at the beginning. A huge thanks goes to Louis Landry, Rob Schley, Andrew Eddie, and Andy Miller for all you've taught me about development, open source, and community. A big thanks also goes to my co-author of the first edition, Ken Crowder, who was my first Joomla "spirit guide" on what was to become quite a journey.

Also a big thanks goes to the amazing Ryan Ozimek for his tireless and endless contributions to Joomla, his relentless pursuit of ways to make it better, and for writing the foreword to this book. A debt of eternal gratitude goes to you for all you do.

—Ron Severdia

Thank you to the Joomla men who taught me so much:

- Brian Watters for introducing me to Joomla all those years ago.
- Andy Van Valer for having such belief in me that he got me to start a business building Joomla websites.
- Roland Hall for teaching me the technical side of Joomla and servers so well I could do it myself.
- James Foreman for tirelessly working with me with clients and the JUG, and for being an excellent colleague and friend.

I send gratitude to my daughter Aurora, who allowed me to give my time to this publication and for her tireless and constant support. You are the best daughter ever and I love you mucho!

Many thanks to my family and my friends who have encouraged me while writing this book and building a business—I wouldn't have done it without you.

Additionally, I want to thank the fabulous people and developers in the Joomla community. You are inspiring, and I am grateful to be a part of such an excellent group of people.

Last but not least, thank you to the entire team at O'Reilly—you are all fantastic. Special thanks to Allyson MacDonald who rocked it doing whatever was needed to make *Using Joomla* happen and be great.

—Jennifer Gress

CHAPTER 1

Overview

There are so many great ideas and purposes for websites. Yet how do you make yours a reality without spending a ton of money? Where do you start? What resources are available to support you? Do you have to know a bunch of code that makes you feel like a deer in the headlights in order to get the result you want?

No, you don't need a lot of money. Just some time. In *Using Joomla*, we'll show you where to start and take you step-by-step along the way. You'll be given resources on where to look for further help if you need it. You won't need to know any code, though a little HTML and CSS will make your journey a bit easier.

All of this is accomplished by using Joomla for your next website.

Joomla is a content management system (CMS) which allows users to add, change, and manage website content with ease. *Using Joomla* is going to give you the directions to build a Joomla website step-by-step: from planning (Chapter 2), installation (Appendix A), setting up the structure (Chapter 4), and creating content (Chapter 5), to more complex operations such as extending Joomla with third-party extensions (chapters 7 to 11), migration (Appendix B), multiple languages (Chapter 7), security (Chapter 14), and more. All of this will use Joomla 3.x, the latest and most exciting release to date!

A Brief History of Joomla

In 2000, the Australia-based company Miro developed a proprietary CMS called Mambo and, a year later, released it for free to the public under the GNU General Public License (GPL) (see "Why Open Source and the GPL?" on page 3 for more on GPL). Mambo quickly garnered a lot of community support and enthusiasm. But in 2005, a copyright dispute with the Mambo Steering Committee caused most members of the Mambo Core Team to resign. The result was a new entity called Open Source Matters and a *code fork* (a point at which a new version of the source code "forks" in a different direction) of Mambo called Joomla. Joomla, which is a phonetic spelling of the Swahili word

"Jumla" meaning "all together," was officially launched with version 1.0 on September 16, 2005. The first version was primarily a rebranding with a few bug fixes, but 14 updates and numerous open source awards followed over the next two years.

On January 21, 2008, the first major revision to Joomla was announced: Joomla 1.5. It was a monumental effort on the part of many and brought a whole new level of power and features to the open source CMS world. Joomla received a new API and became a truly international CMS, with support for extended character sets and right-to-left languages. It grew leaps and bounds in areas like usability, extensibility, and template control—where it was already superior to other options.

In July 2009, the Joomla Project announced a restructuring of its management to increase productivity and efficiency. The Core Team that originally led the project was replaced by the Joomla Leadership Team. This redefined the role of the team leading the project and structured it more around community involvement in events, the Google Summer of Code projects, and other activities. This somewhat federative approach to team-building was also an effort to increase community participation in the development process instead of relying on a small group of coders to do most of the work.

In January 2012, the third revision to Joomla was announced: Joomla 2.5—another fantastic effort by the Production Leadership Team and others in the Joomla Community. Joomla 2.5 brought many vital new features and a new API, giving Joomla greater ease in use, user control, multilanguage abilities, and the ability to update with one-click.

Quickly after the release of Joomla 2.5, work was under way on the Joomla 3.x series. Joomla 3.x focuses on mobile-friendly websites on the frontend, as well as backend administration. With greater ease in navigation and more user-friendly means of editing Joomla sites, Joomla 3 is fabulous and the focus of this book. As of April 2014, Joomla 3.3 is the current release within the Joomla 3 life cycle. Every two to three months there will be a new minor release within the Joomla 3.x series. Minor releases are whatever comes after the dot (3.4, 3.5, 3.6, etc.). When the last minor release for Joomla 3 is released, it will be supported for two years. We do not know how many there will be as of June 2014.

This release structure allows new features to be added to Joomla 3 as they are needed. Additional features and changes to Joomla 3 are to be fully backwards-compatible from Joomla 3.4 on. This means that updating Joomla 3 within the version won't break Joomla and won't break any break third-party extensions.

Checking the information about Joomla CMS versions (*http://bit.ly/cms-versions*) will keep you up to date on Joomla versions and their support dates.

Joomla Series End-of-Life Dates

Nothing lasts forever (except maybe a Twinkie) and that goes for Joomla releases, too. The following is a list of previous Joomla releases and their end-of-life dates:

- Joomla 1.0.x: July 22, 2009. We advise you to migrate to Joomla 3.x in order to stay current.
- Joomla 1.5.x: September 2012. We advise you to migrate to Joomla 3.x in order to stay current.
- Joomla 2.5.x: December 2014. We advise you to migrate to Joomla 3.x before Joomla 2.5 is end of life.

(For more information on upgrades and migration, see Appendix B.)

Why Open Source and the GPL?

The idea behind open source software—that it can be freely used, modified, or even sold—is a powerful one. This doesn't mean that open source software is always cost-free, but users like you and me are allowed to change and improve it, which spurs creativity and innovation.

The Joomla Project believes strongly in the power of the GNU GPL. It's not just because it's the most popular of the open source licenses, but the project also feels it offers the best freedoms for third-party developers and encourages them to follow the project's lead in choosing to make their software open source. Visit the Open Source Initiative (*http://www.opensource.org*) for more information. For more information about the GNU GPL, visit the Free Software Foundation (*http://bit.ly/free-soft-fd*).

The Advantages and Disadvantages of Using a CMS: Static Versus Dynamic

For many years, the traditional way of building a website has been with plain, static HTML. Whenever a change was needed, web designers used tools like Adobe Dreamweaver to perform tasks manually. If the websites were small, it was a fairly simple task. Now that even relatively small sites contain hundreds of pages and the largest ones contain hundreds of thousands, the time and expense involved in maintaining a static HTML website is much greater than when the Web was young. An advantage to static HTML sites is that they are less likely to have security vulnerabilities and require very little ongoing maintenance.

A CMS has many advantages because of its dynamic structure. You can make one simple menu change and have it reflect throughout your entire site—no matter the size. Your content is organized and maintained through a backend system, allowing you to manage templates, content, images, and more. A CMS like Joomla has many powerful features, like contact forms and search, already built in. It can also help teams effectively collaborate, create content based on specified permissions, and manage documents and digital assets.

The disadvantage of using a dynamic CMS as opposed to a static site is that it requires commitment and ongoing maintenance. Software of a CMS must be updated to keep features and security up to date. Frequent security updates happen with the core software and third-party extensions. While some may think it is optional to do these updates, one of the top reasons for problems in a CMS is the core or third-party extensions not being properly updated in a timely fashion. Thus, your commitment is necessary. It's similar to a vehicle. Everyone knows that the oil needs to be changed regularly or the vehicle will not perform optimally or can even break. It is the same with software like Joomla. Getting the oil changed doesn't take very long. It does need to be done, though. Depending on the number of third-party extensions your website is using, your time commitment could be as small as 10 minutes every month. Not bad and very doable! Still, if you cannot commit to the necessary time, perhaps a static site is best for you.

Since you are reading this book, we'll trust that you are totally committed to your Joomla site and will be on your game keeping it up to date. You can get into planning your website in Chapter 2 or you can jump in and start on Appendix A to install Joomla and take a tour of the Administrator Panel (Chapter 3).

Joomla Concepts

Joomla is database-driven. Your content is stored in a database that is created at the time of installation (see Appendix A).

Joomla is menu-based. Your content displays in various ways according to menus and menu items. This is often referred to as the *site navigation* or *site map*.

Menus give your visitors a way to reach your content. Content is most often an article or a group of articles in a specific category displayed in the main content area of your site. Third-party components like a forum or store display in the main content area by means of specific menu item types, which are as part of the component.

Often one wants to display smaller blocks of content above, below, or in the sidebars of the main content area. These blocks are called *modules*. Modules display in module positions defined by the template, and based on their menu assignment.

For example, you may want one or more modules displayed only on the home page above your main content article. You may want a specific module displayed only on your store pages to bring attention to specific products. Each module can display on one or more menu items regardless of their type.

URLs are displayed based on *menu item aliases*. The alias is set within the menu item and displayed on the frontend of your site as the URL for that page.

Figure 1-1 shows an example of a typical site page that includes a module, menu, and main content area.

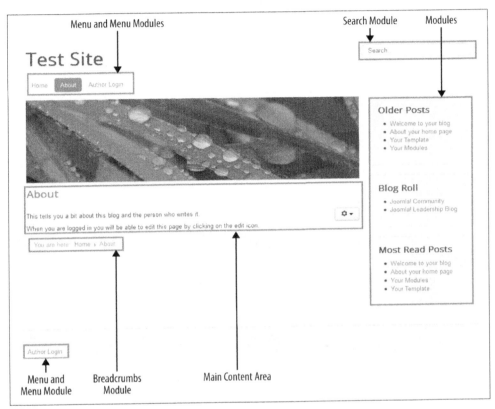

Figure 1-1. Menus, modules, and main content area of a Joomla site

As you can see, a typical page is made up of articles, menus, and modules. Understanding this will make planning your website easier and will help you know the terminology better. Check out the Preface for more on terminology in your Joomla site.

The first step in building a website is to plan. Planning takes patience and decision-making. It's OK for it to take time. The better you plan, the easier it will be to build your site. In Chapter 2, we will take a step-by-step process and plan a website.

CHAPTER 2

Planning Your Website

When you first sit down to create your new Joomla site, a little bit of planning and forethought can save you a lot of time and heartache down the road. But don't worry if you haven't worked out every little detail. Joomla is flexible enough for you to be able to move things around and readjust later on.

Example Website: Joomla Pet Center

We are going to create an example website called Joomla Pet Center for fans of pets. Joomla Pet Center will include articles, a store, social community, and many other elements which together will give you a real-world example of a website with a variety of features. While Joomla Pet Center will be fairly complex, your site may be simpler. Regardless, planning is key.

Goals of the Website

Knowing your business goals is helpful when planning a website. We have to have a good handle on what we want people to do when they get to the site. If you have a marketing plan, or mission statement, this is a good time to pull those out and review them so that the website works with them and the mission of your business.

If you don't have a business plan or mission, no need to worry (though you may want to consider it for the future). Simply ask yourself, "What do I want my website visitors to do when they get to my site?"

Our Joomla Pet Center has several goals:

1. Encourage visitors to buy products from the site's online store
2. Provide helpful information via the Joomla Pet Center blog

3. Give pet lovers a community in which they can meet each other and foster relationships with people of like mind

4. Capture contact information from visitors in order to reach out to them again to achieve future sales

Now it is your turn to think about and write down the goals for your website.

Hands-On Exercise: Write Your Goals

There isn't a wrong or right way to determine your goals and record them somewhere. It is helpful to write them down and revisit them frequently. As a website progresses, sometimes we can get distracted with its functionality, or the design and goals can get lost in the shuffle.

Ask yourself some questions and note the answers. It's OK if you don't know the answers. Just asking the questions will assist in your planning process.

Ask yourself:

- What is my top business goal?
- What are my other business goals?
- What do I want people to do when they get to my website?
- What are the benefits of my product or service that visitors want?
- Do I want the website to be mobile-friendly?
- Will more than one person be administering the website? If so, what will they need to access?
- Will visitors be able to contribute to the site in any way, whether it be commenting, submitting forms, or creating a profile? How will they and their information be moderated?

Having a basic concept of what you ultimately want to achieve for your business and your site will assist you throughout the planning process. Now let's plan your site menu.

Planning Menu Items

It is easiest to begin the planning of your website by figuring out what menu items (or sections) you would like to appear on your site. The Joomla menu system manages the navigation for your website and gives it a framework. A menu can also be referred to as tabs or buttons that often exist at the top of a website and provide navigation throughout the site content. Menus can also be down the side of a page or at the bottom of a website. There can be more than one menu on a website.

In a Joomla menu, each of the linked pages of content is created by adding a new menu item to one of these menus. The *main menu* is typically where visitors will navigate to the main pages of your site. Each of these pages is a menu item within the main menu.

The importance of a good menu structure cannot be overemphasized. If users can't quickly and logically find the information they want, they'll go somewhere else. So when you're building a website, you should spend the extra time to make sure the menu structure (or site map) is just right. On smaller sites, the site map pretty much builds itself because the structure is simple. On larger sites with thousands of articles, time invested up front to get things organized in the best possible way will save a lot of time and headache down the line and also provide for a better user experience.

Joomla makes it easy to organize your information with its menu system. You can create an unlimited number of menus and menu items as needed, with the ability to nest those menu items within each other to go as deep as you want.

 Some of you are probably shaking your head at the "unlimited menus" statement above. Yes, we're just like you in that we question everything, and the truth is that it's not technically unlimited. The maximum number of menu items is actually 4,294,967,295. With a number that big, we think it's safe to say that it is virtually unlimited.

When planning our Joomla Pet Center, we talked together on the phone to determine the menu items for the site and wrote them down on a piece of paper. After several website builds, this will be sufficient for you, too. However, as a beginner, it will be easier for you to draw it out in some way.

Ways to draw out your menu items:

On paper
> Get a piece of paper and leave a little space at the top and then draw a line across the paper either portrait or landscape—it doesn't matter which way. Write the menu items that will appear on your site across the paper above the line. Below the line, write the items that will appear in the drop-down of that menu item. Using sticky notes is a great way to easily try different arrangements of topics to find the most effective sequence and flow of content.

In a spreadsheet
> Start with the top row of the spreadsheet and in each cell type the name of the menu item across the top. Make that row bold. On the next row down under each of the bold cells, type the menu items that will be drop-down items.

Wireframing software
> There are many wireframing tools that will allow you to create menus and page layouts with varying effort, complexity, and cost. You are welcome to take the plan-

ning of your site to any level you wish. In some cases, using wireframing software like wireframe.me, OmniGraffle, or Mockingbird is a very good idea. In other cases, it is overkill and could take more time than paper or a spreadsheet.

Presentation software like PowerPoint or Google Presentations
You can create a presentation-style file with boxes outlining what goes where in a Google Drive document for as many pages as you wish.

If you have a lot of ideas for your website, it might be useful to try this simple exercise: Write down all the sections and ideas you have on small index cards. Lay out all the cards (or stick them on a wall if you're using stickies) and put related items together in the same area, moving them into logical groups so they all create the least number of groups possible. This will help make your site structure and menu system more clear.

Figure 2-1 shows the menu items Joomla Pet Center will have.

A	**B**	**C**	**D**	**E**	**F**	**G**	**H**	**I**
Home	Store	Events	Gallery	Community	Forum	Blog	How to's	About
								Testimonials
								Forms
								Privacy Policy
								Terms & Conditions
								Contact

Figure 2-1. Joomla Pet Center menu items using a Google Drive spreadsheet

Next, we take it a step further and determine the type of each menu item, which will affect its layout/display on the page. The type or the component that will be used is in parentheses next to the menu item in Figure 2-2.

Menu items are likely to change as the site progresses. Flexibility is important as the site takes shape.

Figure 2-2. Joomla Pet Center menu items with types to determine layout

Joomla Pet Center will make use of a few third-party extensions which add to the standard functionality of what comes with Joomla when it is installed. Therefore, a number of the menu items for Joomla Pet Center will display based on Component menu items.

Home

> The home page of Joomla Pet Center will have a gallery, a featured article, and a number of modules guiding the visitor to the main points of the site that achieve our goals.

Store

> The store will use a component called HikaShop, which is an ecommerce component to give shopping cart functionality to the website.

Gallery

> We will use a module and plugin extension called Sigplus Gallery for a gallery of images of various pets.

Community

> JomSocial is the top social extension for Joomla. It can be likened to a mini-Facebook for Joomla.

Forum

> We will use Kunena as a forum for people to discuss various topics on Joomla Pet Center.

Blog

> Joomla is great for blogs. We will use Joomla articles with Joomla's tagging component, along with an extension called Komento so that people can comment on the articles in the blog.

How to

> We'll handle the "How to" section the same way as the blog.

About and Testimonials

Both the About and Testimonials pages need to display multiple articles at a time. To accomplish this, we will use the Category Blog menu item type and pull all the articles in a given category into a page on the site.

Forms

RSForm is the component that will display the various forms needed on Joomla Pet Center.

Privacy Policy and Terms & Conditions

These are both Single Article menu item types that will display one at a time when clicked.

Contact

Using Contact Enhanced, we will build a beautiful contact form for the site.

Now it is your turn.

Hands-On Exercise: Choose Menu Items and Layout

First, using whatever method works for you, draw out or make a list of all the menu items you will have on your site. If this turns into more than one menu, then make more than one list or drawing. If you plan to have a lot of content in your menu in columns, you may want to use multiple pieces of paper or tabs of a spreadsheet so that it can be clearer.

Once you are done making your list of menu items, you will go back and decide what type of content it is, what component can be used to create that content, and then what type of menu item to use to link to that content. The following list describes the most commonly used menu item types.

A page on your website can consist of a single article

As users navigate your website, they view one article at a time on each page, as seen in Figure 2-3.

A page on your website can consist of multiple articles

As users navigate your website, each page they see contains several articles (e.g., an entire category of articles) (see Figure 2-4). These might be full articles or just teasers that require users to click a *Read more* link to view an entire article.

Figure 2-3. Example of a single-article display

Figure 2-4. Example of multiple articles displayed on a page

A page that displays a content type produced by a different component than the Article Manager

As users navigate your website, the page displays content pulled from a component like a store or a calendar, as seen in Figure 2-5.

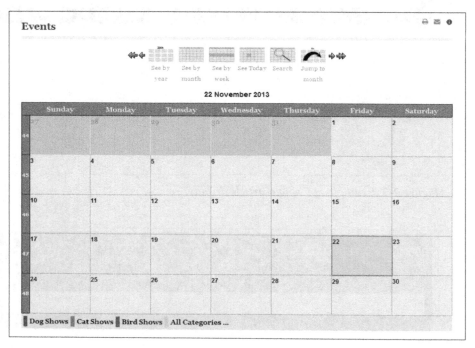

Figure 2-5. Example of the content from a calendar component displayed on a page

Most sites will likely use a combination of all of these options to display articles.

Planning Categories

Categories can be imagined like buckets. Each article (or page) is assigned to a category. You can imagine each article going into the bucket. Categories can have nested categories, or subcategories: buckets inside of buckets. You will get to see this as we create categories for Joomla Pet Center in the next chapter.

With your menu item and types in clear view, you can now plan your categories.

Joomla Pet Center will have the following categories based on the menu items we created in our spreadsheet:

- Blog
- How to
- About
- Testimonials
- Legal

In addition to these, we will have nested categories for the Blog and the "How to" sections, so we can organize the content to be easier for visitors to sort and navigate.

The Blog category will have the following nested categories or subcategories:

- Dogs
- Cats
- Reptiles
- Birds

To keep it simple, we will use the same nested categories for the "How to" category.

Hands-On Exercise: Make Your List of Categories

You can do something as simple as highlight your menu items that will be categories. You can also make a separate list, or use a combination of both. Just have them ready so that when it is time to create the categories, your list will make the process a quick one.

Because there are menu items that can pull articles from a specific category, keep your ultimate display types in mind while planning your categories.

Planning Articles

Just because we only have a few categories on Joomla Pet Center does not mean that we won't have many articles. In the About category, we will use a Category Blog menu item type and show three full articles about the Joomla Pet Center partners.

We'll have three articles for this category called:

1. Helen
2. Diana
3. Mark

Testimonials, the Blog, and the "How to" categories will also need to display multiple articles in the main content area.

In the Testimonial category, we will start out with three testimonials. The article titles will coincide with what the testimonial is about.

Because we don't yet know the titles of the articles that will appear in the Blog and "How to" categories, we will use the following placeholders:

- Testimonial 1
- Testimonial 2
- Testimonial 3
- Blog 1
- Blog 2
- Blog 3
- How to 1
- How to 2
- How to 3

Our Legal category will house the Privacy Policy and Terms & Conditions articles.

This is all just a plan. As the website progresses, it can and likely will adjust. Thank goodness Joomla is so flexible.

Hands-On Exercise: Make Your List of Articles

You can either directly create the articles in Joomla or plan a list using a variety of approaches, such as another spreadsheet tab, sheet of paper, presentation slide, or wireframing software. Whatever approach you prefer, you might want to make some notes about the categories that you'll put the articles in.

Go ahead and make notes about your articles within their categories if you choose to at this time.

Planning Users

If you are the only one managing content on the backend, and website visitors won't need to log in to access special content or do specific actions, then you won't need to plan for additional users.

If you are planning to have multiple users, edit content on the site, or perform certain actions, you will need to think about who is doing what. Joomla is very flexible and can allow or limit permissions to specific *user groups*.

If there is special content or functions you want your visitors (users) to have access to, they will need to register for a user account to be granted specific permissions governing they can do or see.

In some cases, a third-party extension may dictate how users are handled. Each scenario is different and can be very simple or very complex. Joomla can handle both and everything in between.

See "Hands-On Exercise: Creating Users" on page 244 for an entire section to set up users, user groups, and Access Control Lists.

Hands-On Exercise: Write Out Your Users and What They Can See or Do

This is a big topic, so let's just start with some basic definitions to help you understand.

Users
> Anyone registered on the site with frontend or backend access.

User group
> Determines what users can *do* and the permissions they have. Works in conjunction with ACLs.

Access Control Lists (ACLs)
> Determines what users can *see* and works in conjunction with user groups.

For planning purposes—consider, decide, and document the following:

- If visitors will register (have a username and password) on your site to "unlock" content hidden to unregistered (public) visitors.
- If there will be specific content that different registered users can access on your site. For example, students see *abc* content and teachers see *xyz* content.
- If other users will add content via the frontend.
- If other users will edit existing content via the frontend.
- If other users will add or edit content, or manage extensions via the backend.

Get specific. If Helen needs to add events, she will need permissions (controlled by the user group) to do so either via the frontend, the backend, or both.

If Mark needs to edit specific articles on the frontend and not be able to edit others, he will need permissions (controlled by the user group) to do so via the frontend.

If certain visitors should never see specific content, that user group needs special ACLs to control what they are allowed to see.

For step-by-steps involving users, user groups, and ACLs, see "Hands-On Exercise: Creating Users" on page 244.

Choosing Extensions

There are literally thousands of extensions for Joomla that provide just about every feature imaginable. For our Joomla Pet Center and for the sake of this book, we chose extensions that are popular, well-tested, have good support, are ready for Joomla 3.x, and will benefit you as a student of Joomla. They are included in the later chapters of this book.

Because choosing extensions for your website can be daunting and challenging, there is a dedicated appendix to assist you in finding extensions to make Joomla do even more than it does already. Please see Appendix C to learn more about choosing extensions. There are important tips on finding and choosing extensions from third-party developers in Appendix C.

Do find your extensions and plan for them, as they might change your design and site plan. That being said, attempt to use what comes with a Joomla installation first and use a third-party extension only if required.

Choosing a Template

The site template determines the look and feel of a website including colors, fonts, font sizes, and other styling aspects. There are many places to find suitable and attractive templates for your Joomla website.

Included Templates
Joomla installs with a number of default templates for you to use at no additional cost. You can customize them if you have the skillset to do so.

Third-Party Free Templates
You can find many free Joomla templates on the Internet. However, it is important to research a number of things about these before deciding to use one:

1. Does the developer continually update the template for new releases of Joomla?

2. Is there support for the template?

3. Do a Google search on the template name and read the results.

4. Do a Google search on the template name plus the word "vulnerability" and see if anything comes up. Issues should be infrequent and show that it was patched quickly.

5. Are there link-backs to the template developer's website? If so, is that OK with you?

Third-Party Professional or Paid Templates
Joomla templates can be purchased individually or via a subscription from many template companies. Typically, it is fairly simple to alter/customize the template so

that you can have specific colors, backgrounds, fonts, etc. The good thing about paying for a template is that for the most part, these template companies continually update their extensions for the new releases of Joomla. However, if it is a very old or unpopular template, this may not be the case. As a result, research is needed with these companies as well. Here are some items to research about paid templates:

1. Does the developer have a history of providing updates for older templates for the latest releases of Joomla?

2. Most paid template companies do offer support, but you should still read the terms and conditions of the membership or purchase to make sure that support is what you are expecting.

3. Do a Google search on the template company you are considering to see what others say about it.

4. Do a Google search on the template name you are interested in to see what others say about it.

Custom Templates

You may want to employ a designer to design a custom template for you and have a Joomla template developer create it for you to use with Joomla. You may have the skillset to create your own custom template. This is the most time-consuming option and could be the most expensive, but you will be more likely to get exactly what you want with this option.

Twitter Bootstrap

A couple of guys from Twitter got tired of doing the same steps over and over to build a website from scratch so they came up with an open source framework to make things easier, faster, and more consistent. Released in 2011, they called this frontend framework Bootstrap (*http://getbootstrap.com/*). Earlier versions of Joomla (1.6–2.5, included with the *Atomic* template) used a similar framework called Blueprint (*http://www.blueprintcss.org/*), but Bootstrap took flexibility and mobile compatibility to the next level.

Fortunately, Bootstrap has progressed quickly since its initial release and is already at version 3.1. Joomla 3.0 was released with Bootstrap 2.1 and unfortunately, Joomla 3.2 uses the legacy Bootstrap 2.3.2 version which is incompatible with Bootstrap 3 and Joomla 3. So you can't really use the latest Bootstrap version (which has tons of improvements) without a lot of work (including modifying core Joomla files) or by using a "bridge" template containing elements and overrides from both. Templates like Joostrap (*http://www.joostrap.com/*), T3 (*http://t3-framework.org/*), or Wright (*http://wright.joomlashack.com*) are a great way to build your own template on the latest framework.

Not all template companies use Bootstrap. Many don't. But that doesn't mean that third-party extensions can't use Bootstrap to work with them. They still work. A few template companies may actually block certain Bootstrap files, which may require a few CSS work-arounds to display correctly. This is rare, but possible.

For Joomla Pet Center, we are going to use a free template from a very reputable template company called RocketTheme. The template name is *Afterburner2*. RocketTheme has very good support and a flexible framework (the framework gives additional function-ality to the template) that is easy for beginners to configure.

Home Page Layout

Going back to paper, a spreadsheet, a presentation slide, or wireframing software, we will now sketch out our home page layout. This is a guide so that we can create the elements required and have something to look at. Chances are good that the finished home page will look different than our sketch, and that is just fine.

Using a new tab of our spreadsheet called "Home page," we will use outlined cells to lay out our home page. It is absolutely fine to use a piece of paper (perhaps even easier).

We already know that we want a gallery and an article with content for our home page. We also want to have a number of modules (think of modules as boxes) to direct people to various functions of our site that mesh with our site goals.

See Figure 2-6 for our projected home page layout.

The spacing of modules is not exact. This is a quick, easy, and fairly low-tech way of sketching out a projection of what the home page layout will look like. As content goes into the modules, things will change.

Hands-On Exercise: Draw Out Your Home Page

Take a few minutes to decide what you want on your home page. This isn't something you have to treat as a contract. It is to be done as an exercise in planning. If you want a Twitter feed on your home page, then make a box for it.

Sometimes it is easier to figure out what to display on the home page after the rest of the site is laid out and content exists. It becomes clearer as the site is built as to what has its proper place on the home page. If you want to wait to sketch out your home page layout, that is acceptable and perhaps even preferred.

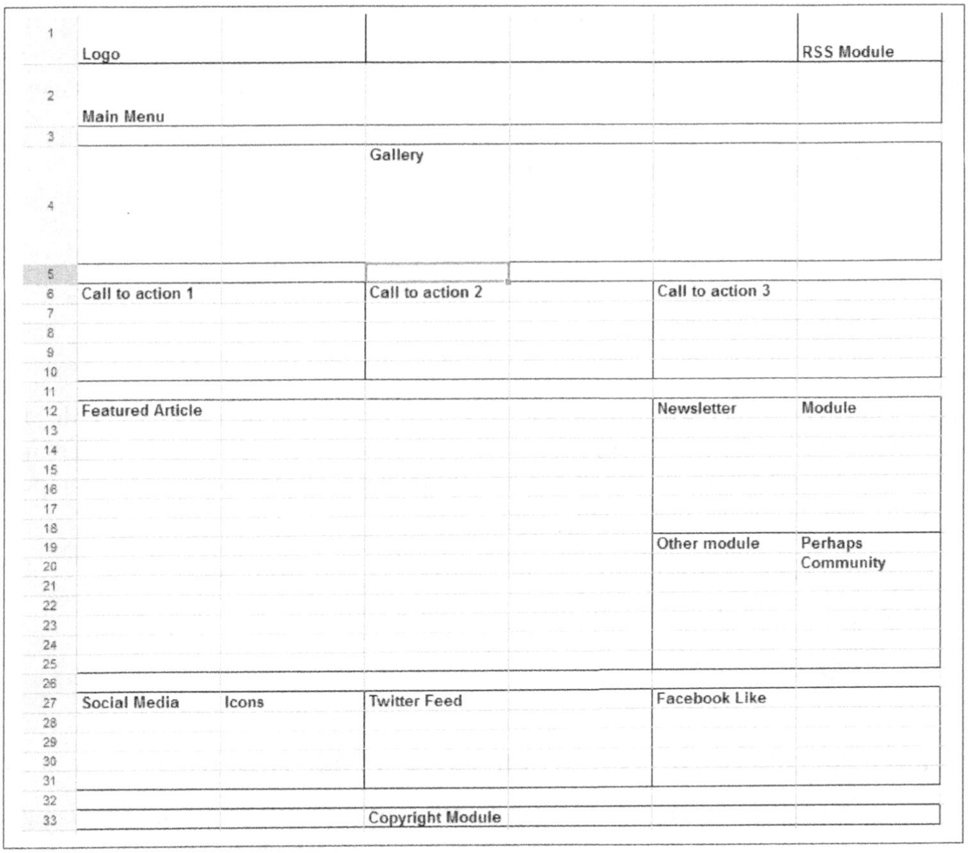

Figure 2-6. Joomla Pet Center home page layout

Internal Page Layout

Using a similar approach as the home page layout, we have to figure out how our internal pages will be laid out. The difference between the home page and the internal pages is that typically, the home page gallery won't display on the internal pages. The three modules beneath the gallery also will not typically display on the internal pages. It could be that different modules will appear at the top of the internal pages depending on what page was being viewed.

Often there are different sidebar modules on internal pages than there are on the home page, which would highlight content or give additional calls to action depending on the content being displayed.

For example, on the Joomla Pet Center testimonial page, we may want to display a module in the sidebar giving people instructions on how to submit a testimonial. Joomla modules provide a lot of power to be able to display different content on different pages.

Planning the internal pages is again just a guide. We may or may not know what we want to display on the sidebars or on internal pages until the content is entered.

 You may have several different internal page layouts. Extensions will often dictate the layout as well as specific modules to be published on those pages. The key is to plan things out so you have a basis from which to work.

For Joomla Pet Center, we assume that we will have a sidebar on each page to display complementary information or action items. This will be the right sidebar so that on a mobile device it will appear after the main content item. The left sidebar would appear first on a mobile device prior to the content item.

 On a mobile device, sidebar modules generally display before or after the main content area. Each template works differently, so check the template demo from a mobile device to see how the module positions display.

Hands-On Exercise: Draw Out Your Internal Page Layout

Think about your internal pages. If you offer white papers on your products, you might want to have a different module on each product page that allows people to read that product's white paper. You may want to display your contact information in a module on every page.

You can draw on a piece of paper to lay out each page of your website or you can make a new slide for each page in presentation software. You can make a new tab of a spreadsheet. Plan out what modules you want to display on your internal pages, and whether they will be the same on all pages or if you want different modules on each page.

This exercise is to give you an opportunity to think about what modules you might want, if any, to accompany the content that displays on a page.

Now that we have spent some time planning the site, we can be more efficient and quickly get building. Let's take a short tour of how Joomla works on the backend before setting things up.

CHAPTER 3

A Tour of the Administrator Panel

If you want to follow along in this chapter, you need to have Joomla installed. If you haven't yet downloaded and installed Joomla, see Appendix A for instructions. We'll be taking a brief tour of the Joomla Administrator Panel and jumping right into setting up the structure of the website.

In any good CMS, the administrator dashboard is where the magic happens. In Joomla, this is referred to as the Administrator Backend and allows site administrators to build and maintain robust websites. This chapter will cover the Control Panel, Menu, and Administrator Module regions of the backend. Other chapters in this book will discuss these items in more detail.

If you haven't installed Joomla yet, you can refer to Figure 3-1 to see the different areas we'll cover.

If you have Joomla installed, you can log in and view your own administrator control panel at *http://www.YourSite.com/administrator* (remember to replace "YourSite" with your URL).

Control Panel

The *Control Panel* is more or less the administrator's home page. It's the launching point from which you will build and manage your website. The Control Panel dashboard is divided into two columns. The column on the left sidebar shows links to commonly used areas of the site. The right column shows the administrator modules. Figure 3-1 shows the Control Panel columns you would see if you were logged in as a Super Administrator. Depending on whether you are logged in as a Manager, Administrator, or Super Administrator, there may be fewer quick links and administrator modules on your screen.

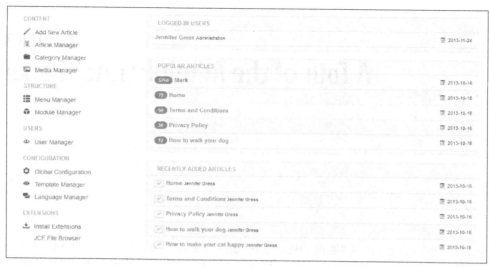

Figure 3-1. Joomla 3.x Administrator Backend

The links in the left column provide you with quick access to the following areas:

Add New Article

> This link will take you to the new article page. This is the same as clicking Content→Article Manager and then New.

Article Manager

> Displays a list of all of the articles that have been created in Joomla by you or any other user. You can also manage, add, edit, and delete articles from this screen.

Category Manager

> Managing, adding, editing, and deleting categories takes place here. Categories are used to organize groups of articles.

Media Manager

> Allows you to upload files into Joomla. Examples of file types are images, documents, videos, audio files, etc. Once uploaded, you can embed and link to them from various places within the CMS.

Menu Manager

> This is mainly used for creating new menu items, but it can also be used to create new menus.

Module Manager

> Used for creating, editing, or deleting modules published both on the frontend of the site and in the Administrator Backend.

User Manager

The *User Manager* allows you to manage user accounts, user groups, and access levels.

Global Configuration

A lot of high-level Joomla settings can be modified here.

Template Manager

Used for managing and configuring templates, template styles, and template files.

Language Manager

If English is not your first language or if you prefer a different language, you can use the *Language Manager* to change the default language for the frontend, the backend, or both. You can also allow each user to set their own language preferences and override language keys.

 Additional languages are now available from the backend of Joomla. They can be installed from the *Extension Manager*. The Joomla Translation Working Group has translated Joomla's core language files into more than 100 world languages. Translations are available for download from JoomlaCode (*http://bit.ly/jc-translate*).

Extension Manager

Used to install optional third-party extensions, update extensions, manage extensions, discover extensions, run a fix on the database, view warnings, and install additional language packs. Third-party extensions are packages that provide additional features or customize how Joomla works. See Appendix C for more on third-party extensions.

Administrator Menus

The menu at the top of the Administrator Control Panel serves as a launching point to virtually every area of Joomla's backend. A super administrator will have access to and see the menus that follow. If a user is in a different user group (administrator or manager), they will see some of these menus but not others. See "User Groups" on page 245 for more information on user groups and the privileges granted to each group.

System

The System drop-down menu contains links to pages that facilitate the management of configuration settings, system information, cache, and checked-out items (see Figure 3-2).

Figure 3-2. System menu drop-down

The following items are found in the System drop-down menu:

Control Panel
This links to the Administrator Control Panel.

Global Configuration
Many high-level Joomla settings can be modified here, such as system-wide editor and captcha, Search Engine Friendly (SEF) URLs, mail options, meta description and keywords, text filtering, access to global site, system, server, permissions, and text filter settings.

Global Check-in
This gives you the ability to check in articles, modules, menu items, and more in the database tables that may be locked/checked-out by another user who didn't check their item back in or may have been booted out of the system before exiting the article (or other item) properly.

Clear Cache
This does just what it says—it clears your site's cache.

Purge Expired Cache
Deletes any cache files that are no longer current.

System Information
Contains information about your server settings and key Joomla information. This is most helpful when troubleshooting an issue that may be caused by your server not being set up properly to run Joomla effectively.

Users

The Users drop-down menu contains links to manage and configure users, user groups, user access levels, user notes, and user note categories. Each menu item in the Users menu drop-down has a submenu item that allows you to instantly "Add a new" of each menu item type for swift additions in the Users menu. Below are the items with descriptions of what you will find in the Users menu drop-down. For more information on using the items in the Users menu drop-down, see Chapter 4.

User Manager
> Allows you to manage user accounts.

Groups
> Allows you to view default user groups or add new groups that can be configured with specific permissions that dictate what users can do on the site. (See "User Groups" on page 245 for more information.)

Access Levels
> Allows you to view default access levels (or access control lists—ACLs) and create new access levels, to control which user groups can view what content on the sites, frontend or backend. See "Access Control Lists (ACLs)" on page 246 for more detail on ACLs.

User Notes
> Create notes about specific users that will appear in the User Manager, with the ability to view or add a note on the fly about that user.

User Note Categories
> Add *User Note Categories* to organize User Notes more effectively.

Mass Mail Users
> Provides an easy way to send email to all your users or specific user groups.

Menus

The Menus drop-down menu allows you to access pages where you will have the ability to add, edit, and delete menus and menu items. Figure 3-3 shows the Menus drop-down menu as it would look if sample data was not installed during Joomla installation. If you installed sample data during installation, you'll see other menus below Main Menu.

As with the Users drop-down, the Menus drop-down has submenu items so that you can quickly add a new menu or a new menu item to an existing menu by utilizing the "Add a new" submenu item. For more information, see "Creating Menu Items" on page 47.

Menu Manager
> Add, edit, and delete menus.

Main Menu
> As the name suggests, Main Menu is the name of the main menu shown on the frontend. By clicking on Main Menu from the drop-down menu, you will be able

to add, edit, and delete menu items. If you have more than one menu, they will all be listed separately within the Menus drop-down.

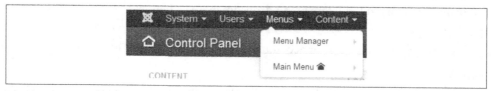

Figure 3-3. Menus drop-down menu

Content

Some would call content the heart of any CMS. The Content drop-down menu (shown in Figure 3-4) gives you access to fundamental parts of Joomla that facilitate managing your articles as well as your site's hierarchical structure. Other content types such as events and contacts are managed using the Component drop-down menu (see the following section). For more information, see Chapter 4 and Chapter 5.

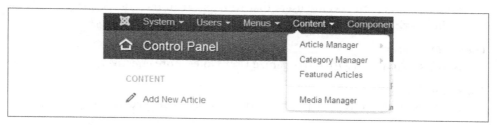

Figure 3-4. Content menu drop-down

Article Manager
> Displays a list of all of the articles that have been created in Joomla. You can also manage, add, edit, and delete articles from this screen.

Category Manager
> Add, edit, or delete categories.

Featured Articles
> Shows the articles that have been designated to display as Featured. This is often content intended to show on the home page of your website, but it is not limited to this. Featured articles can be configured for any categories and then configured through the menu item to define how the content displays on the frontend of the site.

Media Manager
> Allows you to upload files into Joomla. Examples of file types would be images, documents, videos, audio files, etc. Once uploaded, you can embed and link to them from various places within the CMS.

Components

The Components drop-down menu lists all the installed components. Figure 3-5 shows the components that are available from Joomla. Any additional components you install will also show up in the Components drop-down.

Starting with version 3.4, components that are supported by Joomla will be available via the Joomla Extensions Directory or the Install from Web tab in the extension manager. These "core supported" extensions include Banners, Contacts, Finder, Messages, Newsfeeds, Redirect, Search, and Weblinks.

Figure 3-5. Components menu drop-down

Extensions

The *Extensions* drop-down menu shown in Figure 3-6 shows links to install and manage your extensions, including modules, plug-ins, templates, and languages. Components are installed and managed from the Extensions drop-down menu as well.

Here are the descriptions of each of the Extensions drop-down menu items:

Extension Manager
> Install and uninstall extensions, manage extensions, update extensions, discover extensions, fix the database, view warnings, and install additional language packs.

Module Manager
> Add, edit, and delete instances of installed modules. You can also move and reorder them.

Plugin Manager
> The Plugin Manger allows you to configure installed plugins. Options include enabling, disabling, order of execution, and access levels.

Template Manager
> Here, you can change the look and feel of your website as a whole or just for specific pages. You can also modify the templates and template styles that have been previously installed. You may have multiple configurations of the same template on your Joomla site.

Language Manager
> If you've installed any other languages, the *Language Manager* is where you can change the default language to the language of your choice. You can also create and manage language overrides here.

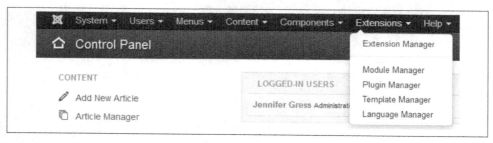

Figure 3-6. Extensions menu drop-down

Help

The *Help* drop-down menu (shown in Figure 3-7) provides access to help documents.

Joomla Help
> This links to Joomla's internal help guide.

Official Support Forum
> This links to Joomla's vast support forum. Be sure to read the forum rules and the Absolute Beginner's Guide to Joomla (*http://docs.joomla.org/Beginners*) before posting. Utilize the Forum Post Assistant (*http://bit.ly/postassist*) tool to help others help you.

Figure 3-7. Help menu drop-down

Documentation Wiki

This links to the Joomla official documentation.

Joomla Extensions

This links to the famous Joomla extensions directory (JED). For more about third-party extensions, see Appendix C.

Joomla Translations

This links to the Joomla Translations page, where language packs for all releases of Joomla can be found.

Joomla Resources

Find resources for education, extensions, templates, hosting, books, and more.

Community Portal

The latest blog posts and information from the Joomla Leadership Teams, as well as local Joomla User Groups (JUG), events, and the Joomla Community Magazine (JCM).

Security Center

This links to the Joomla Security Center, where you can sign up for the Security News Feed to receive notices about security releases for your Joomla site. Whenever these become available, you should upgrade them immediately (if not sooner!). For more on security, see Chapter 14.

Developer Resources

Links to the Joomla Developer Network. There are many ways to help!

Joomla Shop

You know you want a t-shirt. This links to the Joomla Shop where you can fulfill that desire—and then some.

Personal Information Settings

The top righthand corner of the Control Panel shows a gear icon. This provides access to a drop-down menu that lets you quickly edit your account or log out (see Figure 3-8).

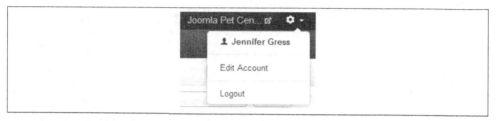

Figure 3-8. Personal Information drop-down menu

Edit Account
> Here you can edit your account information.

Logout
> Click logout to close the Backend Administrator Control Panel.

Administrator Modules

Administrator Modules are located in the main column of the Control Panel, as shown in Figure 3-9. By default, Logged-in Users, Popular Articles, and Recently Added Articles are installed and enabled for all users who have access to the backend.

Logged-in Users
> Shows you a list of all of the users who are currently logged in to your website. You can also see when they were last active or log them out. You cannot log out other Super Administrators.

Popular Articles
> Lists the 10 most popular articles along with the number of hits they have received.

Recently Added Articles
> The Recently Added Articles module lists the 10 most recently added articles, along with the date on which they were created and the name of the author.

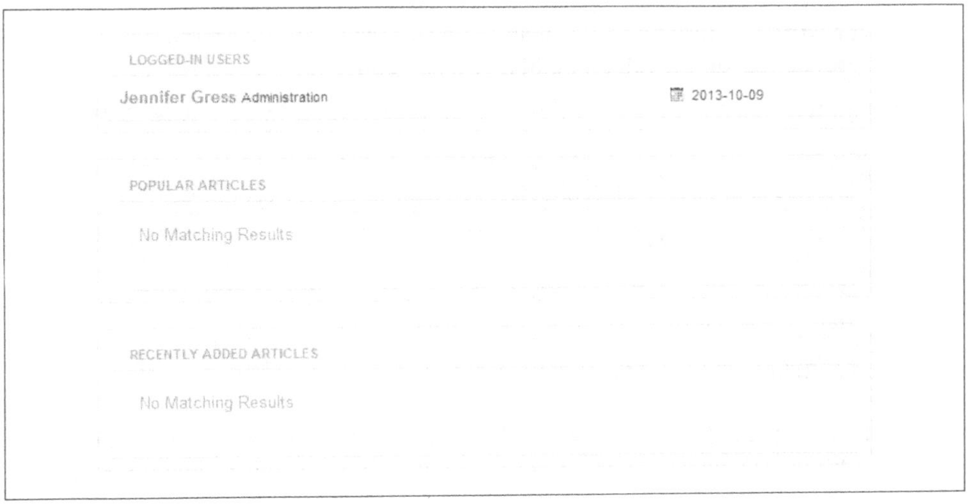

LOGGED-IN USERS

Jennifer Gress Administration   2013-10-09

POPULAR ARTICLES

    No Matching Results

RECENTLY ADDED ARTICLES

    No Matching Results

Figure 3-9. Administrator modules

Top Toolbar

In the top left area of the Article Manager, Menu Manager, and almost every Joomla extension, you will see the top toolbar. The top toolbar (Figure 3-10) contains buttons to Save, Edit, Trash, and perform a variety of other functions depending on which area of the backend you're working in. In some cases, you will see different buttons than are shown in Figure 3-10 until you select an item. After selecting a checkbox for an item, new buttons will appear that allow you to perform other functions. You will be using items in the top toolbar throughout this book and often on your Joomla journey so it's a good idea to get familiar with it.

Figure 3-10. Article Manager toolbar

Filtering and Display

When you have a lot of articles, categories, menus, or modules, finding a specific one would be difficult without filters. Take a look at the Article Manager by clicking Content→Article Manager. By clicking the Search Tools button next to the search bar at the top of the manager, two rows of drop-down items will display to filter content (see Figure 3-11). You can filter articles one of two ways:

- Enter a word in the article title, alias, or the article ID in the Search box on the left and press Enter or click the magnifying glass icon.

- Select one or more items from the drop-down menus to filter articles by Status, Category, Max Levels, Access, Author, Language, or Tag.

Figure 3-11. Article Manager filters

Filters are also available in the Category Manager, Menu Item Manager, Module Manager, and Plugin Manager. Many components use filters to customize the display or locate specific items.

Footer Menu

The lower left corner of the Backend Administrator Control Panel shows you how many visitors and admins are logged into the site at any time. It also shows you if you have any mail and gives you the ability to log out (see Figure 3-12).

Figure 3-12. Footer menu

Here is a brief description of the items in the Footer menu:

View Site
    Opens a new tab/window and shows you the frontend of your website.

 Clicking the name of your website in the top right corner of the Control Panel has the same preview effect. Clicking the Joomla icon in the top left corner of the Control Panel will take you back to the backend Control Panel view.

Visitors
    Shows you the number of visitors logged in to the frontend of your website.

Admins
    Shows the number of administrators signed into the backend of your website.

Mail Envelope icon and number
    Shows if you have any messages/mail.

Logout
    Logs you out of the Backend Administrator Control Panel.

Now that you have a brief overview of the Joomla backend, get ready to start building the structure of your website.

CHAPTER 4

Setting Up the Basics of Your Website

In this chapter, we're going to set up the basic structure that we planned in Chapter 2. The very first step is to install Joomla. See Appendix A to accomplish this if you need to and then come back here to dive in.

For setting up Joomla Pet Center, we will start from a blank site with no sample content loaded. You may have chosen to install the sample content during the Joomla installation, and you can follow along using that (for information about sample data, see Appendix A). If you did not, then have your own planning sketches available so that you can set up your website structure while we do so for Joomla Pet Center.

The order of creating content for your website is as follows:

1. Create categories

2. Create articles

3. Create menu items

Content Categories

One of Joomla's strengths is its simplicity, and that's reflected in how it manages contenet, using categories and articles. It really is as simple as thinking of categories as being like buckets, and articles as like rocks. You can't have the same rock in multiple buckets, but you can have many rocks and buckets.

The Category Manager displays the categories of your site. These are the "buckets" for your articles. If your site is small, you may only need one or two categories. You'll organize your articles within them. But most sites will have a number of categories (e.g., About, Products, Services, Blog) to give more control and flexibility over how your articles are displayed. The Category Manager enables you to copy, edit, create, and delete categories. Before you can create articles, you'll need to first create a category.

Creating Categories

You must create at least one category before you create any articles. For example, in Joomla Pet Center, we will be creating the categories we came up with in "Planning Categories" on page 14.

Joomla Pet Center Categories:

- Blog
- How to
- About
- Testimonials
- Legal

Blog and "How to" nested Categories:

- Dogs
- Cats
- Reptiles
- Birds

Hands-On Exercise: Create Your Categories

1. Log in to the backend of your website.
2. Click on Content and hover over Category Manager, then click on Add New Category. This opens the Category Manager: Add A New Articles Category (Figure 4-1) screen.
3. Enter a title for the category. We will start with the category Blog.
4. Leave the alias blank, and Joomla will fill it in for you.
5. Optionally, you may also enter a description of the category in the text box. This information will show up on category pages when the appropriate menu item parameter is enabled. See "Category Blog Layout" on page 51 further along in this chapter for more information about this parameter.
6. Another option is to associate an image that displays with the category. Simply click on the Images button at the bottom of the text editor to add an image to the category.

7. In the details panel on the right, select a parent category if the category you are creating is nested. In our case, it is not.

8. Leave the Tags field for now. We will be setting this up in Chapter 8 when we set up our Blog.

9. Leave the Category as Published.

10. Choose an access level—either Guest, Public, Registered, Special, or a custom access level if you have created any. Most often this will be set to Public. If set to Registered, registered users or higher will have access. Special means only administrators will have access. Custom ACLs will have different access permissions. (See "Access Control Lists (ACLs)" on page 246.)

11. For other Publishing Options, Options, Metadata Options, and Category Permissions, click the tabs next to the Category Details tab and fill them in as desired.

12. Click Save & Close to return to the Category Manager or Save & New to create an additional category or nested category.

Figure 4-1. Create a new category

We have added all the categories and nested categories for Joomla Pet Center. When complete, our Category Manager will look like Figure 4-2. Yours should look similar.

Figure 4-2. Joomla Pet Center categories in Category Manager view

If you installed Joomla with the sample data, you can use the existing categories and change the title, alias, and other settings to utilize what was installed with your site. Or you can follow the instructions above to create new categories and then unpublish or trash the sample data categories.

You will not be able to delete categories unless you first move or delete all articles within those categories. This includes archived articles and articles that are in the trash.

Publishing and Unpublishing Categories

In the Category Manager, you also have control over the published state of each category or nested category. To publish or unpublish a category, click the icon in the Status column, as shown in Figure 4-3. You can also unpublish a category in the Category Editor.

1. Go to the Category Manager and click the category name to open it in the Category Editor. You can also click the checkbox by the category name and select the Edit button in the toolbar.

2. On the Details panel on the right, click the drop-down menu for Status and set its status from Published to Unpublished, as shown in Figure 4-4.

3. Click Save & Close.

Figure 4-3. Publish or unpublish a category in the Category Manager

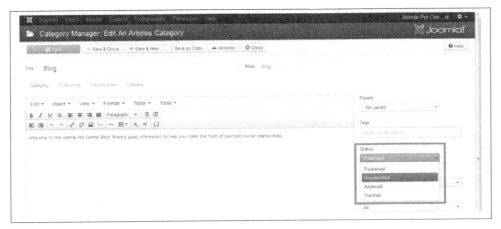

Figure 4-4. Publish or unpublish a category in the Category Editor

Copying Categories

There are times when you may want to duplicate a category. To copy a category:

1. Go to the Category Manager and open the category you want to duplicate.

2. Click the Save as Copy button in the toolbar.

3. This will open a copy of that category, which you can now give a new title and alias. You can simply erase what is in the alias field after copying and Joomla will assign a new alias upon saving the new category.

 The Alias field is used to manage how a page's URL is constructed. Each category must have an original alias (each article and menu item must have original aliases as well). If in doubt, empty the alias field and Joomla will fill it in for you. For more on how to work with the alias field, see "SEF URLs" on page 238.

4. Make any other changes to the items in the Details panel on the right or in the additional tab items next to Category Details as appropriate.

5. Click Save & Close.

You may copy multiple categories (or articles) at a time using the Batch function. Simply check the categories you want to copy (or move) and click the Batch button in the top toolbar. Select where you want to copy them to and make sure the Copy option is selected. Then click Process. Batch functionality is available in multiple instances of your Joomla website.

Uncategorized Category

You may have noticed the option of using the Uncategorized category when creating new articles. Uncategorized articles are limited in how they can be displayed on your website, so we don't recommend keeping finished articles in this category.

If you do use the Uncategorized category, it should be limited. The only articles that might be appropriate to have in the uncategorized category are:

- The home page
- Custom 404 page
- Thank you page for form submission
- Draft articles submitted by site authors

Aside from those, your articles should be placed into applicable categories you create. This reduces heartache down the road when you want content to display a certain way, and the articles need to be moved into categories which then breaks links and is just a pain overall.

Now that our categories are all set up, we can create articles.

Creating Articles

You can create and manage articles in the Article Manager.

Creating a new article is as simple as clicking the Add New Article link on the left sidebar of the Control Panel. You can also create a new article by clicking on Content, hovering over Article Manager, and clicking Add New Article. If you are already in the Article Manager, simply click the New button in the toolbar. All of these methods open up the Article Editor screen (Figure 4-5) where you can add text, images, and other content. When you click Save, your article is saved and kept open for editing. If you are done editing, click Save & Close, and you'll be taken back to the Article Manager. Clicking Save & New saves the article you are working on and opens a new article to be added to the system.

Figure 4-5. The Article Editor

In setting up the basics of our website, we will first create all of our articles at once without adding content to them. We will add content in Chapter 5.

Hands-On Exercise: Create Your Articles

We will use the spreadsheet we created when planning our website to create our articles. You will use the planning sketch of your website and create yours.

Joomla Pet Center will have the following articles, which we decided in "Planning Articles" on page 15:

- Helen
- Diana
- Mark
- Testimonial 1
- Testimonial 2
- Testimonial 3
- Blog 1
- Blog 2
- Blog 3
- How to 1
- How to 2
- How to 3
- Privacy Policy
- Terms & Conditions
- Home

Follow these steps:

1. Click on Add New Article in the Control Panel.
2. Enter an article title in the Title field. We'll start with Helen.
3. Leave the Alias field blank and Joomla will fill it in for you.
4. Select Category from the drop-down menu. In our case, the category is About.
5. For the time being, we are going to leave everything else as is and click Save & New to create the rest of our articles.

The Featured button is what tells Joomla to display any Featured articles on a page that is set up to be a Featured Article menu item type; this is most typically the home page. Even though "home" is the most popular use of Featured articles, it is not the only way they can be used. Featured articles are associated with the Featured menu item type, which is installed by default by Joomla as the Home menu item in the Main Menu.

None of our articles will be Featured articles except our home page, which we will mark as Featured and leave in the Uncategorized category. This will be denoted by a yellow star in the Status column of the Article Manager.

When we are done adding articles for Joomla Pet Center, the Article Manager will look like Figure 4-6.

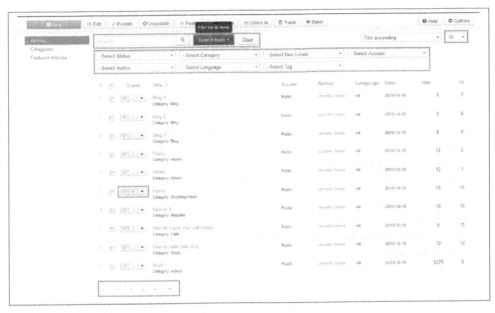

Figure 4-6. Joomla Pet Center articles

You can see in the Article Manager that we have a list of articles. At the bottom of the list, you can navigate to a second page of articles. You can select the number of articles to show in the list in the top right corner. There is a red box around it.

There are a number of tools, including filters, that can save you time when looking for your articles to edit them in the future. You can type a portion of the title into the search box at the top of the Article Manager. You can select Search Options at the top of the Article Manager, which will toggle the display of several filters that you can set when looking for articles in a certain Category, Status, Access Level, and more. You can also click on a column heading to sort by a heading. Clicking twice will reverse the results. For example, clicking on the Title column heading once will sort alphabetically with the letter A first. Clicking the Title heading again will sort reverse-alphabetically with the letter Z first.

Once you set your filters, the system remembers that they are set, visits other pages, and returns. In order to display your entire list of articles again (unfiltered), you need to clear the filters by choosing Select from the drop-down menu.

Article Publishing and Unpublishing

New articles are set to Published by default—meaning they are visible to your site users. Unpublishing an article removes it from view. Publishing and unpublishing articles is straightforward, but there are a number of ways to do it and customize the process. The first (and most common) way is by clicking the publish/unpublish icon in the Article Manager.

Find the icon in the Status column. A green checkmark means the article is already published on your site. A red circle with a white x in the center means the article is unpublished and not viewable on your website. The star icon denotes that the article is both published and Featured.

The second way to toggle the published state is in the Article Editor where you edit the article. Go to the Article Manager and click the name of the article you want to edit. Find the Status drop-down under the Details column at the far right of the screen. Select either Published, Unpublished, Archived, or Trashed from the drop-down menu, as seen in Figure 4-7.

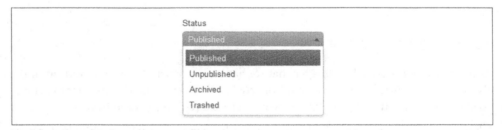

Figure 4-7. Change the status of an article

Click the Save button or Save & Close button to save your changes.

Now that we have added our categories and articles, if you were to check the frontend of our website, you would see that there is no difference in how the site looks. Now that we have our categories and articles created, we get to move to the fun part of having them display on the frontend of the website by creating menu items.

Creating Menu Items

Menu items are the primary tools for navigating to and controlling the display of content in Joomla. Joomla Pet Center has a lot of menu items that will depend on an extension to display content stored in the extension itself. Since we are only setting up the basics of our site structure right now, we will create placeholders for menu items that will utilize extensions.

We will focus on the most popular menu item types for Joomla Pet Center: the Category Blog, Single Article, and our placeholders that utilize the Text Separator menu item type.

For now, we are working with the Main Menu, which was installed with Joomla.

Let's start by taking yet another look at our sketch, spreadsheet, or file of the menu that we created in Chapter 2 so we can create our menu items.

Text Separator Menu Item type

Aside from Home, our first five menu items are extensions. Because we haven't yet installed and configured these extensions, we will create placeholders for them using what's known as the *Text Separator* menu item type.

The Text Separator menu item type is also often used as a main tab, or Parent menu item with submenu or child-menu items. This forces a visitor to choose from the drop-down because the Text Separator isn't clickable.

Hands-On Exercise: Create Text Separator Menu Items

1. Click on Menus from the backend Control Panel, hover over Main Menu, and click on Add New Menu Item, as seen in Figure 4-8.

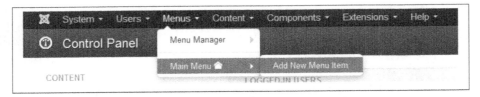

Figure 4-8. Add a new menu item to the main menu

2. In the Menu Manager: New Menu Item screen, enter the menu title.
3. The alias will autogenerate when you save the menu item. See more about using an alias in "SEF URL Settings and SEO Basics" on page 238.
4. Click the blue Select button to the right of the Menu Item Type field to select the type of menu item, as seen in Figure 4-9.

Figure 4-9. Enter the title and click Select to choose the menu item type

5. Click on System Links and then on the Text Separator menu item type, as seen in Figure 4-10.

Figure 4-10. Select Text Separator from the System Links menu item types

6. Click Save & New from the top toolbar and repeat for the next menu items that have the Text Separator menu item type. When you get to the last one, click Save & Close.

You may not have the same menu items next to each other as we do. Feel free to create your menu items in the order your menu calls for and with whatever types are required. Items can be ordered after they are entered.

We are going to continue and add our Text Separator menu item types for events, gallery, community, and forum. Forms and Contact will also be extensions, so we will create Text Separator menu items for those when we get to the About portion of the menu items.

Creating Single Article Menu Item Types

The Privacy Policy and Terms & Conditions for Joomla Pet Center are both simple Single Article menu item types. Single Article menu item types are by far the most commonly used menu item type. We just happen to be using a lot of extensions and Category Blog layouts (which you'll see in the following hands-on exercise) in Joomla Pet Center. Chances are good that you will have more Single Article menu item types than we do.

Let us create a couple of Single Article menu items.

Hands-On Exercise: Single Article Menu Item Types

Open a new Menu Manager: New Menu Item. Then just follow along.

1. Enter the title of your menu item. Ours will be Privacy Policy.

2. Leave the Alias field blank, as Joomla will fill it in for you.

3. Click the Select button for the Menu Item Type.

4. Click Articles and then click the Single Article menu item type. (Figure 4-11.)

5. Click the Select button next to the Select Article field.

6. A list of articles will appear in a pop-up window. You can filter by Access, Status, Category, or Language. You may also type a portion of the title of the article into the *Filter* field at the top and press Enter. Articles matching your search will appear in the box. Click on the desired article. See Figure 4-12 to see articles in the Legal category.

7. Leave the Link field alone unless you really know what you are doing. It will be automatically populated for most menu item types.

8. Leave the Target Window as Parent.

9. Leave the Template Style as Use Default unless you are using a different template for specific pages.

Figure 4-11. Click Article, then Single Article to choose the menu item type

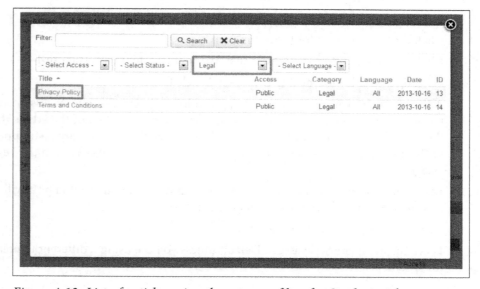

Figure 4-12. List of articles using the category filter for Single Article menu item type

10. Leave the Menu Location as Main Menu.

11. Click the Parent Item drop-down menu and select About as the Parent Item. This means that the Privacy Policy menu item will be a drop-down menu item under the About tab in the main menu.

12. Leave the Status as published.

13. Leave the Default Page set to No. Only one menu item will be Yes on your website. That menu item will be the main page that your domain directs to. Typically, this is the home page.

14. Leave the Access set to Public unless it is intended for registered users or content to display to a specific access level.

15. Click Save & New to save and move on to creating a new menu item or Save & Close if complete.

It is possible to change menu item types. If you create a Single Article menu item type and then decide you want to make it Category Blog, you may do so simply by clicking the Select button next to Menu Item Type and selecting a new menu item type. Keep in mind that the system will then erase the settings you had created for the original menu item type. So if you decide to go back to Single Article, you will have to input your original settings again. You may want to take a screen capture of your original settings so they are easy to access in case you want to revert back.

You may want to use the Save as Copy button to test a new menu item type before changing menu item types. Just remember that whichever you choose, you may need to change the alias and title so that the original title and alias are properly reflected in the new menu item type that may be a copy.

We left most of the settings alone while creating the basic structure of this site. The reason for this is because when we add our chosen template, the look and feel will change. After we install and configure the template we are going to use, we will be better able to decide how we want things to display. Adding content to the articles may also change what we want to display and how. Just getting the basics in place helps us. Then we will go back and fine-tune.

Category Blog Layout

Blog, About, and Testimonials are our next menu item types and they are all going to be Category Blog menu item types. We will configure each one differently so that you can see the flexibility of this type.

We are going to skip some aspects of the menu item settings. We could write an entire book just on menu items if we were to go through every field. Hovering over any field will provide you with a tooltip describing what that field does.

Global settings for some parameters of the Category Blog layout can be found in the Global Article Options, which we cover in "Joomla Pet Center Article Options Hierarchy" on page 85.

Hands-On Exercise: Category Blog

We'll start with our Category Blog menu item for our Blog. Start by having a Menu Manager: New Menu Item up on your screen.

1. Enter the title; in our case, the title is Blog.

2. Leave the Alias field blank. For more information on how to work with the alias field, see "SEF URLs" on page 238.

3. Click the Select button for the Menu Item Type.

4. Click Articles and then click the Category Blog menu item type. (Figure 4-13.)

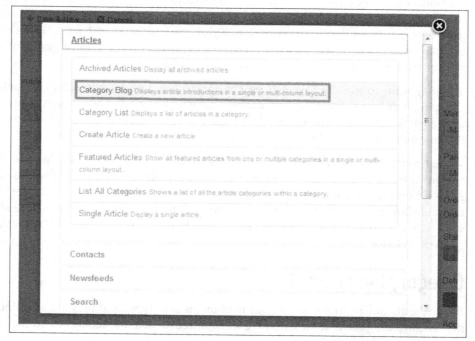

Figure 4-13. Select Article, then Category Blog to choose the menu item type

5. Choose the appropriate category from the "Choose a category" field. We will choose Blog, which will include all our nested categories within the Blog category.

6. Leave the Link field alone unless you really know what you are doing. It will be automatically populated for you for most menu item types. It just states what the internal link will be to that menu item minus the Itemid parameter.

Changing the default value can break links and lead to unexpected results if you're not sure how Itemid parameters work.

7. Leave the Target Window as Parent for most cases.

As a guideline, if you are linking to a page on the same website, you should open it in the *Parent* window (which refers to the browser window or tab you are currently viewing). If you are linking to a different website, you should almost always open that page in a new window so you don't take the user away from your website.

8. Leave the Template Style as Use Default unless you are using a different template for specific pages.

9. Leave the Menu Location as Main Menu.

10. Leave the Parent Item as Menu Item Root. This means that it will be a parent menu item having a main "tab" or "button" in the main menu. If it were a drop-down item (a child item), then clicking the drop-down of the Parent Item would give you the opportunity to select which parent item to have the new item drop down under.

11. Leave the Status as Published.

12. Leave the Default Page set to No. Only one menu will have a Default Page state of Yes on your website. That menu item will be the main page that your domain directs to. Typically, this is the home page.

13. Leave the Access as Public unless it is intended for registered users or is meant to be displayed to a specific access level. Figure 4-14 shows the Details tab.

14. Click on the Blog Layout tab.

15. Enter the following and see Figure 4-15 to see the Blog Layout fields of this tab.

- **1** in the # Leading Articles field
- **4** in the # Intro Articles field
- **2** in the # Columns field
- **10** in the # Links field

16. For now, leave the rest of the fields set to Use Global. We will go over what this means in Chapter 5.

17. Click Save & New to create another menu item or Save & Close if you are done creating menu items.

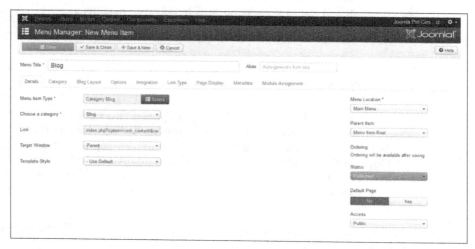

Figure 4-14. Category Blog Details tab for Joomla Pet Center blog

Figure 4-15. Category Blog Layout tab for Joomla Pet Center blog

What we have done in this menu item is tell the Blog menu item to show one Leading Article in its entirety. We want four articles to show only their intros, and then folks can pursue the ones they're interested in by clicking on the title or the "Read more" button.

At the bottom of the main Blog page, there will be a list of up to 10 links to additional articles in the Blog category or any of its nested categories.

The About Category Blog menu item will be created the same way as the Blog menu item, except we'll choose About as the category and in the Blog Layout tab we will select the following:

- # Leading Articles = **3**
- # Intro Articles = **0**
- # Columns = **1**
- # Links = **0**

This will cause the articles for Helen, Diana, and Mark to appear one after another in their entirety on the About page of the website.

We'll do it again with the Testimonials Category Blog menu item by choosing the Testimonials category and clicking the Parent Item drop-down and selecting the About category. In the fields on the Blog Layout tab, we will choose the following:

- # Leading Articles = **0**
- # Intro Articles = **100**
- # Columns = **3**
- # Links = **0**

This will create a display that appears to be three columns of testimonials. We want them all to show, so we set the number of Intro Articles relatively high and display zero links.

Category List Menu Item Type

We will set up the "How to" menu item differently, as "cat people" typically do not want to see "How to" articles about dogs. This is a change from the original spreadsheet we created. A *Category List* menu item type will be ideal for this area of the site so that people can easily find the "How to" article that means the most to them.

We've created the menu item similarly to the Category Blog, except that we selected Category List from Articles for the menu item type.

We left it entirely default for now. Once the template is installed, we will be able to fine-tune it and get it looking the way we want it to look, displaying the correct information.

Mastering Backups

We have added a lot of information to our site now. Before we install our template, we want to make a backup of our website and the database.

 It is highly recommended that you run a backup of your site before you install or uninstall any extension, do an update, or after you do any work on your site. Otherwise, if an unlikely problem were to occur, you would need to either start over or restore an earlier backup and have to do your work over again. Back up!

The easiest way to run a backup of your site and database is with a brilliant extension called Akeeba Backup. Jenn (and thousands of others) are extremely impressed with the developer of Akeeba Backup as a result of his witty sense of humor, excellent documentation, stellar products, and brilliant mind.

Thanks to the new Install from Web feature in Joomla 3.x, we can install Akeeba Backup from the Extension Manager.

1. Click on Extensions in the top menu and then on Extension Manager.

2. You will see a blue bar across the top of the screen with a button directing you to add the install from Web tab.

3. Click that button and wait while the system installs the appropriate plugin to add the Install from Web tab. You will now see a list of categories and a number of pretty, colorful icons for different popular extensions from the Joomla Extensions Directory (JED). Since Akeeba Backup is one of the most popular Joomla extensions available, it will be listed in one of these boxes. Scroll down until you find it.

4. Click on the Akeeba Backup Core box. Core implies that it is the noncommercial (free) version of Akeeba Backup.

5. You will now see the rating, software version, the type of extension (component, module, plugin) and buttons for download, directory listing, and developer website.

6. Click the Download button and you will be taken to the appropriate page of the Akeeba Backup website to download the Akeeba Backup package.

 Just because you see an extension in the Install from Web tab, don't feel complacent about its safety. You still need to do research on extensions and only install those you need on your website. If you install an extension you do not need, uninstall it immediately (after taking a backup). Extensions need to be maintained and updated; scripts not being updated are one of the top reasons that sites get hacked. See Chapter 14 and Appendix C for more information on extensions.

---

7. Once you download the latest stable version of Akeeba Backup and save it to your computer, go back to your Extension Manager.

8. Click on the Upload Package File tab.

9. Click the Browse button and navigate to where you saved the Akeeba Backup package and double-click on it.

10. Click the Upload & Install button.

11. When complete, you will see the "Installing component was successful" message. See Figure 4-16. It is highly recommended that you spend some time watching videos and reading the documentation for Akeeba Backup, and learning how to restore backups. The documentation is so thorough that it isn't necessary to cover it here. The author/developer has done better than we ever could.

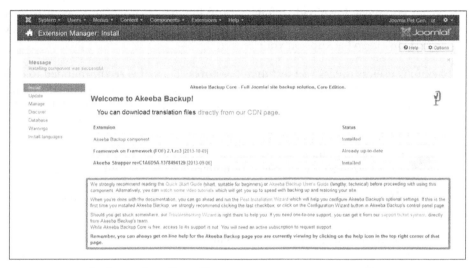

Figure 4-16. Akeeba Backup "installing component was a success" screen

12. Click on Components and then on Akeeba Backup.

13. Because this is our first time accessing Akeeba Backup, it wants to run us through the configuration wizard and make sure we know a few important things. Leave the two boxes checked to run the configuration wizard and update all profiles to ANGIE. Then, read all three boxes under Mandatory Information and be sure you understand them. This is very important!

14. When complete, click "Apply these preferences."

15. Akeeba Backup will perform a bunch of scans and do its magic to configure itself on your server. Do not browse away from the page while it's processing.

16. You will see a Finished message, and from here you can click the Backup Now button. On this screen, you can simply click the Backup Now button, or you can enter a note in the Backup comment field. In our case we will type before template install. This comment appears in the Manage Backups tab of the extension and can be helpful.

17. Click Backup Now and the site will back up. Do not navigate away from this page until it is complete.

18. When complete, use an FTP client such as FileZilla and copy the backup file off the server and onto your local device, an external drive, or DVD. The default location of the backup file is *public_html(httpdocs)/administrator/components/com_akeeba/backup*. Your default backup location may (and should) be elsewhere, yet that is the default location.

19. After you have downloaded your backup file, make sure you delete it from your server. If someone gets their hands on your backup, they can find ways to hack your site. Don't keep backups on your server!

A backup is useless unless you test that it restores. Thus, it is recommended to create a subdomain or subdirectory on your server and test restoration of your backup. Full documentation can be found at Akeeba Backup (*http://www.akeebabackup.com*).

 The Pro version of Akeeba Backup provides many more features, including automated backup and storage in an external location like Amazon S3. This is highly recommended. As humans, we have great intentions of keeping our site regularly backed, up and then guess what? It doesn't happen. The Pro version is worth every penny.

Now that you have your backup, you can safely install the template.

Template Parameters

We've decided on the Afterburner2 template by RocketTheme. The first step is to download the package from RocketTheme's website (*http://bit.ly/afterburner2*). We are downloading the Afterburner2 Template bundled with Gantry. You may be using a different template company or a custom template. Once you have the package (typically a *.zip* file), follow these steps to install your template:

1. Log in to your Backend Administrator Control Panel.

2. Click on Extensions and then on Extension Manager.

3. Click the Browse button, navigate to where you saved the template installation package, and select it. This will fill in the filename to replace the "No file selected" text.

4. Click the Upload & Install button (Figure 4-17) and wait for the success (or failure) message (Figure 4-18).

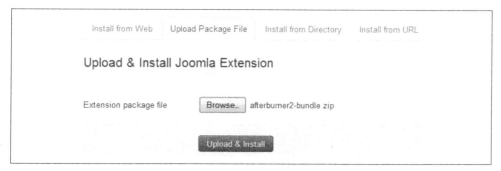

Figure 4-17. After selecting the file package, click the Upload & Install button

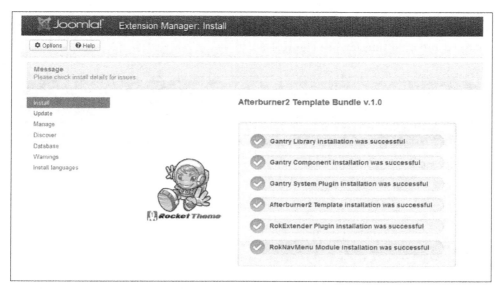

Figure 4-18. Success message after installing the template package

With our template installed, we will now set it to be the default template and set up the parameters for it.

1. Click on Extensions and then click on Template Manager.

2. Click the button with the star to the right of the Style called Afterburner2 - Default. This action makes the Afterburner2 template the default template for our website (See Figure 4-19).

Figure 4-19. Set Afterburner2 as the default template

At this point, we can go to the frontend of our website and see the structure we have planned and built thus far. See Figure 4-20.

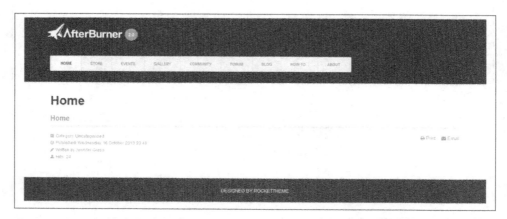

Figure 4-20. Frontend of Joomla Pet Center after installing template and setting it to default

There are several things we want to change and customize in the template for Joomla Pet Center. We want to change the logo, the "Designed by RocketTheme" in the footer, and the color from the pink accent color to a lovely green.

We make these changes in the parameters of the template. From the Template Manager, click on the Style Afterburner2 - Default to access the configuration of the template. The Overview tab appears. See Figure 4-21.

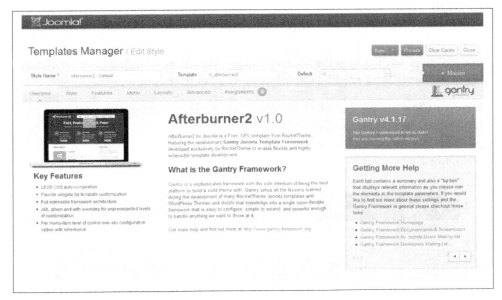

Figure 4-21. Overview tab of the Afterburner2 template configuration

The overview tab gives you just that: an overview of the template and the Gantry Framework that the template runs on top of. There are links to get more help and a notification as to whether the installed version of Gantry needs to be updated or if it is up-to-date. For more on third-party extension updates, see "Updating Third-Party Extensions" on page 291.

There are other tabs for the Afterburner2 configuration. They are:

- Style
- Features
- Menu
- Layouts
- Advanced
- Assignments

Each template company has a different way of making changes to template parameters. We will be going through each of our tabs and making changes that give us the look and configuration we are looking for on Joomla Pet Center. You will want to do the same thing with your template. The template company should have documentation and tutorials to assist you in making the template "your own."

The Style Tab

The Style tab starts with the ever-important logo. Currently, the template is pulling the Afterburner2 logo, and we want it to pull our logo instead. To do this, we need to upload our logo image to the site in the Media Manager. We will be covering media in detail in "Media Manager" on page 127, but for now, we want to see our logo on the site.

1. Click Close in the Template Manager/Edit Style screen (unless you have made changes, in which case click Save & Close).

2. Click on Content and then on Media Manager. By default, you will see a screen like Figure 4-22.

Figure 4-22. Media Manager screen in thumbnail view

3. Create a new folder by clicking the Create New Folder button in the top toolbar as seen in Figure 4-23. Name it *logos*.

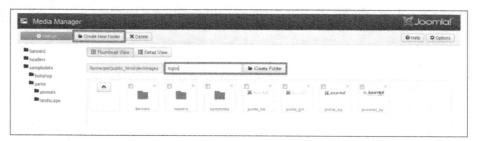

Figure 4-23. Add a folder for logos in the Media Manager

4. Click on the new logos folder you just created.

5. Click the green Upload button in the top toolbar.

6. Navigate to where your logo file is located and select it.

7. Click the Start Upload button.

Now we'll go back to our template parameters by clicking Extensions and again on Template Manager. Select the Afterburner2 template and then click the Style tab.

We will be making a number of changes to this tab to address the logo and the accent color.

To change out the logo:

1. Leave the Show setting as On.

2. Leave the Position at top-a.

3. Click the Type drop-down and select Custom. This creates a new line where you can select your logo that was just uploaded to the Media Manager.

4. Click the Select button, which opens a new window in a popup box with the folders and files in your Media Manager.

5. Scroll down to your folder called *logos* and click on it.

6. Click on the logo file you just uploaded which will force the Image URL to appear below in the Image URL field.

7. Click the blue Insert button. See Figure 4-24.

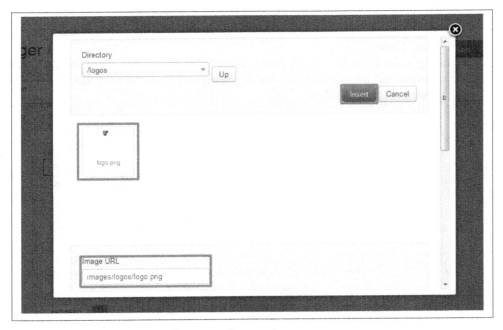

Figure 4-24. Insert your own logo into the template

Some templates will require you to create a Custom HTML module to display your logo. If this is the case, simply create a new Custom HTML module as described in "Hands-On Exercise: Create Custom HTML Placeholder Modules" on page 74 and insert an image as described in "Hands-On Exercise: Adding Folders and Uploading Images from the Editor" on page 132. To hyperlink the image of your logo, follow the directions in "Hands-On Exercise: Hyperlinking an Image" on page 136.

Now we'll address the rest of the parameters on the *Style* tab:

Header Style

> Leave as Dark. You may want to change it to light if your logo has dark text that wouldn't otherwise show up on a dark background. The light header style will create a different look that you might prefer.

Menu Style

> Leave as Light. You may want to change it to dark or grey. This is all a matter of preference.

Footer Style

> Leave as Dark. Same as above on personal preference. Image background colors may dictate how you want this to appear.

Link & Accent Color

> Click the color swatch to the right of the hexadecimal code field to use the color picker provided. You can also directly enter a hex code into the field. See Figure 4-25 as an example.

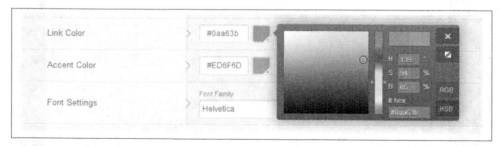

Figure 4-25. Using the color picker to change the accent and link color in the template

Most browsers have add-on tools that give you the ability to grab hex codes from web-based sites or images. These can be great tools to find the exact color of a hue in your logo or other resource. ColorZilla is an example of one of these tools for Firefox.

Font

Here you can choose from the drop-down many of the standard fonts and a plethora of Google Fonts.

Figure 4-26 shows how the Style tab looks after our changes.

Figure 4-26. Style tab with completed parameters

Now let us take a look at the frontend with our new settings in Figure 4-27.

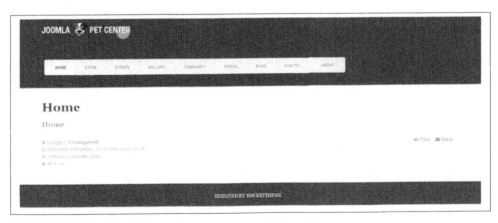

Figure 4-27. Frontend of Joomla Pet Center with logo changes

The logo looks good, but as you can see, there's a dot under it; the CSS in the template is creating this. We don't want that there, so we'll need to find the CSS code that makes it appear and alter it.

Using a Firefox add-on tool called Firebug, we'll inspect the element to find the applicable code. Chrome has a similar Inspect Element function that you can access by right-clicking on a browser window and choosing Inspect Element.

Firebug creates a panel under the website that shows the code and CSS of the website. When we inspect the element over the logo area, we can see the code that creates the style of the logo—including that circle, which is called `<span id="rt-logo-accent">` `</span>` in Figure 4-28. That is what we need to see, so we'll click on that `span` line.

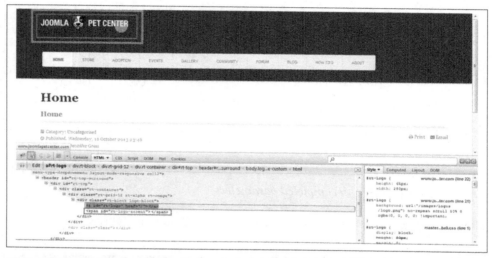

Figure 4-28. Firebug inspecting the logo area to find proper CSS code to change

In Figure 4-29, we can see the CSS code on the right. If we change the height to 0, the dot disappears, and that's what we want. Another way to state this is `display: none;`. We will copy the code from Firebug and create a template override file to make this change permanent.

 Changes made in Firebug or in Chrome's Inspect Element function are not permanent. They show you what your changes would look like before committing them. If you refresh, your changes will disappear.

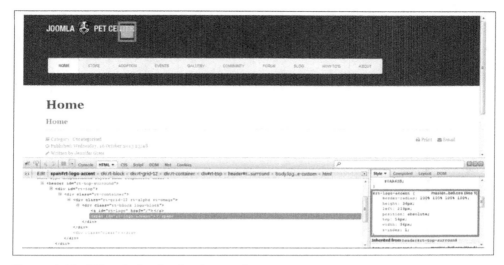

Figure 4-29. CSS code for the dot that we do not want

Template CSS Overrides

Many template companies have specific files that changes to the template CSS can be placed into. The benefits to this are many:

- One place to make changes
- Won't be affected by template updates
- Often, CSS changes desired for other extensions can be added to the template overrides which then wouldn't be affected by extension updates
- We won't forget that we changed the individual files—because we didn't

To create an override file for RocketTheme templates, we will follow these steps:

1. Click on Extensions and then on Template Manager.
2. Click on Templates in the left sidebar.
3. Scroll down and select the Afterburner2 Details and Files.
4. Create a new *.css* file by clicking New File from the top toolbar.
5. Select the *css* folder.
6. Select the File Type css from the drop-down.
7. Name the file *rt_afterburner2-custom.css*.
8. Click the blue Create button. See Figure 4-30.

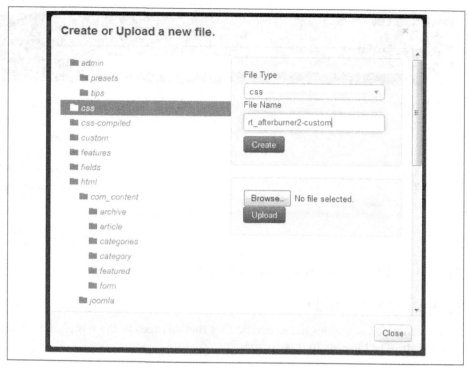

Figure 4-30. Create a new CSS file

9. Navigate to the file on the right sidebar and place the following code into the file.

```
#rt-logo-accent {
    display:none;
}
```

10. Click Save & Close and refresh the frontend.

11. Using FTP, copy this new file onto your local device so you have it as a backup in case it is needed in the future.

With the code in our overrides file in place, the green dot is gone.

We could have gone into the *logo.php* file and erased the line for rt-logo-accent except that, in that case, any template update would put the green dot back. Using the CSS override file, we avoid future problems.

Templates that operate on top of a framework will almost always have some kind of override file system. Look for documentation from your template company or search in their forums.

Remember that if you want to change something in your template, chances are good that someone else has wanted to as well. Search for what you want to do and you will likely find the answer.

Features Tab

The Features tab is where we can change the copyright, change the module position, turn off the System Messages, and add our Google Analytics tracking code.

We are going to leave everything as default on the Features tab except Designed by RocketTheme, which we will change to "© 2014 Joomla Pet Center. All rights reserved." This field takes HTML, so if we wanted a blank line under the copyright, we could add it with a break. Perhaps something like:

© 2014 Joomla Pet Center. All rights reserved.
Built by Jenn & Ron

This would appear as:

© 2014 Joomla Pet Center

Built by Jenn & Ron

When we save the new settings, the completed *Features* tab looks like Figure 4-31.

Figure 4-31. Features tab of template for Joomla Pet Center

The frontend of the site reflects our new copyright in Figure 4-32.

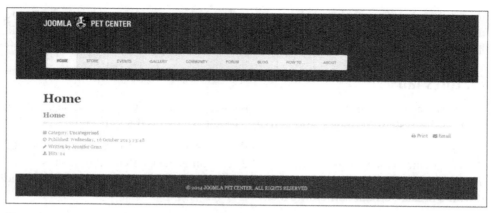

Figure 4-32. Page with Joomla Pet Center copyright in place

Menu Tab

In the *Menu* tab, you can control the menu type and what menu is being used. We are leaving them all as default, as seen in Figure 4-33.

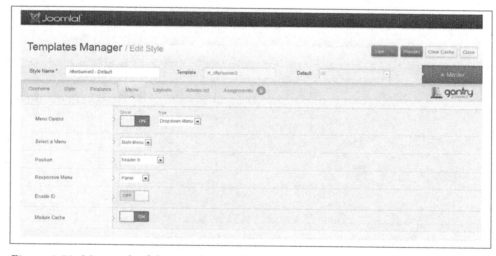

Figure 4-33. Menu tab of the template configuration for Joomla Pet Center

You can select Split Menus in the Menu tab by choosing it from the drop-down. A *split menu* eliminates the drop-down for child menu items (submenu items) and instead only shows the parent menu item in the main menu bar. When the parent menu item is clicked, a secondary menu appears in the module position chosen in the Menu tab of the Afterburner2 template parameters.

Layouts Tab

There is extraordinary flexibility with the Gantry Framework, which quickly becomes apparent in the Layouts tab. See Figure 4-34.

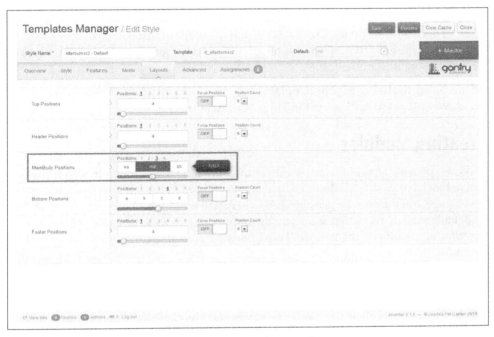

Figure 4-34. Layouts tab in Afterburner2 template configuration

Most templates for Joomla operate with a 12-grid system. Modules and the main content area can be set to span a specific number of columns of the 12 available grids. This creates a lot of flexibility in your layout display.

We've left everything at the default values except the MainBody Positions. We know that we are going to have sidebars. In order to accommodate this, we needed to change the configuration.

1. Click the number of Positions. We selected 3 so that we could have a sidebar a (sa), a mainbody section (mb), and a sidebar b (sb). If a sidebar is not in use, it will collapse. This gives us a lot of flexibility.

2. Click, hold, and slide the slider below the positions to determine the ratio of space for each position. This can be changed as the design takes shape.

3. Click Save.

Advanced and Assignments Tabs

We are going to leave both the Advanced and Assignments tabs at their default settings. You are welcome to change them. Feel free to read more of the RocketTheme documentation (*http://www.rockettheme.com*).

Assignments come into play if you want a different look and feel to appear on different pages. This is a powerful feature that is beyond the scope of this book, yet very cool. You can create different variations of this template and have them appear on different menu items by using Assignments.

At this point, the basics of your template are configured and your site should look pretty good. We will get to further customizing of content in Chapter 5.

Creating Modules

Modules provide a sort of window into your content by displaying it in small, customizable blocks or boxes. Modules are usually positioned in the left and right columns of a web page, but they can be just about anywhere you want. Joomla comes with a number of default module types that show you the most recent news items, a login form, breadcrumbs, or an advertising banner. Third-party extensions provide options do a whole lot more.

At this point, you should have a few menu items created (see "Creating Menu Items" on page 47 if you jumped ahead) as a prerequisite for getting your modules to appear.

Module names and their positions are determined by their location in your template. If you're using the default Protostar template and you installed the sample data, you already have a few modules in various positions set up on the frontend of your website.

The Module Manager provides an overview of your modules, their positions in your template, type of module, and status (see Figure 4-35).

In the Module Manager, you can reorder modules when you have more than one module in the same position by dragging and dropping into the desired order. See "Ordering Modules" on page 79 for more detail.

Figure 4-35. The Module Manager

As your site grows, you'll end up with a lot of module positions, and finding them can be tough. Have you ever looked at a module and wondered which position it was in? Here's how to find out.

To enable the preview of module positions (which is disabled by default):

1. From the backend, click on Extensions and then on Template Manager.
2. Click on the Options button at the top of the screen.
3. Click Enabled for Preview Module Positions.
4. Click Save & Close.
5. Click the eyeball icon at the left of the template title to view the preview of the module positions available for that template.

On the frontend, add the tp parameter with a value of 1 on the end of the website URL. An example of that would be: *http://www.<yourwebsite>.com/index.php?tp=1*

That's it. Now you can see the module types and positions from the frontend of your site.

Placeholder Custom HTML Module

We know that we will have modules on our site based on our layout, which we saw in Figure 2-6. Because we don't have our extensions installed yet and we haven't yet learned how to create content and manage images (this will be discussed in Chapter 5), we are going to create a few placeholder modules so that the layout of Joomla Pet Center can take shape.

The module positions for the Afterburner2 template can be found on RocketTheme's demo website (*http://demo.rockettheme.com*). Once we select the Afterburner2 template, we can navigate to the module positions page of the demo to see which are built into the template for us. In our case, these module positions are available on the RocketTheme demo website (*http://bit.ly/rocket-demo*) under the "Features" tab.

Afterburner2 is a free template. Free templates often have less functionality than paid ones, which is the case with Afterburner2. Afterburner2 doesn't have as many module positions as RocketTheme's Club templates. We are going to make it work, as there are still many module positions to choose from.

The Top module positions are going to be utilized by our logo and our RSS module. The menu bar occupies the Header positions so we are unable to use it for additional modules.

 More than one module can be used in the same module position, as they can stack or be side-by-side. We are not choosing to do so because of aesthetics. You will need to try different positions in order to achieve the layout you want.

Our gallery will occupy the Breadcrumbs module position. This is not normally a position we would use for a gallery, but since we are low on positions, and breadcrumbs are not necessary on the home page, we will use it. See "Adding an Image Gallery" on page 140 for instructions on how to create a gallery.

We will place our three calls to action in the module positions Content Top and use content-top-a, content-top-b, and content-top-c.

We will use the Sidebar position sidebar-b for our newsletter (see "Getting the Word Out with a Newsletter" on page 231) and other modules.

The Bottom positions will house our social media modules. See Chapter 12.

We will create placeholders for each of these modules.

Hands-On Exercise: Create Custom HTML Placeholder Modules

Creating placeholder modules is generally the same process no matter the type or position. Because we only need to place a little text in a module as a placeholder, a Custom HTML module is the perfect type of module for this purpose. A Custom HTML module is also good for pasting a bit of HTML code on your site outside of the main content area. This module allows to you paste any text, image, or HTML you want and have it show up in a module position. To create a Custom HTML module:

1. Click on Extensions and then on Module Manager.

2. Click the New button in the top toolbar.

3. Choose the type of module you want to create; in our case, we will choose Custom HTML (see Figure 4-36).

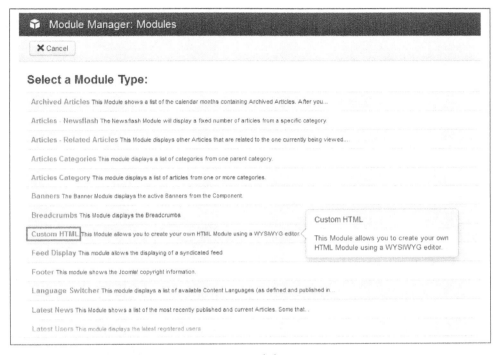

Figure 4-36. Selecting the Custom HTML module type

In the Module tab:

1. Enter **Gallery** as the module title (show or hide the title on the right sidebar) and choose a position from the drop-down. We will create a placeholder for the gallery in the Breadcrumbs position.

2. Change Status to **Unpublished** if you don't want it to appear at this time. (You can also trash the module with the Status drop-down).

3. If you want your module to turn on or off automatically, set the Start Publishing and Finish Publishing date and time.

4. Choose the Access level if different from public.

5. Select your Language if different languages are being utilized on the site.

6. Add a Note, which will appear in the Module Manager list if desired.

See Figure 4-37 for how our placeholder looks with the Module tab filled out.

Figure 4-37. Custom HTML module tab

If your desired module position isn't in the position drop-down, you can create one on the fly by typing the name.

You can also type the name of a module position to save time scrolling through the drop-down, as it shows the positions for all loaded templates in the Template Manager. You may also want to uninstall unused templates from the Template Manager so that module positions are faster to select from the list.

Adding a note in the Notes field for a module will help clarify what a module is if the title is obscure. Notes are a great way to make your life easier in the future. You could add a note like "home page advertisement" or "contact page sidebar." Use whatever makes it easier to find the module, because the titles don't always make sense when editing or aren't shown on the frontend.

In the Menu Assignment tab:

In order for your modules to appear on your website, they must be associated with one or more menu items. Since menu items essentially point to pages on your site, you're deciding which modules will show up on which pages. To assign a module:

1. In the Menu Assignment tab (Figure 4-38), leave the Module Assignment set to "On all pages" to have the module show up on all pages. Select "No pages" to have the module be hidden. Choose "Only on the pages selected" to choose specific pages for the module to appear on. Or choose "On all pages except those selected" to have the module publish on all pages except the ones checked.

2. We will only be showing the slideshow on the home page. We will select the option "Only on the pages selected," which brings up a list of all menu items on the site.

3. Uncheck all boxes except the Home menu item by deselecting all other menu items or clicking the link None at the top and then only ticking the Home box. Check out Figure 4-39 for how this looks.

4. Click Save to save the module and stay on the screen. Click Save & Close to save and go back to the Module Manager list.

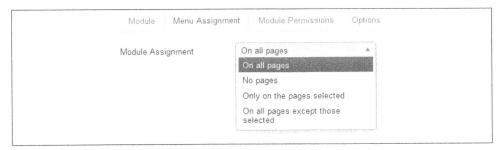

Figure 4-38. Menu Assignment options for modules

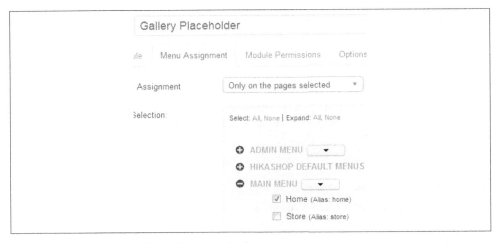

Figure 4-39. Module published only to the home page

If you were to use the "Only on the pages selected" Module Menu Assignment, then as you add articles to the menu, you would also have to go into each module and select the menu item in the Module Menu Assignment for each module you want to appear on your new page. It's a real time saver and a real confusion saver if someone other than you is adding pages but doesn't have the permissions to edit modules.

The great thing about "On all pages except those selected" is that as you add pages to your menu, modules will automatically publish on them with this option selected, except on the pages that are checked.

Within the Menu Assignment tab, you can save time by using the Select: All, Select: None, Expand: All, Expand: None either at the top of the Menu Selection or the drop-down arrow button next to the menu name and checking the Select or Deselect checkboxes to check or clear all menu items in that menu with a click.

In the Advanced tab:

1. Enter a Module Class Suffix in the Advanced Options tab if you want to apply specific CSS styles to this module. Module Class Suffixes are appended to the normal module CSS class. If you have an off-the-shelf template like we do, the template designer may have included alternative color schemes, borders, and styling for modules that are activated by adding one of the available Module Class Suffixes in the template demo. If you are using a custom template, to check with your template designer about the suffixes available to you.

It is important to note that a leading space before a suffix leaves the preprogrammed CSS class intact and adds an additional class, so that two sets of CSS rules apply. A suffix without a leading space causes the existing class to be renamed so that a different set of rules apply.

2. Afterburner2 has a number of module suffixes with the main style suffix as box1. For the purpose of the slideshow placeholder, we will not use a suffix.

3. Click Save to save the module and stay on the Edit Module screen. Click Save & Close to save and go back to the Module Manager list.

Hovering over any of the titles in the Advanced tab will tell you what each field is for. Module Class Suffix is the most frequently used field in the Advanced tab.

See Figure 4-40 as an example.

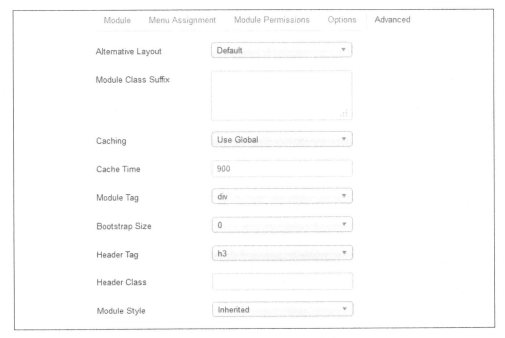

Figure 4-40. The advanced tab of a Custom HTML module

Depending on which type of module you created, you'll have a few module-specific options available. Go ahead and play around with the options, choosing the ones that best fit your needs, and see how they affect the frontend of your site.

Ordering Modules

Ordering modules in the same module position is a breeze in Joomla 3. From the Module Manager, use the position filter to display the position you want to order. Click the up/down arrows at the top of the first column on the left to activate the ordering function. Then simply drag and drop the modules in the order desired.

Duplicating Modules

Since we are creating a number of placeholder modules, we are going to simply duplicate our modules and change the following items on each so that they appear on our frontend.

- Title
- Module Position
- Show Title

- Text in the description
- Notes field
- Menu Assignment
- Add a Module Class Suffix if applicable

Duplicating modules is also very helpful if you have modules with a lot of customizations and you need more than one of these modules. You can save a lot of time by duplicating it rather than starting from scratch. To copy a module:

1. From the Module Manager, click the checkbox next to the module name you want to duplicate.

2. Choose Duplicate from the top toolbar. See Figure 4-41.

Figure 4-41. Duplicate a module

Your new copy will be saved with the same title and "(2)" added (e.g., a new copy of Gallery Placeholder will be named Gallery Placeholder (2)). Your new module will be unpublished by default.

You can then go into the module and change the title and other specifics to make it appear on the proper pages and publish it to the frontend according to our list as previously stated in this section.

We have created the rest of our placeholder modules (See Figure 4-42). One of the top reasons to create placeholders is so that as we create content, we have a proper idea of layout in the design. If you think you might have a sidebar, adding a placeholder for it is a wise move. It may determine the optimum or maximum width for images that you place in articles.

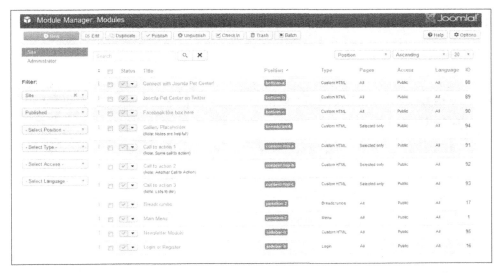

Figure 4-42. Placeholder modules in the Module Manager

Deleting Modules

Ultimately, we will be deleting some of our placeholder modules. Here are the step-by-step instructions on how to delete modules.

If you make a mistake or create a module you no longer need, you can simply delete it. To delete a module:

1. Click on Extensions and then on Module Manager and click the checkbox next to the module name you want to delete.

2. Choose Trash from the top toolbar.

 You can still access trashed modules by choosing Trashed in the Status filter drop-down. You can restore or permanently delete modules from the Trashed module list.

Frontend Layout After Building the Structure

See Figures 4-43 and 4-44 for how our site looks after the work we did in this chapter.

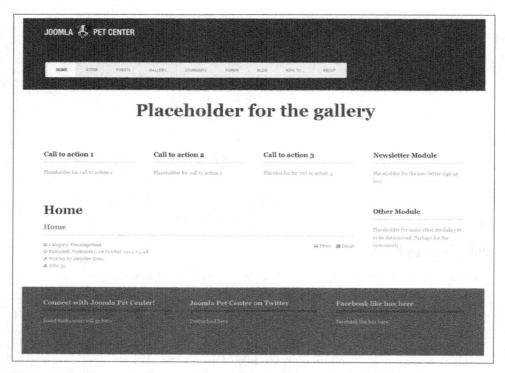

Figure 4-43. Home page layout with articles, menu items, and modules

Now that you have gotten this far, it is time to run a backup. See "Mastering Backups" on page 56 and remember to do backups regularly, not to keep backups on your server, and that a backup is only good if you are sure it can be restored.

Next we will rock on and work with the content and fine-tune the site further.

Figure 4-44. Interior page layout with sidebar modules

CHAPTER 5

Creating Content

Because Joomla is a CMS, it goes without saying that content is at the heart of everything it does. Whoever said "Content is king" was very right. Attracting site visitors requires compelling content that is regularly updated.

The basic content type in Joomla is the article. In this chapter, we're going to explore article content in depth as the basis for understanding how Joomla organizes content as a whole.

Joomla Pet Center Article Options Hierarchy

When we look at the frontend of Joomla Pet Center, we can see that each article has some data being displayed by the system. See Figure 5-1.

This information and the display of an article on your Joomla website is controlled by three sets of parameters: Global Article Options, Menu Item Article Options (see "Creating Menu Items" on page 47), and Article Options. In many cases, the same parameter can be specified for all three. A specific cascading hierarchy is used to determine which parameters are actually used when an article is displayed.

Global Article Options

The Global Article Options are accessible in the Article Manager. In the top toolbar, click the Options button. These parameters should be set to whatever you desire for the majority of your articles. Wherever you see Use Global within Article Options, Category Options, Menu Item Options, and even Permissions, it is pulling from the parameters that are set in the Global Article Options—thus the term Use Global in the drop-downs. You can override what is set in the Global Article Options via the Menu Item Article Options.

Menu Item Article Options

These options override the Global Parameters and they're located in the Advanced Options tab of the Single Article menu items (pointing to individual articles). They can be adjusted by going to Menus in the top menu and choosing the menu that contains the menu item you want to edit. Then click the name of the menu item in the Menu Item Manager to open it for editing. Make your changes in the Options tab.

Article Options

These parameters will not display on your site unless the menu item type is Category Blog or Featured Articles, and Use Article Settings is selected. If this is the case, then the article options settings will take effect. To do this, go to the Article Manager and click the article title to open the article for editing. Click the tab Options, and change the desired fields. In the menu item associated with your category of articles, click the Options tab and change desired settings to Use Article Settings.

Figure 5-1. Article display showing category, date, author, hits, and icons

For our articles, we do not want the category, date published, author, or hits to show up except in the Blog and the "How to" articles. This means that for the majority of our articles, we want those turned off. We will leave the Print and Email icons published.

Hands-On: Setting the Global Article Options

Joomla comes out of the box with the Author, Created Date, Category, Hits, and the Print and Email icons set to show on all articles. So unless you desire that, you have to venture into the Global Article Options and change them in the Articles tab. You might not need to change anything else in the Global Article Options.

1. Click on Content and then on Article Manager.

2. Click on the Options button in the top toolbar on the right (Options are also accessible through the Category Manager and Featured Article Manager).

3. Change the Show Category and Link Category to Hide and No (Figure 5-2).

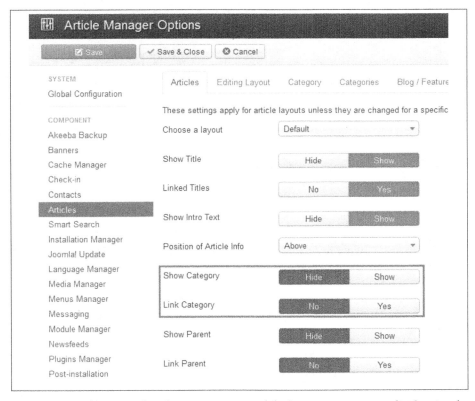

Figure 5-2. Changing the show category and link category to not display in the Global Article Manager Options

4. Scroll down and change the Show Author, Show Publish Date, and Show Navigation to Hide (Figure 5-3).

Figure 5-3. Changing the Show Author, Show Publish Date, and Show Navigation to not display in Global Article Manager Options

5. Scroll down more (this is a long page) and change Show Hits to Hide (Figure 5-4). If you want to not show the icons or words for print and email, they can be changed to Hide in this screen.

6. Click Save or Save & Close.

7. Refresh the frontend of your site and you should see your changes take effect.

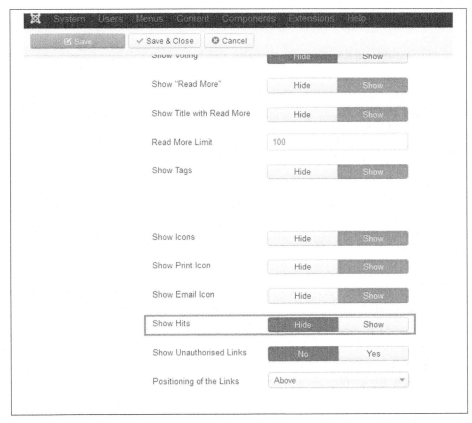

Figure 5-4. Changing the Show Hits to not display in Global Article Manager options

The Global Article Options are a very powerful way to accomplish other settings on a site-wide level. If you are using the same Category Blog display settings on multiple menu items, it would be brilliant to set the parameters here before setting up your menu items. By doing so, the site will pull what is in the Global Article Options, saving you time.

Note all the various tabs in the Global Article Options (Figure 5-5). Here's a brief description of each of the tabs and what they do. If you hover over each setting within each tab, a tooltip will describe what the setting is for. .

Figure 5-5. Global Article Options

Global Article Manager Options are divided into the following tabs:

Articles

The settings selected here apply to all article layouts.

Editing Layout

These settings control some options so that users editing articles may or may not be able to alter Publishing Options, Article Options, Frontend Images and Links, Administrator Images and Links, and URL Target Windows. They also dictate how Intro and Full Text Images float—giving articles a consistent look and feel despite who is editing them.

Category

These settings globally decide various options based on categories. You can choose a default layout, and show or hide Category Titles, descriptions, images, etc. These apply unless they are changed in the individual categories or in the menu item settings.

Categories

Settings apply for Categories when they are displayed as one or more subcategories within a parent category unless altered in the individual category or menu setting.

Blog/Featured Layouts

Here you can set a global setting for all blog or featured menu item layouts. This is helpful if you have a number of Category Blog or Featured Article menu items and you want to keep the look consistent site-wide and make setting up of those menu items faster.

List Layouts

A number of different menu items create lists of categories and/or articles within a category, contacts, and more. This tab allows you to globally set whether you want certain common list attributes to show or not.

Shared Options

These settings are for shared options in the list, blog, and featured menu item types so that if you always want to follow one consistent method, you can do so with ease instead of having to change it in all menu items associated with list, blog, or featured menu items.

Integration

This tab is mainly regarding the Feed component built in to Joomla's core.

Permissions

Review the notes at the bottom of the permissions tab and "Users, User Groups, Access Control Lists (ACLs), and Frontend Editing" on page 244 for additional information about using permissions.

Next we need to change the menu items for the Blog and "How to" articles so that the author and published date appear. While we are at it, we will remove one of the instances of "Home" from the home page. That can drive you nuts!

Changing Menu Item Options

We want the author and published date to appear in the Blog and "How to" articles, so let's make that happen:

1. Click on Menus and then on Main Menu.
2. Click on the title of the Blog Menu Item.
3. Click on the Options tab.
4. Change Show Author to Show.
5. Change Show Publish Date to Show (see Figure 5-6).
6. Click Save or Save & Close.

Figure 5-6. Set the author and publish date to show in the menu item options

Do the same thing with the "How to" articles.

See Figures 5-7 and 5-8 for how these articles now display. The "How to" articles show the author and date when they are clicked from the category list view.

Figure 5-7. Blog articles with author and date displayed

Figure 5-8. "How to" articles with author and date displayed

To get that second "Home" title out of the home page, follow these instructions:

1. From the Main Menu Manager, click on the Home title.
2. Click on the Page Display tab.
3. Change Show Page Heading from Yes to No.
4. Click Save & Close.
5. Check to see how it looks on the frontend.

If you don't want to show the title at all on the home page, simply change the Show Title field to Hide in the menu item Options tab. It is pulling the article title. If you want to change the title of the article, do so in the Article Manager.

You will probably be visiting your menu items on more than one occasion to fine-tune how your article displays. This is normal. Just remember that if you are experimenting with how displays look, only change one setting at a time. Save that one change and check it from the frontend. If it doesn't do what you want it to do, change that one setting back and then change another one. It can be easy to get confused and wish you could start over. "One change at a time" is a good motto while you are learning to use Joomla.

The WYSIWYG Editor

WYSIWYG (What You See Is What You Get) editors make it really easy to create and format your site content. If you're familiar with most word processing programs, you're already familiar with how the "B" button makes text bold and how to make text bigger or smaller. The editor included with the basic installation of Joomla is TinyMCE (*http://tinymce.moxiecode.com*). It's a lightweight and powerful WYSIWYG editor that not only allows you to write and format your text, but supports image management, Flash/media embedding, and tables.

You can change the editor in the Global Configuration to either set your choice of editor on a site-wide basis or in a user's profile to set on an individual basis. To change the WYSIWYG editor for all users, visit Global Configuration and select the Site tab in the secondary toolbar (if it isn't already selected). Under Site Settings, you should see a drop-down menu to select an editor to use globally. Select No Editor if you want to turn the editor off completely.

There is a new editor in Joomla 2.5 and 3.x called CodeMirror (*http://codemirror.net/*). This gives coders an easy way to enter their HTML and have it color-coded to assist in finding errors.

 You can install other third-party WYSIWYG editor extensions and they will appear in this same drop-down menu. You'll find a few editor options in Appendix C.

We will be installing a third-party editor called the Joomla Content Editor (JCE) (*http://www.joomlacontenteditor.net*). It is the simplest editor for beginners to use, and its noncommercial (free) edition has a ton of functionality. JCE has additional plugins with more features, which can be purchased via a subscription.

Installing JCE

In much the same way that we installed Akeeba Backup ("Mastering Backups" on page 56), we will install JCE. Back up your site before performing the installation.

1. Click on Extensions and then on Extension Manager.
2. Click the Install from Web tab.
3. JCE will be on the list (Figure 5-9). Click on it.
4. Click Install. See Figure 5-10.
5. Click Install again to confirm the installation.

Now we will assign JCE as the global editor.

1. Click on System and then on Global Configuration.
2. On the Site tab, select Editor - JCE from the drop-down (Figure 5-11).
3. Click Save & Close.

Figure 5-9. Install JCE from the backend of Joomla

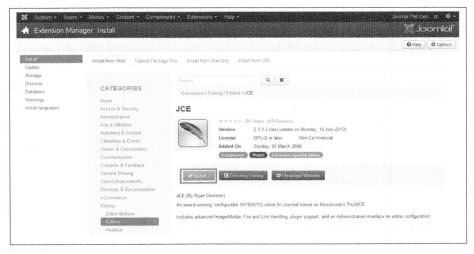

Figure 5-10. Step 1 of installing JCE.

Figure 5-11. Site Settings in Global Configuration showing WYSIWYG editor options selecting JCE

When you click on the Extensions menu, you will see that JCE Editor appears in the drop-down. JCE is extraordinarily flexible. We are going to leave all the default settings as they are at this time.

JCE allows you to create various profiles for different users or user groups that determine which buttons appear in the editor for them. This is a powerful feature if you want some users to not have certain abilities and others to have them.

JCE allows you to add styles and classes to the editor, which adds incredible functionality.

Our editor in articles now looks like Figure 5-12. You will see that there is more functionality there than you will likely use.

Figure 5-12. The JCE editor toolbar

Ron prefers TinyMCE to JCE. Joomla can handle this beautifully by assigning a different WYSIWYG editor for just one user.

1. Click on Users and then on User Manager. See "Hands-On Exercise: Creating Users" on page 244 for directions on creating users.

2. Find a user that is at least Author-level or higher (the minimum required to author content) and click their username to edit their user profile. In our case, we will click on Ron's user account.

3. In the Basic Settings tab, change the setting for Editor from Use Default to Editor - TinyMCE. See Figure 5-13.

4. Click Save & Close when you're done.

Now Ron can use TinyMCE and the rest of the users can use JCE.

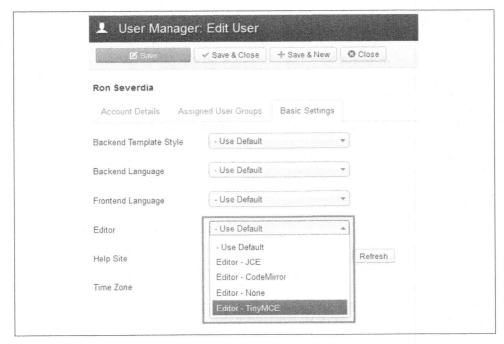

Figure 5-13. Editing a user to assign a WYSIWYG editor

Customizing Articles: Recommended Guidelines

The best way to enter your text into an article is to type it directly into the Content tab. Allow your sentences to wrap naturally and press Enter for a new paragraph.

Out of the box, the text you type into the Content tab will not look exactly as it will on the frontend of your website. "What You See" is not always "What You Get," despite the Content tab being called a WYSIWYG editor. It's close, though. The template CSS dictates the color and size of your text on the frontend as well as some additional styling, which will differ from template to template. You can use documentation from JCE to make the CSS of your template available through the editor by utilizing an *editor.css* file (*http://bit.ly/editor-ss*) so that "What You See" more closely matches the final result for the currently active template. Here are some suggestions:

- Type text first with no formatting
- Format text
- Add hyperlinks
- Add images

Copying and Pasting

Many people like to work on their website content in a word processing program and then paste it into an article. This creates inconsistencies in the site, because when you copy and paste from another application like a word processing program, it will bring in the formatting from that program and try to render it with HTML (and usually add a lot of "junk" code behind the scenes, which makes things difficult to fix without coding knowledge). What then happens on the frontend of your website is that you will have a page that looks one way, another page that looks different, and perhaps some pages with multiple font types, font sizes, and font colors—resulting in an inconsistent design or layout. If you paste from a word processing program and then try to add content to your article, you may end up with spacing issues and wonder why that has happened—and how on earth do you fix it?

Here is how to avoid some of these problems if you want to work on your content in a word processing program and then paste it into your website articles.

First off, do not format your writing in your offline program. Just type the text. Do the formatting part in the article with the editor. You will save yourself frustration. Promise! You will find it helpful to know some keyboard shortcuts working with editors. Here are the most commonly used keyboard shortcuts:

- Copy = Ctrl+C on a PC or Cmd+C on a Macintosh
- Cut = Ctrl+X on a PC or Cmd+X on a Macintosh
- Paste = Ctrl+V on a PC or Cmd+V on a Macintosh
- Undo = Ctrl+Z on a PC or Cmd+Z on a Macintosh

We have copied a small amount of text from a Word document by pressing Ctrl+C on a PC or Cmd+C on a Macintosh. This is not a complex article, and it will go on the home page of Joomla Pet Center. We will go step-by-step to show you how to properly paste this into our article:

1. Copy desired text.

2. Open desired article in Joomla.

3. Click the "Paste as plain text" icon in the editor (see Figure 5-14).

Figure 5-14. Paste as plain text selection in the JCE editor

4. In the new window that has opened, use the "Paste" keyboard shortcut and paste your content into the window. See Figure 5-15.

You can work with your text from inside this window. If you indented in your word processing document, you can remove those in this window. We don't indent paragraphs on the Web. If you have breaks instead of paragraph tags, they can be fixed in this window.

5. Click Insert.

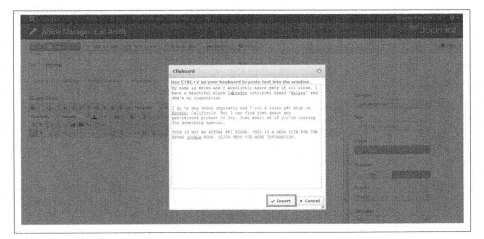

Figure 5-15. Paste as plain text into the window and insert

Your text will now appear in the main content area as seen in Figure 5-16.

Save what you have, and the rest of the chapter will help you make your content take shape and look more attractive.

You can make the content area of the editor larger by dragging the lower righthand corner down and to the right.

Figure 5-16. Text after pasting as plain text

Pasting Lists

The most common types of lists are an unordered list (bullets) and ordered lists (numbers). You can create lists using the JCE Editor with ease by using the icons showing an unordered list or an ordered list.

We are specifically bringing them up because when you paste from a word processing program and you have lists formatted, they may appear fine. Yet, if you try to add a line or remove a line it can get messy quickly.

Here's how to best handle it:

1. Don't format your list in a word processing program in the first place.

2. Leave each line of your list as a plain old line of text.

3. After you paste as plain text into the article, highlight the lines you desire to be in a list and click the appropriate list icon in the editor.

Here's how a list can look before you format it (Figure 5-17):

This will give you nice clean code (even though you can't see it) that will allow you to change your list items with greater ease.

If things are so screwed up that it is frustrating you massively, then highlight all of the text and click the Remove Formatting button, then retry the Unordered List button. If that still doesn't work, then retype those items one at a time pressing Enter between each one. Then follow the three steps listed previously. If the formatting persists at being a pain, you are going to need a clean line of code, because every time you press Enter, it is taking code with it to the next line and that is messing up your list.

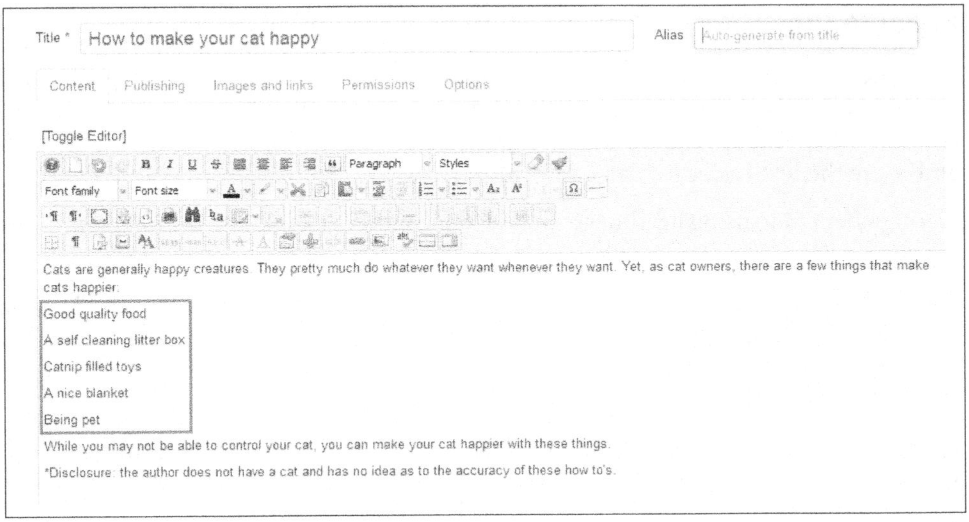

Figure 5-17. List items before formatting into an ordered or unordered list

To do this, click Toggle Editor at the top left of the editor icons. This shows you the HTML for your article. Scroll down until you get to the part of the content that is giving you trouble. When you get there, put your cursor at the beginning of the line and press Enter. Arrow up to your clean row and type **<p></p>**. See Figure 5-18 for how this looks. Click Toggle Editor again and scroll down to where you just put your clean line. Put your cursor there and type it again as instructed previously.

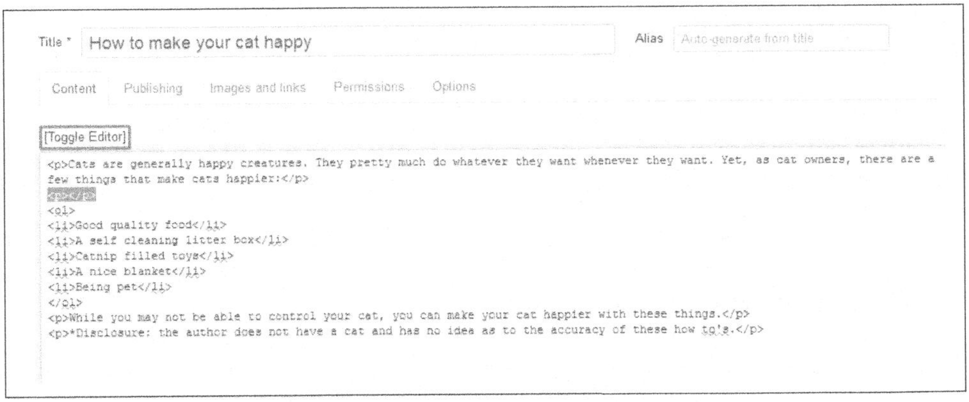

Figure 5-18. How to add a clean line to your content

Learning some basic HTML code will help you in the long run. Visit w3schools (*http:// w3schools.com/*) for free learning resources.

Heading Tags

Using headings (also called heading tags or h tags) is a great way to make specific bits of content stand out and have a consistent look and feel site-wide. Typically, headings are used when there is a fair amount of content in an article and headings divide it up and make the text easier to scan and read.

Another benefit to using headings is that search engines do look at them when they scan the site.

Do not use Heading 1 in your content, as it is dedicated for your titles. Do use Heading 2 through Heading 6 liberally. You may use the same heading consistently throughout the article or graduate down in size (Heading 1 is the largest heading and Heading 6 the smallest) as you move through depth levels in your content.

In our next example, we take one of our "How to" articles and change the title from How to 3 to How to walk your dog. We cleared the alias field so that it would autogenerate using our new title.

See Figure 5-19 for the text for this article.

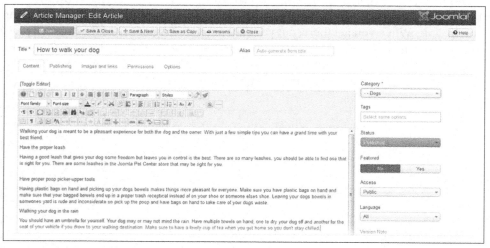

Figure 5-19. "How to walk your dog" text

Likely you can see by looking at the text that we have three phrases that would benefit the reader/visitor by having a larger size and weight of font. A heading tag does exactly this. We will change the three phrases "Have the proper leash," "Have the proper poop picker-upper tools," and "Walking your dog in the rain" to Heading 2, Heading 3, and Heading 4 so that we can see how each one looks and choose one for our article.

How to add a heading tag:

---

1. Highlight the text you want to be a heading.
2. Click the Paragraph drop-down in the top row of the editor.
3. Scroll down and select Heading 2 (see Figure 5-20).

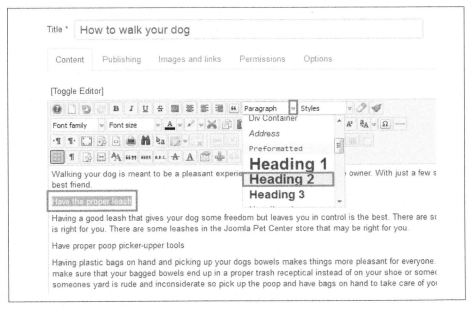

Figure 5-20. Creating text with a heading tag

4. Repeat and substitute Heading 3 and Heading 4 for the other two phrases.
5. Save the article.
6. Go to the frontend of your website and navigate to the article being edited.
7. Check out how the article looks (see Figure 5-21).

In the Afterburner2 template, the heading tags look like Figure 5-21. Heading 2 has that nice line underneath it. Heading 3 has a larger font than Heading 2 and doesn't have a nice line. Heading 4 is a slightly smaller font than Heading 3 and does not have the nice line either.

Based on how these styles look, we are going to stick with Heading 4 for this article and most of our articles in the site. You will have to decide for yourself what Headings you use and for what purposes. We will use the other Heading tags, just less often and with specific purpose.

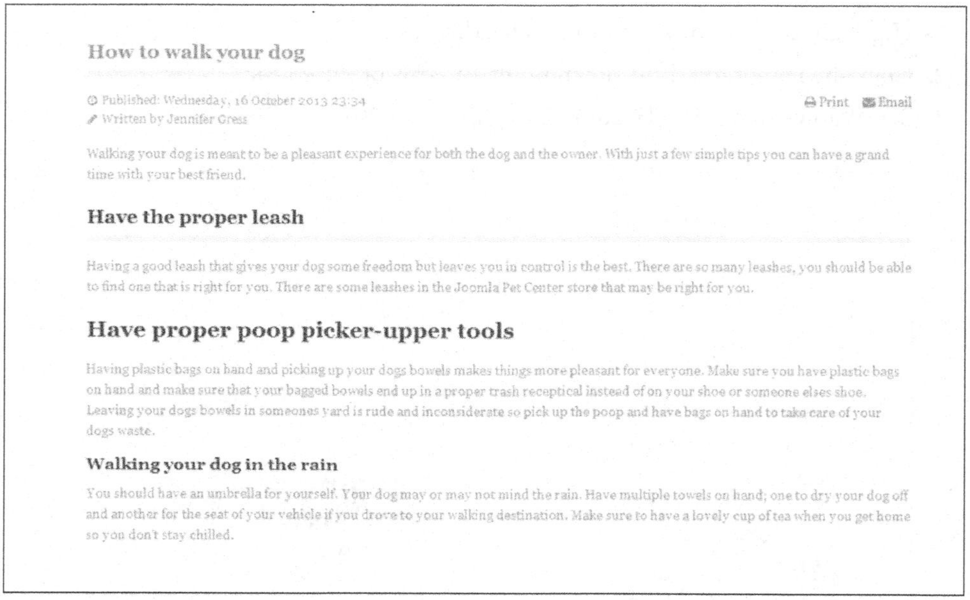

Figure 5-21. Different looks of headings 2 through 4

We will highlight the text we formatted as Heading 2 and Heading 3 and change them to Heading 4, and Save & Close our article.

If you would like to change how your Heading tags look, you may. It will require a modification of your template and knowledge of Cascading Style Sheets (CSS).

Text Color and Underline

While the editor has the ability to create text of any color, it is not recommended that you use this function. If you do use it, use it minimally and with very specific purpose.

Your template has specific CSS styles that dictate the font and hyperlink color for your website. When you manually change the color of text in your article, your website visitors assume it is a link. If the visitor has to wonder if something is a link or not, you risk them leaving your site. On a mobile device, they may think that the colored text is a link that is broken, making them think you don't care about your site and wonder why they should stay, browse, shop, or do whatever you want them to do.

Do not change the color of text just because you can! Let your template do its job and take care of the coloring of text for your site.

The same concept goes for using the underline function of the editor. When text is underlined, it will confuse a visitor as to whether the text is a link or a broken link, and this will just frustrate them.

If you would like your main body font to be a different color site-wide, you may. It will require a modification of your template and knowledge of CSS.

Tables

Tables do not work very well on mobile devices. One of two things will happen:

1. The visitor will have to scroll back and forth on their phone/tablet to see the data.
2. The table will not allow someone to scroll back and forth on their phone/tablet to see the data.

Different size tables without a set width might work well. Do not have a fixed-width table if you want to have any hope of it working on a mobile device. Try it with limited text and without spending much time, and test it from a mobile device to see if it works. If not, try something else, like:

- Create an image of the information
- Find a different way to display the information
- If you are very savvy with HTML and CSS, find articles online about making tables responsive

Hyperlinking

Hyperlinking in a website is as normal as breathing is for a human body. Having internal links from one page of your content to another guides your visitors to the information they want and to what you want them to see to accomplish your business and website goals. Having external links to other websites can navigate the visitor to even more resources than your website provides. Having email links can help visitors contact you or other people with ease—and often if you can get visitors to contact you, it is a step in the right direction to meet your goals.

Internal Links to Content Items

Hyperlinking to other pages on a website like an article or menu item (e.g., contact page or store) is common practice with content. As an example, we will use an article for Helen in the About category.

Read through the text for the Helen article. We have made **bold** the words that are opportunities for hyperlinking to internal pages.

"Helen loves dogs—all dogs. Her love of dogs is what has spurred this website into existence, to bring other pet owners together and provide resources to others who share her passion. By partnering with **Diana** and **Mark,** the website also provides valuable information about **cats** and **reptiles.** Helen has been the proud recipient of the **Doggy Society's Doggy Lover Award** every year since its inception in 1912. Helen's joy is sharing. Helen is an active member of the Joomla Pet Center **forum** and **blog.** Feel free to send Helen a message via the **contact** page or by sending her an **email.**"

Hands-On Exercise: Hyperlinking to Internal Content

"Diana" is the text we will link first. "Diana" is a single article. Follow along as we link the word "Diana" to the article associated with her.

1. Type your text into the article if not typed already.

2. Highlight the text you want hyperlinked.

 For better search engine indexing of your content, hyperlink the words that most exactly match the content item or article you are linking to. For example, if you are linking to the contact page which has the title "Contact," your text in the article may say, "Contact us for more information." Highlight only the word "Contact" and hyperlink only that one word.

3. Click the Insert/edit link button in the editor with the chain link icon (see Figure 5-22), which will open a pop-up window.

4. In the pop-up window, click the word Content in the Links section. You will see the different categories of your website. Clicking on a category will then open up the articles within that category.

5. Click the category that the article you want to link to is in. For example, we are linking to "Diana," which is an article in the About category.

6. Click the Diana article from the list under the About category. You will see that the URL at the top of the window has filled in with the relative URL of the article. See Figure 5-23.

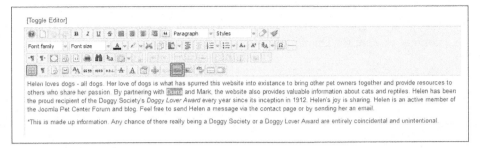

Figure 5-22. Highlighted text and the insert/edit link icon

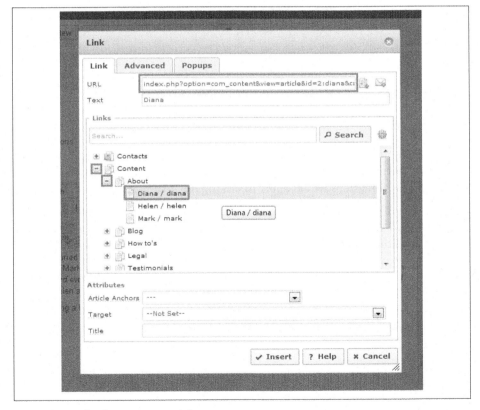

Figure 5-23. Linking to an article

7. Leave all other settings as they are.

8. Click Insert at the bottom of the window.

9. Click Save in the top toolbar.

10. Go to the frontend of the website and test the link. See Figure 5-24 for our text and the word "Diana" linked to her article. The link indeed works, though there is no content present for Diana's About page yet.

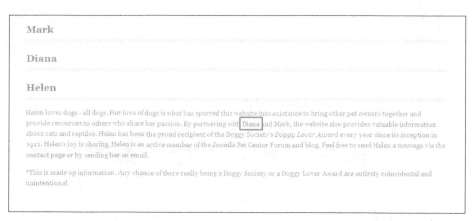

Figure 5-24. Article with hyperlink to another article within the site

11. Repeat with any other hyperlinks in the article, then click Save & Close.

Hyperlinking to the blog or an extension like the forum or the store have similar yet slightly different steps. Follow along while we link the word "blog" in Helen's article to the blog. The same steps would apply to linking the forum, store, or other component.

Extensions and menu items for extensions need to be created before you can link to them. Because our store and forum extensions are not yet installed, we cannot link to them at this time. Once the extensions are installed and the proper menu item types are created, they can be linked by following these same steps.

1. Follow steps 1–3 in the preceding list.

2. Click on Menu in the Links section of the pop-up window. Each of the menus of your website will appear.

3. Click on Main Menu, which will then display a list of all your menu items.

4. Click on the Blog menu item, which will automatically fill in the relative URL in the URL field at the top of the pop-up window.

5. Leave all other fields as they are.

6. Click Insert at the bottom of the window.

7. Save the article and test your link from the frontend. See Figure 5-25.

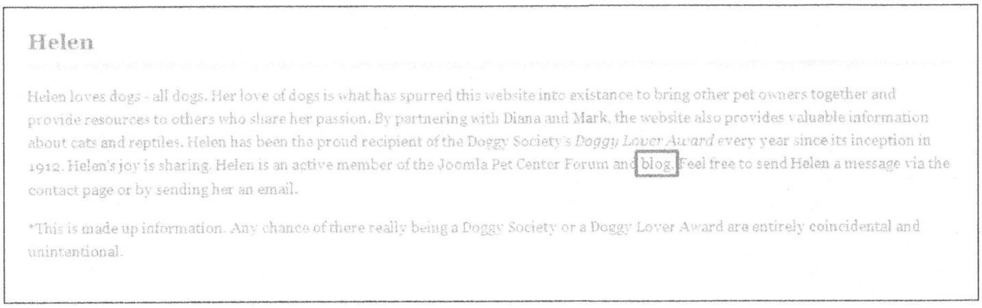

Helen

Helen loves dogs - all dogs. Her love of dogs is what has spurred this website into existance to bring other pet owners together and provide resources to others who share her passion. By partnering with Diana and Mark, the website also provides valuable information about cats and reptiles. Helen has been the proud recipient of the Doggy Society's *Doggy Lover Award* every year since its inception in 1912. Helen's joy is sharing. Helen is an active member of the Joomla Pet Center Forum and blog. Feel free to send Helen a message via the contact page or by sending her an email.

*This is made up information. Any chance of there really being a Doggy Society or a Doggy Lover Award are entirely coincidental and unintentional.

Figure 5-25. Hyperlink to a blog-style menu item within the site

8. Click Save & Close when complete.

Hands-On Exercises: External Hyperlinks

External links take visitors away from your website to a different website. The steps are very similar to linking to internal content with a few minor adjustments.

1. Follow items 1–3 on "Hands-On Exercise: Hyperlinking to Internal Content" on page 106.

2. Copy the URL of the website page you desire to link to.

3. Paste the URL into the URL field of the link pop-up window. Make sure the URL is complete and begins with either http:// or https:// to signal that the link is a connection to an external website.

4. Set the Target to "Open in new window" from the drop-down. See Figure 5-26.

5. Click Insert.

6. Click Save from the top toolbar.

7. Test your link from the frontend and verify it opens in a new tab or window (depending on browser configuration).

Figure 5-26. Hyperlinking to an external website address

The reason we set the target to open in a new window is the hope that by opening the external website in a different tab, the visitor may come back to our website and do what we want them to instead of leave forever and never come back. Distracted browsing and Internet addiction is very common.

Hands-On Exercise: Email Address Hyperlinks

If you would like to hyperlink the word "email" with an actual email address or *address@yoursite.com* to an email address, it is a simple process.

1. Again, follow steps 1–3 in "Hands-On Exercise: Hyperlinking to Internal Content" on page 106.

2. Click the envelope with the little green plus sign to the right of the URL field (Figure 5-27).

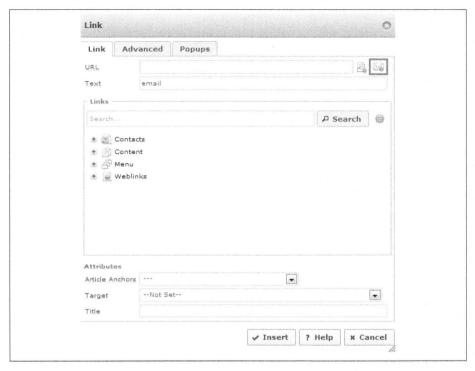

Figure 5-27. Hyperlink to an email address icon

3. In the pop-up box that appears, enter the email address (and any cc or bcc addresses) and the desired subject line (Figure 5-28).

Figure 5-28. Entering email addresses and subject line for email hyperlink

4. Click OK.

5. Set the Target to "Open in new window."

6. Click Insert at the bottom of the link pop-up window.

7. Click Save from the top toolbar.

8. Test from the frontend. See Figure 5-29.

Helen

Helen loves dogs - all dogs. Her love of dogs is what has spurred this website into existance to bring other pet owners together and provide resources to others who share her passion. By partnering with Diana and Mark, the website also provides valuable information about cats and reptiles. Helen has been the proud recipient of the Doggy Society's *Doggy Lover Award* every year since its inception in 1912. Helen's joy is sharing. Helen is an active member of the Joomla Pet Center Forum and blog. Feel free to send Helen a message via the contact page or by sending her an email.

*This is made up information. Any chance of there really being a Doggy Society or a Doggy Lover Award are entirely coincidental and unintentional.

Figure 5-29. Email hyperlink in an article

 If you do not have an email client configured to automatically open and compose an email, this link will not work for you. It will work for people who do. Those that don't use such email clients can simply copy the address into their browser-based email client.

Adding Embedded HTML Code and Text Filtering

There are times that you may want to embed HTML code into an article (or module). Common uses of adding HTML code to an article are to embed a YouTube video, a PayPal button, or an affiliate code onto your site.

Because code can sometimes include malicious additions that you do not want on your site (for example, an <iframe> can sometimes be used to attempt site hacking), Joomla applies specific text-filtering profiles based on the user group a user is in. This is to protect your site. Super Administrators and Administrators have no filtering and can safely embed code into articles without any code stripping. Other user groups may have filtering set differently. As a result, before you embed code in an article or instruct other users in user groups with lesser permissions to embed code in articles, you will want to make sure that they have the ability to add code without it being removed upon saving the article.

If a user without permissions to embed code into an article does indeed embed code, the code will be stripped out of the article upon saving.

If a user without proper filtering permissions accesses an article with embedded code already in place and makes an edit anywhere in the article, the code that was in place will be stripped out when they save.

Text-filtering settings are found in Global Configuration. Click on the Text Filters tab. Reading the description of what is in the default blacklist at the bottom of the page will help you to know what is allowed and disallowed for various user groups.

We want the Editor user group to be able to embed videos from YouTube. Embed code from YouTube is an iframe. Thus, we will change the editor user group filter type to White List and type `iframe` into the Filter Tags field. Then click Save & Close. See Figure 5-30.

Filter Groups	Filter Type[1]	Filter Tags[2]	Filter Attributes[3]
Public	No HTML		
⊢—Guest	Default Black List		
⊢—Manager	Default Black List		
⊢—⊢—Administrator	No Filtering		
⊢—Registered	No HTML		
⊢—⊢—Author	Default Black List		
⊢—⊢—⊢—Editor	White List	iframe	
⊢—⊢—⊢—⊢—Publisher	Default Black List		
⊢—Super Users	No Filtering		

1. Black List allows all tags and attributes except for those in the black list.
  — Tags for the Default Black List include: 'applet', 'body', 'bgsound', 'base', 'basefont', 'embed', 'frame', 'frameset', 'head', 'html', 'id', 'iframe', 'ilayer', 'layer', 'link', 'meta', 'name', 'object', 'script', 'style', 'title', 'xml'.
  — Attributes for the Default Black List include: 'action', 'background', 'codebase', 'dynsrc', 'lowsrc'.
  — You can black list additional tags and attributes by adding to the Filter Tags and Filter Attributes fields, separating each tag or attribute name with a comma.
  — Custom Black List allows you to override the Default Black List. Add the tags and attributes to be black listed in the Filter Tags and Filter Attributes fields.

White List allows only the tags listed in the Filter Tags and Filter Attributes fields.

No HTML removes all HTML tags from the content when it is saved.

Please note that these settings work regardless of the editor that you are using.
Even if you are using a WYSIWYG editor, the filtering settings may strip additional tags and attributes prior to saving information in the database.

2. List additional tags, separating each tag name with a space or comma. For example: p.div,span.

3. List additional attributes, separating each attribute name with a space or comma. For example: class,title,id.

Figure 5-30. Customize how code is filtered by user group in Global Configuration

This ought to do it. Yet, there is still a chance that upon saving, the code could be stripped. If this occurs, there is a setting in the WYSIWYG editor for JCE that may need to be changed.

1. Click on Extensions and again on JCE Editor.
2. Click on Editor Profiles and then on the Default link to access the default profile.
3. Click on the Plugin Parameters tab.
4. Scroll down just a bit and click on the tab on the left that says Media Support.
5. The second item on the list says Allow IFrames and is by default set to No. Change this to Yes. See Figure 5-31.

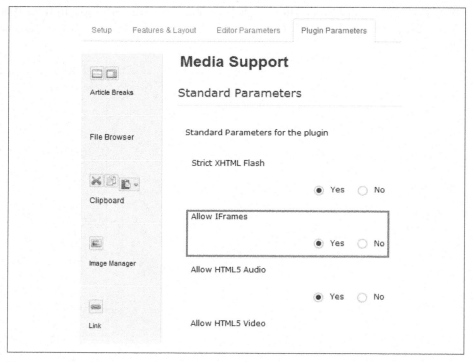

Figure 5-31. Setting JCE editor to allow iframes

6. Click Save & Close from the top toolbar.

Now that we don't run the risk of stripping out our YouTube code, we will add a video to the home page of Joomla Pet Center as an example.

Hands-On Exercise: Add a YouTube Video

1. Go to YouTube and navigate to the desired video.

2. Beneath the video will be a link that says Share and then another link that says Embed. Click the Embed tab.

3. Choose the size of the player you desire from the options listed, and then copy the embed code provided in the box.

4. In the backend of your website, click on Content and then on Article Manager.

5. Click on the article you desire to insert the video. In our case, the article is called Home.

6. In the main text area for the article, put your cursor where you want the video to be and type the words **embed here**—this makes it easier for the next step. If you want the video to be centered, then center that text with the editor.

7. Click the Toggle Editor text at the top left of the editor above the icons. You will now see all the HTML code from the page in the text area of the article including the text **embed here** that you just typed.

8. Highlight the line of code, `<p>embed here</p>`. See Figure 5-32

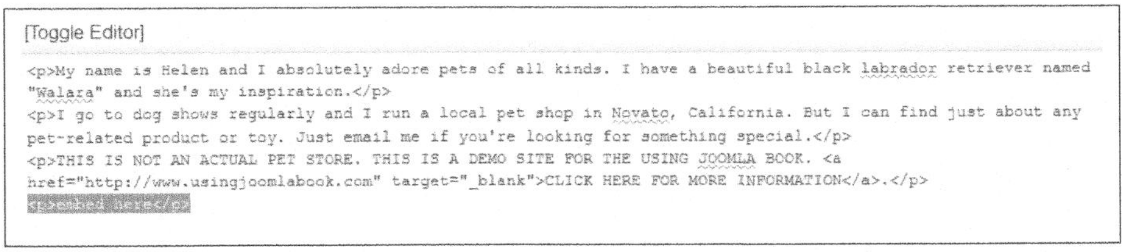

[Toggle Editor]

`<p>My name is Helen and I absolutely adore pets of all kinds. I have a beautiful black labrador retriever named "Walara" and she's my inspiration.</p>`
`<p>I go to dog shows regularly and I run a local pet shop in Novato, California. But I can find just about any pet-related product or toy. Just email me if you're looking for something special.</p>`
`<p>THIS IS NOT AN ACTUAL PET STORE. THIS IS A DEMO SITE FOR THE USING JOOMLA BOOK. <a href="http://www.usingjoomlabook.com" target="_blank">CLICK HERE FOR MORE INFORMATION</a>.</p>`
`<p>embed here</p>`

Figure 5-32. Use the Toggle Editor to see where you will paste the embed code

9. Paste your embed code from YouTube over the line you highlighted in the previous step.

10. Click Toggle Editor again and you should see a beige box, which is your video as seen in Figure 5-33.

11. Click Save in the top toolbar.

12. Go to the frontend and refresh, or navigate to the page you just embedded the video and test it.

13. As long the video works as expected, go to the backend and click Save & Close.

Our video on the frontend looks like what is seen in Figure 5-34.

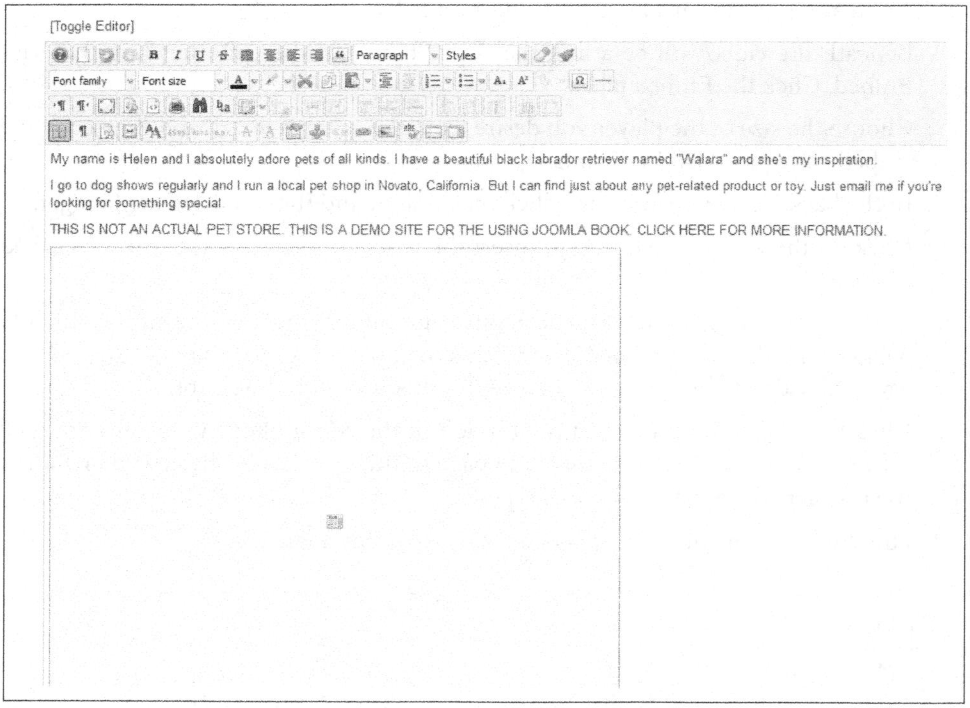

Figure 5-33. How videos look in the Edit Article screen after inserting an embed code

We embedded a playlist. Within YouTube, you can specify whether to embed an entire playlist or an individual video. You may want to create your own playlist to embed, so that you have more control of what is displayed when the video ends.

Figure 5-34. Video displayed on the home page

Read More and Pagebreak

Under the text editor area in the Article Editor, you've probably already noticed four article-related buttons (Figure 5-35). These buttons are inserted by Joomla and appear regardless of which editor you have selected, so they may be redundant. If your selected editor provides a more feature-rich version of a button at the top of the editing window, that's the one to use. Because JCE Editor increases functionality beyond that of these buttons, we will only be looking at Read More and Page Break. Let's take a closer look at both:

Figure 5-35. The default editor extended toolbar

Read More

When you have a few articles displayed on a single page, a common practice is to display just a teaser of each article. When a user finds an article of interest, they can click a Read More link to see the full article.

To add a "Read more" link to the article, place your cursor where you want to "break" your article (usually after the first sentence or paragraph) and click the Read More button. The following HTML will be automatically inserted into your article.

```
<hr id="system-readmore" />
```

There will now be a horizontal rule with a break, as shown in Figure 5-36. When this article is loaded on the frontend of your site, Joomla will add a "Read more" link at that point.

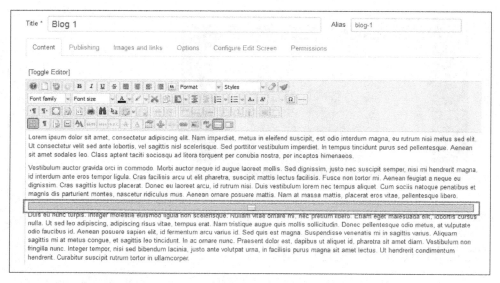

Figure 5-36. "Read more" line in an article

Page Break

    Page breaks are often added to reduce scrolling when reading long articles. You can add a page break to your articles where your cursor is placed. Clicking the Page Break button gives you the option to add a Page Title and Table of Contents Alias. The following HTML code will be automatically inserted into your article: `<hr title="My Page Title" alt="MY TOC Alias" class="system-pagebreak" />`

When this article is loaded on the frontend of your website, Joomla will automatically generate a table of contents in your article with links to any other page breaks you've added. By accessing the Content - Pagebreak plugin via the Plugin Manager, you can select page breaks to display either plain, or as tabs or sliders with the Presentation Style setting.

Meta Description and Keywords

Each article, category, and menu item have fields for entering a Meta Description and Meta Keywords. Meta Description is a summary sentence that outputs in the HTML and is sometimes rendered in search engine results. Meta Keywords output in the HTML of each article.

The Meta Description is more important than the keywords because of how search engines scan the text in the article these days.

You will want to enter a Meta Description for each of your articles.

1. In the desired article, click on the Publishing tab.
2. Enter a value for the Meta Description in the field.
3. Click Save & Close.

When adding meta keywords to your site, they can be all lower-case and separated by commas. Keywords need to be directly related to the content of the article.

Article Management

The following pointers will help you manage articles on an ongoing basis.

Versioning/Revisions and Editing Articles

Joomla 3.x has the ability to save revisions of your articles when you edit them. To use this functionality, you must first enable it in the Global Article Options (Figure 5-37).

1. Click on Content and then on Article Manager.
2. Click on the Options button on the top toolbar.
3. Click on the Editing Layout tab.
4. Change the Save History button to Yes.
5. Change the Maximum Versions number to the number of versions you would like to keep. The default is 10.
6. Click Save & Close.

Figure 5-37. Enable versioning in Global Article Options

When you edit an article, you will see that there is a new field on the right sidebar under the Language drop-down called Version Note, as seen in Figure 5-38.

Figure 5-38. Add a version note to save a revision of your article

We added a link to the article and added "Add link" as the version note. After saving the article, when we click on the Version button in the top toolbar, we can see our new version saved, as in Figure 5-39.

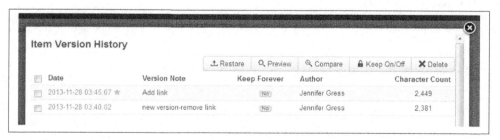

Figure 5-39. Item version history of article

From here, we can mark a revision to keep forever, restore a revision, delete revisions, and compare revisions. If you do not enter a version note, the system will still keep a revision for you. It won't have a note, however. The star shows which version of the article is live.

This is a handy feature that will enable you to revert to an earlier version (for example, if you mess up—and we've all messed up—or if the code gets stripped out). We set our maximum number of versions to keep at 10, but you will have to decide what works for your site. It is possible that keeping a large number of revisions could perhaps get a little out of hand.

Check In

When you edit an article, Joomla "checks out" the article from the database so multiple users don't try to edit the same article at the same time. When you're done editing an article, it must be "checked in." If this doesn't happen for some reason (for example, closing your browser window without saving your work, trying to save changes after your login session has expired, or using your browser Back button), Joomla will assume that the article is still checked out and will prevent anyone from editing it. If you discover that an article remains inappropriately checked out, you can check it back in by clicking on the checkbox to the left of the status column in the Article Manager and then clicking the Check In button in the toolbar.

If you find that multiple items are checked out, you can check in multiple articles at one time by clicking on System and again on Global Check-in. Using this tool will check in all of your articles and any other items that are checked out.

 If you use this tool to check articles back in, make sure none of your users have open articles, or else their work will be lost.

For more detail on checking in items, see "Global Check-in" on page 284.

Ordering Articles

You can display articles in the order in which they appear in the Article Manager. You only need to set your article order here if you're going to use this order to display your articles on your website. This is applicable for Category Blog, Category List, and Featured Menu Item types, which give you the option to "Use Article Manager Order." You can also set the parameters to display your articles in a specific order (e.g., by date or title).

If you're not there already, click on Content and again on Article Manager to view your articles. Article ordering is handled on a category level, and you can see the article's position within that category by selecting the category from the category filter and looking at the Order column, which has two up/down arrows in the heading and three dots prior to the checkbox for each article title.

To make ordering easier to see, let's use the filters to view a specific category. Choose a category from the article filter drop-down menu. We will use the category Blog for our example. Once you've selected a category, you should see only the articles in that specific category—something like Figure 5-40.

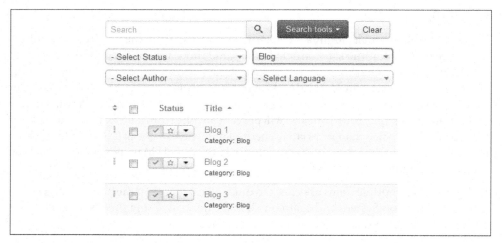

Figure 5-40. Ordering a category of articles in the Article Manager

You can reorder the articles by first clicking the up/down arrows at the top of the column and then simply clicking the three dots at the left of the checkbox and dragging the articles into the desired order. Ordering menu items, modules, and categories are done this same way site-wide.

Permissions

Permissions are determined by one of three default Access Levels: Public, Registered, and Special. You may have more custom Access Levels. We will be looking only at the three default Access Levels. The default Access Levels correspond to the following user groups and determine their access:

Public

> This level applies to general users and site visitors who don't have an account. It could also be defined as guest users.

Registered

> This level applies to all users that have logged in. These users are associated with user groups that are Registered or higher. This includes Authors, Editors, Publishers, Managers, Administrators, and Super Administrators.

Special

> This level applies to users that are any level above Registered, including Authors, Managers, and higher.

Category Permissions

> To set permissions for an entire category, go to the Category Manager and choose the category you want to edit. Choose an Access Level in the field on the right and click Save & Close.

Article Permissions

> To set permissions for a single article, go to the Article Manager and choose the article you want to edit. Choose an Access Level from the drop-down menu in the righthand column under Details and click Save & Close.

For detailed information on permissions, Access Levels, and user groups, see "Users, User Groups, Access Control Lists (ACLs), and Frontend Editing" on page 244.

Archiving Articles

Archiving articles is the best way to remove your articles from view, but still keep them. *Archived* articles aren't deleted, but they aren't visible on the frontend unless you create direct links to them or create an Archived Article List menu item. Archived articles are not visible in the backend Article Manager unless you set the Status filter to specifically show Archived Articles.

Trashing Articles

When you no longer need an article, you can remove it from the Article Manager by moving it to the trash. The *Article Trash* behaves like the recycle bin or trash can on your desktop computer. Once you trash an article, you can still recover it until you empty the trash. Trashed articles are not visible in the backend Article Manager unless you set the Status filter to specifically show Trashed articles. From there, you can set an article's status back to Published or permanently remove trashed articles from your site.

To permanently delete articles, go to the Article Manager, filter the status by Trashed, click the checkboxes next to the articles you want to delete, and then click the Empty Trash button in the toolbar.

Joomla does not ask you to confirm emptying the trash a second time. Deleting articles from the Article Trash actually deletes the information from the database. As a result, if you accidentally delete an article from the Article Trash, it is gone forever.

Adding Content to Modules

Adding content to Custom HTML modules is exactly like adding content to articles or category descriptions. You can apply all the principles in this chapter and in "Media Manager" on page 127 to make your Custom HTML modules look great.

Hands-On Exercise: Showing Modules Inside an Article

Modules are usually associated with menu items, but sometimes you'll want to associate a module within a specific article. Modules are commonly assigned to module positions, and these positions appear on the web page as defined in your template. But sometimes it's useful to have a module actually "embedded" in the article itself, which gives you a great deal of flexibility over where you display your modules. To do so, follow these steps:

1. Go to Extensions and then Module Manager, and create a new module or open an existing module.

2. Add the desired content.

3. Make sure the module is Published.

4. Instead of choosing a module position that is defined in your template, create a new one just for use inside an article. Let's say `inarticle` is the name of the new module position we'll use. It doesn't exist yet so it will not be selectable in the drop-down, so just type in the new position name.

5. In the Menu Assignment tab, make sure the module is set to display on all pages.

6. Click Save & Close.

7. In the Article Manager, locate the article you want the module to appear in.

8. Click the article name to open it for editing. Find the place where you want the module to be.

9. Enter *{loadposition myposition}* where you'll replace *myposition* with the name of the module position you used in step 4 (Figure 5-41). Using the name `inarticle`, the text you enter into the article would be *{loadposition inarticle}*.

Any module assigned to the `inarticle` position will now load in that article. Check your results by viewing the article on the frontend. Your module should now load directly into the body of the article. If it doesn't, check the settings of the module to verify that it is Published and that the Menu Assignment tab shows All pages.

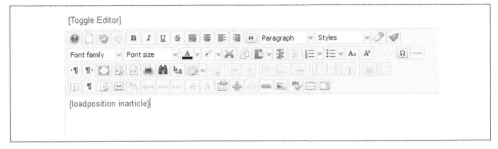

Figure 5-41. The loadposition module tag inserted into an article

CHAPTER 6

Managing Media and Creating Galleries

Media Manager

Using media on your site makes it much more engaging than just plain text. With Joomla, you can add images, audio, video, or even Adobe Flash to your web pages with just a few clicks. In this section, we'll cover how to upload media, add it to your articles, and delete media.

The *Media Manager* (Figure 6-1) is a simple tool for not only managing your media files, but also incorporating them into the pages of your website. To open the Media Manager, click on Content and then on Media Manager to open up the default Thumbnail View.

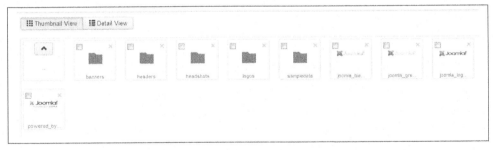

Figure 6-1. The Media Manager default Thumbnail View

The Media Manager displays images, folders, and other files inside the */images* directory. The folders on the left sidebar are all subfolders within that directory. The little folder symbol next to each expands and collapses each folder of the tree. Clicking on each of these folders displays their contents.

The Media Manager doesn't manage images or other files that are used in your template. Those should be stored in the template folder.

Navigating Views and Managing Media

The Thumbnail View (Figure 6-1) might not show the information you want to know about each file. The Detail View (Figure 6-2) in the Media Manager shows a little more detail about each file, including the file size and pixel dimensions.

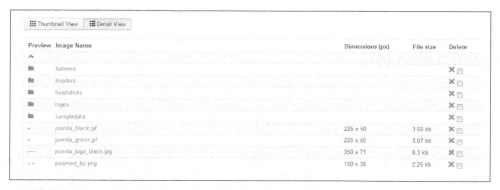

Figure 6-2. The Media Manager Detail View

In both views, only a small thumbnail of each image is shown. If you want to see the full-size image, click the image thumbnail, the icon, or the filename to open the image in a larger view.

Uploading and Deleting Media

In this section, we will go over how to upload media and how to delete it. Storing unnecessary media files on your website takes extra storage and creates confusion, so we will cover the best ways to go about it.

Hands-On Exercise: Uploading Media

We're now going to walk through the basic steps of uploading an image. To upload an image using the default form uploader:

1. Click on Content and then on Media Manager.

2. Select the folder on the left where you want to upload the image. If you need to create a new folder, you can do so by using the Create Folder button in the top

toolbar. Then click that new folder and be sure you have it accessed before proceeding.

3. Click the Upload button in the top toolbar. This will create a field and buttons just above the thumbnails or details (depending on which view you are in).

4. Click the Browse button and select the file on your computer. You can select more than one image if they are in the same folder or section of your computer (Figure 6-3)

5. Click the Start Upload button.

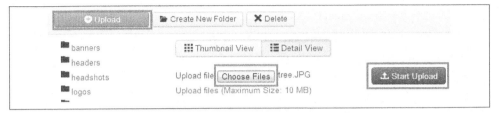

Figure 6-3. Uploading in the Media Manager

These same steps apply to uploading documents like PDFs or other file types to the Media Manager. You may need to use an FTP client to upload very large files to your image folder.

 The upload functionality is limited by the POST limit set by your hosting provider. To check your limit, go to System→System Information→PHP Information and look for the `upload_max_filesize_` (individual files) and `post_max_size` variable (total files) to see the maximum upload size in megabytes.

The time it takes to upload a file will depend on the speed of your connection, the speed of your web server, and a number of other factors.

Hands-On Exercise: Deleting Media

To delete a single media item in the Media Manager:

1. Click on Content and then Media Manager.

2. Select the folder on the left to locate the item you want to delete.

3. Click the X icon next to that item (Figure 6-4).

Figure 6-4. Deleting a single item in the Media Manager

To delete multiple media items at once from a single folder:

1. Click on Content and then Media Manager.
2. Select the folder on the left to locate the items you want to delete.
3. Click the checkboxes next to each item (Figure 6-5).
4. Click Delete in the top toolbar.

Figure 6-5. Deleting multiple items in the Media Manager

 You cannot move media around in the Media Manager. If you need to move an item to another folder, you will need to delete that item and upload it to the proper folder using the previous steps. You might be able to move media from your hosting dashboard file manager. Just remember that when you move an image, any link to the image in your website will break until the URL is changed to reflect the new location.

Using Media in Your Articles

Adding media to your articles is a good way to spruce up the look of your website.

Hands-On Exercise: Adding an Image to an Article

We're now going to add an image to Helen's article. To insert previously uploaded images and other types of media to your articles:

1. Click on Content and then on Article Manager.

2. Click the name of the article to which you want to add an image.

3. Insert your cursor in the article body where you want the image to be placed.

4. Click the "Insert/Edit image" button in the JCE Editor's toolbar. It looks like a small photo of a tree. This will open the Image Manager in a pop-up window.

5. The bottom half of the image manager is called *File Browser*. This shows everything in your root image folder. Navigate to where you uploaded your image in the Media Manager on the left side of the window called *Folders*. When you select your image, the *Details* will appear on the right. This will fill in the *URL* in the top field of the Image Manager. See an example in Figure 6-6. A preview of your image should appear at the top right of the window in the *Preview* area.

6. Replace the Alternate Text with something familiar for people to read. This assists those with disabilities viewing the site. It also improves search engine optimization (SEO).

7. Click Insert. (For more on aligning images or wrapping text, see steps 14 and 15 in "Hands-On Exercise: Adding Folders and Uploading Images from the Editor" on page 132).

8. Click the Save button to save the article or Save & Close to save the article and proceed to the Article Manager List.

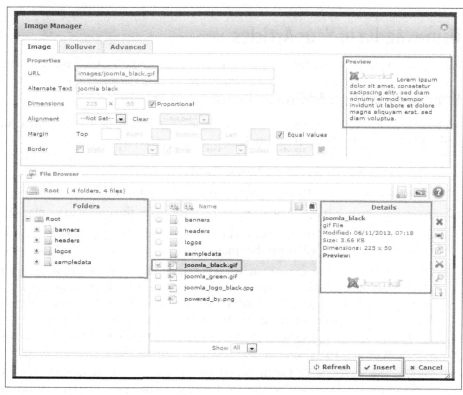

Figure 6-6. Insert an image with the JCE Image Manager

Hands-On Exercise: Adding Folders and Uploading Images from the Editor

You can add folders and multiple images at a time from the Image Manager with the JCE Editor. It is a similar process to working with the Media Manager and adding an image in the previous section.

1. Click on Content and then on Article Manager.

2. Click the name of the article where you want to add an image.

3. Insert your cursor in the article body where you want the image to be placed.

4. Click the Insert/Edit image button in the JCE Editor toolbar. It looks like a small photo of a tree. This will open the Image Manager in a pop-up window.

5. To add a folder, navigate to the folder that will contain the new folder and then click the button above the details with the folder icon and a green plus sign.

6. Type the name of the folder (all lowercase with no space). We will add a folder for headshots. See Figure 6-7.

Figure 6-7. Adding a folder to the image directory using JCE from within an article

7. Click OK.

8. In the middle section, navigate to your new folder. Make sure you are in the correct folder before uploading your image(s).

9. Click the *Upload* icon above the Details panel. This will open a pop-up window for you to drag and drop image files or browse to select images. You can upload multiple images at a time as long as they don't hit the size limit. See Figure 6-8.

10. Click Upload, and the X in the upload screen will turn to a checkmark as each file upload completes, and then the window will close.

11. Back at the Image Manager, select the file you just uploaded or one you wish to insert into the article. This will automatically fill in the URL, Alternate Text, and Dimensions.

12. Replace the Alternate Text with something normal for people to read. This assists those with disabilities viewing the site, plus it improves SEO.

13. Do not resize images in the browser using the Dimensions field, even though you can. Resize and optimize your images with a photo editing application prior to uploading to your site. See "Resizing, Optimizing, and Naming Image Files" on page 139.

14. If you would like your text on the page to wrap around the image, click the drop-down next to the word Alignment and choose to the right or left. You will be able to see an example of this in the Preview pane.

15. If you need to stop the text from butting right up against the image, add some margin to the right or left (depending on which direction the image is aligned). We want to align our image to the left, so we will add 10 pixels of margin to the right side of the image. See Figure 6-9.

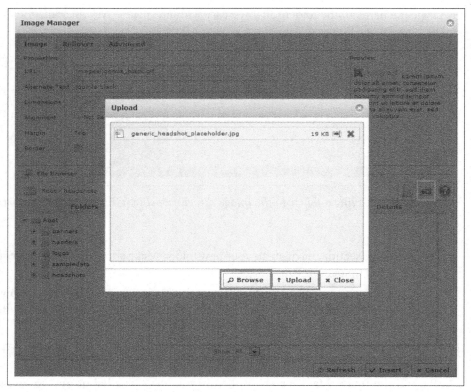

Figure 6-8. Upload images via JCE Image Manager

16. Click Insert.

17. You will now see your image inserted into the article editor. Click Save from the top toolbar and check your article from the frontend of your website (Figure 6-10).

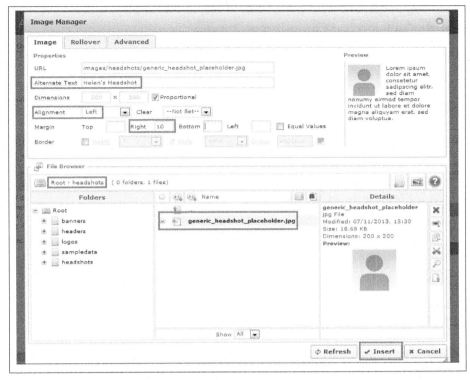

Figure 6-9. Inserting an image with left alignment and right margin

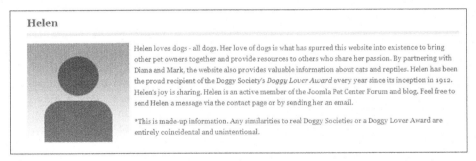

Figure 6-10. Image added to article as viewed from the frontend

Hands-On Exercise: Changing an Image

Make a mistake or want to update an image? To change an existing image:

1. Go to the Article Manager and click the name of the article that contains the image you want to change.

2. Select the image you want to replace by clicking on the image.

3. Click the "Insert/Edit mage" button in the JCE Editor toolbar. It looks like a small photo of a tree.

4. Select or upload the image you desire. A preview of your image should appear after you select the desired image.

5. Click Insert.

6. Click the Save button to save the article or Save & Close to save the article and proceed to the Article Manager List.

7. Refresh and check your change from the frontend.

Hands-On Exercise: Removing an Image

Deleting the image is like deleting text. Follow these steps:

1. Go to the Article Manager and click the name of the article where you want to remove an image.

2. Select the image you want to delete by clicking on it.

3. Press Delete on your keyboard.

 When you delete an image from an article, it does not delete it from the Media Manager. If you know that you will never use that image on your site again, it is best to also remove it from the Media Manager. You may also delete an image from the JCE Image Manager by selecting it and clicking the Delete icon to the right of the Details pane.

Hands-On Exercise: Hyperlinking an Image

1. Insert your image by following the instructions in "Hands-On Exercise: Adding an Image to an Article" on page 131.

2. Click the image in your content text so it is outlined.

3. Click on the "Insert/Edit link" button in the editor toolbar.

4. Follow the instructions for "Hands-On Exercise: Hyperlinking to Internal Content" on page 106.

Hands-On Exercise: Linking Documents

Linking to downloadable files, PDFs, and documents is very similar to inserting images in an article.

1. Create a new folder (see "Organizing Media" on page 137) named *documents* in Media Manager. Folders and filenames should have no spaces and be all lowercase.
2. Upload documents to the applicable folder via FTP, Media Manager, or even JCE unless the file is too large.
3. Go to the Article Manager and click on the article in which you want the document linked.
4. Type the display text for your link (caps and spaces are fine here).
5. Highlight the text and click on the "Insert/Edit link" button; it is the same button with the chain link icon used to add a hyperlink.
6. Click on the button with the paper document icon to the far right of the URL bar that says Browse when hovered over.
7. A pop-up window will open with the root folder displayed.
8. Click on the applicable folder and navigate to the file you want to link to.
9. Click Insert, which will close this pop-up window.
10. Set the Target to open in a new window from the drop-down in the Link pop-up.
11. Click Insert at the bottom of the pop-up window.
12. Click Save in the article.
13. Refresh and test from the frontend.
14. Go back to the backend administration and click Save & Close.

Organizing Media

Taking some time to think through your media before haphazardly uploading is wise. Even in a small site, media can quickly become a mess, making it difficult to find images when you are working in an article.

Here are some tips to help you:

1. Do not upload large quantities of images into the root of the */images* directory (where you land when you go to Media Manager).

2. Create folders often.

3. Create a folder specifically for logically categorized images.

4. Examples of folder names could be:

- *logos*
- *social-icons*
- *affiliation-logos*
- *documents*
- *videos*
- *news*

You can create subfolders within these folders. For example, inside of the documents folder could be folders for:

- *past_newsletters*
- *press_releases*
- *data_sheets*

Within the news folder could be:

- *2014*
- *2013*
- *2012*
- *2011*

You may need to break it down further or in different ways. Make it logical for the people working with your site. There are few things more frustrating than looking for an image in the root of the Media Manager with 900 images in it. Trust me, after 45 minutes looking for one image, you'll wish you had made folders. So make folders.

 When naming files and folders, use only lowercase letters and no spaces.

Resizing, Optimizing, and Naming Image Files

In "Hands-On Exercise: Adding Folders and Uploading Images from the Editor" on page 132, we recommended that you resize images before uploading them to your website. This is important because:

Page speed
> It takes browsers longer to load the page and render an image that has an original size of 1000 pixels by 1000 pixels compared to 200×200.

File size
> An image that is 1000×1000 will be much larger than a 200×200 image. This occupies unnecessary space on your server.

They look better
> When images are resized in the browser, they often look grainy and pixelated. When the image is properly resized, it makes a beautiful difference in how the image looks on your page.

An additional guideline for images on websites is to optimize them for the Web. The reasons are the same as for resizing images. The idea behind this is that an image on a website does not need to be the same quality as one you would take to a photo processing store and have blown up into an 8×10 image.

Photoshop makes it easy to crop, resize, and optimize images. Yet not all people have the luxury of Photoshop. A cheaper alternative is Photoshop Elements, which is a stripped down version of Photoshop that still does cropping, resizing, and optimizing images beautifully. Your computer may have a basic image editing program like Paint that can resize but not optimize images, but other, better options exist.

Here are some web-based services to help you resize and optimize your images:

- Webresizer (*http://www.webresizer.com/*): resizes and optimizes images.
- Imageoptimizer (*http://www.imageoptimizer.net*): only optimizes images and does not resize them.
- Gimp (*http://www.gimp.org/*): Gimp is an open source alternative to Photoshop. It is a big program and will have a learning curve, but it is worth it.

These are other resources as well. Doing a Google search for "resize and optimize images" will turn up an onslaught of options.

Learning to work with images is important. Take the time to master it, as it will make your website load faster and be more attractive.

While you are at it, practice naming your images and document files in a way that search engines like. Search engine crawlers do not see the colors on your site, nor do they see the images on your site. Search engine crawlers see text and code. When it comes to image and document filenames, the search engines only see the filename and the alternative text (which we showed you how to change when adding an image in "Hands-On Exercise: Adding an Image to an Article" on page 131).

The image filename *IMG1234.jpg* is ineffective. If instead you renamed the file to *cute-black-labrador-swimming.jpg*, you will get better results from people searching for this type of image. You really don't know how people will find your site. This does take more time and effort. Yet it is important and since you are committed to your website, you will do the best you can, right?

Just remember, filenames have no spaces and are all lowercase.

Global Media Manager Options

There are several global settings for the Media Manager that can be accessed and set by clicking on Content→Media Manager, and then clicking the Options button in the top toolbar.

The most commonly used are:

Legal Extensions (File Types)
> When uploading files with the Media Manager, this field tells Joomla what extensions to allow. You can add new extensions as needed, but be sure to add both the lowercase and uppercase version of the extension separated by commas, and avoid spaces. Generally, you wouldn't allow users to upload scripts that might be accessed by a third party to execute code on your server (e.g., any executable files like *.php*, *.rb*, or *.asp*).

Maximum Size (in bytes)
> This is the largest file size users with upload permissions can upload. If you run into an issue where you can't upload a file smaller than the Maximum Size, look at the System Info under the System menu. It's possible that the `upload_max_file size` in PHP is set to a smaller number. To fix this, either edit PHP's *php.ini* file or contact your host.

Adding an Image Gallery

Images and how they are presented make a big difference in the look of a site. Images create an inviting environment and create personal connections with visitors. A picture is worth a thousand words, isn't it?

We will add two types of image galleries to Joomla Pet Center. One will be in a module position on the home page. The second will be embedded into an article.

To do this, we will use a third-party extension called sigplus (*http://bit.ly/sigplus-ext*). Sigplus has both a module and plugin available, and we will use both. Sigplus is a free download. You will need to pay to get developer support. If you like sigplus, a donation to the developer would be a good way to help ensure the possibility of future development.

The following is not a substitute for reading the developer's documentation (*http://bit.ly/sigplus-docs*). Always read documentation.

Hands-On Exercise: Installing sigplus

Installing sigplus is a breeze with the Install From Web feature of the Extension Manager.

1. Click on Extensions and then on Extension Manager.
2. Type **sigplus** into the filter and press Enter, or click the magnifying glass button.
3. Click the sigplus entry and then the green Purchase & Download button.
4. This will take you to JoomlaCode, where you can download the package for Joomla25+.
5. Back up your site.
6. Go back to the Extension Manager and click the Upload Package File tab.
7. Browse to find your download of sigplus and click the Upload & Install button.

This installs the module and plugin to the site. Now let's get some image galleries added to Joomla Pet Center.

Hands-On Exercise: Creating a Gallery in a Module

We are going to add an image gallery to the Joomla Pet Center home page in the drawer module position, as we planned in Chapter 2.

First we need to get our images ready as explained in "Resizing, Optimizing, and Naming Image Files" on page 139. Because they have been taken with a nice camera, the images are over 4,000 pixels wide and almost 4 MB in size. We do not need any image that huge on the website. All it will do is bog everything down. Prepare all images to be no more than 1,000 pixels wide and optimize to no more than 100 KB. For most images, anything larger is overkill.

With your images resized and optimized, let's get our home page gallery up.

1. Click on Content and then on Media Manager.
2. Add a new folder for your gallery images. We'll call ours *home-gallery*.

3. Upload your images to the new folder as described in "Hands-On Exercise: Uploading Media" on page 128.

Now that the images have been uploaded, we'll configure the module to display them.

1. Click on Extensions and again on Module Manager.
2. Click on the module Title that says "sigplus."
3. Change the Title to Dog Gallery or choose Hide the Title if desired.
4. Select the Drawer Module Position.
5. Set the Status to Published.
6. On the lefthand side, change the *images* path to the folder you just created for your gallery, *images/home-gallery*.
7. Change the number of Columns to the number of images you want set in the row. We have four images, so change the Columns to *4*.
8. Click on the Menu Assignment tab and set the Module Assignment to show only on the home page.
9. Click Save and then see how it looks from the frontend of your website.

If you like the gallery, click Save & Close. If you want to make more changes, make changes one at a time and save after each of them. This is a very flexible module. Have some fun with it. Our home page gallery looks like Figure 6-11.

Figure 6-11. Home page gallery with sigplus gallery module

Hands-On Exercise: Embedding a Gallery in an Article

You can easily add galleries to an article using the sigplus image gallery plugin. Adding an image gallery to an article is a great way to add some flavor and variety to a lot of text without taking up a lot of space.

1. Click on Extensions and then on Plugin Manager.

2. Locate the "Content - Image gallery - sigplus" plugin.

3. Enable it by clicking the red X.

4. Create a new article or open an article in which you wish to embed a gallery.

5. In the location in the article where you would like your gallery to appear, type *{gallery}home-gallery{/gallery}*. (Remember to change home-gallery to the name of your folder.)

6. Save your article and check it from the frontend.

The tag `{gallery}folder{/gallery}` defaults to looking for subfolders of */images*. If you want to pull images from a folder that is further down the tree, perhaps in a folder inside a folder, you would add that to the tag. For example, if you wanted to pull the images in the */images/sampledata/parks* folder, you would have a tag that looks like `{gallery}sampledata/parks{/gallery}`. See Figure 6-12 for how this looks in our article and Figure 6-13 for the frontend view of the article.

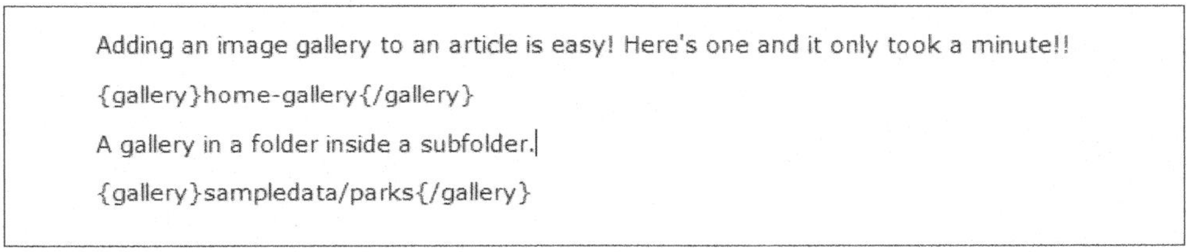

Adding an image gallery to an article is easy! Here's one and it only took a minute!!

{gallery}home-gallery{/gallery}

A gallery in a folder inside a subfolder.|

{gallery}sampledata/parks{/gallery}

Figure 6-12. Use the sigplus gallery to embed a gallery into an article

To change the parameters of how the galleries look, go back to the Plugin Manager and click on "Content - Image gallery - sigplus" and make changes similar to the parameters that are in the module.

The order of the images is determined by the filename. If you want to order them, name your images with perhaps a number in front to denote the order in which they will appear. Using a leading zero (01, 02, … 12, 13) will sort alphabetically, as will using 10010, 10020, 10030, giving you plenty of room to add pictures between each other if the need arises.

You can add captions to your gallery images as well. See the developer's documentation (*http://bit.ly/sigplus-docs*) for instructions.

Figure 6-13. How galleries in an article appear from the frontend

Other Gallery Resources

A favorite extension of Jenn's is JFBAlbum (*http://bit.ly/jfbalbum*). JFBAlbum pulls albums from Facebook in a beautiful gallery type of display. The extension is 20 bucks. The beauty of this extension is that Facebook houses your huge 4,000-pixel images and resizes them for you. The parameters of the extension display them on your Joomla site perfectly.

Another popular gallery is IgniteGallery (*http://www.ignitegallery.com*). This is a big component that is great for managing massive galleries. For many people, though, it is more than they need. Yet it's worth a mention if you need a lot of controls for multiple galleries.

If you want a slideshow, you may want to try YooTheme's Widgetkit (*http://www.yootheme.com/widgetkit*) or Slideshow CK (*http://bit.ly/slide-ck*).

CHAPTER 7

Making Your Website Speak Multiple Languages

The Internet is a global platform, and users will likely visit your website from places that you've never heard of before. Joomla has made it very easy to provide your site information to visitors in their own language.

We've set up our pet store, and while looking at our site analytics, we discovered that many people from the Czech Republic visit. To make our site friendlier to those users, we will translate the site content into Czech. Since Czech users are increasing and one person in particular, Karel, has been very helpful in providing suggestions, we have decided to ask him to help out in the site administration. He prefers Joomla to be in Czech instead of English, so we will customize the Joomla interface to support multiple languages.

Offering Your Site Content in Multiple Languages

Older versions of Joomla required a third-party extension to support sites with multiple languages (both frontend and backend). That's no longer necessary, because Joomla 3.x was built from the start with multilingual support in mind. Let's set up a few languages to see how it works.

Hands-On Exercise: Installing Multiple Languages When Joomla is Initially Installed

If, when installing Joomla 3.x and setting up a new website, you know you want to make your site available in multiple languages, you can choose to install additional languages and activate the required plugins during installation. (If your site is already live, jump to "Hands-On Exercise: Installing Additional Site Languages After Joomla is Installed" on page 147 for the usual process of setting up additional languages.)

Upon successful installation, you will see the option to install additional languages (Figure 7-1).

Figure 7-1. Joomla successfully installed

Click the "Extra steps: Install languages" button to start the process.

1. Choose the language packs you want to use and they will automatically be downloaded and installed. Click Next.

2. Click Yes to activate the multilingual feature. Then click Yes for Install Localized Content, which will automatically create a category for each language. This is a good way to keep your content organized by language in Joomla.

3. Click Yes to Enable the Language Code Plugin. This will give you unique URLs using a language code (en-GB) to improve your site's SEO.

4. Choose both a default language for the administrator backend and the site frontend or leave them as the default. Click Next. See Figure 7-2.

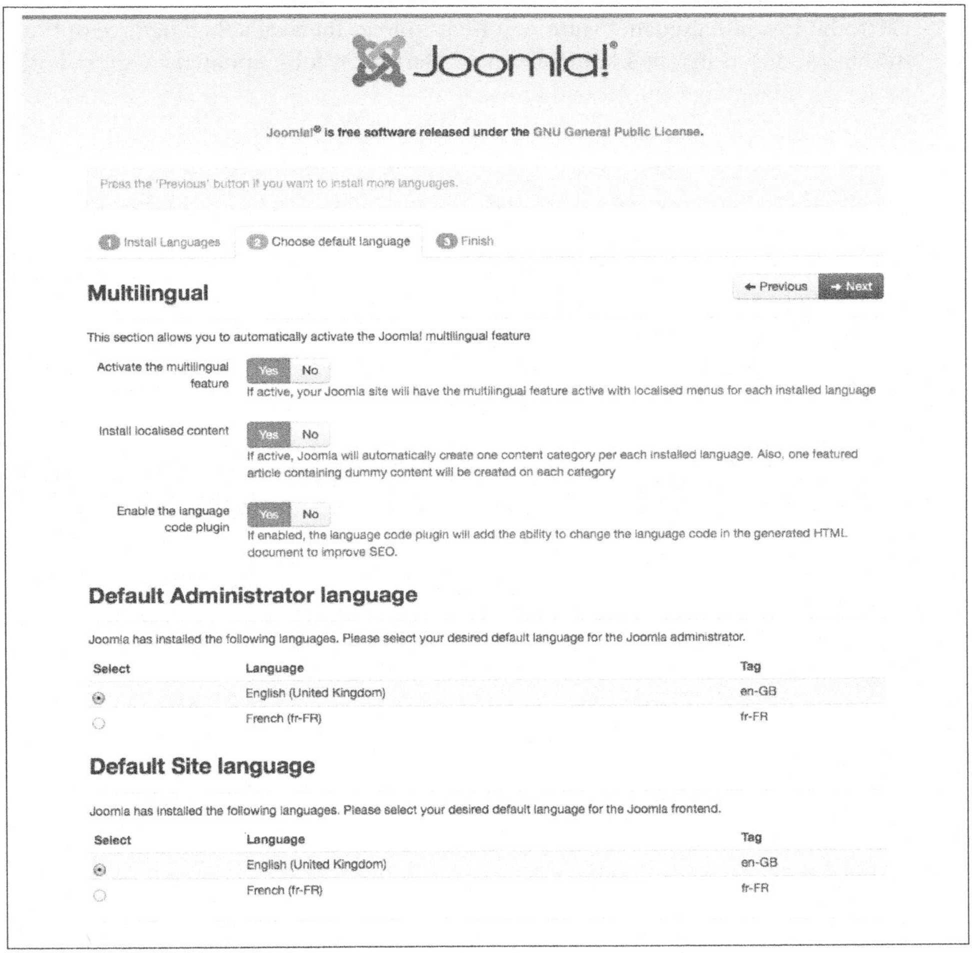

Figure 7-2. Activate all the options and set the preferred primary language

Your site is now set up to use multiple languages. See "Translating Your Content" on page 149 for an overview on how to best create and structure your content.

Hands-On Exercise: Installing Additional Site Languages After Joomla is Installed

If Joomla has already been installed and you want to add another language, the Joomla Extension Manager can autoinstall many accredited language translation packs.

1. Click the Install Languages submenu item to load the available language options. Be careful not to install a language that hasn't been fully updated. A short notice under each language will let you know:

   ```
   Language pack does not match this Joomla version. Some strings may
   be missing.
   ```

   Usually, the version number of the pack will match the Joomla version number, but not always, so it isn't a reliable indicator. If you don't see the language you want, click the Find Languages button to refresh the list (see Figure 7-3). It might already be installed or it might not be available. Check the language site (*http://bit.ly/joom lang*) for additional details on whether it's available (or if it isn't available, feel free to volunteer to contribute a translation). At this time, there are translations in almost 50 languages.

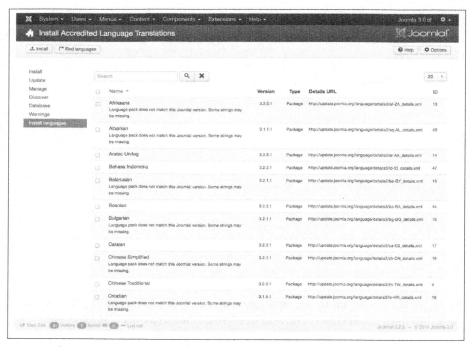

Figure 7-3. Choose the language(s) to install

2. Check the language(s) you want to install and click the Install button, as seen in Figure 7-4. This will install the language for both the site and administrator.

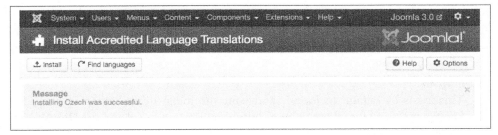

Figure 7-4. Successful installation of the Czech language pack

Uninstall a Language

To uninstall a language, go to the Extension Manager. Choose Manage from the left submenu and then choose Package from the Type drop-down menu (not Language) to locate the language pack to uninstall (see Figure 7-5). You can't uninstall the languages themselves; this can only be done by uninstalling the package.

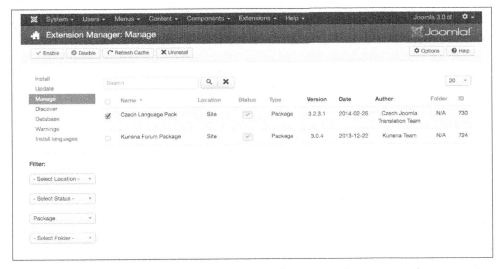

Figure 7-5. Choose Package from the filter drop-down to see language packages

Translating Your Content

If you'd like to offer your site content to users in other languages, we recommend it be translated by someone who is a native speaker of that language, because good translation is really an art. Each translation requires a separate article, so if we are translating our entire website in English to Czech, we will need a Czech article for every corresponding English article.

Since menu items handle URL routing in Joomla, we will need to create additional menu items that point to the translated articles. To keep track of our languages, we will organize and group them into separate menus as seen in Figure 7-6. In the Menu Manager, create the following menus:

Main Menu

> This exists by default in Joomla and your site menu items belong in here. The Language setting for all menu items here should be set to All and the Default Page option set to Yes.

Main Menu (English)

> If your website is in English, this may be a duplicate of the items in the Main Menu. The Language setting for all menu items here should be set to English (which can be changed all at once if you copy the menu items using the Batch option).

Main Menu (Czech)

> If all the content of your website has been translated into Czech, this may be a duplicate of the items in the Main Menu. The Language setting for all menu items here should be set to Czech (which can be changed all at once if you copy the menu items using the Batch option).

See "Copying Categories" on page 42 for how to use the Batch option.

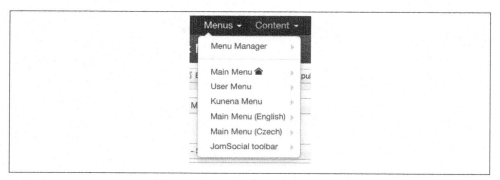

Figure 7-6. Create two new menus, one for each language supported

Depending on the size of your site and how much you want to customize your SEF URLs (see "SEF URL Settings and SEO Basics" on page 238), you might want to separate your articles into language categories as well. To do this, create your categories in the Category Manager as you normally would (see "Creating Categories" on page 38), create an extra category called English, and put all your content categories nested inside the English category. Do the same for the other languages, so all your top-level categories are language names and site content is structured underneath each. This can also help prevent URL conflicts. See Figure 7-7.

Figure 7-7. Create a default category and a separate one for each additional language

Users can switch between languages using the Language Switcher module that comes with Joomla. Enable this module in the Module Manager and make sure the language setting is set to All.

Activating the Language Filter system plugin enables automatic content switching. We could set the same language for all users, but we will let the plugin automatically set the language based on the user's browser settings as shown in Figure 7-8. In order to do this, Joomla needs to know the connection between the English and Czech menu items. In the Menu Item Options, go the the Associations tab and select the corresponding menu item. If you select it in one, it will automatically be set in the other. Improve your SEO by activating the Language Code plugin (don't forget to add the custom language codes in the settings).

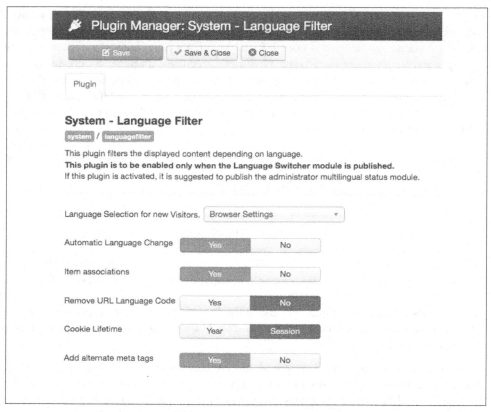

Figure 7-8. Configure the Language Filter plugin settings

Using the Joomla Administrator Interface in Another Language

Our Czech users are increasing, and one person in particular has been very helpful in providing suggestions. We have decided to ask Karel to help out in the site administration, and he prefers Joomla in Czech instead of English. If we have already installed the Czech language pack, there's no need to install anything else. See Figure 7-9.

Figure 7-9. We already installed the Czech language pack so we're ready to go

Hands-On Exercise: Setting the Language Options for Site Administrators

From the administrator backend, we will go to the User Manager under the User menu, and find the user for whom we want to change language settings. Click the user's name to open their settings and switch to the Basic Settings tab as shown in Figure 7-10.

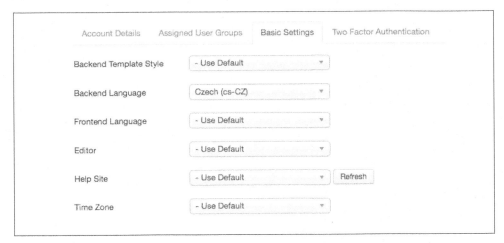

Figure 7-10. Change the user's language setting in their profile

Change the Backend Language to the preferred language. Karel speaks Czech. If the language doesn't appear here, it may not be installed, so verify that it's present in the Language Manager, and follow the steps in "Hands-On Exercise: Installing Additional Site Languages After Joomla is Installed" on page 147 if you need to install a new language. You can also change the Frontend Language for this user in these settings if your content is translated into those other language(s). Click Save & Close when you're done.

Karel should now see the administrator interface in Czech, while the default administrator will see it in the default language.

In the next chapter, we'll start creating our blog in English (which Karel writes in Czech).

CHAPTER 8

Starting a Blog

Blogs nowadays are used for much more than personal diaries. They're a way to communicate ideas, business news, and even critical information to the world. They are your own "personal newspaper" or corporate newsletter that dynamically updates and allows for a two-way conversation with your audience.

At its inception, Joomla didn't have many blog features—and is still missing quite a few —but it can be used effectively as a blog with a few customizations. In this chapter, we'll walk through how to use Joomla as a blog, as well as explore a few other installable blogging options.

Joomla Articles as a Blog

A blog is essentially a collection of articles displayed with the most recent article first. Because Joomla uses articles to organize content, this is easy to set up. In fact, you've probably done the steps already.

1. Create a category for your blog articles by going to Content→Category Manager and clicking the New button. We'll call ours Blog.

2. Add a description if you'd like to display a text introduction at the top of your blog. Otherwise, leave it blank. Leave the other settings at their defaults and click Save & Close.

All that's left to do is to create a new menu item pointing to the blog as described in "Category Blog Layout" on page 51 in Chapter 4. Make sure you edit the menu item and update the Article Order setting in the Blog Layout tab to Most Recent First, so your latest blog post will always be at the top of the page.

If your blog is in a different language than your site or it's in multiple languages, see "Translating Your Content" on page 149 for information on creating multiple categories for multilingual content.

Hands-On Exercise: Creating a New Blog Post

Now you're ready to create your first blog post. Create a new Joomla article in the Article Manager (see "Creating Articles" on page 43 for a review on creating articles) and select your Blog category.

To submit blog articles from the frontend of your site, you'll need to create a new menu item (called Submit an Article) and add it to a module visible on your website. Set the permissions of that menu item so only users who will be blogging will be able to see it (usually this goes in the User Menu, which is displayed in a Menu Module). Then all the user has to do is log in to the frontend and submit an article.

Using this setup with the default Joomla categories, you could have multiple users sharing the same blog or set up separate Joomla categories for individual users to have their own blog.

Hands-On Exercise: Scheduling an Article to Publish and Unpublish

A handy way to publish or unpublish an article is to auto-publish on a specific date and time. There are many situations where this could be useful (maybe you're going on vacation and you want an article to auto-publish while you're away). Alternately, you might want an article to expire on a certain date and *unpublish* automatically.

Start by going to the Article Manager and clicking the name of the article to edit it. In the second tab, Publishing, you'll see the options for the article (see Figure 8-1).

Adjust the following parameters to automate publishing:

Start Publishing
> This is the date and time the article will be automatically published. Clicking the calendar icon will display a calendar date picker, as shown in Figure 8-1. The default value for this field is the Created Date.

Finish Publishing
> This is the date and time the article will be automatically unpublished. Clicking the calendar icon will display a calendar date picker, as shown in Figure 8-1.

Figure 8-1. Schedule publishing and unpublishing in the Article Manager

Remember, these parameters are based on your web server's internal clock. Check with your web hosting provider to see if there's a time zone difference you need to account for when scheduling.

Also note that the time is in 24-hour format—HH:MM:SS.

The Finish Publishing parameter also recognizes the term Never for items with no end date. The default value for this field is Never, or 0000-00-00 00:00:00.

Click Save or Save & Close to save your changes.

Adding Comments, Tags, and Modules to Your Blog

By default, Joomla doesn't come with commenting capabilities, so we'll have to use a third-party solution. Fortunately, there are several very good options for comments.

Hands-On Exercise: Adding Comments Using Komento

Komento (*http://stackideas.com/komento*) is a free extension that adds commenting functionality to any article on your site. While the paid pro version offers a few themes and a number of other features, you might not need those to add simple comments. To use Komento, follow these steps:

1. Download and install the Komento extension in the Extension Manager. Open Komento under Components.

2. By default, Komento enables comments on all Joomla articles, but we only want comments on our blog posts. So open the Integrations section and click the Joomla Article button to adjust the settings.

3. In the Workflow section, change the Komento assignment to "On selected categories" and choose the Blog category we created (see Figure 8-2).

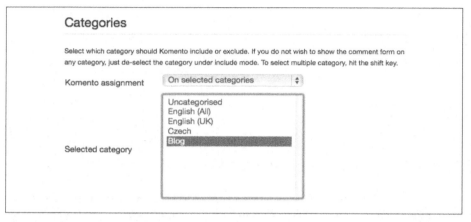

Figure 8-2. Select Komento categories

4. You can change layout options in the Layout section, but this is not required. However, you should set up the antispam options that are supported. Flood control, Akismet, and reCaptcha are all very helpful at preventing spam comments.

5. Click Save & Close when you are done.

Now switch to the articles on the frontend of your site to see the comment fields. Any new posts will also be visible under the new comment section.

 Make sure to enable Clear Captcha on page load in the Komento configuration settings. That will delete old captcha files on a regular basis.

Hands-On Exercise: Adding Comments Using the Kunena Forum

Yes, it might sound odd at first, but if you think about it, a discussion forum is really just a series of comments organized into categories and threads. And the Kunena (*http://www.kunena.org*) forum component has a special plugin that adds a comments feature to your blog posts and centralizes all that discussion on your forum. You don't need to actually use the forum if you don't want to (you can hide it from your site visitors), but adding a forum might be a great way to facilitate even more user interaction on your website (see "Creating a Discussion Forum with Kunena" on page 224 in Chapter 12 for details on how to set up and manage the Kunena forum).

1. After installing Kunena, download (*http://www.kunena.org/download/*) and install the Kunena Discuss plugin.

2. Comments on articles are "mapped" to specific forum categories. We have a blog category called Dogs, and we also have a forum category with the same name. So we'll go to the Category Manager and note the category IDs in both Joomla and Kunena.

 Note that you have to use an ID of a Kunena category, not a section. So if it says Section next to the ID in the Kunena Category Manager, it won't work.

3. Go to the Plugin Manager and open the Content - Kunena Discuss plugin (Figure 8-3).

Figure 8-3. Add the category mapping to the plugin settings

4. Enter the pairs of IDs (Joomla Category ID first, Kunena Category ID second) separated by a comma (e.g., **13,1**). If you want to map multiple categories, separate the pairs with a semicolon (e.g., **13,1;15,6;18,2**). See Figure 8-4.

Figure 8-4. Define default category for comments

5. If you don't have a forum category that corresponds to the content category in Joomla, you can create a general "catch-all" default forum category for all other comments. Enter the category ID from Kunena under Default Forum Category.

6. Enable the plugin and click Save & Close.

Now, site visitors will see a comment field at the bottom of each article in the Dogs category. When comments are added to articles in that category, a new topic will be created in the corresponding forum category. So users will see the same comment in both places, though it actually only exists in the forum.

Hands-On Exercise: Adding Joomla Tags to Your Blog

Tags are a great way to display related content on your website. In Joomla 3.1, content tags were introduced and they can be used to tag any content, contacts and any other core Joomla extension. Tags are quite robust, and they are almost Joomla articles themselves, supporting descriptions, images, and more. For our purposes, we will just use the basic tagging feature. So let's quickly create a few new tags:

1. Go to Components→Tags and click the New button.

2. Add a Title (e.g., **Dogs**) and click the Save & New button. Repeat this to create a few tags.

3. Click Save & Close when you've created your last tag.

Tags can also be created on the fly when creating a new article, so you don't have to create all of them now. Just type a new tag name into the Tags field and click Save & Close.

Now when you create new articles, you'll see the option to add tags. Click the box to see a drop-down menu or start typing in it to see tag matches. When users click on these tags, they will see all the articles related to the tag.

Tor Tags (*http://bit.ly/tortags*) will auto-add tags to your content and includes a tag cloud module. It is also compatible with a number of other Joomla components, like JEvents and K2, if you want to use tags with those extensions. There are paid upgrade options for more features, and Joomla 3.x compatibility.

Hands-On Exercise: Adding a Popular Tags Module

Since we're tagging our blog articles with keywords, let's give users a way to search for all the articles with a specific tag. So let's create a tags module in the Module Manager:

1. Go to Extensions→Module Manager and click the New button.

2. Choose the Popular Tags module by clicking on it.

3. Add a title for the module (Popular tags) and adjust the "Maximum tags" value to show the number of tags you want. You may want to change a few other things like "Display number of items" to Yes.

4. In the Cloud Layout tab, you can change the minimum and maximum font size, but we'll leave them at the default.

5. In the Position drop-down, choose the template position where the module should appear. The module will appear on all pages by default, but if you only want the module to appear on specific pages, switch to the Menu Assignment tab and choose the specific pages in the Module Assignment options.

6. Click Save & Close. Switch to the frontend of your site to see the module (Figure 8-5).

Figure 8-5. The Popular Tags module showing the most popular tags

This now displays a list of tags in order of popularity (the most items tagged with this keyword). Also, the Similar Tags module will display a list of articles with the same tag as the article currently viewed.

Hands-On Exercise: Adding a Latest Posts Module

Say we want to add a "latest news" module to the side column of our website. Joomla has made this easy with the Latest News module. To create the module:

1. Go to Extensions→Module Manager and click the New button (make sure the Site option is selected in the left column; otherwise, you'll be creating an Administrator module).

2. Select the Latest News module type from the list of available modules.

3. As shown in Figure 8-6, add a title for the module ("Latest Blog Posts"), select the blog category, and enter the number of posts to show in the module. We'll use five.

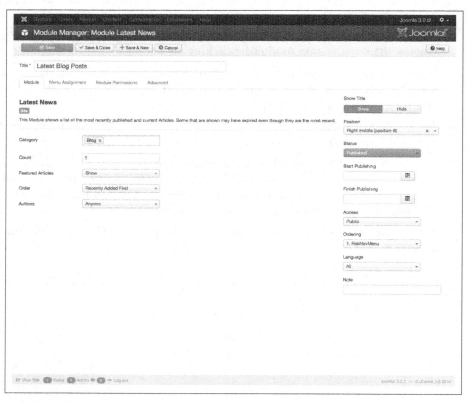

Figure 8-6. Creating a new Latest News Module

4. In the Position drop-down, choose the template position where the module should appear. The module will appear on all pages by default, but if you only want the module to appear on specific pages, switch to the Menu Assignment tab and choose the specific pages in the Module Assignment options.

---

5. Click Save & Close.

6. Switch to the frontend of your website to see the new module showing the latest posts, as seen in Figure 8-7.

Figure 8-7. See the latest articles in a module

CHAPTER 9

Create and Share an Event Calendar

Helen travels to dog shows and other pet events year round. She needs a way to keep track of those events and let her site visitors know about them. The best way to do this is to add an events calendar to the site. We will use a third-party extension called JEvents for this purpose.

JEvents (*http://www.jevents.net/*) is a free extension. The documentation and support are a bit lacking unless you purchase a membership. That being said, JEvents is straightforward to install and to use for simple implementations of an events calendar.

Hands-On Exercise: Installing and Configuring JEvents

1. Back up your site.
2. You can install JEvents through the Install from Web tab in the Extension Manager just as you did with Akeeba Backup (see "Mastering Backups" on page 56).
3. After installation is complete, navigate to Components and then JEvents.
4. Click on Configuration.
5. You will see three buttons for "Config options to show." Click on the Advanced button.
6. The left sidebar shows the different sections to be configured in JEvents. In the Component section, leave every entry at the default except for the following:

   - Change Show Headline to Menu entry
   - Change Show Copyright Footer to No
   - Change JEvents Project News to No
   - Change "Timezone for site" to our time zone

7. Click Save and then click on Permissions in the left sidebar.

8. Chose the groups and what they are allowed to do. For Joomla Pet Center, the default permissions are fine as is.

9. Click on Event Editing from the left sidebar. Read this section thoroughly and make whatever changes you'd like. We are leaving all at the defaults except for the following:

   • Change "Required fields" to include Description and Location
   • Change "Show time details before description?" to Yes

10. Click Save when complete, and then click on Event Detail View from the left sidebar. Again, here is what we are changing:

    • Change Display Creators to Name

11. Click Save and then click on Main Monthly Calendar.

 Some complain that their event titles get cut off in calendar view. This is the section of the configuration that you can change by increasing the "Title length" and Max Events. As the tooltip says, changing these numbers to be very high could destroy the layout of your calendar. Just keep it in mind so it can be altered if need be.

12. We are going to leave everything at the defaults in Year/Category View and iCal Import/Export.

13. In the RSS section, we will brand it for Joomla Pet Center instead of JEvents for the RSS Title and RSS Description.

14. We are going to leave the SEF/Performance Options at their default settings.

15. Both Calendar and Latest Events are specifically geared toward modules for JEvents. We will leave both as is at this time.

16. Click Save & Close to return to the JEvents Control Panel.

Hands-On Exercise: Creating a Calendar

In JEvents, you can have a virtually unlimited number of calendars. We're going to create a single calendar for the entire site, but each user could have their own private calendar. To create a new calendar:

1. From the JEvents Control Panel, click Manage Calendars.

2. We are going to use the default calendar. To create an additional calendar, click New and enter the new calendar information.

3. Change Unique Identifier to a different name if you wish.

4. Change any of the other settings you want. We're leaving it all at the defaults.

5. Click Save & Close.

That's it! Now let's add some categories.

Hands-On Exercise: Creating Event Categories

Separating events into categories makes it easier for visitors to sort through events they want to see. Since this calendar is mainly for Helen's dog shows, we want a category for Dog Shows. We will add additional categories for Cat Shows and Bird Shows.

1. From the JEvents dashboard, click Manage Categories.

2. We will first use the Default category and change it to Dog Shows.

3. Change the name of the category.

4. Enter a description of the category if desired.

5. Click on the Options tab and select a color for the category and add an image if desired.

6. Select a user that administers the category if desired.

7. Click Save & Close or Save & New to create another category.

8. Choose a different color for each category so it is easier for visitors to distinguish between the categories.

Hands-On Exercise: Adding JEvents to the Menu

At this point, you may want to see what your configuration and categories for your first calendar looks like. To do this, you need to add it to a menu to be able to access it.

1. Click on Menus and then on Main Menu.

2. You already have a placeholder menu item for events, so you should click on that and change the menu item type. If you do not have a placeholder set, you will click New and continue with the instructions.

3. When you click the Select button to choose a menu item type, you will see an accordion item with the label jevents. Click on it to see the options for displaying your events via a menu item (Figure 9-1).

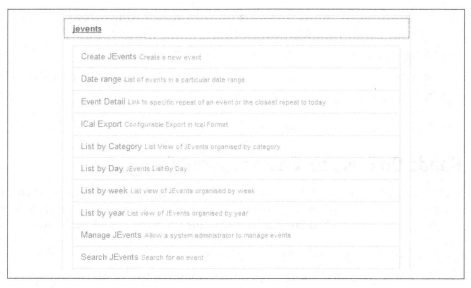

Figure 9-1. Options for JEvents menu item types

4. Choose a menu item type by clicking on it. We chose View by Month, which gives a month calendar view as seen in Figure 9-2.

5. You have many options for displaying your calendar. Try different types by selecting them and then clicking Save from the top toolbar.

6. Refresh from the frontend to see how it will look.

7. Repeat until you have a display style you are happy with, and then click Save & Close.

It may help to have some events in your calendar as you try out the various options.

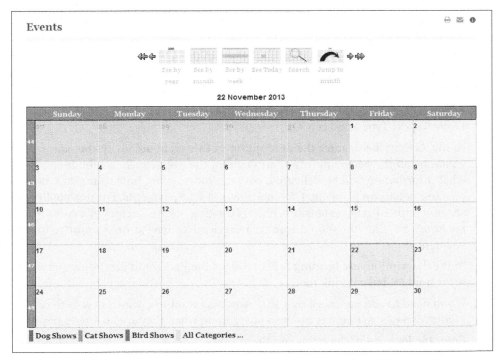

Figure 9-2. JEvents view in a month calendar

Hands-On Exercise: Adding Events to JEvents

New events can be created in a snap in a variety of ways. The two types of events are either one-time events or recurring events. We'll step through both types of event creation.

Create One-Time Events

1. From the JEvents dashboard, click Manage Events.
2. Click New from the top toolbar.
3. In the Subject field, enter the title of the event.
4. Change Event Creator to a different user if desired.
5. Select the category for the event from the Category drop-down.
6. Leave access level set to Public. For more information about access levels, see "Access Control Lists (ACLs)" on page 246.
7. Leave State set as Published.

8. Click the calendar icon to select the start date for your event. Then enter the time the event starts. Select the button to denote a.m. or p.m.

9. The end date should automatically set itself to the same as the start date, though you will want to confirm this and change it if necessary. Click the Calendar icon and select the end date. Enter the end time and select the button to denote a.m. and p.m.

10. Leave Repeat Type as no repeat.

11. In the Activity field, enter the description in this main area with the editor. This would be all the pertinent information about the event, such as who is speaking, what information will be delivered, contact information, how to register, how to pay, and details on payment. (JEvents does not take payments. For this you'll need another third-party extension like JTicketing (*http://techjoomla.com/jticket ing.html*), or else you should link to a service like PayPal or Eventbrite to take payments.)

12. In the description, use heading 2, 3, or 4 from the Paragraph drop-down as well as some bold to make it look nice.

13. If you need to add an image or a PDF, you may want to create a new folder in the Media Manager so that it is easier to purge them when they are no longer required.

14. Enter the location of the event and the address.

15. Enter the contact information for the event.

16. Any extra information can be entered here, such as a price if applicable (though I would also put it in the description).

17. Click Save (it might say Apply) at the top and check out how your event looks on the frontend.

18. Make any changes you want to after you check it out from the frontend.

19. If you're happy with it, then click Save & Close.

Our one-time event can be seen in Figure 9-3. We used heading 2 and heading 3 for the first four lines. We made the size of the text in the fifth line 12 points. We used some built-in typography found in the Afterburner2 template for the buttons.

Figure 9-3. One-time event using JEvents

Create Recurring Events

Organizations often have recurring events that happen, for example, or on the second Tuesday of the month. JEvents makes it very simple to add recurring events. Here's how to do it:

1. Enter the event exactly as if it is a one-time event except change "Repeat type" to the event's frequency (daily, weekly, monthly, or yearly).
2. JEvents will present additional options that only apply to recurring events. Adjust these options as you wish.

Here are some examples of common recurring events and how to create them:

Weekly recurring event on Saturdays from 10 a.m. to 2 p.m. (see Figure 9-4):

1. In the "Repeat type" field, select the Weekly radio button.
2. Leave Repeat Interval field set at 1 weeks.
3. Enter the number of repeat counts (how many times the event will recur) you would like to have. If it is unlimited, then leave it blank and the field will set itself to 999 when you save (or you can just type in 999 into the field yourself).

4. Click the Repeat Until radio button and click the arrow in the calendar next to the year until you find your chosen date.

5. In the By Day field, ensure that the correct day of the week is selected. For example, if your event is on Saturdays, make sure Saturday is what is selected in the By Day field.

6. Click Save & Close and check your results from the frontend.

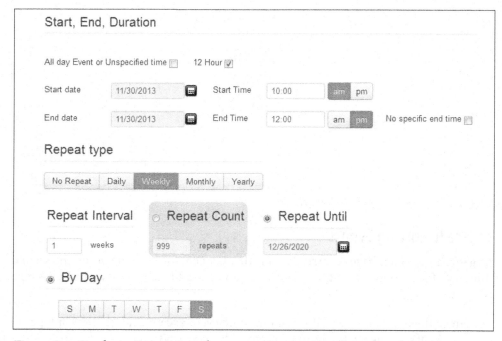

Figure 9-4. Configuration settings for a recurring event on Saturdays from 10 a.m. to 2 p.m.

You can see in the calendar view that we have our one-time event and four recurring events for April of 2014 in Figure 9-5. When you click on one of the recurring bird cage sale events, you can see the event detail view in Figure 9-6.

Figure 9-5. Calendar view of a one-time event and a recurring event

Figure 9-6. A recurring event in JEvents

Follow these steps to set up an event happening on the third Thursday of each month from 6 p.m. to 8 p.m. (see Figure 9-7):

1. In the "Repeat type" field, select the Monthly radio button.

2. Leave the Repeat Interval set at 1 months.

3. The Repeat Count field will set itself to 999 when you save, or you can just type it in.

4. Click the Repeat Until radio button and click the arrow in the calendar next to the year until it gets to 2020, or whenever you want the repeat to end. Then click the third Thursday of the month there.

5. Ignore By Month Day in this example.

6. Click the By Day radio button and make sure that the Thursday button is selected.

7. In the Which Week(s) field, uncheck the week 1, week 2, week 4, and week 5 buttons leaving ONLY week 3 checked.

8. You should not need to use the "Count back from month end" checkbox.

9. Click Save & Close and check your results from the frontend.

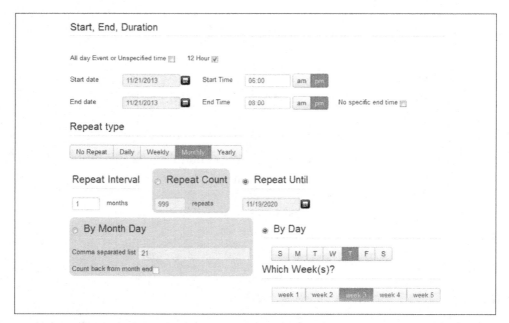

Figure 9-7. Configuration settings for recurring events every third Thursday of the month

Follow these steps to set up an event happening on the 17th of each month from 1 p.m. to 3 p.m. (see Figure 9-8):

1. Set "Repeat type" to Monthly.

2. Leave Repeat Interval at 1 months.

3. Repeat Count will set itself to 999 when you save, or you can just type it in.

4. Click the Repeat Until radio button and click the arrow in the calendar next to the year until it gets to 2020, or whenever you want the repeat to end. Then click the 17th of the month there.

5. In the By Month Day field, the date (number of the day) of the event should be listed in the field "Comma separated list." That is perfect. Just confirm that the number in the field is the date on which you want the recurring event to happen each month.

6. You should not need to use the "Count back from month end" checkbox.

7. Save and check your results from the frontend.

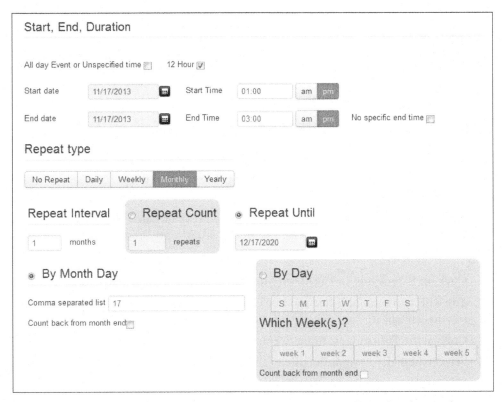

Figure 9-8. Configuration settings for recurring events on the 17th of each month

Adding Events from the Frontend by Visitors/Registered Users

Would you like your visitors or registered users to be able to add events from the frontend of your website? If so, JEvents makes this easy to do.

To add events from the frontend:

1. Log in to the site on the frontend.
2. Navigate to the event calendar.
3. At the bottom of the calendar, you will see a link called "Add an event." Click on it.
4. Create your event. Examples can be found in the previous three sections of this chapter.
5. If you need to edit an event, click on the orange pencil icon at the top of the right side and edit the event.

 You cannot edit the time and date for recurring events from the frontend. If you make a mistake and cannot resolve it from the edit screen, you will have to log in to the backend to resolve it. If you do not have access to the backend, you will need to contact whoever does to assist you.

Add a Module Showing Latest Events on Other Pages of the Site

We want to have a module that lists the latest events, so that people can easily see at a glance what is coming up.

The JEvents package includes such a module, called JEvents Latest Events. We will publish this module in the sidebar-a position, where we currently have a placeholder titled Other Module.

1. Click on Extensions and again on Module Manager.
2. You will see an unpublished module called JEvents Latest Events. Click on the title so you can edit it.
3. Change the Title to Upcoming Events.
4. Select whether you want the title to show or be hidden. We chose Show.
5. Select sidebar-a as the Module Position.
6. Change the Status to published.

---

7. In the Menu Assignment tab, select the pages you want the module to appear on.

There are a number of options for this module. We recommend you save it without changing any of the other settings. Then take a look at it and decide what you want to change. Only change one setting at a time, and then click Save to view your changes. This way you will know exactly how each setting affects the frontend. Click Save & Close when you are happy with your module. The module on Joomla Pet Center can be seen in Figure 9-9.

Figure 9-9. Latest events module

Having an attractive and effective events calendar can be a great addition to your site. As you can see, it's very simple to add events that your visitors can appreciate and participate in. Next, we'll create a contact form.

CHAPTER 10

Creating Forms

Forms are very common on websites. Contact forms are the most popular. Often there is a need for highly customized forms in order to get the information you need from visitors.

In this chapter, we will add a contact form and a donation form with fields to accept payments via PayPal. This will give you a brief idea of what is possible for your website.

Contact Form with Contact Enhanced

Contacts and contact forms are included with Joomla when it installs. The contact form isn't particularly flexible and doesn't always look very pretty. Thus, we are going to use a third-party extension for the Joomla Pet Center contact page/form.

Contact Enhanced (*http://idealextensions.com/ce/*) is one of many extensions available from Ideal Extensions. Contact Enhanced is a commercial extension and worth every penny for the increased flexibility and ability to customize your contact page by adding extra contact detail fields—and to customize your contact form by adding form fields. With Contact Enhanced, you can put a contact form into a module position, which is helpful on many sites where you may not want the form to take an entire page. The support for Contact Enhanced is fantastic.

 The following exercises are not a substitute for the developer's documentation (*http://idealextensions.com/ce/doc/*). It is recommended that you read the developer's documentation as well.

For Joomla Pet Center, we are going to keep the contact form pretty basic. We will add a field in the form to collect the specific topic that the visitor is contacting us about.

Hands-On Exercise: Installing Contact Enhanced

After purchasing and downloading Contact Enhanced, you will need to unzip the package and extract it so that you can access the installation package required for Joomla 3. Typically this is done by double-clicking on the zipped file and choosing Extract. Save the extracted folder. Inside will be packages for multiple versions of Joomla and a captcha plugin created by Ideal Extensions, called SecurImage.

1. Log in to the backend of Joomla.

2. Back up your site.

3. Click on Extensions and then on Extension Manager.

4. Click the Upload Package File tab.

5. Browse to the folder where your Contact Enhanced packages are located and select the desired zipped package for Joomla 3.x. It will look similar but not identical to *pkg_contactenhanced_3.x_regular_package.zip*.

6. Click the Upload & Install button.

That's it. Now Contact Enhanced is installed. In general, when working with third-party extensions we would configure the extension next. With Contact Enhanced, we find it easier to get the contact created first, see it, and then alter the configuration as needed.

Hands-On Exercise: Creating Beautiful Contact Pages with Forms

The first step in creating a contact page is to create a category for your contact. Any and all contacts must be in a category.

Creating Contact Categories

1. Click on Components and then on Contact Enhanced, and you will reach a very empty dashboard.

2. Note the menu on the left sidebar and the Options button at the right side of the top toolbar, as seen in Figure 10-1.

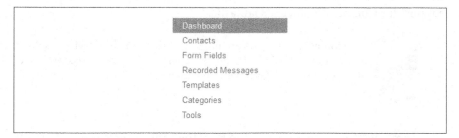

Figure 10-1. Contact Enhanced sidebar menu

3. Click on Categories on the left sidebar menu, as we need to create a category before we can create a contact.

4. Click the New button from the top toolbar.

5. Enter the title of your contact category. You are going to create a category called Contacts.

 If you have multiple contacts or types of contacts, you may want to create multiple categories. For example, perhaps you want to create a Board of Directors and an Associates category. If you have multiple locations represented on your site, perhaps you want to add a category for each location.

6. Enter a Description for your category if you wish.

7. Click Save & Close.

Create a Contact

When you click on the Contacts menu item on the left sidebar, there are two choices when creating a new contact:

1. Create a contact.

2. Import Contacts & Categories from Joomla Core Contacts.

   The second option is handy if you have tried to get the Joomla Core Contacts to work and found you just needed more functionality than it could provide. All your work and settings will import right into Contact Enhanced. Simply click the link if you would like to import from Joomla Core Contacts.

Create a New Contact

1. Click "Create a contact."

2. Enter the name of the contact.

3. Leave the Alias field blank, as Joomla will fill it in for you.

New Contact Tab

1. Enter information on the New Contact tab as needed and see how it looks for you. We like to have a lot of flexibility over display and like to use the Extra Contact Detail Fields for all our display information.

2. You must enter an email address in the Email field in order for the contact to save.

3. Verify that the correct category is selected from the drop-down.

Maps Tab

1. If you have entered an address in the New Contact tab, click the "Locate in map" button and it will automatically put your location in the Google map.

2. Enter the Latitude and Longitude if they are different from the address field.

3. You can drag and drop the marker to get the exact location and choose the zoom level.

Miscellaneous Info Tab

The Miscellaneous Info field can be utilized for any purpose. It does require a Language Override to override the title of the field. See "Language Overrides" on page 241 for how to add a Language Override to your site.

Sidebar Tab

Contact Enhanced gives you the ability to have a sidebar on your contact form without having to create an additional sidebar module position in your template. This is nice if you would like a column-like look on your contact page. The width and position of the sidebar can be set in the Contact Form tab. Enter the information you would like in your sidebar just as you would any article. The sidebar displays next to the form.

Extra Contact Detail Fields Tab

Extra Contact Detail Fields are very handy for adding information that doesn't fit into the default fields. These can be for anything. The labels can be changed via the Language Manager Overrides (see "Language Overrides" on page 241). Using an Extra Contact Detail Field for everything on your contact page above the form is a simple way to get things to display exactly how you want them to.

Display, Contact Form, and Template Tabs

All of these settings pull from the Options button, which we haven't addressed yet. If you have multiple forms, you will want to manage the settings accessed via the Options button before controlling the display for Contact Forms from their tabs. See "Hands-On Exercise: Configuring Contact Enhanced" on page 185 or refer to the developer's documentation.

Integrations Tab

Contact Enhanced offers integrations with other software. We will not be addressing this tab. However, it would be good for you to take a look, so that as your business grows, you know how you can further take advantage of your existing technology.

In Figure 10-2 we use the fields in the Edit Contact tab, including the Image field with a koala bear. We change the Setting field on the Icons tab in the Global Options to Text for this view. There is no extra field in use.

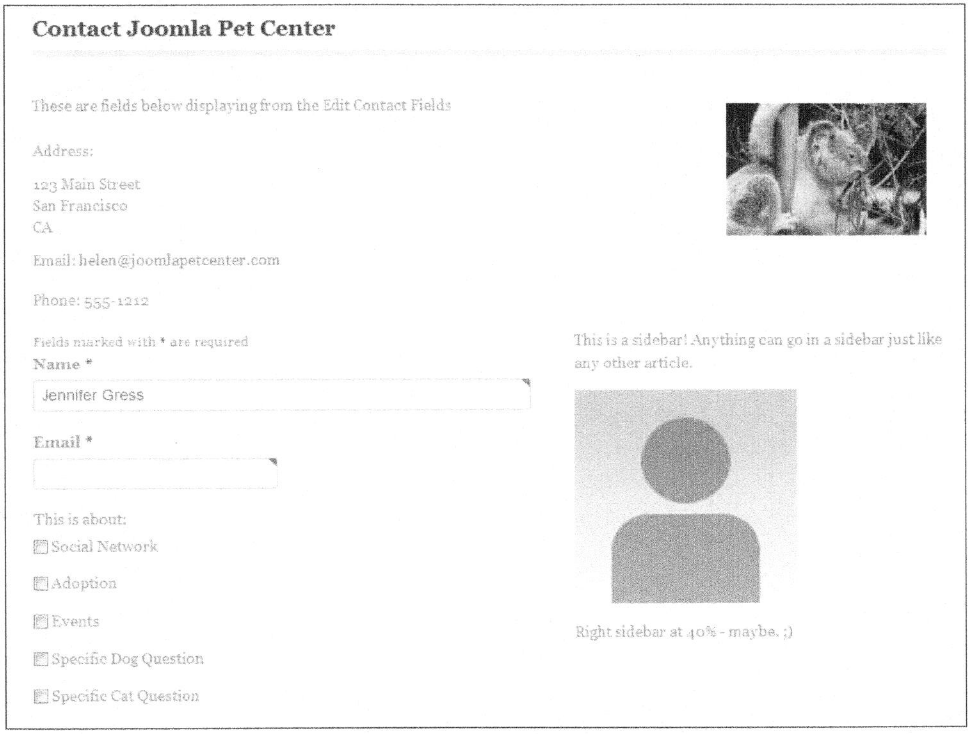

Contact Joomla Pet Center

These are fields below displaying from the Edit Contact Fields

Address:

123 Main Street
San Francisco
CA

Email: helen@joomlapetcenter.com

Phone: 555-1212

Fields marked with * are required
Name *

Jennifer Gress

Email *

This is about:
- Social Network
- Adoption
- Events
- Specific Dog Question
- Specific Cat Question

This is a sidebar! Anything can go in a sidebar just like any other article.

Right sidebar at 40% - maybe. ;)

Figure 10-2. Display of contact form when using fields for the contact

In Figure 10-3, we add all the contact data to one Extra Contact Detail Field. Everything above the form is in one Extra Contact Detail Field. We have not shown the email address required in the Edit Contact tab.

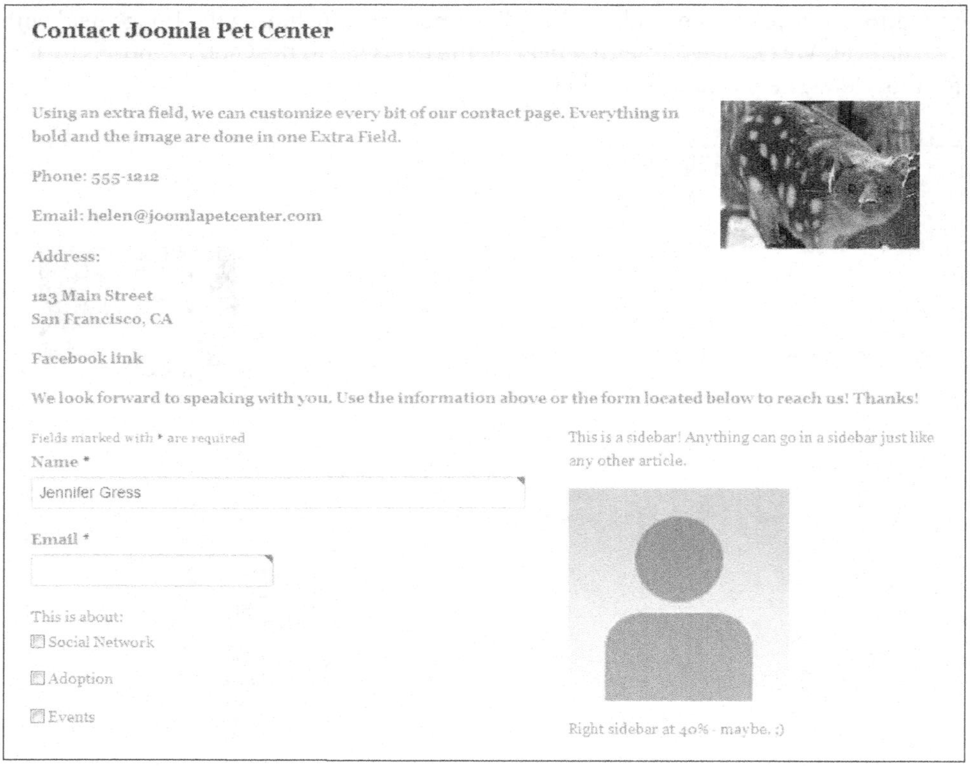

> **Contact Joomla Pet Center**
>
> Using an extra field, we can customize every bit of our contact page. Everything in bold and the image are done in one Extra Field.
>
> Phone: 555-1212
>
> Email: helen@joomlapetcenter.com
>
> Address:
>
> 123 Main Street
> San Francisco, CA
>
> Facebook link
>
> We look forward to speaking with you. Use the information above or the form located below to reach us! Thanks!
>
> Fields marked with * are required
>
> Name *
>
> Jennifer Gress
>
> Email *
>
> This is about:
>   Social Network
>   Adoption
>   Events
>
> This is a sidebar! Anything can go in a sidebar just like any other article.
>
> Right sidebar at 40% - maybe. :)

Figure 10-3. Display of contact form when using one Extra Contact Detail Field

Hands-On Exercise: Adding a Contact Form to the Menu

We need to add the contact form to the menu so we can see what we want to change.

1. Click on Menus and then on Main Menu.
2. Click the Contact menu item that was created as a Text Separator menu item type.
3. Click the Menu Item Type Select button.
4. Click the Contact Enhanced accordion heading and select the Single Contact Form menu item type.
5. Click the Select button next to the new Select Contact field and select the contact you wish to display.
6. Click Save & Close.
7. Review your Contact from the frontend.

How does yours look? What about ours? Not bad, but not super. Let's get it fixed up by addressing the configuration.

Hands-On Exercise: Configuring Contact Enhanced

Click on Components and then on Contact Enhanced. Click the Options button on the right side of the top toolbar. Here you see a ton of options for many parameters to display your forms. Here's what we will change from the defaults:

Single Contact Tab

1. Change Email to "Show email as a mailto link."

2. Set Country to Hide.

3. Set Extra Contact Detail Field 1 to "Show, but hide label."

Icons Tab

- Change the Settings to None. You can load custom icons to show instead of the default icons that load with Joomla.

List Tab

- Set the Extra Contact Detail Field 1 to Show.

Contact Form Tab

1. Set the Email Sender to Contact. This will enable you to reply directly to the visitor who submitted the form by clicking Reply in your email account.

2. The Redirect field allows you to add a page to which to redirect the visitor after submitting the form. Only use this field if the value will be the same for each of your contacts/forms. If you intend to have a different redirect page for each contact/form, then use the Redirect field within each of the individual contact's parameters.

Maps Tab

- Set Show Map to "After the form." You may want to put the map in the sidebar.

Now our form looks pretty good. We want to do a few more things, though.

Hands-On Exercise: Adding a Contact Form to an Article

If you would like to add the form to an article, you can do that using the plugin Content - Contact Enhanced Form. To make it even easier, do this:

1. Click on Extensions and then on Plugin Manager.

2. Look for the plugin Button - Contact Enhanced Form and make sure it is enabled.

3. Go to the article into which you want to add the form.

4. Put your cursor where you want to insert the form.

5. Click the button "Add CE form" below the description area.

6. Select the contact you desire, and it will insert the form into the article.

You can get very specific with this syntax on what you want to appear in the article using the tag. Check out the Content - Contact Enhanced Form plugin and click on the Description tab for all the details and options that are available in an article.

Hands-On Exercise: Add a Form Field to the Contact Form

We want to get more specifics from our visitors when they submit a contact form. In addition to the standard fields, we will add a field titled "This is about" and give them a series of checkboxes to select. We are choosing checkboxes instead of a drop-down because it's a little easier for visitors browsing from a mobile device to navigate.

1. From the Contact Enhanced dashboard, click on Form Fields from the left sidebar menu.

2. Click New.

3. Enter the name of the field.

4. Select the field type. We will select Checkbox.

5. Click the Save button from the top toolbar.

6. In the Value field, we will add the options we want people to be able to check. Ours will look like Social Network|Events|Specific Dog Question|Specific Cat Question|Specific Reptile Question|Other.

7. Add a Tooltip in the Tooltip tab.

8. Add any Attributes into the Attribute tab.

 Attributes can be any HTML attribute. For example, if you want to make the fields wider, you can add `style="width:90%"`. We have done this with the Names Form Field as an example on the Joomla Pet Center Contact form.

9. We'll set the General and Checkbox parameter tabs to how we want them to display. You can select the number of columns and the custom field's container width in these tabs.

10. Save the Form Field and view the form from the frontend.

We want this form field to appear before our subject line, so we'll go back to the Form Fields manager and drag the "This is about" field to above the subject field. The custom fields reorder exactly the same way we order articles, categories, and modules.

Depending on the template you are using, you may need to change the Width type in both the General Parameters tab and the Checkbox Parameters tab (or whatever type of custom field you are adding) from Bootstrap to Percentage.

In our case, because our template is blocking some bootstrap files, we also need to add some custom CSS to the custom fields so that our sidebar appears, as our template was blocking it. We did this using the following steps:

1. Add a new form field with the type CSS Code.

2. Save the form field.

3. Add this custom code:

```
.row-fluid{width:100%;zoom:1}
.row-fluid:before,.row-fluid:after{display:table;line-height:0;content:""}
.row-fluid:after{clear:both}
.row-fluid [class*=span]{display:block;float:left;width:100%;
min-height:30px;
margin-left:2.07446808511%;-webkit-box-sizing:border-box;
-moz-box-sizing:
border-box;box-sizing:border-box}
.row-fluid [class*=span]:first-child{margin-left:0}
.row-fluid .controls-row [class*=span] + [class*=span]
{margin-left:2.12765957447%}
.row-fluid .span12{width:99.9468085106%}
.row-fluid .span11{width:91.4361702128%}
.row-fluid .span10{width:82.9255319149%}
.row-fluid .span9{width:74.414893617%}
.row-fluid .span8{width:65.9042553191%}
.row-fluid .span7{width:57.3936170213%}
.row-fluid .span6{width:48.8829787234%}
.row-fluid .span5{width:40.3723404255%}
.row-fluid .span4{width:31.8617021277%}
.row-fluid .span3{width:23.3510638298%}
.row-fluid .span2{width:14.8404255319%}
.row-fluid .span1{width:6.32978723404%}
```

4. Leave the rest of the parameters at the defaults and click Save & Close.

5. Refresh and test it from the frontend.

You may add fields for very useful items like dates, free-text boxes, custom PHP and CSS, and integration with Constant Contact, MailChimp, and AcyMailing. Contact Encanced also integrates with SalesForce. See all custom field options and their descriptions on the Ideal Extensions website (*http://bit.ly/cust-f-opt*). This makes Contact Enhanced very flexible to use.

Hands-On Exercise: Adding Captcha to the Form

Joomla comes with Google's ReCaptcha integrated. Sadly, this doesn't always keep spammers out and can often be difficult for visitors to read.

The Contact Enhanced component comes with a different captcha plugin called Secur-Image. It's in the same package as Contact Enhanced, and we'll install it the same way through the Extension Manager.

Here are the steps:

1. Install SecurImage captcha through the Extension Manager.
2. Click on Components and again on Contact Enhanced.
3. Click on the Options button.
4. Click the Contact Form tab.
5. Change the Captcha Plugin to Captcha-SecurImage.
6. Click Save & Close.
7. Check it from the frontend of your form.

This is a highly configurable captcha plugin. To change its appearance, go to the Plugin Manager and click on Captcha - SecurImage. Here you can alter color, how many lines appear, if you want it to display a math problem, etc. Remember, change one thing at a time and check each change from the frontend. Because Joomla Pet Center gets a lot of traffic and we really don't want anyone emailing through our forms, we are going to make it very difficult to get through the captcha.

You can use SecurImage in other forms or other third-party extensions on your site by setting the captcha default in Global Configuration.

Testing Your Contact Form

Next, make sure you test your form by filling it in and submitting it. The submitter will receive a copy of the email if they select the box. The email address assigned in the contact will receive the form. You may add email addresses to receive the form results in the Contact Form tab. The email received looks like Figure 10-4, which is the Plain Text email. You can also configure Contact Enhanced to send HTML emails. On your email, the email address and IP address will appear. They have been removed from this screen capture.

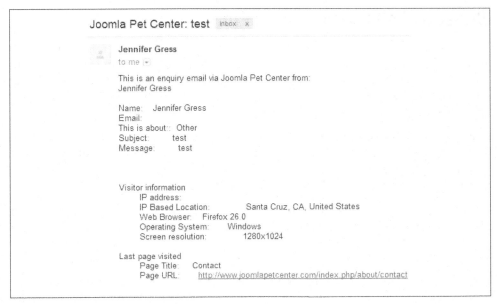

Figure 10-4. Email received when a visitor submits a form

You may view recorded messages in the backend of Joomla in the Contact Enhanced dashboard and reply to them from there if desired.

It is easy to make very customized contact forms using Contact Enhanced. Jenn often uses them as regular forms. There are a few things that would require a different forms extension, so we'll go forward and investigate.

There is even more you can do with Contact Enhanced, including:

- Google Spreadsheet integration
- QR code integration
- SalesForce integration
- Send a copy of an email to a specific user group
- Display menu items in many styles
- Frontend editing of contact information forms
- Use with Joomla's multilingual features

Donation Form with RSForm Pro

There are times that you may need to use a third-party extension for other types of forms. Thus, we are briefly going to share RSFormPro (*http://bit.ly/rsformpro*) by RSJoomla. RSForm Pro is also a paid extension that costs about the same as Contact Enhanced. There are some "free" form extensions out there, but many of them require the presence of "link-backs" to the developer site, and Jenn just doesn't like that.

There are many aspects to RSForm Pro, as it is highly customizable. In this chapter, we will tell you what aspects of the configuration you should address. We will not give you step-by-step instructions for each aspect. RSForm Pro has very good documentation (*http://bit.ly/rsform-docs*) and support. Read the documentation.

RSForm Pro has an incredible features list, including PHP manipulation, accepting PayPal payments, SalesForce integration, vTiger integration, and much more. Check out RSForm Pro Features and Benefits (*http://bit.ly/rsform-feat*) to see more that can be done with RSForm Pro.

Joomla Pet Center doesn't really need another form, so we're going to do a very short form with a PayPal button, since that is a common need for sites. We will pretend that Joomla Pet Center accepts donations and create a form for that. We'll get right into it.

Installing RSForm

Before purchasing RSForm, you will want to download and install the RSTester to make sure that your server is compatible with its extensions. If it all checks out fine, purchase the extension. After purchasing RSForm Pro, download the proper version and install it via the Extension Manager after making a backup.

Configuring RSForm

1. Click on Extensions and then on RSForm Pro to get to the dashboard.
2. Click on Configuration on the left sidebar menu.
3. Click on the Update tab and enter your license code in the field, so you can get extension updates.
4. Click Save & Close.

Installing Plugins and Modules for RSForm Pro

Unlike Contact Enhanced, each plugin for RSForm needs to be individually installed.

1. Right-click on Plugins from the RSForm dashboard and choose "Open in a new tab"—or it will take over your backend and take you to the RSJoomla website.

2. Download any of the modules and plugins you will require.

3. Install applicable modules and plugins via the Extension Manager just like you did with the extension.

4. Go to RSForm Configuration and click on the PayPal tab.

5. Fill in the PayPal tab with the appropriate information. Ours looks like Figure 10-5. Leave the Tax Type field blank for no tax.

6. Click Save & Close.

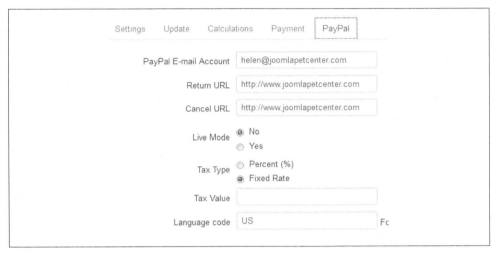

Figure 10-5. PayPal configuration for RSForm Pro

Creating a Donation Form with PayPal Payment Integration

There are two example forms that install with RSForm Pro. Definitely check them out, as each field can be copied to another form. We suggest you keep these two example forms as they are for reference—just unpublish them so that they aren't accessible from the frontend.

Now we'll create the form with a PayPal payment field. The basic steps are:

1. Make sure you read the documentation for the PayPal plugin (*http://bit.ly/paypal-docs*).

2. Make sure you have downloaded and installed the PayPal plugin from RSJoomla.

3. Make sure the plugins are enabled in the Plugin Manager.

4. Create a new form from Manage Forms and use the wizard to set up your new form.

We chose the simple contact form during our wizard. Now we will fine-tune it.

We want to keep the Name, Email, and Send fields. We will delete the Subject and Message fields by clicking the red Delete icon next to each of those fields. We will add fields for Header, Address, Phone, Captcha, and PayPal, which is a series of fields. See Figure 10-6 to view the fields added from the backend. See RSForm Pro documentation on setting up the PayPal fields (*http://bit.ly/paypal-fields*).

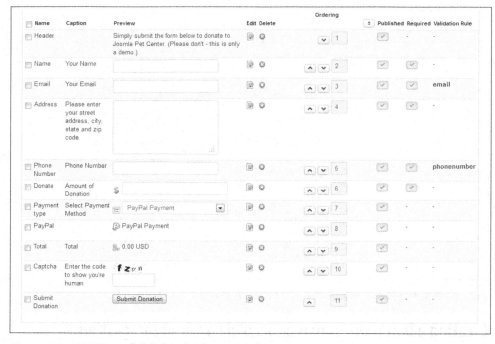

Figure 10-6. RSForm fields for the donation form

Next you will need to address the properties of the form so that the emails that go to the visitor and the administrator of the form give the desired information.

1. From the form edit mode, click the Properties tab.
2. Click the User Emails menu item on the left sidebar to edit the email sent to the visitor/user.
3. Click the button Toggle Quick Add on the top right.
4. Click Edit the Email Text, which will open the email text in a new window.
5. Copy the desired caption and value tags from the Quick Add options on the right and paste them into your Email Text window.

6. Format them how you want them to look. Make sure you test the form and make sure it isn't too small and is legible. On the backend, ours looks like Figure 10-7.

```
Thank you for your donation. We appreciate your contribution!
{Name:caption}: {Name:value}
{Email:caption}: {Email:value}
{Address:caption}: {Address:value}
{Phone Number:caption}: {Phone Number:value}
{Donate:caption}: {Donate:value}
{Payment type:caption}: {Payment type:value}
{Total:caption}: {Total:value}
```

Figure 10-7. Values to be included in emails sent to the visitor and the admin

7. Copy the email text and paste it into the Admin Emails email text. Add or remove text and fields as desired. This way you don't have to format both of them which can be time-consuming.

8. Save both of these emails.

9. Save & Close the form itself.

A glance in the Properties tab shows that there are obviously many, many things you can do with these forms. Right now, we want to see our form and test it. We'll move on and add it to a menu item so we can check it out.

Adding a Form to the Menu

1. Click on Menus and then on Main Menu.

2. Click on the Forms menu item and click the Select button for Menu Item Type.

3. Click on RSForm Pro.

4. Change the menu item type to Form.

5. You will see a new field labeled Form appear under Menu Item Type.

6. Select your form from the drop-down.

7. Click Save.

8. Check the form from the frontend.

9. Test the form with your own email address and make sure the emails you altered look how you want them to.

Our form looks fine (Figure 10-8). It might be nice to add a PayPal icon to the form, which can be accomplished by adding an image field. We grabbed PayPal's source code from its approved logo page (*http://bit.ly/paypal-logo*) and entered the HTML in a free-text form field in RSForm Pro.

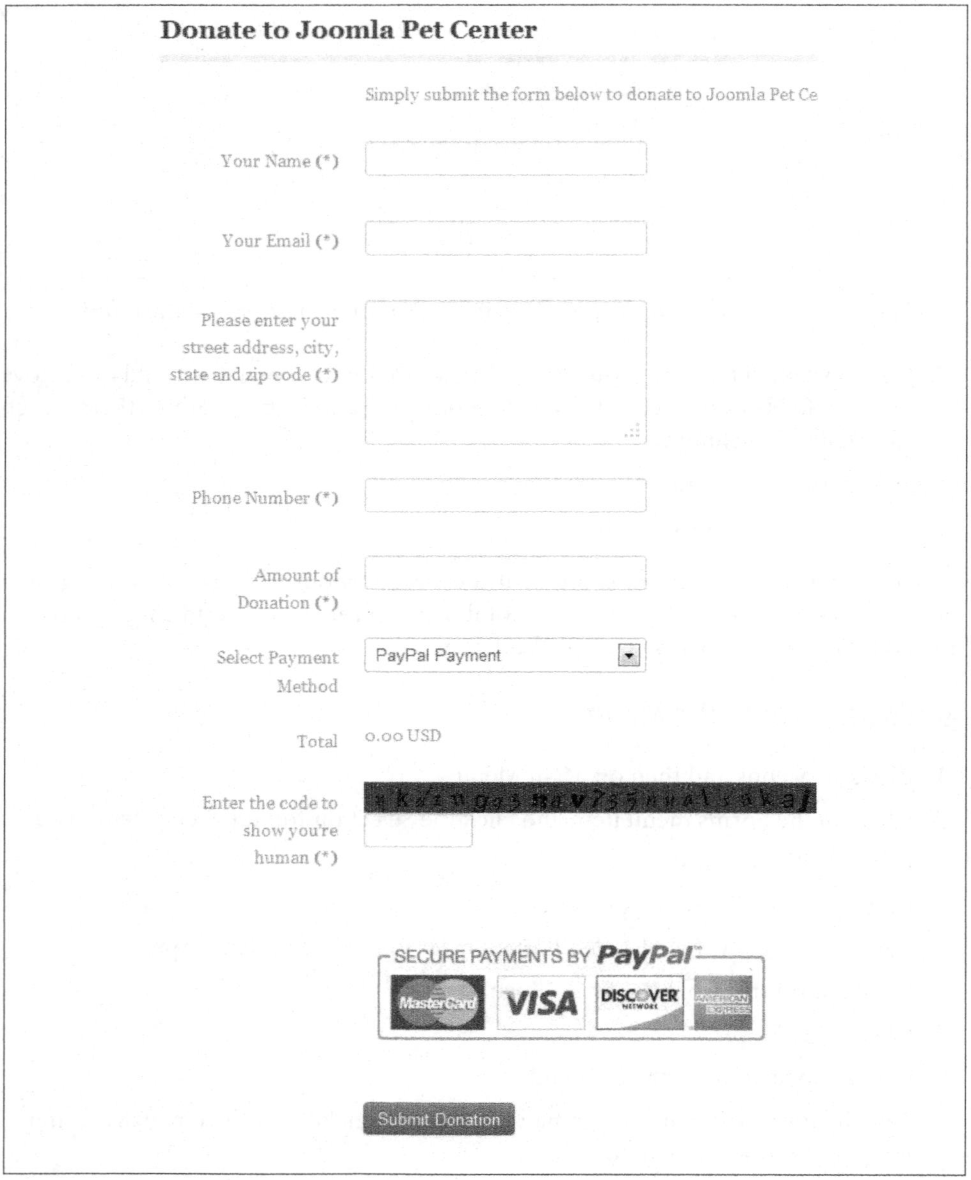

Figure 10-8. Donation form from the frontend

We'll leave it up to you to investigate the properties, fields, and other functionality of RSForm Pro beyond this brief example. RSForm Pro makes so much possible using forms on your Joomla website.

CHAPTER 11

Building an Online Store

An online store using Joomla is a great way to get your products out into the world and make money. Stores can offer physical products or virtual products available for download only. Payments can be taken via credit card with a payment gateway, or hosted solutions like PayPal or Google Checkout can be used. Benefits to using PayPal or Google Checkout are that you don't have to be concerned with store security, as you'll see later on in this chapter.

Stores are almost always more complex to configure than you realize going into it. While YouTube may have a video showing you how to set up a store in a few hours, it rarely is as simple as that. Planning is required to set up your store. Thinking ahead is also required. We do not yet know what will be necessary when going from Joomla 3 to Joomla 4. We might need to migrate third-party extensions. If you know you don't want to take on migrating your store in the future, you may want to think about utilizing a hosted shopping cart like Shopify, AmeriCommerce, or MagentoGo. When you choose a hosted solution, typically security issues such as those discussed in "Notes About Security, SSL, and PCI Compliance" on page 208 are taken care of for you.

If your website is selling products (or subscriptions), you will need to budget for expenses. Online stores like Amazon or eBay have IT staff/programmers employed to run, manage, and administer their online stores. Even "simple" products can require the ongoing expense of working with trusted programmers. If you decide to hire a freelancer or contract help, they may or may not follow the best practices or rules in the process of your online store project. This could create pain down the road around upgrades and/or security.

That being said, Joomla makes it much easier to build online stores at a lower cost by using existing third-party extensions that accomplish much that is necessary for the online store owner. Even if a third-party extension doesn't do exactly what you want out of the box, you can often find a reputable Joomla integrator to extend those third-party extensions. Yes, it may cost you, yet it is less than it would be to start from scratch.

We are going to show you the basics of setting up an online store for Joomla Pet Center using the third-party extension HikaShop (*http://www.hikashop.com/*). HikaShop has a free version called HikaShop Starter and two "paid" versions: Essential and Business. You can compare versions on the HikaShop website. The starter version of HikaShop requires that visitors register as users on the Joomla site in order to check out. If you don't want people to register in order to check out, you will want to go for one of the paid versions.

There are good reasons for using a paid version of a shopping cart for your store:

- Features
- Support
- Updates

In planning, you will need to consider several things for your online store. Here are some questions to ask yourself:

1. Will you offer physical products that need to be shipped?
2. How will shipping work? Cost? Flat fee? Based on weight? Are there complex shipping configurations?
3. How will tax work? Every country is different in how it handles taxes. You will need to check with your accountant or local government to determine how your tax configuration will need to be set up.
4. Will you offer virtual products?
5. How will you control the delivery of that virtual product to your customer?
6. Will you require visitors to register and log in to the system in order to make a purchase?
7. What types of payment options will you offer?
8. If you will accept credit cards without the aid of a service like PayPal, do you have a merchant account set up at your bank? Do you have a payment gateway like Authorize.net?
9. If you will accept PayPal or Google Checkout or something more common in your region, do you have that account set up properly?
10. Will you have images for your products?
11. What attributes will those products have (size, color, etc.)?
12. Are there custom options that you offer that might affect the flow or the extension you use?

The Joomla Pet Center store will be using the "free" starter version of HikaShop. We don't want people to buy any products. Nor do we want anyone to register or check out. As a result, if you were to take a look at Joomla Pet Center and attempt to check out, you won't be able to. This is on purpose. Joomla Pet Center will simply use PayPal as a payment option.

 The following hands-on exercises are not a substitute for thoroughly reading the developer's documentation (*http://bit.ly/hika-docs*), which is very good.

Hands-On Exercise: Installing HikaShop

With our planning done, we are now ready to install HikaShop on our Joomla website.

1. Download the applicable package for HikaShop from the website.

2. Back up your site.

3. Install the extension via Upload Package File in the Extension Manager.

4. You will automatically be taken to the HikaShop Installation Assistant, a delightful walkthrough of some of the main configuration options of HikaShop.

5. Shop Access determines how the frontend of HikaShop looks on your website. We are choosing the menu item for products.

6. For Products Layout, choose whether you want your products to display in a grid, list, or table. We are choosing a grid.

7. In the Location field, enter your country, state, and address.

8. For the Main Parameters, enter your main currency, tax name, and rate. We are choosing USD $ for the currency, Tax for the tax name (make it something that describes the tax so you know what it is), and 8.75 for the rate. We may need to change these later in System→Taxes→Manage Rates button. There you would create a new rate, unpublish the old rate, and edit your tax rule to choose the new rate.

9. Enter your PayPal email address in the "PayPal configuration" field.

10. Select the "Product type" you will be selling on your site. The options are "Virtual goods," "Shippable goods," or Both.

11. Click the "Save & go create your first product!" button.

This takes you to a new product screen. Close out of it. We aren't quite ready to add a product.

Hands-On Exercise: Configuring HikaShop

We need to make a few refinements to our configuration after the walkthrough we just completed.

1. Click on the HikaShop menus System and again on Configuration.

2. You'll want to confirm each of these settings with the configuration documentation from HikaShop (*http://bit.ly/config-docs*) and change whatever needs to be changed. We changed the Tax section by changing our "Main tax zone" to the United States of America, and the "Show taxed prices" to "Display both" and to "Apply discounts" before taxes.

3. Note that there are tabs across the top as seen in Figure 11-1. Check them all.

4. Click Save & Close when complete. It's good to know where these settings are, as you will probably need to revisit them as you set up your store.

Figure 11-1. Tabs of the HikaShop configuration

Hands-On Exercise: Setting Up Payments, Shipping, and Taxes

While many people want to jump right into creating their products, there are three very important aspects of your store: payments, shipping, and taxes. All three must be in place in order for your store to function and sell products. Let's start with Payments.

Payments

We are only going to use PayPal so our configuration is simple. Using PayPal Pro will keep the transaction on your site rather than taking visitors off to PayPal to complete their transaction. PayPal Pro needs to be a Business-type account from PayPal.

If you want to use more than one payment method, go for it. Many people offer an option of either using a credit card on the site or going off to PayPal. This may or may not increase your sales. Both PayPal and taking credit cards have fees associated with them through either PayPal, the bank, and/or the gateway. Know that a portion of your sales will go toward these services.

1. Click HikaShop's System and again on "Payment methods."

2. PayPal is already entered because we set it up in the walkthrough. Clicking on the title will allow you to set up even more configuration options for this payment type. Definitely do this, as you will want to verify your currency type at the very least. Again, checking the HikaShop Documentation for PayPal (*http://bit.ly/hika-paypal*) is key to your success.

 From any screen in the HikaShop extension, you can click the Help button and your help will show up in a handy split screen, making it simple to read and make changes at the same time.

3. Click Save & Close when complete.

To add a new payment option:

1. Create a new payment option by clicking the New button.

2. Select one of the plugin options and enter all your applicable data. Use the documentation from HikaShop by clicking the Help button from any screen.

3. Click Save & Close when complete.

Zones

Zones are utilized for both shipping and tax configuration. By clicking on System and then on Zones, you will see a huge list of zones. Within each country zone are subzones with their states. From the main Zones screen, you can get documentation by clicking the Help button.

If you want a zone with all of Europe, you can use a default zone called Europe, which already has all the European countries added to it.

You could do the same if you have the same shipping or tax rule for the Americas. Create a new zone called Americas and then add each of the countries to it.

Shipping

You will want to think about your shipping fees. For some, a flat fee based on the shipping or billing address may be fine. Others with awkward or complex shipping parameters will need to do more preparation and configuring. HikaShop has a number of plugins for shipping, which can be found through its documentation.

Joomla Pet Center will have two shipping options:

1. National $5.00
2. International $15.00

To get started, simply:

1. Click on System and again on "Shipping methods."
2. Click the New button.
3. Select the plugin you would like to use for your shipping method. We are choosing the Manual Shipping Plugin.
4. Make it Published.
5. Name it. We are naming ours National Shipping and International Shipping.
6. Enter the amount of the shipping in the Price field and select $ USD from the drop-down.
7. Edit other fields as desired.
8. Click the box next to Restrictions, which will open an additional set of fields for you to enter your rules.
9. Assign a Zone by clicking the Edit icon and selecting the appropriate zone, as shown in Figure 11-2.

Figure 11-2. Add a zone to a shipping method

10. Fill in any of the other fields you desire.
11. Click Save & Close.
12. Repeat for another shipping method.

If you are using the USPS, UPS, or FedEx shipping plugins, you must enter your account information so that HikaShop can pull the shipping calculations from those sources. You must also specify the weight and dimensions, so that the shipping entities can calculate the rates for the products.

HikaShop has pretty flexible shipping parameters. See what the owner/lead developer has to say:

If you want different shipping prices based on the location of the user, you can create several instances of the plugin with different "zone" restrictions and different prices. If you want different prices based on both the location and the weight of the products, you can create one instance of the plugin per combination of zone and weight range with the corresponding price in each. The system will then filter out the shipping methods that don't match on the checkout and only display the relevant(s) one(s).

Alternatively, you can also create one manual shipping method with the "shipping price per product" option turned on. Then, in each product, you'll be able to set the shipping price for the product and the system will sum the shipping prices of all the products in the cart for the shipping method.

On top of that, you can have combinations of all of these shipping method settings (some shop owners do have complex requirements) to be able to have almost any kind of shipping method selection on the checkout. I'm not even talking about HikaMarket Multivendor, which allows you to have different shipping methods for different vendors *and* have different shipping method selections for different vendors on the checkout (that's something that few multivendor systems allow for).

— Nicolas Claverie
HikaShop owner/lead developer

Tax

We need to charge sales tax in the state of California only. To set this up, we will:

1. Click on System and again on Taxes.
2. Click on the "Manage tax categories" button.
3. Click on New and add a new category. We will name ours California Sales Tax.
4. Click on System and again on Taxes.
5. Click on New and create a new tax rule.
6. Select your new product tax category from the drop-down.
7. Make sure your rate is selected.
8. Select "Cumulative tax" and the post code if required.
9. Click the edit icon to add the zone of California by filtering by state and entering California into the filter.
10. Click OK.
11. Select the customer type if desired.
12. Change Published to Yes.

Hands-On Exercise: Adding Categories, Products, and Attributes

We need to have categories for the products to go into. We're going to have just a few categories for Joomla Pet Center for dog, cat, and reptile accessories.

To add a new category, from the HikaShop dashboard/menu:

1. Click Products and then Categories.
2. Click the New button.
3. Enter the name of the category.
4. Click Save & New.
5. Repeat until you have added all your categories.
6. Click Save & Close.

To add a new product, from the HikaShop dashboard/menu:

1. Click Products and then Add a Product.
2. Enter the name of your product.
3. Add a product category by clicking the Add button in the Categories box.
4. Enter the product description in the field below the editor.
5. If you have related products, they can be added in the "Related products" box.
6. We will address Characteristics in the next section.
7. Enter the price in the Prices box and any minimum quantity you may want to add.
8. Add your images into the Images box.
9. Add files to the Files box if you have downloadable files as part of the product.
10. To the left of the Files box, select your Product tax category from the drop-down. For us, we select California Sales Tax.
11. Look at each of the additional fields and alter what is required.
12. Click Save & Close.

To add characteristics (also known as attributes or variants) to a product:

1. Click on Products and then on Characteristics.
2. Click the New button.
3. Enter the Name of the Characteristic, such as **Size**.
4. On the right in the Values box, click the Add button.

5. Enter the size itself, such as **Small**.

6. Click OK.

7. Repeat until you have added all the variants of your characteristic.

8. Order the characteristics how you want them to appear on your product page.

9. Click Save & Close or Save & New to create a new characteristic.

To add the characteristic to a product:

1. From inside the product, scroll down to the Characteristics box.

2. Click the Add button.

3. Select the characteristic you want associated with this product.

4. Click OK.

5. Repeat for as many characteristics that you want to add.

6. Click Save & Close.

If you would like to manage the variants of a characteristic by product, use the Manage Variants button to override the main product information for each variant (for example, having a different price per variant).

Process orders from the Orders drop-down and create discount codes from the Discounts drop-down. Don't forget about the Help button on every screen and visit HikaShop's site for more documentation and a support forum.

 If you would like to do A/B testing to see if one product image performs better than another, there is a great extension that can help you. Google Website Optimizer (*http://bit.ly/google-optim*) helps you put together A/B tests with Google to determine what gets your store the most sales.

Adding the Shop to the Menu

If you didn't get a menu item created during the initial walkthrough, simply go to your main menu and add one. Select from the options and check them all out.

When we installed HikaShop, an additional menu was created called "HikaShop default menus." If you would like that menu to appear, you'll need to create a module for it.

1. Click on Extensions and then on Module Manager.

2. Click on New.

3. Select Menu from the module types.

4. Enter a title and whether you want it to show or not.

5. Select a module position.

6. Choose Menu Assignment and select the option to only show on the Store menu item.

Now that we can see our store, we need to test all functions. We've added a product to our cart after selecting our characteristics. Enter a billing address. Make sure that based on that billing address (or shipping address if that is how your cart calculates shipping and tax), the correct shipping and tax appear. You can set up multiple billing and shipping addresses by clicking the New button from the checkout screen.

Indeed, when an Australia address is entered, the shipping method for International Shipping appears, as seen in Figure 11-3. No sales tax is added to the order, as shown in Figure 11-4. When a California address is entered, then the National Shipping option appears, as seen in Figure 11-5. Sales tax is added to the order, as seen in Figure 11-6.

Figure 11-3. Australian address charges the international shipping rate

Figure 11-4. No sales tax charged to addresses outside of California

Billing address

○ Ms Jennifer Gress
who cares
4067 brisbane Queensland
Australia
Telephone: 831-227-3522

◉ Ms Jennifer Gress
123 Main Street
95060 Santa Cruz California
United States of America
Telephone: 831-227-3522

NEW

Shipping method

National Shipping $5.00
◉

Figure 11-5. California address charges the national shipping rate

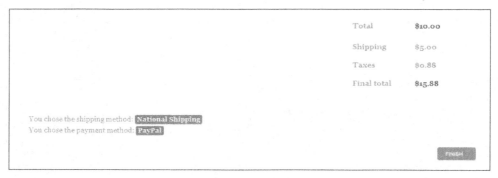

Total	$10.00
Shipping	$5.00
Taxes	$0.88
Final total	$15.88

You chose the shipping method: National Shipping
You chose the payment method: PayPal

FINISH

Figure 11-6. Sales tax is charged to California addresses

Adding HikaShop-Specific Modules

HikaShop installed with several modules. They are listed in the Module Manager and are unpublished.

We are going to publish a couple. We're going to publish the HikaShop Cart Module and the HikaShop Random Products modules to our sidebar.

Just go in and edit the settings and publish.

Notes About Security, SSL, and PCI Compliance

Keeping your online store and your customer's sensitive data safe is of utmost importance. It needs to be the first and most constant thing on your mind. Many thanks to Matt Simonsen (one of our technical reviewers; read about him in "About the Technical Reviewers" on page xix) for his assistance and expertise on this topic.

Make these tasks a priority in your security routine:

- Keep all scripts patched and up to date. That means Joomla and all third-party extensions.
- Use trusted third-party extensions. Tips on choosing third-party extensions are found in Appendix C.
- Use strong passwords and change, regularly. We know it's a pain, but it increases good security.
- Choose a reputable host with secure and encrypted protocols. This means using SSH or SFTP and not regular FTP.
- Use a third party to regularly scan and audit your site.
- Use security-based extensions like those discussed in Chapter 14.

- Consider adding `mod_security` (discussed in this chapter), or a cloud security solution like CloudFlare (*http://www.cloudflare.com*) in front of your hosting company.

- Keep minimal services exposed by firewalling all nonpublic services (talk to your host about this).

- Regularly review server logs.

- Larger companies have maximum security because of multiple networks with dedicated database server(s) and firewalls as well as separate applications on HTTP servers.

Below are several security terms, definitions, and tips for your online store and server environment:

SSL (Secure Sockets Layer)

SSL is a protocol for encrypting information over the Internet. The visible manifestation of this is the addition of the letter *S* in the URL of at least the checkout process pages of your website. You will see *https://www.yourdomain.com* instead of plain *http://*. This encrypts the data submitted by your visitor/shopper.

If you take credit cards on your site or are utilizing PayPal Pro, which keeps visitors on your site throughout the transaction process, you need to have an SSL certificate. You can get SSL certificates from your host or a third party.

 Unless you're also using encrypted protocols, using SSL can give you a false sense of security. Still, you need it in combination with other security measures.

ModSecurity

ModSecurity (*http://www.modsecurity.org/*) (`mod_security`) is an Apache module that helps keep your server secure. It is not typically something installed by the average user. Rather, it is utilized and managed by your host to help protect your server (and thus your site) from intrusions and vulnerabilities. You will want to contact your host and make sure they have the ability to use ModSecurity to help keep your customers, information private. Many hosts have the ability to use ModSecurity as well as other server-hardening techniques to help keep stores and their visitors secure. Ask about it.

`mod_security` can break many applications and/or may require carefully tuned rulesets to be effective. If you use `mod_security` and have trouble with extensions, disable it before discussing with vendor support for the affected third-party extension, as `mod_securi ty` could be the cause of your issues.

PCI Compliance

Payment Card Industry Data Security Standard (PCI DSS) is mostly used in the US and is gaining momentum worldwide. PCI Compliance is a set of requirements that are designed to ensure that all companies that process, store, or transmit credit card information maintain a secure environment. There are various merchant levels which each have unique requirements to satisfy PCI Compliance. Being that this is a gigantic subject, we encourage you to research and then make sure you are compliant and ready for self-assessment or PCI Scans. Both are set up through your merchant account. See PCI Compliance FAQs (*http://bit.ly/pci-faqs*) and its accompanying page PCI Myths (under the PCI 101 tab) for more information.

Very few shared hosting companies are PCI Compliant, and very few virtual private servers are PCI Compliant. It doesn't mean you won't pass a scan. It's just that normally, it's not the server that will be PCI Compliant.

Never keep credit card numbers. Make sure your online store doesn't either. Protect your visitor. Be paranoid about this. It is a healthy paranoia if you are accepting credit cards through your online store.

So that we don't end on a total downer note, many people create very successful online stores using Joomla and third-party extensions like HikaShop. Take your time, do the research, plan well, and you can have a great online store selling physical or virtual products to the world.

CHAPTER 12

Engaging and Keeping in Touch with Your Users

Everywhere you go on the Internet, you see ways to connect to social networks like Facebook, Twitter, Pinterest, and many others. These networks give users a common home to connect and share their ideas, photos, videos, and more. If your website is also a place where users with a shared interest come together to interact, you'll want to add some of these social sharing features. This makes your site more engaging and improves the "stickiness" factor—reasons for your users to keep coming back.

Getting Social with JomSocial

There are a few nice social extensions available for Joomla, but JomSocial (*http://www.jomsocial.com*) has done it better than the others. Originally developed by Azrul, it's now run by the folks at iJoomla.

Hands-On Exercise: Installing and Configuring JomSocial

Let's set up a social website for pet owners by first installing JomSocial. Go to Extension Manager→Install and choose the installation package. After JomSocial is installed, go to Components→JomSocial and click on Configuration to see the subsections as seen in Figure 12-1.

Adjust anything you think you might need, but here are a few things we'll customize for our site. First, we'll set up user profiles and custom profile fields, and configure a few basic settings.

1. Under Site, we will enable the ability to use multiple profiles, so we can have Dog Lovers, Cat Lovers, and Reptile Lovers. We will configure the specific options for each in a moment under the settings for Profile.

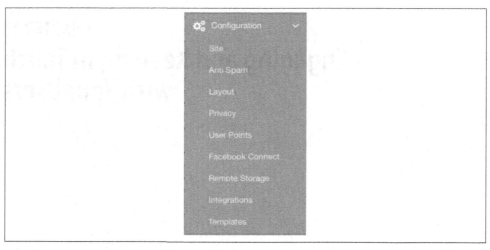

Figure 12-1. First adjust the JomSocial configuration

2. If you're not planning on using a separate ReCaptcha extension, you will want to enable the one here. Go to Google ReCaptcha (*http://www.google.com/recaptcha*) and register to get your public and private keys to add to the configuration.

3. To help prevent spam, we are going to sign up for Akismet (*http://akismet.com*) and enter the key provided in the Anti Spam section of the Configuration.

4. We like the default template, but the blueface template better suits our website, so we'll change that in the Templates section of the Configuration. Click on the name to adjust any specific parameters, like hiding Who's Online (see Figure 12-2).

Figure 12-2. See which users are online

Hands-On Exercise: Setting Up a Custom User Profile

Now that JomSocial is configured the way we want, we'll move on to setting up custom user profiles in the Profiles section:

1. Go to Multiple Profiles and click the New button.
2. Add **Dog Lovers** to the title field and the short description, **We are lovers of all types of dogs. Ruff!** (see Figure 12-3).

Figure 12-3. Adding multiple profiles in JomSocial

3. Don't forget to publish the profile, and we'd like to allow users with this profile to create events and groups, so we'll enable those before saving.

Now we want users to share more details about their dogs, so we give them the ability to add dog breeds and names to their profiles. Go to the Customize Profile section.

1. We want to create a new field group called My Dog by clicking the New Group button and leaving the default settings as is.
2. Next, create a new field for the dog breed by clicking the New Field button.

3. Enter **Breed** for the Name, and for the Field Code enter `FIELD_DOGBREED` (this could be anything, but it's best to be consistent with the naming scheme used by default; see Figure 12-4).

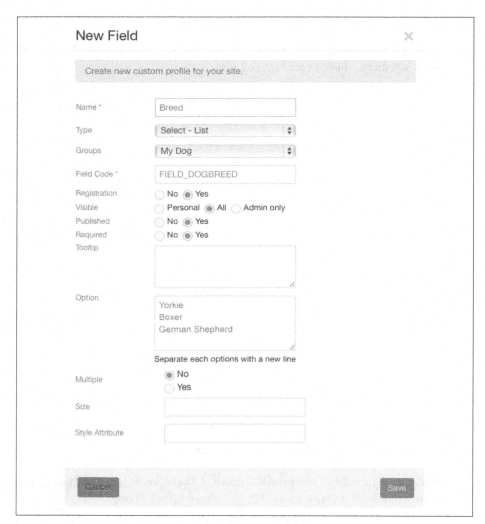

Figure 12-4. Add a new profile field for dog breed

4. For Type, we want to only provide a few specific breeds to pick from, so choose Select - List and enter three items in the Option box: `Yorkie`, `Boxer`, and `German Shepherd`. When a user registers or edits his profile, he will see a drop-down with these options in them. For Groups, choose the new My Dog field group we created in step one.

5. Click Save when done (see Figure 12-5).

Figure 12-5. Now you have a new field group and a custom field

6. Let's create one more custom field to enter the dog's name. This time we will choose Textbox as the type, so a user can enter in her preferred name without any constraints. Type **Dog's Name** for the Name field and **FIELD_DOGNAME** in the Field Code (see Figure 12-6). Click Save when done.

Figure 12-6. Create a custom field to enter a dog's name

7. You need to do one final step to make these custom fields available to users. Return to the Multiple Profiles sections and open the Dog Lovers' profile you created earlier. Open the Fields tab and activate the two new custom fields you created (Breed and Dog's Name).

Now we'll set up a few groups for our members to join.

Hands-On Exercise: Setting Up Groups in JomSocial

Groups enable people with common interests to share and discuss. We are going to set up a few groups, but first we need to set up our group categories, so you'll have to give some thought to how to structure the groups on your site. If you don't have enough interest groups to justify using categories, you can have just one category for all your groups. To set up group categories:

1. Go to Components→JomSocial and choose Group Categories from the left submenu.

2. Click the New button and enter a name and a description, as seen in Figure 12-7.

Figure 12-7. Creating a new group category in JomSocial

3. Click Save when you're done.

Repeat these steps for any other group categories. We'll create two, named Dogs and Cats. Then we'll create our individual groups for animal breeds (see Figure 12-8).

Figure 12-8. Create a new group in JomSocial

1. Click View Groups from the left submenu and click the New button.

2. Add a name and description for your group. We'll add Yorkshire Terriers and upload a cute avatar.

3. Select the group category we created earlier.

4. Make sure you publish the group.

5. Click Save & Close when you're done.

We recommend you enable photos, video, and events, so group members will be excited about returning to your site to share them.

You can also create groups from the site frontend (see Figure 12-9). Navigate to JomSocial, click Groups in the menu, and then click the Create link on the right side of the submenu and follow the same steps as you did to create a group on the backend.

Figure 12-9. Create a JomSocial group on the site frontend

We'll now create groups for other dog (Bulldog, Dalmatian, Labrador Retriever, Poodle) and cat (Persian, Burmilla, Siamese, and Manx) breeds. We recommend you add some seed content (like photos and videos) to get the group started, so it doesn't look empty. You may want to do this on a regular basis for groups that are just getting started, so your users can see the full features and benefits of joining and sharing. Users can now join your groups when visiting the Groups section of JomSocial on your website.

Hands-On Exercise: Creating Events in JomSocial

Events in JomSocial are organized into categories in the same way groups are, so we'll create two Event Categories: one for dog shows and one for cat shows.

1. Go to Components→JomSocial and choose Event Categories from the left submenu, as seen in Figure 12-10.

2. Click the New button and enter a name and a description. Our description is Dog Shows.

Figure 12-10. Create a new event cateogry in JomSocial

3. Click Save when you're done.

Let's create an event for the annual Westminster Dog Show. Events in the latest version of JomSocial can only be created on the frontend of your site, though you can manage existing events from the backend. To create an event, navigate to the JomSocial section of your website and do the following:

1. Click the Events menu and then click the small Create Event link underneath it, as seen in Figure 12-11.

Figure 12-11. Create events in JomSocial on the site frontend

2. Add a title and brief summary for the event. See Figure 12-12.

Figure 12-12. Create a new event in JomSocial

3. Select the Event Category "Dog Shows" that we created earlier.

4. Enter the event location. Make sure this is correct, because it will be linked to a Google Map on the event page once it goes live.

5. Enter the start and end time and date. Select the All Day option if there are no specific times.

6. For Number of Seats, enter the number of people that can sign up for the event. This will help limit attendance if the venue has a certain capacity.

7. Click Create Event when you're done. That's it.

After you save the event, you can customize the appearance of the event page by uploading a header/cover image.

Now, we'll create events for our other favorite dog shows, the Golden Gate Kennel Club and Cape Cod Kennel Club. You can save a little time in creating events if you already have them in your calendar and can export them as ICS files. A few calendar applications support this format—Apple iCal/Calendar, Google Calendar, Mozilla Thunderbird, and some versions of Microsoft Outlook. The Import button is right next to the Create Event button.

To keep in touch with everyone who has confirmed attendance, remind them the event is coming up, or ask them to RSVP, click the Options link on the event page to send out an email reminder to all participants (see Figure 12-13).

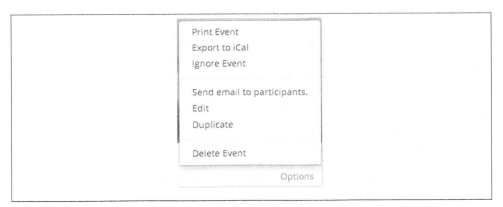

Print Event
Export to iCal
Ignore Event

Send email to participants.
Edit
Duplicate

Delete Event

Options

Figure 12-13. Configure event options in JomSocial

 Many extensions like JomSocial and Kunena have built integrations with each other. To take full advantage of those integrations, go to the extension settings and turn on integration. For Kunena, activate the Kunena - JomSocial Integration plugin in the Plugin Manager.

Here are some additional social feature options:

- Community Builder (*http://www.joomlapolis.com*)
- Easy Social (*http://stackideas.com/easysocial*)

Social Media Sharing

Promoting your site through social networks is a standard practice these days. This involves making your content as easy as possible for users to share. You could create a Joomla module from scratch to accomplish this, but the free service AddThis makes this really easy.

Hands-On Exercise: Adding an AddThis Module

AddThis (*https://www.addthis.com*) is a free service that adds sharing buttons to your website so users can share your content on sites such as Facebook and Twitter. You have three main options, and each has premade Joomla extensions that you can quickly install:

Smart Layers
> Sharing buttons "float" in a layer above your content in the margins. On the Get the Code page under Options, choose Joomla as the platform to download the module. Install this module in Joomla as you would any other, configure its options (adding your Facebook profile and other user profiles), and make sure to enable it once installed. See Figure 12-14.

Share Buttons
> Sharing buttons are located in a group, which can be customized and placed anywhere on your site. On the Share Buttons page under Options, choose Joomla as the platform to download the plugin and module. Install them in Joomla as you would any other module, making sure you enable them. See Figure 12-15.

Follow Buttons
> Follow buttons are directly linked to your social networking accounts, so users can follow you with a single click. On the Follow Buttons page under Options, choose Joomla as the platform to download the module and plugin, making sure to enable both once installed.

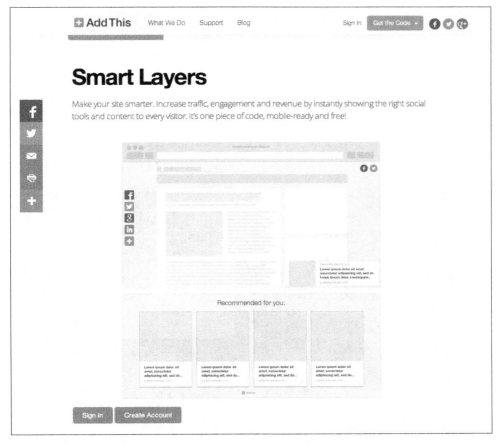

Figure 12-14. Download the Smart Layers module for Joomla

Figure 12-15. Easily add sharing buttons to your website

Creating a Discussion Forum with Kunena

Kunena (*http://www.kunena.org*) is much more than a discussion forum. It's a communication platform. The name comes from the Swahili word "to speak" (like "Joomla" comes from a Swahili and means "all together as one") and originally was a fork from another forum that fizzled out years ago. The Kunena team has done an amazing job of making the free forum extension a fast, robust, and highly integrated solution. Kunena supports multiple languages, and there are quite a few Kunena-specific extensions available from developers who wanted to extend the features in new ways. See Figure 12-16.

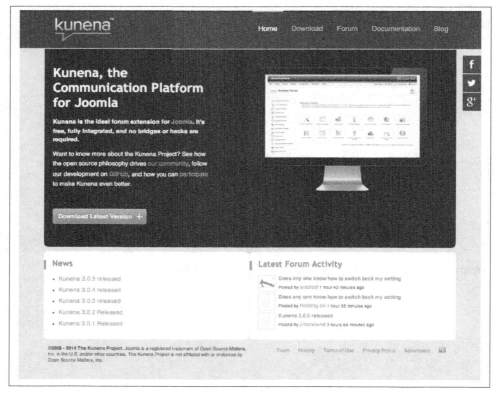

Figure 12-16. The Kunena main page

Let's create a simple forum for visitors of Joomla Pet Center to share their pet experiences.

Hands-On Exercise: Creating Forum Categories

Just like Joomla, Kunena uses categories to create a forum. We'll create three new forum categories for a few different types of pets—Dogs, Cats, and Reptiles.

1. Go to the Components Menu and choose Kunena Forum to go to the dashboard.

2. Go to the Category Manager, which is shown in Figure 12-17. You'll see three items (one section and two categories) there already. These are installed by default, and you can delete them later. You might want to keep them and just disable them, so you can use them as an example if you get stuck and your forum isn't working as expected.

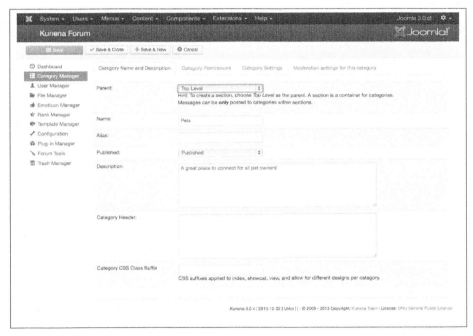

Figure 12-17. Create a new forum category in Kunena

3. Click the New Category button to create a section. Yes, this is a little confusing, but we need a section to "contain" the categories we'll create in a minute. We'll name this Pets and add a short description. Leave the alias blank (it will be auto-created on Save).

4. We will leave the options in the other tabs (Permissions, Settings, and Moderation) as the default. That means this section will be accessible by the general public, but only registered users will be able to post messages. Polls are disabled by default.

5. Don't forget to change the Published option to Published and click Save & Close when you're done.

Now we'll create the categories where users will post messages:

1. Click the New Category button to create a Dogs category and add a short description.
2. Select the parent section called Pets that we just created and select Published.
3. Leave the other options at the defaults, and click Save & Close when you're done.

We'll create two more for Cats and Reptiles. When you switch to the frontend of your site, it should look like Figure 12-18.

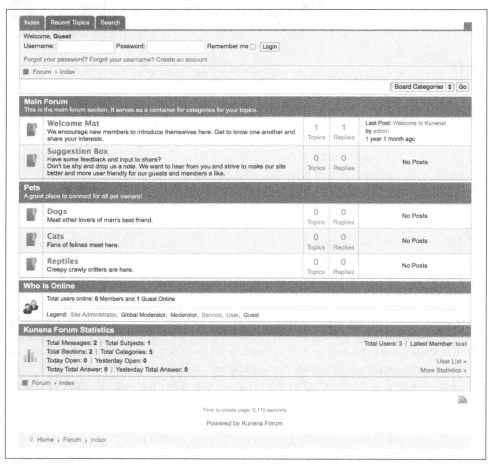

Figure 12-18. New forum categories for our Joomla Pet Center

Oops. We just discovered that reptile pet owners hate being lumped in together. Apparently, there's a rivalry between snake owners and turtle owners, so we'll create separate subcategories for them. Follow the same steps as above, except call one Snakes and another Turtles. Choose the Reptiles category as the parent for each, select Published, and click Save & Close when done. It will look like Figure 12-19.

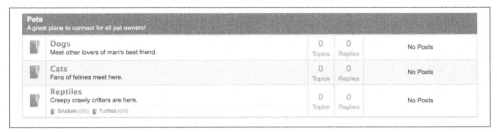

Figure 12-19. New forum subcategories for our Joomla Pet Center

You'll now have two new subcategories under the Reptiles category. If you want to prevent users from posting in the general Reptiles category now, you can lock it in the Kunena Category Manager. Click the icon in the Locked column next to Reptiles.

Now let's disable the default categories created when Kunena was installed. In the Kunena Category Manager, click the little green checkmarks to the left of each category name to disable them, as seen in Figure 12-20.

Figure 12-20. Disable a forum category

The disabled forum categories should now look like Figure 12-21.

Figure 12-21. Forum sections and categories are now disabled

If you switch to the frontend of your website, you'll see that the default categories are no longer visible. If you want special forum categories that are not visible in the main forum, but want to give users a special URL to see them, you can disable only the parent section and leave the categories under it published.

 Disabling the parent section is not a substitute for having a secure forum category and should only be used if there is not a security risk with the information being posted there. See the next section for how to set up permissions if you want to customize how users access your forum.

Hands-On Exercise: Creating Category Permissions and Moderating Users

Sometimes you need a private forum for team discussion. Helen has decided that she and her forum moderators need their own section, to discuss problem users and debate plans for the future of the forum. She has already created a new category under Pets called Pet Center Team Discussion, but she needs to make it private.

1. Go to Users→Groups→Add New Group to create a new group for the forum moderators.

2. We'll name this group Forum Team Members and make the group parent Registered. This essentially means users in this group will inherit the basic access rights of all users in the Registered group.

3. Click Save & Close.

4. In the Kunena Category Manager, click the Pet Center Team Discussion category name to edit it.

5. Switch to the Category Permissions tab to see the permissions options. The Access Control Types are which system Kunena uses to control access. The default option

is Access Level, and that uses the basic groups/levels Joomla has predefined. We want custom options, so we'll choose User Groups as the type.

 If you have JomSocial, Community Builder/GroupJive, or another supported third-party system installed, you will see it here as an option. Other extensions may have their own groups, and you can use the permissions built into them to manage what users can and can't see.

6. A few new selection boxes will appear, and you should see the Forum Team Members group in each of these boxes. Select the group in the boxes for Primary User Group, User Groups Allowed To Post, and User Groups Allowed To Reply (see Figure 12-22).

7. You can control access to child groups here, but we are only setting up our category and don't need to adjust anything. Click Save & Close when done.

Now any user in the Forum Team Members group will see this forum category. To add a user to this group, go to the User Manager to edit their profile and assign them to this group. We'll do this for each member of our team.

Preventing Spam in Your Forum

Unfortunately, forums are prime territory for spam, and even though no spam prevention tools are 100% effective, Kunena has a few good options in the configuration to help prevent it.

Go to the Security tab of the configuration and make the following changes:

Flood Protection
This helps block spambots that actually get into your forum and prevents them from posting many times quickly. Setting this at 120 means the user has to wait 2 minutes between posts. If that doesn't seem right for your forum, make an estimate based on how quickly you think your average user will be posting on the forum and set this value just under that limit.

Captcha Configuration
If you're not planning on using a separate ReCaptcha extension, you will want to enable the one here. Go to Google ReCaptcha (*http://www.google.com/recaptcha*) and register to get your public and private keys to add to the configuration. Set the Challenge option to Yes, and you might want to change the "User posts" setting from 0 to 2 so users with fewer than 2 posts will have to enter the captcha until they are trusted.

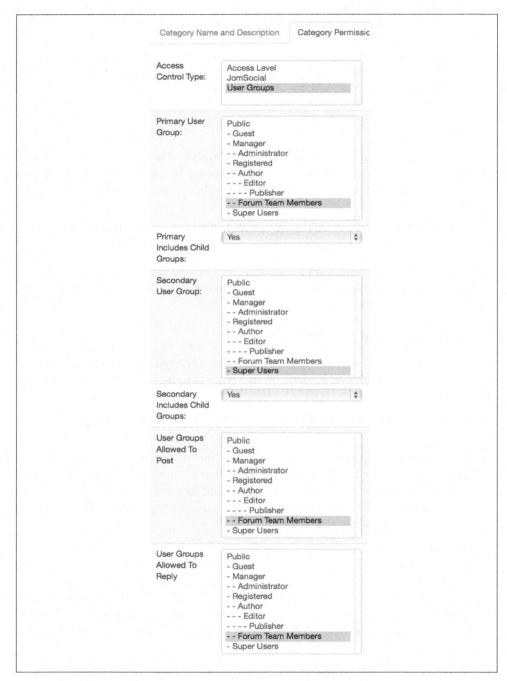

Figure 12-22. Change the forum category permissions

Stop Forum Spam is a great service dedicated to, well, stopping forum spam. Once you register, you can retrieve an API key from their website to add to the configuration.

If you do these few steps, you will eliminate most or all of the forum spam on your website.

By default, you should never make posting to your forum a public option. Registration helps filter out unwanted spammers.

Customizing the Look of Kunena

Kunena has two basic templates: Blue Eagle and Bootlicker. You can see them in the Kunena Template Manager. Clicking on each will display the color customization options, but the easiest way to get Kunena looking more like the rest of your site is to enable the Blend with Joomla Template option at the bottom. Do that first, and then customize the other colors (not the other way around). You might not need to change anything at all.

By default Kunena is the forum title, and it's displayed in a few places on our forum. To customize that for Joomla Pet Center, go to the configuration section of Kunena and select the General tab to enter your preferred name. This affects page titles, the statistics box header, notification sender name, and a few other places.

You can use the Kunena Discuss plugin as a commenting extension on your Joomla articles. See "Hands-On Exercise: Adding Comments Using the Kunena Forum" on page 159 for details on how to set up comments.

Getting the Word Out with a Newsletter

An email newsletter is a great way to reach out to users who may not have visited your site in a while. It's also a great way to alert your users to new site features, deliver news targeted to specific user interests, and see what kinds of topics visitors respond to. Acyba AcyMailing (*http://www.acyba.com/acymailing.html*) is a powerful newsletter component, and the basic version is free.

Hands-On Exercise: Setting Up and Creating a Mailing List

The first thing we have to do is configure a few options, so AcyMailing can send emails and set up a mailing list for users to subscribe to when they register.

1. In the Extension Manager, install the AcyMailing Starter extension.

2. Go to Components→AcyMailing to open the AcyMailing configuration. We will adjust the Sender Information to match our site settings, as seen in Figure 12-23.

Figure 12-23. Configure the reply address in AcyMailing

3. Switch to the Queue Process tab. You can leave the defaults here as is, but you should check with your web hosting provider to see what their email send limit is. Nearly all hosting providers have a limit on the number of emails you can send per hour. They may be able to increase that limit if you ask them.

4. Click Save & Close when you're done.

By default, AcyMailing has a mailing list called Newsletters set up and ready to use, but you can have multiple lists for multiple topics. We will create lists for Dog, Cat, and Fish topics:

1. Go to AcyMailing→Lists and click New.

2. Enter a List Name and Description as seen in Figure 12-24. Users will see these on your website and decide which newsletters(s) to sign up for, so make them sound interesting. Click Save & Close when you're done.

Figure 12-24. Create a new email list in AcyMailing

3. Repeat steps 1 and 2 for each new newsletter list. (See the result in Figure 12-25.)

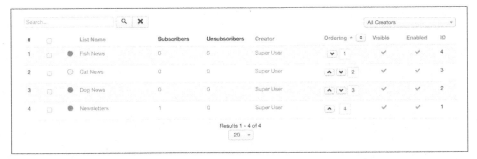

Figure 12-25. Our lists are now set up in AcyMailing

Now we're ready to send our first newsletter to people who have subscribed to the Dog News list.

Hands-On Exercise: Send Your First Newsletter

There are four templates included in the basic version of AcyMailing, and you can create your own by copying the code from one of those into a new template. For our purposes, we will use the existing Newspaper template to send out our first email to all the users currently subscribed to the Dog News list.

1. Go to Components→AcyMailing→Newsletters and click New (Figure 12-26).

Figure 12-26. Create a new newsletter in AcyMailing

2. Create your newsletter in the HTML Version field. This should be something newsworthy for your users. We'll let them know about an upcoming dog show by adding text and images.

3. Leave the Text Version field blank. It will be automatically generated from the HTML Version.

4. Select the list this newsletter will be sent to.

5. Changing the Published setting to Yes will make the newsletter available on your website. Click Preview/Send when you're ready to send or Save & Close if you want to come back to it later.

6. Preview your newsletter to make sure everything looks good. If not, click the Edit button to make any changes and return back to the preview by clicking Preview/

Send. If you're ready to send, you should send a test to yourself first (see Figure 12-27).

Figure 12-27. Send an email test in AcyMailing

7. Once you've confirmed that the email looks good, click the Send button. You will see a status modal with a confirmation of each recipient on the list.

Congratulations! You just sent your first email blast. Check the statistics in the Statistics section of the extension to see how your newsletters are performing based on number of views and clicks.

 AcyMailing uses a queue system to send out email newsletters in batches, in order to not go over your hosting provider's limit. You can adjust the batch sizes in the Queue Process tab of the configuration. Also, your hosting provider may prefer that you use a different sending protocol (e.g., SendMail instead of PHP Mail). Consult the support documentation for your host to make sure you're using the right configuration.

Hands-On Exercise: Letting Users Manage Their Subscriptions with the AcyMailing Module

The AcyMailing module was installed (but unpublished) when you installed AcyMailing. All you have to do is configure and activate it to give users the ability to manage their own subscriptions.

1. Rename the module title to `My Newsletter Subscriptions` or something users will easily understand.

2. For the Display the Lists option, select all or some of the lists you want to show. Make sure you unselect the options for "Automatically subscribe to" or your users won't be able to select specific lists on the frontend.

3. Adjust any other settings and click Save & Close when done.

Now switch to the frontend of your site to see the module (Figure 12-28).

Figure 12-28. The module style may be different depending on your template

Troubleshooting AcyMailing

The developers of AcyMailing have created a fantastic tool to test your newsletters (*http://www.mail-tester.com*) to see if you've been put on any blacklists, or if improvements can be made to your setup. Whether you use AcyMailing or an entirely different newsletter system, it's very helpful.

Additional Newsletter Options

- ccNewsletter (*http://bit.ly/joom-cc*)
- jNews (*http://bit.ly/jnews-ext*)
- Use MailChimp (*http://www.mailchimp.com*) or Constant Contact (*http://www.constantcontact.com*) and embed signup forms on your site.

CHAPTER 13

Solutions to Common Problems

We've compiled a collection of problems users commonly run into and some good solutions for each.

Database Fix Tool

The Database Fix tool checks that your database table structure is up to date with your Joomla website, and lets you attempt to fix any problems that are found. It is great to check this and run the fix after updating Joomla or third-party extensions.

Here's how to run it:

1. Click on Extensions and again on Extension Manager.

2. Click Database on the left sidebar.

3. You will see a screen similar to Figure 13-1 or one saying that things aren't OK.

4. Click the Fix button in the top toolbar.

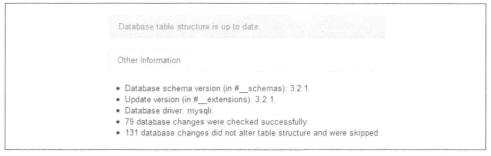

Database table structure is up to date.

Other Information

- Database schema version (in #__schemas): 3.2.1.
- Update version (in #__extensions): 3.2.1.
- Database driver: mysqli.
- 79 database changes were checked successfully.
- 131 database changes did not alter table structure and were skipped.

Figure 13-1. Database fix tool

That's it. Simple and very useful.

SEF URL Settings and SEO Basics

Both Search Engine Friendly (SEF) URLs and Search Engine Optimization (SEO) are key to identifying and classifying your content. Here are a few key points.

SEF URLs

SEF URLs are also known as "human-friendly" URLs, which means site visitors can read them and they make sense. When you first install Joomla, your URLs will look something like this: *http://www.joomlapetcenter.com/index.php?option=com_content&task=view&view=article&id=11*. What a mess! There's no way you'd know what information is on that page. But when you activate SEF URLs, the same URL would look like this: *http://www.joomlapetcenter.com/dogs/collies*.

That makes much more sense. Users will have a very good idea of what to expect when they see that URL—and search engines use these URLs to help rank your content. The URLs are determined by the alias that is used in the menu item and/or the category and article.

The options for SEF URLs in Joomla are:

Search Engine Friendly URLs
> Friendly URLs are human-readable and are better for search engine ranking. This setting turns them on and off.

Use Apache `mod_rewrite`
> This indicates whether you want to use Apache's Rewrite module, an extension for Apache that rewrites URLs. This requires the use of the included *.htaccess* file. This is the only way to remove *index.php* from URLs.

Add Suffix to URLs
> When turned on, the file suffix *.html* will be added to the end of all friendly URLs.

Unicode Aliases
> If set to Yes, then non-Latin characters are allowed in the alias and URL. If no, then a title that includes non-Latin characters will produce the default alias of the current date and time. The default setting is No.

Include Site Name in Page Titles
> This will include the site name in the page titles. For example, if set to Before, the browser tab would read My Website Name - Menu Title. You can select the site name to display either After, Before, or No.

To activate SEF URLs in Joomla:

1. Go to System→Global Configuration.

2. Under SEO Settings (Figure 13-2), click the button on the right to enable Search Engine Friendly URLs. This will append your menu item alias to the end of the URL and make it readable. For more information on setting up menu items, see "Creating Menu Items" on page 47.

3. If your web server is running Apache, change "Use URL rewriting" to Yes to use Apache `mod_rewrite` to enable Apache's URL rewriting functionality. This will give you hierarchical URLs. This also requires you to rename the *htaccess.txt* file included in the home directory of Joomla to *.htaccess* (notice the period in front of *htaccess* in the filename). See more in the Joomla docs on Enabling Search Engine Friendly URLs on Apache (*http://bit.ly/sef-apache*).

4. If you want your URLs to have an *.html* suffix appended on to each, click the button next to Add Suffix to URLs to enable it.

5. Click Save & Close to save your changes.

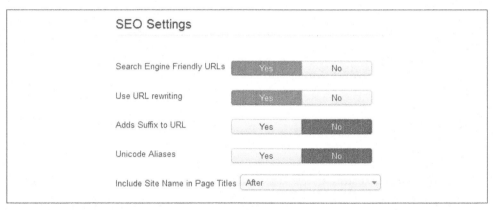

Figure 13-2. Enabling Search Engine Friendly URLs in Joomla

You should now test your website to make sure the URLs are working properly.

 If SEO or SEF settings are not working correctly, you might need to check with your hosting provider to see whether or not their server meets the basic requirements to run Joomla.

Search Engine Optimization (SEO) Basics

Entire books exist about SEO. What's even lovelier is that the rules change frequently. It's a moving target. Yet there are certain guidelines that hold true no matter how algorithms change.

1. Create good, quality content that has value to the visitor. This is *always* number one!

2. Page structure matters. There should only be one h1 tag and the other h tags should accurately represent how your content is presented. More on heading tags can be found in "Heading Tags" on page 102.

3. Good metadata is important, especially the Meta Description found in every article, category, menu item, and many extension fields.

4. Descriptive page titles matter. The <title></title> tags are added by menu item in the Browser Page Title field, as seen in Figure 13-3.

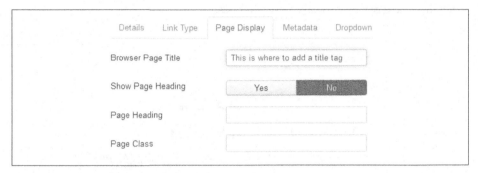

Figure 13-3. Add the title tag into each menu item

5. Search Engine Friendly URLs (see "SEF URLs" on page 238).

6. Image filenames should be considered (see "Resizing, Optimizing, and Naming Image Files" on page 139). Alternate text tags for images as described in "Hands-On Exercise: Adding an Image to an Article" on page 131.

7. Include a site map.

8. Submit site map to search engines.

Certainly you can research and learn more, and test various SEO practices. It is a huge and ever-changing world. You might want to leave all this up to a specialized Joomla extension, like iSEO from iJoomla (*http://seo.ijoomla.com/*), which guides you through the setup process to generate metatags, optimize your content, and even automatically link keywords in your content. This can save you a lot of manual work (even more so if you have a lot of third-party components installed). iSEO also comes with an online course, plus a few other guides to get you up to snuff on SEO best practices for any website.

 Use caution around email or phone scams that claim that they can get you ranked number one on Google. You should do your best to steer clear of these types of claims. Google has even issued a warning on their blog (*http://bit.ly/google-scam*):

"Google never guarantees top placement in search results or AdWords—beware of companies that claim to guarantee rankings, allege a special relationship with Google, or advertise a *priority submit* to Google. There is no priority submit for Google."

Favicon

What is a favicon you ask? It's that little icon in the browser tab, as shown in Figure 13-4.

Figure 13-4. Favicons are small icons that appear in the browser tab

Typically you can create a favicon from a portion of your logo or some kind of branding for your site. Look at other websites for examples. Once you know what you will use, follow these steps:

1. Crop the portion of your logo you will use.

2. Go to a favicon generation website like Favicon (*http://www.favicon.cc*).

3. Upload your image and create the favicon.

4. Download the *favicon.ico* file.

5. Upload the *favicon.ico* file to the root of your *public_html* directory or to the template root. You can view the existing favicons in your site by going to your file manager in your hosting provider's control panel (commonly called the *cPanel*).

When you upload the new *favicon.ico* file, it won't appear immediately in the browser that you normally use. If you use a different browser or clear your browser cache/history, you will be able to see your new favicon. People who have never visited your site will see your new favicon immediately.

Language Overrides

There are times that you might like to override a Joomla or third-party extension language file. An example of this might be the message seen when a contact form is submitted. The message that Joomla gives by default is Thank you for your email. If instead you wanted to say Thank you for your message, you would do so with a *Language Override*.

To do a Language Override:

1. Click on Extensions and again on Language Manager.

2. Click on Overrides in the left sidebar.

3. Click the New button.

4. On the righthand side of the screen, enter the text you want to change. In our example, it is Thank you for your email, which is the Value.

5. Leave the "Search for" drop-down set at Value.

6. Press Enter or click the Search button.

7. You will see a list of language Constants (see Figure 13-5). Select the one you want to change.

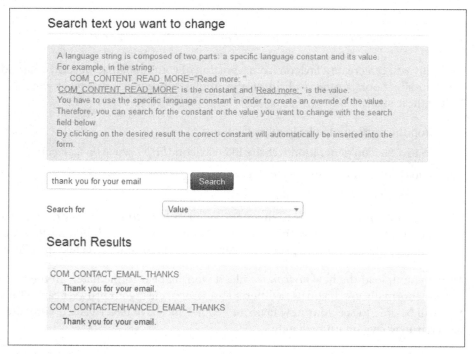

Figure 13-5. List of language constants for our value

8. When you select the one you desire, it will automatically fill in the left side of the screen with the necessary data.

9. In the Text field, change the text associated with the constant, as shown in Figure 13-6.

Figure 13-6. Changing the text of a language constant

10. Click Save & Close.

11. Test from the frontend.

Sometimes it's difficult to know which language constant is the right one. This is especially the case when attempting to override the language constant for a Search module. In those cases, instead of erasing the text that appears for the constant, add something to it to make sure it's the correct language constant. Jenn often adds a question mark to the Text field as a test. Then she saves the override, and refreshes from the frontend to verify the correct language constant has been selected to change.

Language Overrides are a powerful way to make changes to the language files without having those changes be overridden during an update. Happy overriding!

Users, User Groups, Access Control Lists (ACLs), and Frontend Editing

Even the simplest websites involve some aspect of users, user groups, and ACLs. In this section, we are going to briefly cover creating users, user groups, and ACLs and how they can be used. This can be a complex topic used for a plethora of applications. Know that you can go deeper than what we cover here.

Hands-On Exercise: Creating Users

Many times, users need to register themselves on the frontend, but sometimes you may want to add them yourself from the backend. To add users:

1. Click on Users and then on User Manager.
2. Click the New button on the top toolbar.
3. Fill out their relevant details in the Account Details tab.

 Login Name and Password cannot have spaces.

4. Click the Assigned User Groups tab and select a user group for your user. By setting the group, you are defining what the user can and can't do in Joomla. The different permissions and group types are detailed in "User Groups" on page 245.
5. Click the Basic Settings tab.
6. Change any of these settings if applicable. Backend Language & Frontend Language allows you to set a language preference when navigating the backend and frontend of your website. Leaving this as Select Language will keep it as the default language, which is set in the Language Manager. The User Editor can be assigned by user, as we did in Chapter 5. Leaving this as Select Editor will keep it as the default editor set in Global Configuration. The Time Zone can be set by user as well. Because servers are set up all over the world, time zone shifts need to be accounted for. The standard is to set servers to Greenwich Mean Time (GMT) or UTC+0, but not all servers adhere to that standard. Greenwich Mean Time is based on the current time in Greenwich, Greater London, England.
7. Click Save & Close. Once you click Save, an email will be sent to the email address of the new user with their account details.

User Groups

Each group is designed to control what your users can do. The predefined groups are Super Administrator, Administrator, Manager, Publisher, Editor, Author, Registered, and Guest. Table 13-1 outlines the permissions each group has by default. Each group inherits the permissions from all groups below it. As an example, Registered users can not only view content in the Registered ACL, but they can also perform basic browsing, as can the Guest group.

Table 13-1. User groups and their permissions

Group	Backend Permissions	Frontend Permissions
Super Administrator	Global Configuration	All below
	Template Manager	
	Language Manager	
	Mass Mail	
Administrator	User Manager	All below
	Trash Manager	
	Extension Manager	
	Module Manager	
	Plugin Manager	
	Global Check-in	
	Clean/Purge Cache	
Manager	Article Manager	All below
	Featured Articles	
	Category Manager	
	Media Manager	
	Menu Manager	
	Components	
	Private Messaging	
	Help	
	System Info	
Publisher	No access to backend	Can publish articles
Editor	No access to backend	Can edit all articles
Author	No access to backend	Can create articles
		Can edit own articles
Registered	No access to backend	Can view registered content
Guest	No access to backend	Basic browsing

These user groups are not fixed in Joomla. They are the user groups that install with Joomla. You can add user groups for specific tasks if desired (see "User Groups" on page 245). Make sure you only add a user group if you must. User groups (and ACLs) can get confusing quickly. Only add user groups if what installs with Joomla doesn't fit your site's needs. An alternative is editing an existing user group so that it is allowed or not allowed to do what you want to limit permissions to that user group.

Access Control Lists (ACLs)

Let's get clear first.

ACL stands for Access Control List. In the Joomla backend, in the Users drop-down, they're called Access Levels. Go figure that one out. Regardless, ACLs control what a user can see; that is, what they can view on the frontend of your website. ACLs work in conjunction with user groups. They require each other.

The default ACLs installed with Joomla are:

Guest
Anyone who visits the frontend of the site. This is a child of the Public ACL.

Public
Anyone who visits the frontend of the site.

Registered
Only users who are logged in to the frontend of the site.

Special
Manager, Administrator, and Super Administrator can view content on the frontend or backend of the site.

You can keep the default ACLs and use them just as they are. Or you can customize them to suit your needs (see "Hands-On Exercise: Control What the User Sees with ACLs" on page 248). The ability is there to show content to the users you desire.

Hands-On Exercise: Allowing a User Group to Edit Specific Content

Let's say that you have someone helping you add content to your site. You want them to be able to add and edit a specific category but not other categories. You can do that.

Because this is something that a user will do, we will need to add a user group for the user or users that have permission to add and/or edit that category.

1. Click on Users→Groups→Add New Group.
2. Enter a name in the Group Title field.
3. Select Registered for Group Parent. See Figure 13-7.

4. Click Save & Close.

User Group Details

| Group Title * | Blog Editor |
| Group Parent * | - Registered ▾ |

Figure 13-7. Add a new user group

Next, create a new user as described in "Hands-On Exercise: Creating Users" on page 244 and select the user group as the new group you just created.

To give permission to your new user to perform tasks in the category desired:

1. Click on Content→Category Manager.

2. Click on the category you want the user(s) to be able to add or edit.

3. Click on the Permissions tab.

4. On the left sidebar with tabs, select the user group you just created to give permissions to.

5. Read the notes at the bottom of the page.

6. The main section of the page gives three columns for Action, Select New Setting, and Calculated Setting. Change the Select New Setting drop-down for each of the actions you want to change (see Figure 13-8 for the settings to allow the user group to Create, Edit, Edit State, and Edit Own. They are not allowed to Delete).

7. Click Save & Close.

Action	Select New Setting [1]	Calculated Setting [2]
Create	Allowed ▾	Not Allowed
Delete	Inherited ▾	Not Allowed
Edit	Allowed ▾	Not Allowed
Edit State	Allowed ▾	Not Allowed
Edit Own	Allowed ▾	Not Allowed

Figure 13-8. Giving a user group permission to create and edit articles in a specific category

When the user logs in through a login module (see "Hands-On Exercise: Login Module" on page 249) on the frontend of the website, they will only be able to edit the category they have permission to edit or add to. The articles in that category will have an Edit icon that allows the user to edit the content or change the state (published, unpublished, archived).

In order for that user group to add an article, you will need to create a new menu (in either the Registered or Special access level) with a menu item that gives them the ability to create a new article. You can set the default category to only the category they have permission to create for.

A single user may be in multiple groups, which will allow them to add or edit content in multiple categories. If that's the case, when they use the menu item to create a new article, they will have any category they have permission to add to available to select from the category drop-down.

If you want a certain user group to have permission to edit a module, they can do so from the frontend after logging in (see "Hands-On Exercise: Login Module" on page 249 for directions on creating a Login module for your site). However, they must have backend permissions as well. This means their user group must be a child group of one of the user groups that have backend access, as seen in Table 13-1.

Hands-On Exercise: Control What the User Sees with ACLs

ACLs work with user groups. We'll explain with a scenario of a school. For this school website, we want to have a section of the website to be accessible to only students, another area for only parents, and a third area that only teachers can access.

Before we can create access levels for our students, parents, and teachers, we need to create new user groups for each using the instructions in "User Groups" on page 245.

Once we've added our user groups, we can add new access levels for each. To create a new access level:

1. Click on Users→Access Levels→Add New Access Level.
2. Enter the Level Title of **Students**.
3. Check the box for the User Groups Having Viewing Access of Students.
4. Click Save & New to add access levels for Parents and Teachers.
5. Click Save & Close.

Next we need to set certain content to only be viewed by the appropriate access level. Most every component has the ability to set the access level.

Set the Access Level of Your Content

If you want to set a specific category to a certain access level, open the category from the Category Manager and select the Access to Students from the drop-down (Figure 13-9).

Figure 13-9. Access drop-down with Students selected

You will also set access levels for articles from the Access drop-down. The menu items have the same parameters. Set them for the access level desired.

Next, the user itself needs to be placed into the user group(s) associated with the ACL it needs to view. So, if you have a student who creates an account as Registered on the frontend, in order for that user to see the Student content, you will need to add them to the Student user group in the User Manager before they will be able to view the Student content. The same is true for the Parents and Teachers user groups and ACLs. The group that the user is in will tell the ACL what to show to them.

We always recommend using the functionality built into Joomla before using a third-party extension. However, user groups and ACLs can get complicated quickly. If you find yourself getting confused, we recommend using ACL Manager (*http://aclmanag er.net/*) to help you set up your user groups and ACLs. You can uninstall the extension when you are done creating your user groups and ACLs, and all that you created will remain in Joomla core without the third-party extension. Such a great extension!

Joomla's user group and ACL structure makes for a highly customizable experience for your site's users and visitors. Use it if you need it. Do not use it if you don't need it.

Hands-On Exercise: Login Module

Joomla Pet Center is going to require a way for visitors and frontend editors to log in to the site. Joomla installs with a login module already created in the Module Manager. We simply need to set it up to display in our template by assigning it to a module position.

We also want to change a few of the user settings to prevent unwanted people from registering on our site.

1. From the Module Manager, find the module with the title Login Form and click on it to open the module.

2. Change the title of the module if you want to display a title. We will change our title to Login or Register.

3. Add any inviting words you want to appear on the form in the Pre-text or Post-text fields.

4. Change any of the other settings you desire.

5. Select a position for the login module to appear. We will select module position sidebar-b.

6. Click Save and test from the frontend. See Figure 13-10 for how our module looks.

Figure 13-10. Login module from the frontend of Joomla Pet Center

Setting User Options

Now for an adjustment. Because Joomla Pet Center is an example website created for this book, it is particularly vulnerable to attack. Thus, we are going to eliminate the ability for people or automated bots to create an account via the login module.

We do this by changing a setting in the User Manager Options:

1. Click on Users and then on User Manager.
2. Click on the Options button on the top toolbar.
3. The first option on the Component tab is Allow User Registration. Change from Yes to No.
4. Click Save & Close, and the link "Create an account" in the login module on the frontend of the site will no longer appear.

Other notes regarding login from the options in the Users menu:

- You can set the default user group into which new accounts should be placed.
- You can choose whether the system sends the user an email containing their newly created account's password. For security purposes, you may want to switch the Send Password field to No.
- You can choose whether a new user does not need to activate the account, whether the system sends them a link they must click on to activate, or whether an administrator needs to approve their new user account. You would then want to have the system send a notification message to administrators.
- Joomla 3.x comes with captcha integration through ReCaptcha. This needs to be initially set up by going to Extensions and then Plugin Manager. Search for captcha in the filter field, and follow the directions in the plugin to set up captcha. Then go to Global Configuration and set the Default Captcha to Captcha - ReCaptcha. Click Save & Close.
- Set the number of times a user can reset their password and in what amount of time.
- Set the required length of the password along with the requirement for integers, symbols, and uppercase letters. This can do much to increase security on your site. We recommend a password length of eight digits or more.

CHAPTER 14

Making Your Website Secure and Optimized

Security is something that should be taken very seriously. Joomla itself provides regular updates, and one easy thing you can do is always make sure you are using the latest versions of Joomla and that any extensions you use are updated. The Joomla Security Center (*http://bit.ly/joom-secure*) provides updates on any vulnerabilities discovered in Joomla, and we recommend that you sign up for the mailing list (*http://bit.ly/joom-mail*) to receive notifications when a security update is released. See Figure 14-1.

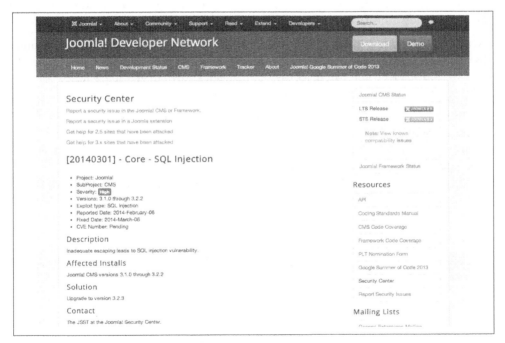

Figure 14-1. The Joomla Security Center

Tips and Best Practices

There are so many great Joomla extensions and it's tempting to try them all, but you should do your homework first. If you find an extension you want to use, check to see if it has any known vulnerabilities on the Joomla Vulnerable Extensions List (*http://vel.joomla.org*). Also, browse around the help section of the developer's site and see if users have reported issues. Is the developer responsive to support questions? Has the developer made regular, timely updates to fix and improve the extension? What kind of support can you expect? Is there a paid support option? These are important questions you need to consider before choosing an extension. Doing some research and searches on Google will help you form a picture of the safety and security of that extension.

You also need to do similar research on your web hosting company. Is it responsive to server issues? How quickly? What is its uptime guarantee? Does it use antivirus software? Does it have a policy for Joomla upgrades that requires you to upgrade regularly? Some hosting providers force you to update your Joomla installation on their schedule, and you should be prepared for that.

Using Security Tools and Performing Health Checks

Joomla development and testing is community-driven and is only secure as the community makes it. If you want to be more proactive, which we recommend you do, here are a few handy tools to help protect your site.

JAMSS (*http://bit.ly/jmass-script*) is a simple tool that regularly checks your Joomla installation for malicious PHP code (Figure 14-2). It's a PHP script that you upload to your website via FTP and run in a browser. It's been known to give a few false positives, but it should provide some protection.

The Brute Force Stop (*http://bit.ly/brutestop*) plugin is a sentry-like tool that checks for incorrect login attempts, records the attempts, and can block the IP of the user (temporarily or permanently). It can also send out an email to notify you that this has happened. See Figure 14-3.

```
Joomla! version: 3.2.3 Stable JAMSS - Anti-Malware Scan Script for Joomla! - v.1.0.4
Welcome to JAMSS, the Anti Malware Scan Script Joomla!
```

Here are the suspicious parts of code found in this scan process :

In file ./plugins/system/gantry/overrides/3.2/2.5/mod_wrapper/default.php-> we found 1 occurence(s) of Pattern #18 - IFRAME element
---> **Details:** *"Found IFRAME element in code, please check if it's a valid code."*

Line #: 28:

```
...  <iframe <?php echo $load; ?>
        id="blockrandom"
        name="<?php echo $target; ?>"
        src="<?php echo $url; ?>"
        width="<?php echo $width; ?>"
        height="<?php echo $height; ?>"
        scrolling="<?php echo $scroll; ...
```

---> ./plugins/system/gantry/overrides/3.2/2.5/mod_wrapper/default.php is a **file**. It was last **accessed**: 2014-03-27T11:53:36-05:00, last **changed**: 2014-03-27T11:53:36-05:00, last **modified**: 2014-03-27T11:53:36-05:00.
File permissions:0644

In file ./plugins/system/gantry/overrides/3.2/2.5/com_wrapper/wrapper/default.php-> we found 1 occurence(s) of Pattern #18 - IFRAME element
---> **Details:** *"Found IFRAME element in code, please check if it's a valid code."*

Line #: 37:

```
...  <iframe <?php echo $this->wrapper->load; ?>
        id="blockrandom"
        name="iframe"
        src="<?php echo $this->escape($this->wrapper->url); ?>"
        width="<?php echo $this->escape($this->params->get('width')); ?>" ...
```

---> ./plugins/system/gantry/overrides/3.2/2.5/com_wrapper/wrapper/default.php is a **file**. It was last **accessed**: 2014-03-27T11:53:36-05:00, last **changed**: 2014-03-27T11:53:36-05:00, last **modified**: 2014-03-27T11:53:36-05:00.
File permissions:0644

Figure 14-2. JAMSS in action

Figure 14-3. Don't forget to enable the plugin

The Joo ReCaptcha (*http://bit.ly/joo-recap*) plugin helps prevent the most common way spammers attack your site—creating dummy accounts so they can post spam in your comments, forums, and anywhere else they can. ReCaptcha is a great service that helps prevent malicious spambots by forcing them to enter a series of letters shown in an image. At the same time, the user is entering letters from a poorly scanned document, and they are helping to perform Optical Character Recognition (OCR) on that document to digitize it. So you're keeping spambots out and doing good by preserving books at the same time! Register for ReCaptcha (*http://www.google.com/recaptcha*) private and public keys to add this plugin (illustrated in Figure 14-4).

Figure 14-4. Use Google ReCaptcha to protect your site

Akeeba Admin Tools (*http://bit.ly/akeeba-admin*) is described as the "Swiss Army knife for your site" because it does many things to make your job as a site administrator much easier. Want to know when an update for Joomla is available? Admin Tools will send you an email. Want to easily create complex *.htaccess* rules? Do it in an easy user interface. Admin Tools will also optimize your database tables and even create custom URL redirects. Figure 14-5 shows the display page for the plugin.

Additional Resources

Here are a few key online resources for helping to secure your Joomla website:

- Joomla Security Checklist (*http://bit.ly/admincheck*)
- Joomla Security and Performance FAQs (*http://bit.ly/sp-faq*)
- Joomla Security Checklist - Getting Started (*http://bit.ly/checklist-gs*)
- Joomla Security News Feed (*http://bit.ly/joomla-secnews*)
- Joomla Vulnerable Extensions Feed (*http://bit.ly/joom-vel*)

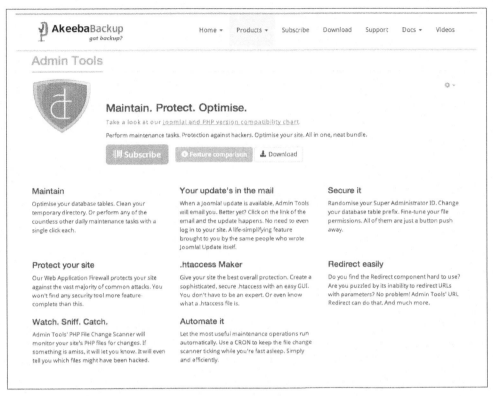

Figure 14-5. AdminTools can help you in a pinch

Enable Two-Factor Authentication

Joomla 3.2.x introduced two-factor authentication to further boost security. This requires the user to verify their identity in two stages before gaining access to a Joomla site. Facebook also uses this to verify you based on your IP as well as your username/password. It can be a minor annoyance for users, but it makes a big difference.

There are two options for authentication, and they are both Joomla plugins installed by default. You only need to activate the one you intend to use. We prefer the Google Authentication option, but here's how to set up both:

To use Google Authenticator (*http://bit.ly/google-auth*), you need to get a free app from Google for Android, iOS, or BlackBerry (see Figure 14-6). Search the app store for your device and download/install the Google Authenticator app. Now we'll set up authentication in Joomla.

Figure 14-6. Set up Google Authentication

1. Go to Extensions→Plugin Manager and enable the Two Factor Authentication - Google Authenticator plugin by clicking the Status button. By default, it's for both the site frontend and backend, but you can configure this in the plugin settings.

2. Go to Users→User Manager and click a username to edit its profile. This user will be required to use two-factor authentication after this is set up.

3. The Two Factor Authentication tab should now be visible (enable the plugin in step 1 if it isn't). Change the Authentication method to Google Authenticator.

4. Follow the instructions for setting up Authenticator. Either scan the QR code or enter the information manually. Enter the security code provided. You will also see a set of emergency passwords. It's very important that you keep these in a safe place in case you lose your password or need them.

5. Click Save & Close when you're done.

To use YubiKey authentication (*http://www.yubico.com/*), you need to purchase a USB hardware token from Yubico and set it up on your computer in order to link your Joomla account:

1. Go to Extensions→Plugin Manager and enable the Two Factor Authentication - YubiKey plugin by clicking the Status button. By default, it's for both the site frontend and backend, but you can configure this in the plugin settings.

2. Go to Users→User Manager and click a username to edit its profile. This user will be required to use two-factor authentication after this is set up.

3. The Two Factor Authentication tab should now be visible (enable the plugin in step 1 if it isn't). Change the Authentication method to YubiKey.

4. Insert your YubiKey into a USB port and follow the instructions. When the process is complete, you should see a confirmation that your key is linked to your account. You will also see a set of emergency passwords. It's very important that you keep these in a safe place in case you lose your password or need them.

5. Click Save & Close when you're done.

Users can also edit their profile on the Joomla frontend to enable Google Authenticator or YubiKey authentication. Once you've confirmed you have everything set up and working for either Google Authenticator or YubiKey, go to the Plugin Manager and disable the Authentication - Joomla plugin to prevent users from bypassing the authentication. Users will now see a third option called Secret Key under User Name and Password when logging in. Users will have to enter a secret key sent to them at the time of logging in to verify themselves, as shown in Figure 14-7.

Figure 14-7. The Secret Key field, used to increase security

I Was Hacked!

Sometimes a hacker can get in through no fault of your own and deface your website. A popular extension you have installed may have a vulnerability, and before you can update it, a "script kiddie" gets in. Don't panic, because you have regular backups to roll back to, right? No? Well, then let me remind you of the importance of regular backups. They're not just a good idea in the case of a break-in, they're a great idea in case anything else happens. Call it an insurance policy or general peace of mind in case that rainy day ever comes.

If you have backups, you can start to roll each one back to figure out when the hack occurred. First, log in to the site using FTP and see where the hacked files are. Roll back the previous backup and see if the files are still there. If they aren't, you're probably OK with that version of the site (hopefully you caught it quickly). But now you have to do some detective work to see *how* they got in. The most common way of hacking a website is via an outdated Joomla extension, so check all your nonstandard extensions against the Vulnerable Extension List to see if any are listed. Update those immediately. Also, make sure you're using the latest version of Joomla in the series (1.5.x, 2.x, 3.x) to ensure you have the latest security fixes.

Check your *.htaccess* to make sure it doesn't contain anything extra in it. Some hackers won't change a thing on your site except this file, only making you think they've changed your files, and instead they're really redirecting your site users to their URL. When in doubt, download a fresh copy of Joomla and upload a fresh copy of this file to your website. You can also use the PHP File Change Scanner in Akeeba Admin Tools (mentioned earlier in this chapter) to see if any of your files have been altered. When in doubt, upload a fresh copy of those.

If you just can't find the security hole, you can also try Phil Taylor's tool MyJoomla (*http://myjoomla.com/*) to audit your site and secure it.

Once you've cleaned up the mess and updated and verified your files, change all your passwords. Change the password for MySQL (which is stored in the *configuration.php* file), FTP, and anything else important. Use secure passwords at all times. There are many great tools out there, like Strong Password Generator (*http://strongpassword generator.com/*) or Password Bird (*http://passwordbird.com/*), that can generate secure passwords for you.

For the future, it's best to be as proactive as possible. Do a regular check every once in a while on the extensions you're using, and make sure Joomla is up to date. You can also pay services like watchful.li to monitor all your sites via one unified dashboard. Sometimes it takes getting hacked as a wake-up call before a person gets serious about security. Don't let that be you.

How to Install Joomla

This appendix will provide everything you need to know about installing and upgrading Joomla.

We understand readers come from various backgrounds and may or may not have expertise in dealing with server environments. Some parts may get a little technical, but we'll try to put away the super-technical lingo and explain the process in simple terms everyone can understand.

Requirements

Even though Joomla may work on servers that do not meet the minimum specifications outlined in Table A-1, it is not advisable to run your site on a noncompliant server. In fact, you should strive to have your server support the recommended requirements.

Table A-1. Requirements for Joomla 3.3+

Software	Recommended	Minimum	Software website
PHP (Magic Quotes GPC off)	5.3.10+	5.3.10+	*www.php.net*
Supported databases:			
MySQL (InnoDB support required)	5.1+	5.1+	*www.mysql.com*
MSSQL	10.50.1600.1+	10.50.1600.1+	*www.microsoft.com/sql*
PostgreSQL	8.3.18+	8.3.18+	*www.postgresql.org*
Support web servers:			
Apache (with `mod_mysql`, `mod_xml`, and `mod_zlib`)	2.x+	2.x+	*www.apache.org*
Nginx	1.1	1.0	*www.wiki.ngix.org*
Microsoft IIS	7	7	*www.iis.net*

For up-to-date requirements information, visit the official Joomla Technical Requirements (*http://bit.ly/joomlatech*) page.

Do not install an older version of Joomla to get around the PHP 5.3.10 requirement. You will end up with a site you cannot maintain. Instead, find a new host.

Choosing a Host

Choosing a good host is of utmost importance. There are many, many types of servers and services that you will need to select based on your site's needs. You may need a dedicated server, a virtual private server (VPS), or cloud hosting. Perhaps shared hosting is all your site needs.

Most sites running Joomla are using shared hosting. Shared hosting is the most inexpensive type of hosting available. Inexpensive is relative, however. Choosing hosting because it is "cheapest" will probably cost you more in the long run when server configurations don't meet Joomla's requirements or you wind up with performance issues.

One of the top questions we (as Joomla consultants) are asked is "What host should I use?"

Focusing on shared hosts, here are a few hosts that are Joomla-friendly. They are not the "cheapest," nor should they be! They are running your website. Any of the following work very nicely with Joomla.

- Rochen (*http://www.rochenhost.com*)
- Khoza Technology, Inc. (*http://www.khoza.com*)
- Inmotion Hosting (*http://www.inmotionhosting.com*)
- Siteground (*http://www.siteground.com*)
- cloudaccess.net (*http://ccp.cloudaccess.net*)

(Jenn receives affiliate compensation from some of these links.)

Local Web Servers

Some people prefer to develop their website locally on their computer, and then migrate it to their web host when complete. This can be much faster than developing on a remote server, since you do not have to rely on the speed of your Internet connection when interacting with the website. Whether you are on a Windows machine or a Macintosh, there is a solution for you.

For Windows, use XAMPP (*http://www.apachefriends.org*).

For Mac, use MAMP (*http://www.mamp.info*).

After either solution is installed, you will find that you have an Apache/MySQL/PHP web server on your computer ready for you to start building your Joomla website. After the website is developed, you can easily move it from your local web server to your web host. To move your website from one server to another, use Akeeba Backup and Akeeba Kickstart.

One-Click Installers

Many shared hosting providers offer a control panel of some kind with a quick install option, referred to as a *one-click installer*. These one-click installers get your Joomla installation accomplished very quickly, without going through the steps in the following section of this appendix. If your host does not have a one-click installer, you will need to refer to the previous section to install Joomla (which is also very simple, so no fretting).

 We prefer using FTP to upload, install, or update Joomla, since hosting providers don't always have the latest versions of Joomla in their one-click installers and can, at times, create more problems than they are worth.

Database Setup

The database is where all of the information for your website is stored. In this chapter, we're going to create a database and database user, and then give that database user privileges to interact with the database.

Since cPanel is the most popular hosting control panel, we will use it in our examples. If your hosting company is not using cPanel, these instructions should loosely correspond to the process in your host's control panel. You may need to consult your hosting provider for specific information.

Let's get started by logging in.

1. Navigate to: *http://www.<yourdomain>.com/cpanel* or follow your host's instructions for setting up nameservers so that your domain points to your hosting company's servers, so that you can reach your cPanel URL.

2. When prompted, enter your login credentials. If you don't know them, refer to any documentation that you may have received from your host when you signed up.

3. Find and click the icon titled MySQL Databases. The icon looks like Figure A-1. Depending on your version of cPanel, it may look different.

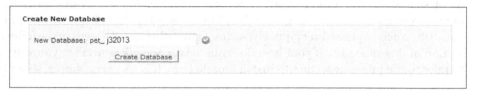

Figure A-1. cPanel icon for MySQL Databases

4. In the New Database: field, enter **joomla** or whatever you would like for a database name, as seen in Figure A-2.

Create New Database

New Database: pet_ j32013

Create Database

Figure A-2. New database

5. Click Create Database.

6. On the success screen, click Go Back to return to the MySQL Databases screen.

 Make a note of the actual database name (an Excel spreadsheet or *.txt* file are good ways to track these). Typically, cPanel will prefix the database name with the account username. In our example, it created a database name of: *pet_j32013*.

7. In the Username field, enter **joomla** or whatever you would like for a database username, as seen in Figure A-3.

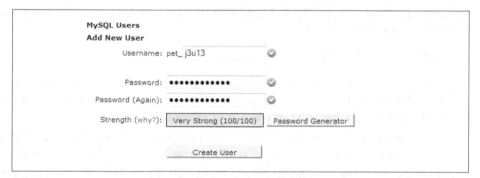

MySQL Users
Add New User

Username: pet_ j3u13

Password: ••••••••••••

Password (Again): ••••••••••••

Strength (why?): Very Strong (100/100)   Password Generator

Create User

Figure A-3. New database user

8. Enter a secure password. Make a note of the database password along with your database username, as you will need them to install Joomla.

Use the cPanel Password Generator to generate strong passwords. Alternatively, if you are not using cPanel, you can generate strong random passwords by using Bytes Interactive (*http://www.goodpassword.com*) or Strong Password Generator (*http://www.strongpasswordgenerator.com*). These give you lots of options for password length, character types, and even the option to exclude characters that can be confused with other characters.

9. Click Create User.

10. On the success screen, click Go Back to return to the MySQL Databases screen.

 Make a note of the actual database username in that same spreadsheet or *.txt* file. Typically, cPanel will prefix the database username with the account username. In our example, it created a database username of: *pet_j3u13*.

11. In the Add Users To Your Databases section, ensure that the correct values are selected for the User and Database fields.

12. Click Add User to Database.

13. Assign All Privileges to the user, as seen in Figure A-4.

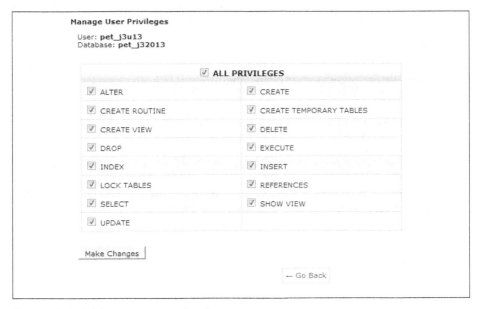

Figure A-4. Add users to your databases

14. Click the *Make Changes* button.

15. On the success screen, click Go Back to return to the MySQL Databases screen.

That's it for the database setup. Now we're ready to begin uploading files.

 Write down the details you just created. You'll need the username, password, and database name during the Joomla installation process.

File Transfer Protocol (FTP)

File Transfer Protocol, often referred to as FTP, is a protocol used for transferring files across the Internet. You are already familiar with another protocol called Hypertext Transfer Protocol, or HTTP.

If you don't already have an FTP client, we recommend using FileZilla (*http://filezilla-project.org*). It is free and works on Windows, Mac OS X, and Linux.

When you open up your FTP client, you will need to enter three pieces of information.

Host/Site
> This tells your FTP client where to find your server. Typically this is your domain name without the *http://www*. An example might be *<yourdomain>.com* or *ftp.<yourdomain>.com*. It may also be an IP address.

Username
> This tells your FTP client what login to use when connecting to your server. This is typically the same as your cPanel login.

Password
> This tells your FTP client what password to use when connecting to your server. This is typically the same as your cPanel password.

Once logged in, you should see something that looks similar to Figure A-5. There are a good number of files and folders. We are only going to concern ourselves with one of them. The *public_html* folder is where all of your website files will go. When you go to a website, it looks for files in that folder to load. On some servers, this folder may not exist. If it does not exist on your server, then look for *www*, *httpdocs*, or *htdocs*. If none of those folders exist, contact your host to find out which folder you should put your website files in.

You may have noticed in Figure A-5 that it has a *public_html* and a *www* folder. Both of these are on our list. How would you have known which one to choose? The *www* folder is not really a folder. Actually it is a symbolic link that points to *public_html*, meaning they are the same folder with two names. Using either would be fine.

Filename	Filesize	Filetype
..		
.cpanel		File folder
.htpasswds		File folder
.mozilla		File folder
.trash		File folder
access-logs		File folder
Backup		File folder
cpmove.psql		File folder
cpmove.psql.1299074234		File folder
etc		File folder
logs		File folder
mail		File folder
public_ftp		File folder
public_html		File folder
tmp		File folder
www		File folder
.bash_logout	33	BASH_LOG...
.bash_profile	176	BASH_PRO...
.bashrc	124	BASHRC File
.contactemail	17	CONTACT...
.cpanel-logs	15	CPANEL-L...
.emacs	515	EMACS File
.gemrc	145	GEMRC File
.lastlogin	14	LASTLOGI...

Figure A-5. Remote files in an FTP client

Now we are ready to get some Joomla files.

Download the latest version of Joomla (*http://www.joomla.org/download.html*) to your desktop and unzip it.

Upload the contents of the Joomla ZIP archive to the *public_html* directory shown in Figure A-5. This may take a while depending on your upload speed. Once everything is uploaded, you're ready to begin the installation steps.

Another way to get the Joomla source files uploaded to your server is to either FTP the zipped package from Joomla or use File Manager upload within cPanel. cPanel allows you to extract the archive with one click. If you are familiar with this method, it is faster.

Don't close your FTP program just yet—there will be one final step at the end where you'll need it.

Web Installer

You're in the final steps of the process, and minutes away from having your very own Joomla website. In your browser, navigate to your website's URL: *http://www.<yourdomain>.com/installation*. You should be greeted with the Joomla Web Installer screen, as shown in Figure A-6.

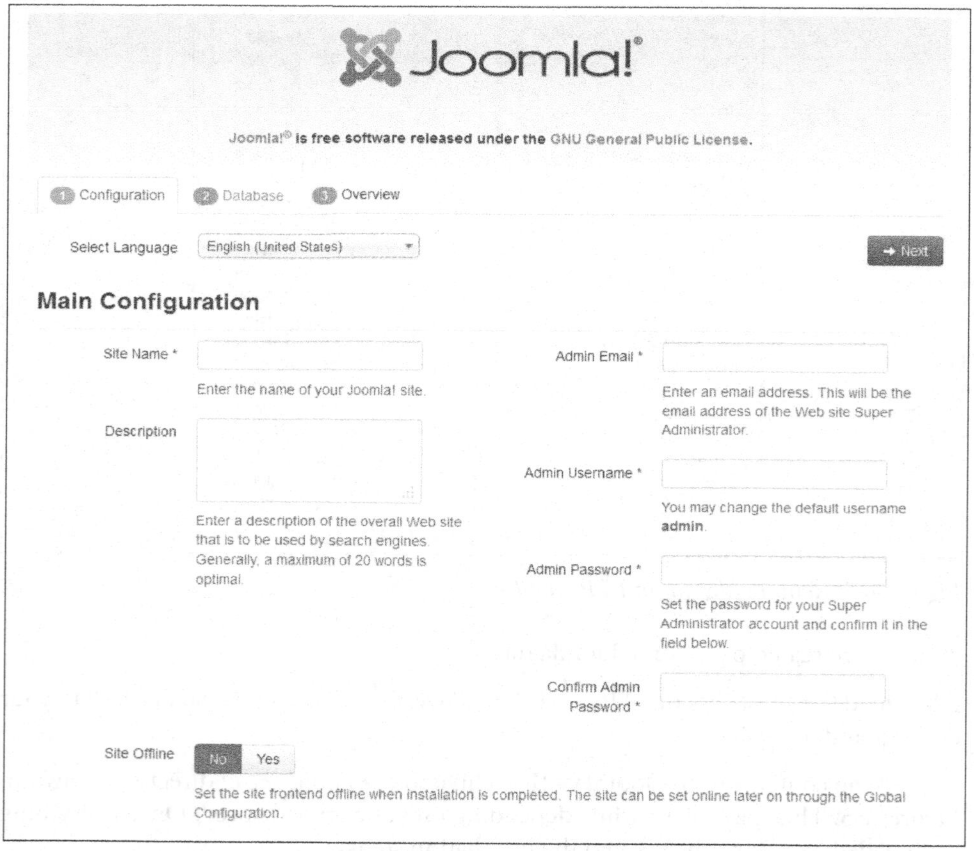

Figure A-6. Joomla Web Installer – Configuration

1. The first step is to select your language from the drop-down.

 If you intend to install multiple languages, it is preferable to do so now. See "Hands-On Exercise: Installing Multiple Languages When Joomla is Initially Installed" on page 145.

2. Enter your site's name.

3. Enter a description of your site. This can be done later if you don't want to think about it right now. It can be found in the Global Configuration.

4. Select if you want your site frontend offline by leaving Site Offline set to No or changing it to Yes.

5. Enter an admin email address.

6. Choose an admin username.

 It is recommended for increased security to not leave the username as the default username admin. Change it to something else. By leaving it admin, you're giving half of your login information away. Don't give it away! Change it!

7. Make up an admin password, enter it in the Admin Password field, and confirm it in the field below. Your password should be secure and include uppercase letters, lowercase letters, numbers, and symbols. It should be a minimum of 8 characters, but 15 is better. The longer the better. This is your website; you want to protect it the best you can. Strong passwords help.

8. Click Next at the top right.

    In the Database Configuration tab (Figure A-7), you will be entering the details of the database you created in a previous step.

    Database Type
    This is almost always MySQLi. If this is not available, then use MySQL. If MSSQL or PostgreSQL are available, they will be listed in the drop-down as well.

    Host Name
    This tells Joomla where the database is located. This is almost always local host, because MySQL typically runs on the same server as your website. If localhost does not work, contact your host to obtain the hostname for your database.

Username

    This is the username we created in step 7 of "Database Setup" on page 263.

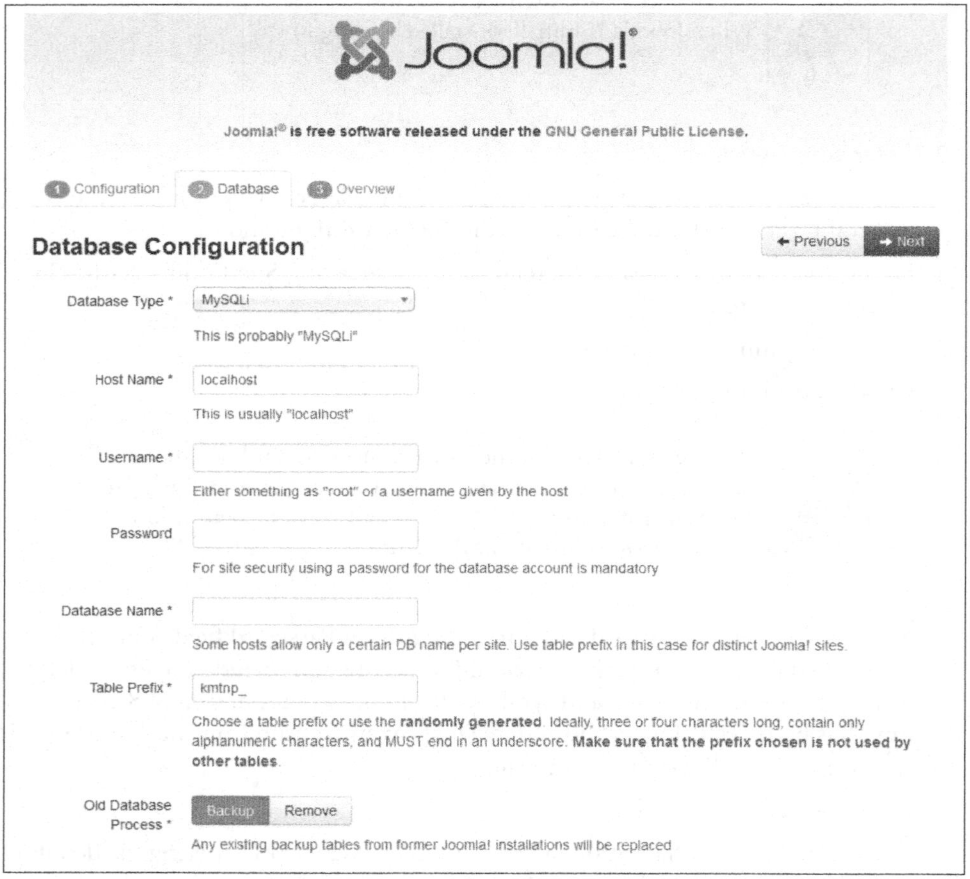

Figure A-7. Joomla Web Installer – Database Configuration

Password

    This is the password to the username we created in step 8 of "Database Setup" on page 263.

Database Name

    This is the name of the database we created in step 4 of "Database Setup" on page 263.

The Table Prefix is randomized so that virtually all Joomla installations will have a different Table Prefix. This is to prevent certain types of SQL injection hacks from working successfully. If you want to choose your own, just pick three or four random letters followed by an underscore. Do not use bak_ as it is reserved for backup tables.

Once everything is entered, click Next. If you receive an error, click Previous and double-check your information.

The next page, seen in Figure A-8, finalizes the installation and gives some options for you to select. Let's go through them.

Figure A-8. Joomla Web Installer – Overview/Finalization

Install Sample Data

If you are new to Joomla, you may want to install the sample data by clicking the Install Sample Data button. The sample data contains articles, menu items, and other forms of content that will display on your site. If you're already comfortable with Joomla, you can choose to skip the sample content. But if you're new to Joomla, you may want to install the sample data to get an idea of how things can be set up.

You can select different types of sample data: Blog, Brochure, Default, Learn Joomla, and Test English (the Test English sample data set is used by community members to help test the software). Pick one and enjoy.

 Once your site has taken shape, you will want to go through and clean up (trash and empty trash) any sample data that you did not use, so it doesn't confuse you or other users on the site. Also, even though pages aren't showing on the frontend of your site, that doesn't mean those pages won't be indexed. Cleanup is helpful in avoiding unwanted content from being indexed and creating confusing other administrators.

Using an extension like OS Content (*http://www.ostraining.com/ downloads/joomla-extensions/oscontent/*) can aid in removing sample data quickly.

Email Configuration

Select whether you would like the configuration settings emailed to the admin email that you set up two screens previously. This emails the admin username and password as well as the database credentials to the email address specified.

Main Configuration

This shows what you entered for the Configuration installation page. You can use the Previous button at the top right to go back to the screen and make changes to it.

Database Configuration

This displays what was entered in the Database installation page. This works the same way as Main Configuration: you may use the Previous button at the top right to go back to the Database screen and make changes to it (though you wouldn't have made it to this screen unless it was correct).

Recommended Settings

As stated, these settings are recommended for compatibility with Joomla, though for the most part, Joomla will often still function if they don't quite match. It would be wise to make a note as to what didn't match, so that if something doesn't work, you have some notes to talk to your host about. For example, "If Magic Quotes are on, Joomla 3.x will not work."

1. Click Install at the top right. We're at the finish line—or rather the Finish page. See Figure A-9.

2. If you would like to install additional languages, you may do so by clicking the "Extra steps: Install languages" button. You would do this before removing the installation folder. This step will install various multilanguage setups for you automatically. If you plan to have multiple languages on your site, this step will save you a lot of time.

3. Remove the installation folder by clicking the orange button that says "Remove installation folder." Alternatively, you may remove the installation folder via FTP or cPanel.

Figure A-9. Joomla Web Installer – Finish

That's it. You now have Joomla installed. The frontend of your website will look similar to Figure A-10.

Figure A-10. Frontend of newly installed Joomla website

Access your site and administrator panel by utilizing your URLs:

- You should be able to access the frontend of your site by going to *http://www.<your-domain>.com*.

- To access the administrator panel, go to *http://www.<yourdomain>.com/administrator* and enter your newly created username and password.

 If you uploaded the Joomla installation package via FTP or cPanel and then extracted the files via the File Manager, you will notice that the zipped package is still located in the root of your site files. It is safe to delete this file. You do not need it. It just takes up space and is no longer necessary in that format.

When you log in to the backend administrator panel, you will find that you have some System Messages. One of them is about Two Factor Authentication. We recommend that you not enable this functionality until you read and understand what this feature does. See more about Two Factor Authentication and Yubikey in Chapter 14.

Global Configuration

Now that you've installed Joomla, you are going to want to make at least a few setting changes in the Global Configuration. Here are the main settings to address after you install Joomla and are logged into the administrator panel:

1. Click on System and then on Global Configuration.
2. In the Site tab, make sure your site name is entered.
3. Scroll down and enter information into the Site Meta Description and Site Meta Keywords fields.
4. Set Robots to "No index, no follow" until you are ready to go live.
5. Change the Show Joomla Version setting from Yes to No.
6. If you are building on a temporary URL that looks like */121.121.12.12~username/*, do not worry about your SEO settings at this time. If you are building on your domain where the site is going to reside, then you can change the SEO settings by following the instructions in "SEF URL Settings and SEO Basics" on page 238 about Search Engine Friendly (SEF) URLs. If in doubt, don't change them right now.
7. In the System tab, scroll down and change your Session Lifetime to 60 (do not set this number too high, as it is dangerous to do so).
8. In the Server tab, verify that the Mail Settings fields for "From email" and From Name are how you would want them to appear when emails are sent from the system, so as to not create confusion for the recipient.
9. Do not touch Permissions or Text Filters for now.

That is all. You can now move on to more exciting aspects of building your website with Joomla.

Global Configuration Expanded

The System menu has settings and tools that affect your website from a global perspective. This includes Global Configuration, Mail Settings, Time Zone, FTP Layer, and more.

The first item in the System drop-down is Control Panel. Clicking this link will get you back to the Control Panel or Administrator Dashboard regardless of where you have been working in the Joomla CMS.

The Global Configuration page contains settings that affect your website from a global perspective.

You must be logged in to the backend as a Super Administrator in order to access the Global Configuration page. It is best to limit the number of people who have access to

Super Administrator accounts. The main difference between Administrator and Super Administrator is that Super Administrators have the ability to break the site more easily. They have the ability to accidentally uninstall needed extensions, and the Global Configuration page is where Super Administrators have the potential to cause the most problems to the site if they don't know what they're doing.

There are two ways to access the Global Configuration screen:

- Click the Global Configuration icon in the Control Panel
- From the top menu, select System and then Global Configuration

It's safe to click around and play with most of the options; however, there are some options that, if changed, would cause your website to cease functioning.

The Global Configuration page is broken down into five main tabs, and those tabs are outlined in the following sections.

Site

The Site tab contains options that affect how the site functions from a usability standpoint.

Site settings

Site Name

Site Name is the name of your website, commonly displayed in the title bar of your browser.

Site Offline

Setting this to Yes will cause the frontend of your website to display an offline message instead of any site pages, based on the selection in the Offline Message field you see below it. If Custom Message is selected from the drop-down, the text in the Custom Message editable box will appear instead of loading your site. A login screen will also appear to allow authorized people to view the site while offline.

Offline Message

You can select whether to display a custom message, the Site Language Default Message, or hide any offline message. This is the message displayed when the website is offline.

Custom Message

This editable box is where you can enter the text you want to display when the site is in offline mode. This box accepts HTML.

If you don't know HTML and want to style your message to look different than just plain text, you can design a custom message using an article with an editor. Toggle the source view and copy the HTML from the article, and paste it into the Custom Message field.

Default Editor

When creating articles, Joomla provides a rich WYSIWYG content editor allowing you to quickly format your content as you would in a word processing program. You can specify the default editor for all users.

Default Captcha

Joomla comes with a delightful ReCaptcha Plugin that can be enabled to provide captcha on forms, to prevent spam and bots from attempting to inject negative items into your site. See Chapter 10 for how to set up ReCaptcha for your site. There are other captcha extensions available. If installed, they will appear in the drop-down here and can be selected as the Default Captcha.

Default Access Level

Select the default access level for content and menu items: this can be Public, Registered, Special, or a custom access level you create.

Default List Limit

When listing content in the Joomla backend, this parameter is the number of items to display per page. This is only the default value, and users have the ability to adjust this when viewing the list.

Default Feed Limit

When syndicating articles or other items using the RSS features of Joomla, this field represents the maximum number of items that will be displayed.

Feed Email

When the feed is generated, the author is shown for each item. This setting allows you to dictate whether you want the feed to show the author's email, the site's email, or no email.

Metadata settings

Site Meta Description

This contains the description metadata. This helps search engines know what your site is about. Some search engines display your meta description under the link to your site within their search results; therefore, it is important not to leave this as the default Joomla description.

Site Meta Keywords

This contains the keyword metadata. Although search engines don't rely on this as much today as they once did, it tells them what keywords you want associated with your site.

Robots

There are four options for directing search engine crawlers on how to handle your content. This information is stored in a file called *robots.txt*. The four options are:

- Index, Follow
- No index, Follow
- Index, No follow
- No index, No follow

Index means that you are telling search engines to index the page. *No index* means that you are telling search engines not to index the page. *Follow* means that you're telling search engines to crawl the links on your page. *No follow* means that you are telling search engines not to crawl the links on your page.

In general, if your site is live and you want people to get to your site, set this option to Index, Follow. If you are in development, then perhaps you want to set this to "No index, No follow" until you are ready to go live.

Show Author Meta Tag

If set to Yes, the author of the article you are viewing will show in the metadata.

Show Joomla Version

If set to No, the version (e.g., 3.x or 2.5) of Joomla will not show in the meta generator. The name Joomla will still appear in the generator.

SEO settings

Search Engine Friendly URLs

Friendly URLs are human-readable and are better for search engine ranking. This setting turns them on and off. "SEF URL Settings and SEO Basics" on page 238 goes into much more detail on the subject of Search Engine Optimization and Search Engine Friendly URLs.

Use Apache mod_rewrite

This indicates whether you want to use Apache's Rewrite module, an extension for Apache that rewrites URLs. This requires the use of the included *.htaccess* file.

Add suffix to URLs

When turned on, the file suffix *.html* will be added to the end of all friendly URLs.

Unicode Aliases

If set to Yes, then non-Latin characters are allowed in the alias and URL. If no, then a title that includes non-Latin characters will produce the default alias of the current date and time. The default setting is No.

Include Site Name in Page Titles

This will include the site name in the page titles. For example, if set to Before, the browser tab will read My Website Name - Article Title. The options for this feature are After, Before, or No. We recommend using After or No.

Cookie settings

Cookies are used to track sessions and are necessary for some operations within Joomla. The settings below are used to further fine-tune cookies set by Joomla. In general, the defaults (leaving the fields blank) will work for most users.

Cookie Domain

This is for telling the system the domain to use when setting session cookies. Precede with a dot (.) to make valid for all subdomains. Example: *.TheDomain.com*.

Cookie Path

Enter the path for which the cookie is valid.

System

The System tab contains options that relate to sessions, debugging, and cache handling.

System settings

Path to Log Folder

This is the path to the Joomla log file where errors are recorded. This path is set by the installer to the */logs* directory.

Help Server

When you choose the server to pull help files from, you are also setting which language to use for help.

Debug settings

Debug System

When debugging is turned on, information to help you troubleshoot a variety of issues is displayed at the bottom of each page.

Debug Language

Similar to Debug System, except that this only displays language information for the Joomla language files. This is useful when writing your own extensions.

Cache settings

Cache

Turning on the cache can help speed up sites with lots of traffic by reducing the number of MySQL queries and the amount of processing power needed to render and return pages. If enabled, however, changes to your site will not appear until the Cache Time (see below) has expired. This setting should not be used in the process of developing a site when many changes are being made and testing is being done.

 Always test cache performance. The cache setting sometimes has unpredictable results depending on the server. Some extensions may break while using cache. Always test and use with care.

Cache Handler

The Cache Handler setting tells Joomla where to store the cache.

Cache Time

This tells Joomla how long to cache a file. After it expires, a new cache file will be created.

Session settings

Session Lifetime

After you have been idle for the given amount of time, the system will automatically log you out. Although it is tempting to make this a really large number so that you never have to worry about being kicked out in the middle of writing a long article, it truly is a security risk. This is especially true if you will be accessing your site from public computers.

Session Handler

The Session Handler setting tells Joomla where to store user session information. Using Memcache is not recommended at this time.

Server

The Server tab contains server-specific options like locale, FTP, database, and mail settings.

Server settings

Path to Temp Folder

This is the folder Joomla uses when storing temporary files. For example, when you install an extension from an archived file, this is the folder where files are extracted before they are actually installed. The default directory is */tmp*. It will appear in this field with your specific server path, with */tmp* as the last part of the path.

GZIP Page Compression

When set to Yes, HTML and other code is compressed before it is sent from the server to a site visitor. For large sites, this setting may improve page loading times.

Error Reporting

Error Reporting sets the level of reporting PHP errors.

Force SSL

This forces your site to run under Secure Sockets Layer (SSL). You can choose Entire Site (frontend and backend) or Administrator Only. Using SSL means that all traffic to and from your site will be encrypted and not readable by hackers using packet-sniffing software. You will need to make sure that you have a valid certificate installed, or end users will receive a warning from their web browser when visiting your site. By default, this is set to None.

Location settings

Server Time Zone

Select your time zone from the drop-down box.

FTP settings

Enable FTP

Most people installing Joomla will not need to enable the FTP layer within Joomla. If you are having permissions issues, then contact your host and have them install the patch suPHP or FastCGI to your server if possible. If they won't do this, then switch hosts.

FTP Host

This is the name of the host for your FTP server. Typically, 127.0.0.1 works.

FTP Port

The default port for FTP is port 21. However, some hosts change this for security reasons, so check with your hosting provider if it doesn't work.

FTP Username

This is the username for the FTP account.

FTP Password

This is the password for the FTP account.

FTP Root

Typically, when you log in to your hosting account via FTP, you won't end up in Joomla's root directory by default. The FTP Root is nothing more than the path from FTP's root directory to Joomla's directory.

Database settings

Database Type

The database type is almost always MySQLi. Changing this field could cause your site to stop working, so it shouldn't be changed unless you know exactly what you're doing and know the type of database created and working for your site. A reason you may want to change it is if you switch hosts to one with a different type of compatible database or change the type of database on your current server.

Host

The hostname is where Joomla can find your database. Most often this is local host, but if your database is on a different server (GoDaddy uses a different server), you'll want to enter it here.

Database Username

This is the username for the MySQLi account that has access and write privileges to your database.

Database Name

This is the name of the database where your Joomla tables are.

Database Tables Prefix

All of the Joomla tables for this installation begin with a database prefix. This is randomly generated by Joomla upon installation for security purposes. See Chapter 14 for more on security. If you wanted to add a second installation to Joomla and not create a new database, you could just give it a different prefix. Prefixes can be lowercase letters, numbers, and underscores. Once this is set, you will probably never change it.

You may have noticed that Password is not an option within the Database Settings. If you want to change the MySQLi password, you'll need to manually change the $pass word variable in the *configuration.php* file located in Joomla's root directory.

Mail settings

Mailer

When Joomla sends out an email, this determines what method to use.

From email

When an email is sent out, this is the return email address.

From Name

When an email is sent out, this name is shown as the sender.

Sendmail Path

If you set Mailer to be Sendmail, this is the path to the Sendmail script on your server.

SMTP Authentication

If you set Mailer to be SMTP Server, this tells Joomla if the SMTP server requires authentication.

SMTP Security

You simply select the security model that your SMTP server uses; either SSL or Transport Security Layer (TSL).

SMTP Port

This is where you enter the port number of your SMTP server. Generally it is 25 for unsecured servers and 465 for secured servers.

SMTP Username

When authentication is required, you must supply a username for the SMTP server.

SMTP Password

When authentication is required, you must supply a password for the SMTP server.

SMTP Host

This tells Joomla where the SMTP server is located. If it is located on your server, you could leave this value as localhost.

Permissions

In the permissions tab you set the permissions settings for the user groups listed there. You would do well to thoroughly review "Users, User Groups, Access Control Lists (ACLs), and Frontend Editing" on page 244 before changing any of these settings. Permissions for user groups get confusing quickly, so read first, read again, and then make changes.

The screen works in the permissions tab like this: you click on one group at a time on the left starting with Public and ending with Super User, and it opens a screen to the right where you can change the permissions for various actions for that user group. You can then change the permissions for those actions in the Select New Setting column.

Check out "Users, User Groups, Access Control Lists (ACLs), and Frontend Editing" on page 244 for detailed information on the wonderful world of permissions.

Text filters

The following Filtering Options are used to control filtering on article submissions. These are essentially security precautions to keep malicious code from being added to your website, but they can also filter unwanted code in articles when an article is submitted or edited:

Filter Groups

Select the user group(s) to which you want the filters applied.

Filter Type
> Select the type of filter you want to apply:
> - Default Blacklist: When selected, this will filter out the following blacklisted tags by default: `applet`, `body`, `bgsound`, `base`, `basefont`, `embed`, `frame`, `frameset`, `head`, `html`, `id`, `iframe`, `ilayer`, `layer`, `link`, `meta`, `name`, `object`, `script`, `style`, `title`, and `xml`. It will also filter out the following blacklisted attributes by default: `action`, `background`, `codebase`, `dynsrc`, and `lowsrc`.
> - Whitelist: This allows only the tags specified in the Filter Tags or Filter Attributes fields.
> - No HTML: This removes all HTML from the article when submitted.

Filter Tags
> List additional HTML tags to filter, separating each with a comma or space. These tags will be either blacklisted or whitelisted, depending on your Filter Type setting.

Filter Attributes
> List additional attributes to filter, separating each with a comma or space. These attributes will be either blacklisted or whitelisted, depending on your Filter Type setting.

These Filtering Options are applied regardless of which WYSIWYG editor is used.

For more explanation on Text Filtering, see "Adding Embedded HTML Code and Text Filtering" on page 112.

 Some third-party editors have their own filter configuration options. See the documentation for your particular editor for more information.

Global Check-in

When an article is edited, Joomla will lock it so that multiple users can't edit it at the same time and accidentally overwrite or delete each other's changes. The article (this also applies to components, categories, modules, and menu items) is unlocked when you click the Save or Close buttons in the toolbar when editing the article. When you close the browser without clicking Save or Close, your session expires, you use the Back button, or you just navigate away from an open article, you never unlock it. When this happens, no one else can edit it. This is actually a great feature and prevents website administrators from having to manage "content conflict." However, we're all human and sometimes we forget to close an article properly.

When items are being edited, a small padlock icon like the one shown in Figure A-11 will appear next to the title.

Figure A-11. Checked-out article in Article Manager

There are three ways to unlock a locked item.

1. Have the person who has it locked finish editing the item and click Save & Close.
2. Use Global Check-in.

> To use the Global Check-in feature, click System and then Global Check-in. Looking at Figure A-12, you'll see that Global Check-in not only checks in articles, but many other types of items as well.

3. If you have the authorized permissions, you can check in the item in the Article Manager, Menu Manager, or Module Manager by clicking on the lock icon or selecting the checkbox in front of the item(s) and clicking the Check In button in the toolbar.

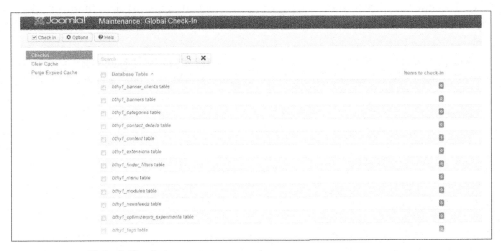

Figure A-12. Global Check-in

If you want to edit an item that is locked and checked out, pay special attention to the time. If you see that it was checked out recently, it is a good idea to check with the person who checked it out to make sure they're not still editing it. If you use Global Check-in and then edit an item while someone else is also editing it, the second person to save the item will overwrite the first person's edits.

Clear Cache

The term *cache* (pronounced like the word "cash") might be a fairly common word, but not everyone knows exactly what it is. Essentially, it's a space where items can be quickly stored and reused in order to save resources and time.

Each time you view a page on your website, Joomla does a lot of work to build each piece of the page, and then puts them together like pieces of a jigsaw puzzle. When the page is complete, the web server sends the rendered code back to your browser, where you actually view the page. When caching is turned on, the individual puzzle pieces are saved to files after they are built. The next time someone needs that puzzle piece, Joomla will get it from the file instead of working to build it again. After a set period of time, that puzzle piece will expire and Joomla will build a new puzzle piece and place it into cache. Typically, cache refresh happens every 15 minutes. Cache settings in Global Configuration can be used to specify the amount of time to cache these puzzle pieces.

On sites with few visitors, caching serves little purpose. On high-traffic sites, caching is vital to minimize server load time, which in turn greatly improves site performance.

To access the Cache settings, click System and then click Clear Cache. Figure A-13 shows the Maintenance: Clear Cache screen with a few cached items. To clear them, check the ones you want to delete and then click Delete in the toolbar.

Figure A-13. Maintenance: Clear Cache - Clear Cache Admin

Clearing the site's cache may need to be done if you have made substantial changes to your website and they aren't appearing on the frontend.

Purge Expired Cache

When the cache refreshes, the old cache files are not removed. To purge expired cache, click System and then Purge Expired Cache. You should see a screen like Figure A-14.

Pay close attention to the warning listed in Figure A-14. If you have a large number of expired cache items, consider performing this action during a time of day with lower traffic.

Once you have read the warning message and are ready to proceed, click the "Purge expired" button in the top toolbar.

Figure A-14. Purge Expired Cache

Depending on site traffic, you should notice that most or all the cache files are now purged.

System Information

System Information provides an overview of certain Joomla and server settings. The tabs in System Information are especially important when troubleshooting problems with your Joomla site.

System Information
> This tab contains basic information about your server and the installed applications needed to run with Joomla.

PHP Settings
> This tab contains PHP settings set by your server administrator that can affect the performance of your website.

Configuration File
> This tab contains the contents of your website's *configuration.php* file. Most of these settings can be changed from within Global Configuration.

Directory Permissions

This tab contains directory permission information vital for proper operation of your website. Every row in the status column should say Writable in green letters. If a directory is not writable, you will see Unwritable in red letters. To correct this, you'll need to change the permissions on those folders, and probably contact your hosting provider for assistance.

PHP Information

This tab gives you an overview of your server's PHP settings.

Updating and Migrating Joomla

Joomla Updates

Things change. This truth is perhaps the only thing that doesn't change. This includes website software like Joomla.

Sometimes you will hear your host tell you that you have outdated scripts or you need to keep your scripts updated. "What is a script? I'm running scripts?" you may ask yourself. And yes, you are. The language Joomla's code is written in is PHP, which is technically a scripting language. A script is a list of commands that are executed by a scripting engine. Joomla itself is a script. Your template is a script. Any third-party extensions are scripts.

The importance of keeping your scripts updated is paramount to the continued health and safety of your website. Outdated scripts can potentially make your site more vulnerable to attack. In fact, the top two reasons sites are hacked are:

1. An improperly configured or vulnerable hosting environment
2. Outdated scripts

We will walk through various means of updating your Joomla site and third-party extensions in this appendix. We will also cover migration from one version of Joomla to another, which is a necessity in order to operate your website with the most recent version of Joomla (a script).

Updating Joomla Within a Release Cycle

Periodically, Joomla will release security and/or feature updates when necessary. It is important to do these promptly. Upgrading Joomla has never been particularly difficult. Since Joomla 2.5, it is even easier for anyone to update Joomla to the latest release.

There are two ways to find out about security updates:

1. Subscribe to receive Joomla Announcements and Security Updates (*http://bit.ly/joom-updates*). You'll receive notification when an update is available.

2. A large pink banner appears across the top of the Control Panel, as in Figure B-1.

3. On the left sidebar of the Control Panel under the heading Maintenance, there is a Quick Link that will state "Joomla 3.2.1 is available: Update now," as can be seen in Figure B-2.

Figure B-1. Update alert banner at top of Control Panel

Figure B-2. Control Panel icon showing a Joomla Update is available

Follow these steps to upgrade your website:

1. The first step when an upgrade to your site is available is to do plenty of due diligence. Read as much as you can about the update by going to Joomla's website and look at the known issues. Click the FAQs for the release link and read what is there. Go to the Joomla Forums (*http://forum.joomla.org*) and see if others are having problems with the update.

2. Back up your website. See "Mastering Backups" on page 56 for instructions on how to use Akeeba Backup in order to create a backup of your site.

3. The pattern of excellence is to restore this backup into a new subdomain or subdirectory as a test site. Visit Akeeba Backup (*http://www.akeebabackup.com*) for documentation on using Akeeba Kickstart (*http://bit.ly/akeebackup*) to restore your backups.

4. Click Components and click on Joomla Update.

5. You will see the version of Joomla you are running and the version available (Figure B-3).

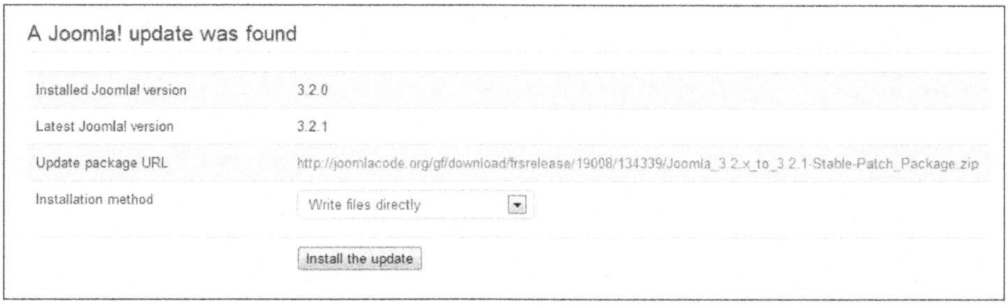

A Joomla! update was found	
Installed Joomla! version	3.2.0
Latest Joomla! version	3.2.1
Update package URL	http://joomlacode.org/gf/download/frsrelease/19008/134339/Joomla_3.2.x_to_3.2.1-Stable-Patch_Package.zip
Installation method	Write files directly ▼

Install the update

Figure B-3. Joomla Update screen

6. Click the "Install the update" button.

You will see the progress of the update and get a notice when it's complete.

Now, test the site. Add an article and add some content to the article with various formatting. Insert some images and do some linking. Add a menu item. Test whatever people do on your site both from a visitor perspective and an admin perspective. If something goes wrong, use a search engine or visit the Joomla Forums to find others who may have gotten the same error you did, or are experiencing the same problem and learn how it was resolved. In fact, it's a pretty good idea to do a search for any update problems before doing the update. Even if you do have problems with the update, you can relax knowing that you are on a test site and not on a production site.

Once you determine that the update has been installed correctly and your components are working properly, back up your live site again and execute the update on your live site. This is also a good time to go through your other extensions and update them if there are updates that have been provided by the developer(s). Maintaining your scripts/extensions is very important. See the next section for more on updating third-party extensions.

We like to run a backup again after the update. Akeeba Backup allows you to associate a note with the backup. You can type **After 3.x.x update** so that you know which backup it is, in case you need to restore it in the future. These notes can be found by hovering over the i icon from the Manage Backups tab of Akeeba Backup.

Updating Third-Party Extensions

There are two types of third-party extensions:

1. Those that notify you through the backend of Joomla and can be updated through the one-click update function.

2. Those that do not notify you through the backend of Joomla and/or must be manually updated via the Extension Manager.

On the Control Panel in the left sidebar under the heading Maintenance, there is notification that Joomla is up to date (see Figure B-4) and another that will say either "All extensions are to up to date" or "Updates are available!" If an extension that can be updated through Joomla has an update available, it will appear here. Clicking on the link will take you to the same place as clicking on Extensions and again on Extension Manager.

 Even if the Maintenance heading states that all extensions are up to date, you still need to check other extensions that do not notify you via the backend of Joomla. Those extensions need to be updated manually.

Figure B-4. The Maintenance section of the left sidebar shows available updates

Click on the left sidebar option Update. Here you will see a list of extensions that need updating, as in Figure B-5. Follow the same routine you would for any update:

1. Read.

2. Back up.

3. Update a test site.

4. Test.

5. Update the live site (button in top toolbar).

6. Test.

7. Back up again.

8. Repeat if necessary.

	Name ⌃	Install Type	Type	Version	Folder	Client	URL Details
	Gantry	Update	Library	4.1.19	N/A	Site	http://www.gantry-framework.org/updates /joomla16/gantry.xml http://www.gantry-framework.org

Figure B-5. A third-party extension update available in the Extension Manager

Some third-party extensions want you to update by installing the new extension package (typically in a *.zip* or *tar.gz* file format) over what you already have. This is done via the Extension Manager on the Upload Package File tab, as we did when installing Akeeba Backup (see "Mastering Backups" on page 56).

In some rare cases, third-party extensions will direct you to uninstall the extension through the Manage section of the Extension Manager and then reinstall the new version of the extension. Never uninstall an extension in an effort to update unless specifically directed by the developer. Uninstalling extensions will mean the loss of your configuration settings in most cases. Use caution and always do a backup first.

You can check with the extension developer's website or the JED to see if newer versions of the extension are available. Check the developer's instructions on updates concerning their extensions, as one approach does not fit all.

Joomla Migrations

Between major releases of Joomla, significant changes take place that sometimes require a restructuring and associated migration of data as opposed to an update. Technology changes not just from the Joomla side but also with the versions of PHP and MySQL that force CMS technology to change with it.

Migrations from one life cycle of Joomla to another give everyone many opportunities to:

- Assess site goals and determine if they are being achieved
- Clean up "great ideas" that didn't turn out so well
- Remove extensions that were installed and not used
- Simplify
- Develop new areas of the site
- Change design and/or flow
- Increase usability
- Increase accessibility to disabled folks
- Increase functionality for visitors on multiple screen resolutions
- Improve SEO
- Take advantage of new features

One of the members of the Joomla User Group (JUG) that Jenn co-organizes used a good illustration that she has altered slightly to more easily describe the process of migration from one major release of Joomla to another.

Imagine in your mind's eye that you have decided to move to a new home. It doesn't matter if this is a new larger home or if you are downsizing to a smaller home. The concept is the same.

In your current home, you have furnishings in each room. Perhaps you have a couch and some coffee tables in the living room. Perhaps you have a table and chairs in the dining room with a big hutch. Let's just say you have a bedroom and an office, each with some furniture in it.

You have found a new home to move into. It's great! Yet, some of the furniture that is working fine in your current home isn't fitting perfectly into the new home. The new home doesn't have a dining room. What are you going to do with that dining room set? The hutch is going to have to be sold.

The living room in your new home is huge! The couch and furniture you have in your current home are going to look like doll furniture. Thankfully, your new home has two bedrooms, and your bedroom and office furniture will fit just fine.

So it is with migration in Joomla. It is moving your data and extensions from one home to another. Perhaps literally if you choose to change hosts at the same time. The articles, categories, menus, and modules are pretty simple to move. The data in extensions perhaps easy and perhaps not so easy. It could be that an extension you have been using hasn't been updated for the new version of Joomla—it will be like that hutch in the dining room. It will have to go. Some other extension or solution will have to be found in order to fulfill the functionality that extension served—if it's still required.

Isn't that a great illustration?

Planning for Migration

The first step in any migration process, whether big or small, is planning. Plan, plan, plan. There is no substitute for planning. If planning takes a week or six weeks, so be it. Planning makes the entire process easier.

The following are considerations for performing a major migration. A major migration would be moving from Joomla 1.0 or 1.5 to Joomla 3.x. A mini-migration, such as Joomla 2.5 to Joomla 3.x, means that Joomla core content is a one-click update, and third-party extensions need to migrate. The amount of work is determined mainly by the third-party extensions in use. Each of the following considerations should be thought about when planning a major or minor migration.

1. Revisit your goals. This is an opportunity to get back on track or change track.

2. Take a look at your existing site from the backend.

3. Make a list of all extensions in use; both the components that install with Joomla and third-party extensions. This includes components, modules, plugins, languages, and templates.

4. Make note if those extensions are used heavily, moderately, hardly ever, or never.

5. Research whether the extensions you rely on are ready for the version of Joomla you are migrating to.

6. Determine if you really need all the extensions you are using. Is it possible that the newer version of Joomla has features that replace an extension you were using?

7. Does the developer of extensions you must keep have a migration path for you to follow from one version of the extension/Joomla to another?

8. Take a look at your sections (if Joomla 1.5) and categories. Sections no longer exist from Joomla 2.5 on. Perhaps there is cleanup that needs to be done so you don't migrate unnecessary sections and categories.

9. Are the categories you have still applicable? Make a list of categories you may want in your "new" site.

10. Take a look at your articles. Is there cleanup that needs to be done? Are there articles in the trash? Best not to move those over. Note or make a list of articles you want to move over.

11. Are you using Joomla Contacts, Web Links, or Newsfeeds? Make note of those, as they will need to move over.

12. Are you going to move over users? If you are using a third-party extension to gather additional data on users, is that going to move over?

13. Take a look at your Media Manager and determine if you need to or want to move it all over. If your Media Manager has become a nightmare, you may want to move your images over manually via FTP or cPanel instead of migrating the entire directory. For more on Media Manager organization, see "Organizing Media" on page 137.

14. Check out your modules. Are there any special modules from third-party developers? You will need to find out whether they are ready for the version of Joomla you are moving to.

15. Look at your template. Has the developer updated it for the version of Joomla you are migrating to? Was it heavily customized? If so, those changes will all have to happen again. Are you using a custom template? It will have to be converted and changed to work with the new version of Joomla. Do you have any desire to have a responsive template? If so, now is the time to decide.

16. Find a template that is compatible with the version of Joomla you are migrating to, or hire someone to migrate your template to work with the version of Joomla you are migrating to.

17. Will your new template have different module positions than your old/existing one? If so, just know to allocate time to change the positions of all of your modules to the new position names.

18. Will your new template require different images? For example, if the header on your existing template is white and the background of your logo is white, and you choose to move to a new template where the header is black, you may need have some image work done so that your images look good. Images with a white background do not look fantastic against black or even off-white, as in a main content area. Keep these things in mind when looking at templates or modifying the template CSS.

19. Check your menus and determine if you will be bringing them all over. Check the trash and ditch any that are there.

20. Are there features of the new version of Joomla that you wish to utilize, like Access Control Levels (ACLs)? If so, now is the time to begin planning for it. Planning ACL structures is a careful and thorough business. Do not rush.

21. Is your existing site using functionality that "hacked the core"? Those changes won't be migrated. This is a good time to clean up "core hacks" by using template CSS overrides or other override techniques.

22. Are the internal links in your content hyperlinked with relative URLs? If not, while in migration mode those links may not work, or they will need to be fixed.

23. Will you have obsolete pages requiring redirects so as to not lose your SEO standing?

The bottom line is that you are determining what stays, what goes, and what changes in every aspect of migrating your existing site to your new site.

Essentially, a migration is a new website—it's just that you already have data. The data will be migrated/moved with minimal effort for the most part. Still, you're building a new website in a new version of Joomla. It will all have to be cleaned up. Migration entails a lot of cleanup. Joomla core data is the simple part of a migration. The more challenging aspects involve the third-party extensions, especially components with data that needs to migrate. Templates are always an important aspect of this.

Each third-party extension developer will have different means of migrating data from one version of Joomla to another. It is up to you to seek this information out and determine the migration path for the individual extension. It will generally fall into one of a few processes:

1. The third-party developer has a documented process to move the data which is fairly simple to follow.

2. The third-party extension is no longer developed for the newer version of Joomla and you must choose a new one.

---

3. Start from scratch or move (copy and paste) data manually (by hand) with an updated version of the extension in the new version of Joomla.

It is outside the scope of this book to describe the thousands of possible migration paths of third-party extensions. There are many articles to assist you on the Internet, and we encourage you to research and read prior to migrating third-party extensions.

Steps for Mini-Migration: Joomla 2.5 to 3.x

The process for Joomla 2.5 sites to go to 3.x is considered a mini-migration. That means that Joomla core extensions (categories, articles, modules, menus, core settings, and plugins) can be updated from 2.5 to 3.x with a one-click update. Third-party extensions may or may not need to be migrated or may only need to be updated.

If the third-party extension includes versions for 2.5 and 3.x in the same *.zip* or *tar.gz* file, it won't require migration and can be updated via the one-click updater.

If the third-party extension has a separate file for a 2.5 installation and a 3.x installation, then you will need to migrate the data according to the developer's documentation.

As of May 2014, the exact verbiage for selections has not been decided by the Joomla Production Leadership Team (PLT). In general the steps below reflect how to perform a mini-migration. They may change slightly. Definitely check documentation provided by Joomla when updating/migrating from Joomla 2.5 to 3.x if anything you see on your screen is different from the list of instructions that follow.

1. Read.
2. Back up.
3. Restore on test environment, subdomain, or subdirectory.
4. Update Joomla to the latest release in the cycle.

 Step 4 must be done in order for the update that will get you to 3.x to appear in your 2.5 site. Failure to update to the latest 2.5.x version could create unknown and perhaps terrible results. Have a backup and be on a test environment to mitigate ill results.

5. Uninstall all extensions (modules, plugins, extensions, templates, packages) that are not ready for Joomla 3.x or do not have a 3.x-ready version inside the same .zip or *tar.gz* file. (Any extensions that aren't ready that you do not uninstall will result in displaying an error and the white screen of death for your update.) If you need to uninstall your template, select a default template like Beez in the Template Manager prior to uninstalling your template.

6. Update all extensions that do have a 3.x version inside the same .zip or *tar.gz* file to their latest release.

7. Back up your site again.

8. Disable the Remember Me plugin via the Plugin Manager.

Failure to disable the Remember Me plugin may throw an error on your update with the infamous white screen of death. Fixing it is a pain, and it's faster to just restore a backup and start over. If you do want to fix it, visit the Joomla Community Form (*http://forum.joomla.org*) and search for "disable *remember.php*" and give it a go.

9. Click on Components and again on Joomla Update.

10. Click on Options.

11. From the drop-down, select the update server option that will get you to 3.x.

The name of the Update server option has not yet been established as of May 2014. Use caution, as there will be as many as three simultaneously maintained release cycles at this time. You want the one that gets you to the 3.x series. As of May 2014, this is labeled Short Term Support.

12. Click Save & Close.

13. Once your available update appears on the Control Panel or in the Joomla Update component, run the update.

14. Click on Extensions and then on Extension Manager.

15. Click on Database on the left sidebar and then click the Fix button.

16. Get ACL Manager and repair your missing assets, orphaned assets, and asset issues. Follow the instructions in steps 23–30 of "Hands-On Exercise: Migrating from Joomla 1.5 to 3.x" on page 301.

17. Check the frontend of your site to make sure you have no white screens of death. If you have a white screen of death, it means that there was an extension still installed that isn't compatible with Joomla 3.

18. Reinstall any necessary third-party extensions, including your template, one at a time.

19. Test everything.

20. Back up your 3.x test site.

21. Move or restore your 2.5 site to a new directory from the root of your hosting for safekeeping until you are sure you no longer need it for anything.

22. Move or restore your 3.x test site to the root of your hosting to make the new 3.5 site your live site.

23. Remove the 2.5 site as soon as possible so you do not have a security vulnerability on your server.

24. Remove the test site in a subdomain if applicable.

25. Remove any unnecessary and unused MySQL databases for the test site or 2.5 site as well.

Steps for a Full Migration from Joomla 1.5 to 3.x

Joomla 1.5 was built with a completely different structure than 2.5 or 3.x. Thus, it is a major migration process to go from 1.5 to 3.x. Thankfully, tools exist to assist us in migrating the areas of the site that install with Joomla, including articles, modules, contacts, etc.

Third-party extensions need to be handled individually, as described earlier.

Migration Tools

The most popular tools to assist with migration are:

SPUpgrade

> We will use SPUpgrade, as it is quick, simple, popular, and an accurate method for migrating Joomla core content and some third-party extensions. SP Upgrade does cost a small amount and it is worth every penny. Check out SP Upgrade on the JED (*http://bit.ly/sp-upgrade*).

JUpgrade

> Many have had good success with this noncommercial (free) extension to migrate between major Joomla releases. Many have not. Its purpose is to move Joomla content, not third-party extensions. Check out JUpgrade on the JED (*http://bit.ly/j-upgrade*).

redMIGRATOR

> redMIGRATOR is a fork of JUpgrade by redCOMPONENT. Check out redMIGRATOR on the JED (*http://bit.ly/redmigrator*).

J2XML and J2XML Importer

> During migration, some decide to rebuild sites entirely from scratch. This is fine if it is a small site; it can be quite time-consuming with a large site. Enter J2XML. J2XML migrates Web Links, sections, categories, and articles. It also migrates users and images associated with the articles while keeping the article IDs, which is

important to most from an SEO perspective. It starts from a clean install of the new version of Joomla from scratch and an empty database, and inserts articles as if they had been hand-entered, which makes for a cleaner move of the data, yet leaves you to create your menus and modules all over again. This is clean and more time-consuming. Check out J2XML (*http://bit.ly/j2xml*) and J2XML Importer (*http://bit.ly/j2xml-imp*) on the JED.

Migrate Me

New to the migration scene is Migrate Me. While we haven't tested this method, we hear there is good success with it and have had success with other extensions by this developer. Check out Migrate Me on the JED (*http://bit.ly/migrate-me*).

Case Study: Migrating www.usingjoomlabook.com from Joomla 1.5 to 3.x

As a supplement to *Using Joomla* First Edition (O'Reilly), *www.usingjoomlabook.com* was created in Joomla 1.5. Now that we have a Second Edition of *Using Joomla*, the content and the Joomla version need to be updated without removing the information from the First Edition.

The case study for this section will be to migrate *www.usingjoomlabook.com* from Joomla 1.5 to Joomla 3.x. We followed the planning guidelines seen in "Planning for Migration" on page 294 and have determined the following:

- System Info shows us that the technical specifications for Joomla 3.x are met on this server. We can proceed.
- There is only one third-party extension installed that is not in use. We will not migrate it.
- There is an additional language pack installed but no content for it. We will not migrate it.
- We will need a new template. We will chose one that is responsive.
- There are a few Web Links in one category. We will bring those over. There are many Web Link categories that do not have any Web Links in them. We will not migrate those empty categories.
- There is one content section with five categories. There are just a handful of articles. We will migrate the section, categories, and articles.
- A handful of Joomla core modules are in use. We will migrate the modules.
- Two menus exist; the Main Menu and a Hidden Menu Links menu. We will bring the menu items from both menus to the 3.x site. It is common to see a menu called Hidden or something to that effect. Often a menu item is created in a hidden menu to create and control URLs for articles that are not displayed to visitors, or to manage which modules display with those articles. While it may appear that the menu isn't in use, and one might be tempted not to bring over the menu items, it could be

important to do so—or certain links within content articles, links published on other websites, or those published in the first edition of the book may not work properly or would require a 301 redirect.

- This is a simple site with only a few images, which are all found in the root of the */stories* directory. */stories* is the default image directory in Joomla 1.5. Changing the image locations will break image links and require reinserting the image with the proper link if you want them to appear. With a lot of images, you will want to keep images in the directories they currently exist in. We will bring over all the images in the */stories* directory along with the directory itself.

- Google Analytics is coded into the template directly. We will need to make sure we add Google Analytics to the new template after the new migrated site goes live.

- We will be changing the menu structure of the migrated site so that the information from the first edition stays intact, with the same URLs, and also includes new pages for the second edition.

The *www.usingjoomlabook.com* site is very simple (see Figure B-6). Yours may be more complex, and it cannot be stressed enough that you should plan accordingly. You must think about everything. Even when you think you've prepared enough, it still could be that something unexpected arises. This is normal, and it is important to not get down on yourself or give up. Ask for help on the Joomla forums if you need to.

Hands-On Exercise: Migrating from Joomla 1.5 to 3.x

1. Create a subdomain, subdirectory, or an environment on your local device where you will install a fresh installation of Joomla 3.x.

2. Install Joomla 3.x using the directions in Appendix A. Do *not* install sample data!

3. Install Akeeba Backup using the directions in "Mastering Backups" on page 56.

4. Take a backup of your clean 3.x site.

5. Take a backup of your 1.5 site and test that it restores properly. Update your 1.5 site to the last release of Joomla 1.5, which is 1.5.26.

 If your 1.5 site does not have Akeeba Backup installed already, you will want to install it to take your backup. See Akeeba Backup's version compatibility (*http://bit.ly/akeeba-backup*) page to determine the version of Akeeba Backup to use. Installing the current version of Akeeba Backup on a 1.5 site will *not* work.

6. Purchase and download the SP Upgrade (*http://bit.ly/dl-spu*) extension. Unzip and extract the files on your local device.

Figure B-6. Frontend of Joomla 1.5 version of www.usingjoomlabook.com

7. Install the applicable SP Upgrade package into your 3.x website (the file package that begins with 3.x.x).

8. Click on Extensions and again on SP Upgrade. You will be greeted by an error and a warning. It's OK—just keep following the directions.

9. Click the Options button.

10. In the Configuration tab (Figure B-7), leaving the Same IDs Handling and the Duplicate Alias fields at their default settings will likely be appropriate for you. By leaving the Same IDs Handling as "Replace existing items" we keep the IDs from the 1.5 site, which is important from an SEO perspective. We have zero existing items, so there is nothing to overwrite. Leaving the Duplicate Alias set to Yes will

add letters and numbers to any duplicate aliases that may exist. In 1.5, duplicate aliases were allowed. From 2.5 on, they are not. The rest will be addressed in future steps.

Figure B-7. SP Upgrade Configuration tab

11. Click the Database tab and enter the 1.5 database credentials. You can find the database credentials in the *configuration.php* file in the root of your Joomla 1.5 site. SP Upgrade automatically fills in the Database Tables Prefix field in with jos. That is the default prefix in 1.5. You may have a different prefix.

12. Enter the FTP credentials into the FTP tab. The correct path to the root needs to be in the FTP Root field. This might be *public_html*, *httpdocs*, or might even be *public_html/directory*.

13. Leave the Permissions tab alone.

14. Click Save & Close.

15. If the banner in the dashboard turns green (see Figure B-8), you're good to go. If it is still red, then something is wrong in your database credentials or FTP login/path. SP Upgrade documentation is quite good. You must be logged in to Cyend's website to access the documentation.

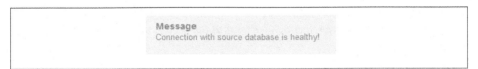

Figure B-8. SP Upgrade healthy connection message

16. The left sidebar of SP Upgrade show the sections of the extension. In the Core Transfer section, select the core components you would like to migrate. Checking the box and leaving the "ID's to transfer" field blank will move all items in that core component. For example, checking the Web Links Category box will bring all Web Links categories. We only want to bring one category, so we will enter the category

ID in the field. The ID can be found in the manager for any component. We only want to move the category ID 35 for Web Links. We will enter that in the field.

 Make sure you bring over sections and categories. If you use the logic that we don't use sections anymore and only bring over your categories, many things will be broken and you will have to start over. Bring sections and categories over and clean them up later.

17. We are bringing over the following: Users (all), Sections (all), Categories (all), Articles (all—see Figure B-9), Web Links Category (35), Web Links (all—see Figure B-10), Menu Types and Items (all), Modules (1,40,42,45,46,47—no spaces between the commas), Images (all—FTP is required to bring over images, see Figure B-11).

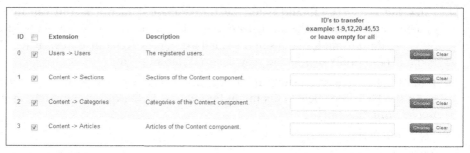

Figure B-9. Migrate all users, sections, categories, and articles with SP Upgrade

Figure B-10. Migrate select categories and all Web Links with SP Upgrade

Figure B-11. Migrate all menus, select modules, and all media with SP Upgrade

We do not recommend attempting to bring your 1.5 template to 3.x. It's not pretty. You can try to bring over your 1.5 template and see how it does migrating it to 3.x. If you do, bring your content first and then make a backup. Bring your template last, so that if it is nothing but a disaster, you can restore the backup and swap out your template to take advantage of newer technology and keep more of your hair.

18. Click the Transfer button and click Yes to proceed. A pop-up window will appear and refresh every 15 seconds. If you have a large amount of data to move, it can take some time. Let it do its thing. It will show Process Completed when complete.

19. Copy this data to a *.txt* file. Some errors show up here, and you will want to go back and resolve them. You can also access this information via the Monitoring Log on the left sidebar.

20. Click on Extensions and then on Extension Manager.

21. Click Database on the left sidebar and run the Fix.

22. Back up your site.

23. Purchase and download ACL Manager (*http://www.aclmanager.net/*). What? When migrating data, some of the assets in the tables get scrambled causing problems down the road. While fixing the asset tables is possible manually via phpMyAdmin, ACL Manager includes a feature for fixing them *so* easily that we recommend using it unless you have experience with databases. See ACL Manager on the JED (*http://bit.ly/acl-manager*).

ACL Manager is a top-rated extension, and while we are using it here to assist with migration cleanup, it does far more. If you have complex Access Control Levels (ACLs) and user group set up on your site, we cannot recommend ACL Manager more. ACLs can get complicated fast. ACL Manager helps you manage them.

24. Install ACL Manager.

25. Click on Components and again on ACL Manager.

26. The ACL Manager dashboard has a box titled Diagnostic Checks. You will see right here if you have asset issues, as we do in Figure B-12.

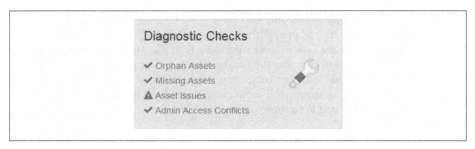

Figure B-12. Asset issues shown easily for us with ACL Manager

27. Click on the Asset Issues link in the Diagnostic Checks box, and it will take you to the Diagnostic page and show you all your problems. This happens in migration. It's OK.

28. Click the Fix Asset Issues button at the bottom of the page to fix them all. This will take a few seconds, and then you will understand why we recommended this extension and the few dollars it costs. It just saved you oodles of time.

29. Back up your site again. Yes, again. If in doubt, back up.

30. Uninstall ACL Manager (unless you have more data to move and will need to fix more asset issues or you intend to use it for ACL management long-term on your site) by going to Extensions and then Extension Manager. Click Manage on the left sidebar. Type **ACL** into the filter. Check the box for ACL Manager and then click the Uninstall button in the top toolbar.

31. Install your new template and customize as desired.

32. Change the positions of your modules if applicable, so they appear where you want them to in your new template.

33. Check the *.txt* file you created with the details from your data transfer. If there are any items that added sp-23908439847 or something to that effect, they need to be addressed as you go through.

34. Make sure all your users are assigned to a group. If they aren't, add them to the applicable group. Do not leave any user groups empty; this could trigger a mail error and send mail to people that you don't intend.

35. Make sure the users' email addresses don't have a 15 appended to them and fix them if they do, so those people will still be able to recover their passwords and receive system mail.

36. Clean up your categories. We are going to change the name of the General category to First Edition and leave the nested categories as is. We also added a category for Second Edition that all our new articles will go into.

37. Clean up your articles. If any of your articles came over with an alias including sp-123235342525, you will want to address it. First, go to your article trash and empty it. Second, check your Archived Articles and see if there are duplicate aliases that would have caused this alias addition to have occurred.

38. Make sure all articles are in a category. If they have an empty category, or a category that says ROOT, that means it was in the uncategorized category and needs to be placed in a new category or nested category.

39. Some article content that looked fine in your 1.5 template may not look fine in an updated template with newer technology. You may need to remove extra spaces and address some messy HTML code. Some tips on this are found in Chapter 5.

40. Look at the frontend of your site and check that your menu items are working properly.

41. Check the frontend of your site and make sure your hyperlinks are working properly. If they are not, you will need to either link them again or verify that they will work again once the site is live. For example, if you linked directly to *http:// www.yourdomain.com/contact* instead of a relative URL, the page will work again when you go live with the proper domain. You just won't be able to use that link to view it until then.

 Broken links after a migration is a lousy problem to find you have. Improper creation of links in your original articles can create hours of work in a migration. If you have the budget to do so, hire someone to check links and update the broken ones. If you don't have the budget or don't trust other people to do it for you, the following items can make it easier for you:

- Have blocks of an hour or two to work at a time
- Have a nice glass of water or iced tea at your desk
- Up-tempo music—play music that can help keep you going
- Make sure you blink your eyes often
- Stand up, stretch, and walk around every hour for 10–15 minutes
- Take it one page or category at a time, and don't think about the others
- Know that you are not alone—lots of link fixing happens at migration

42. Check the frontend to ensure that your images have come through properly and are displaying. If they are not, check them and relink them if necessary.

43. Back up often.

44. If you have third-party extensions, address each one. Back up before you install new extensions. Back up after you are done configuring new extensions. Uninstall extensions you have installed and decided not to use. Uninstall SP Upgrade when you are done migrating data.

45. Make sure your Global Configuration is as it should be and that your Global Metadata is moved over from your 1.5 site.

46. Check the current 1.5 site and make sure that any new content that has been added since the migration started gets moved over to the Joomla 3 site.

47. When you are totally happy with your 3.x site, take a final backup of it.

48. Make a spreadsheet or list of any 1.5 URLs that have changed between your 1.5 site and 3.x site.

49. Move your 1.5 site out of the root to another subdomain or subdirectory, or simply delete it.

50. Use Akeeba Kickstart to restore your 3.x site to the host root.

51. Take another backup.

Then do other little things like:

1. Enable *.htaccess* and SEF URLs.

2. Add Google Analytics tracking code to the new template.

3. Submit any new site map to Webmaster Tools.

4. Create any 301 redirects for new URLs that are different from the 1.5 URLs.

5. Make any other changes that needed to wait until the 3.x site was live.

Before doing any redesign for the second edition of *Using Joomla*, our migrated site's frontend looks like Figure B-13. If you go to *http://www.usingjoomlabook.com* now, you will see the finished product.

Figure B-13. Newly migrated site for http://www.usingjoomlabook.com from 1.5 to 3.x

Migrate to a New Host While Migrating to 3.x

If you decide that it is also time to move to a new host at the same time as you migrate your site, there are a few slightly different setup options that will make your life easier in the long run.

1. Install your fresh build of Joomla 3.x on a temporary domain in the root of your new hosting account.

2. Restore a copy of your 1.5 site in a subdirectory of the root at the new host.

3. Exclude the 1.5 subdirectory from your backup in Akeeba Backup in your Joomla 3 site.

4. Migrate your data from the 1.5 site in the subdirectory to the new 3.x site in the root.

5. When you're ready to go live, change the nameservers for your domain from your old host nameservers to the new host nameservers.

6. Kill the 1.5 site.

Choosing the Right Extensions

It has been said that cooks are only as good as the ingredients that they use. We're not so bold to say that your website is only as good as the extensions you use, but if you use the wrong extensions, you may set yourself up for heartache later.

Which Extension Is Right for Me?

When choosing extensions, there are many questions to ask yourself. This chapter will go through some of those questions.

What Do I Want the Extension to Do?

There are thousands of extensions for Joomla. Chances are that an extension already exists to do what you are looking for. Getting a clear idea of what you want the extension to do will make your search a whole lot easier.

You should first look at the Joomla Extensions Directory (JED) (*http://extensions.joom la.org/*). Categories are broken out logically. Most categories have subcategories that focus on specific needs.

New in Joomla 3.x, you can access and install some extensions from the backend of Joomla. This does not replace the need to take the steps in the rest of this chapter before installing an extension. Any extension installed needs to be maintained. Only use extensions that you need. Uninstall extensions not in use.

If your requirements for an extension are very specific and there is nothing already developed that meets your needs, you may need to hire a programmer to write the extension for you. This may be from scratch or using another extension as a starting point.

What Do Others Say About the Extension?

One of the great features of the JED is that you have the ability to read user reviews of extensions. This is your best source to find out both positive and negative aspects about the extensions. We don't recommend that you rely solely on testimonials the developer posts on its own website.

Am I Willing to Pay for the Extension?

Some people new to Joomla are put off when they find they have to pay for some extensions. Some people think that since Joomla is free, why shouldn't the extensions also be free?

The truth is that it takes time to develop extensions. The developers that write these extensions often devote huge amounts of time in order to provide a product for the world to use. Some developers write and support extensions as their full-time job. So it only makes sense that they are compensated for their time.

Most of the extensions that require payment have very reasonable prices. You may think that $50 seems like a lot of money, but when you compare it to the hourly rate of hiring your own developer to build an equal product, you'll quickly discover that $50 is a bargain.

We're not advocating that you should pay for all of your extensions, or even that extensions you pay for are better than extensions that you do not pay for. We're saying that if you find that a specific extension that costs money and does what you need better than a free one, go with the one that costs a little money. In the long run, we think you'll be glad that you did because of the support you'll receive.

We all know that software piracy is wrong, yet so many people do it. If you download a pirated version of an extension, there's no way to really know what you are actually downloading. The person that pirated the software could have added their code to do something malicious. Let's explore some of the consequences that might convince you not to pirate extensions. A pirated copy of the extension could potentially do one of the following:

- Email each of the users signed up on your website letting them know that the owner of the site likes to steal software
- Blindly create a Super Administrator user for the hacker to log into your website
- Upload a file that could be used to completely delete your website
- Give the hacker the ability to send spam from your server

It is common for the original developer of the real extension not to provide support on pirated versions of their extension.

You may want to consider giving a donation to developers for their non-commercial extension for the same reason that some developers charge—to compensate them for their time and to show some gratitude. Additionally, donating to an extension developer gives them incentive to continue development of the extension in the future. Good reviews on the JED show the developer that there is public appreciation of their extension, which provides further incentive.

Can I Get Support on the Extension If I Need It?

Some extensions provide excellent support. Some extensions provide no support. The ability to obtain support, whether free or paid, is important if you ever have a problem.

Checking the developer's website to see how they handle support is an important point in deciding on which extension to use. Do they have a ticketing system? Do they have a public or private forum?

If the developer's website looks like it has not been updated or the forum is full of unanswered questions, you can pretty much expect that you won't get any help from the developer if you have issues. Also be on the lookout for developers who consistently ask for backend access to your site to resolve some issue and never report back to the forum to explain the fix. Without knowing what was changed on your site to fix a problem, you do not know if an update will override the fix.

If you can see that the support forum offers prompt answers to questions, that is a good sign.

Check the documentation on the developer's website. Good documentation is priceless. If you have permission to access it, read it to help you make a decision. Some developers do not allow you to read the documentation until you purchase the extension, while some others have you pay for a membership to access the documentation.

Changelogs

Investigate the extension version changelogs to get a feel for how often the developer updates the extension. Check the amount of time that passes in conjunction with major Joomla releases. It is important to see the response time to bug fixes and how the developer responds to Joomla releases, which may force the extension code to change.

License

Almost all software made today is released with some license attached to it. The license states what you can and cannot do with the software. Some licenses are very restricting while others are very free.

Joomla is released under the GNU General Public License Version 2 (GNU GPL). The GNU GPL license gives you a lot of freedom when it comes to what you can do with the software. All extensions listed on the Joomla Extensions Directory are licensed under GNU GPL.

Not all extensions for Joomla are released under the GNU GPL license. We are not going to open a GNU GPL debate in this chapter—we will only state that it's the Joomla Project's stance that extensions are derivative works and therefore should also be licensed under the GNU GPL. As a Joomla user, you have to decide whether you want to use extensions that adhere to Joomla's principles or if you're willing to veer away from the GNU GPL license when choosing extensions. We're not going to make that decision for you, but we recommend you get as informed as possible and come to your own conclusion.

To learn more about the GNU GPL, refer to the license information that is included in the root directory of every Joomla web site. Specific filenames are:

- *LICENSE.php* for Joomla 1.5
- *LICENSE.txt* for Joomla 2.5 and 3.x

Even if you only read the Preamble, it is worth it. You will get a good basic understanding of the freedoms that are given to you.

Is It Secure?

Extensions listed on the JED are not audited for security issues in advance of being listed. The JED relies on users to report back their experiences and help with crowd-sourced reviews. While it would be ideal to be able to audit every extension in advance of being listed on the JED, the truth is that it would take a lot of manpower to do a security audit on every extension. Here are some quick things that you can do to check for some basic security issues:

At the top of the extension's PHP files, there should be a check to see if _*JEXEC* is defined. This is to make sure that you cannot call the file directly, since we want all files to be called through Joomla's main *index.php* file.

Example: `defined('_JEXEC') or die( 'Restricted access' );`

Occasionally, there's a good reason why a file would need to be called directly. If you do not see the `defined()` command from above in one or two files, you may want to check with the developer to make sure that it was done intentionally.

`JRequest` should be used to request all variables. If you see `$_REQUEST` = anywhere in your extension, you should be very cautious. You may be vulnerable to SQL injections.

Did you download the extension from a trusted source?

Visit and get the latest list from the Joomla Vulnerable Extensions (VEL) (*http://vel.joomla.org/*) team. Report issues to the developer and possible security issues to the VEL team if you find them.

Is the Extension Encrypted?

In the software industry, many companies encrypt their software so that the code is not visible. Typically, this is done in order to preserve intellectual property. In the open source world, people prefer their source code to be open without encryption. If there's a problem with a component, we want to be able to fix it ourselves if we need to. If there is something we wish worked a little differently, we want to be able to change it.

For the most part, all extensions are open source. There are some extensions that resort to encrypting a single file that performs checks to see if you legally purchased a license to use. Depending on the type of encryption, you may have to have special software installed on your server to interpret it.

Where Can I Find an Extension Used in This Book?

All of the extensions that we spotlight in this book have a link to the website where they can be downloaded. The following is a chapter-by-chapter list:

Chapter 3

- Afterburner2 (*http://bit.ly/afterburner2*) template by RocketTheme
- Akeeba Backup (*http://www.akeebabackup.com*)
- Akeeba Kickstart (*http://www.akeebabackup.com*)

Other popular template companies:

- Joostrap (*http://www.joostrap.com*)
- Joomlashack (*http://www.joomlashack.com*)
- YooTheme (*http://www.yootheme.com*)
- Joomla Bamboo (*http://www.joomlabamboo.com*)

Chapter 4

- JCE Editor (*http://www.joomlacontenteditor.net*)
- CK Editor (*http://bit.ly/ck-editor*)

Chapter 6

- sigplus Gallery (*http://bit.ly/sigplus-ext*)

Chapter 8

- Kunena (*http://www.kunena.org*)
- Komento (*http://stackideas.com/komento*)

Chapter 9

- JEvents (*http://www.jevents.net/*)

Chapter 10

- Contact Enhanced (*http://bit.ly/contact-enhance*)
- SecurImage Captcha (*http://bit.ly/secur-capt*)
- RSForm Pro (*http://bit.ly/rsform-feat*)

Chapter 11

- HikaShop (*http://www.hikashop.com/*)

Chapter 12

- JomSocial (*http://www.jomsocial.com*)
- Community Builder (*http://www.joomlapolis.com*)
- Easy Social (*http://stackideas.com/easysocial*)
- AddThis (*https://www.addthis.com*)
- Kunena (*http://www.kunena.org*)
- Acyba AcyMailing (*http://www.acyba.com/en/acymailing.html*)

Chapter 13

- iSEO from iJoomla (*http://seo.ijoomla.com/*)
- ACL Manager (*http://aclmanager.net/*)

Chapter 14

- JAMSS (*http://bit.ly/jmass-script*)
- Brute Force Stop (*http://bit.ly/brutestop*)
- Joo ReCaptcha (*http://bit.ly/joo-recap*)
- Akeeba Admin Tools (*http://bit.ly/akeeba-admin*)
- watchful.li

Appendix A

- OS Content (*http://bit.ly/OScontent*)

Appendix B

- SP Upgrade (*http://bit.ly/dl-spu*)
- ACL Manager (*http://www.aclmanager.net/*)

Other popular migration components:

- J2XML (*http://www.eshiol.it/*)
- Migrate Me (*http://www.php-web-design.com/*)
- jUpgradePro (*http://matware.com.ar/proyects/jupgradepro.html*)

As time goes by, we expect that some of those links will change or even disappear. If a link from the book changes or no longer works, we will update it on the website that accompanies this book to point to its new location.

Ways Extensions Are Packaged

There are thousands of extensions available for installation with Joomla. They tend to come packaged in four different ways:

Universal Installer
> A single ZIP file with everything required to install in any version of Joomla. Simply upload the ZIP file in the Extension Manager and click the Install button.

Version-Specific Installer
> You are offered a file for Joomla 2.5 and another file for Joomla 3.x. Upload the appropriate file for your version of Joomla in the Extension Manager and click the Install button.

Separate Extension Installers for each feature
> Instead of a single package file, there may be separate ZIP files to download and install for each component, module, and plugin. Just make sure the files you download are for the Joomla 3.x version. These files can be uploaded and installed via the Extension Manager in any order.

A ZIP file that contains a bundle of ZIP files
> These are the only downloads that cannot be uploaded and installed directly. The hint is that the filename will include words like "UNZIPFIRST" in it. If you attempt to install this ZIP file, no harm will come to your Joomla installation. You will get an error saying "No manifest file could be found." Simply unzip the file locally and inside you will find more ZIP files, one of which will be for Joomla 3. Upload and install the file to the Extension Manager.

Disable Install from Web Feature

With the new Install from Web feature in Joomla 3.x, it is easier than ever to install extensions. With this ease comes responsibility. While the feature is fantastic, you don't want others with access to the backend to be able to install extensions haphazardly. You will want to disable it when not in use. Here's how to do it:

1. From the administrator Control Panel, click on Extensions and then on Plugin Manager.

2. Type **web** into the filter/search bar.

3. For the Plugin Name Installer - Install from Web, click the green checkmark button in the Status column so that it is disabled.

4. Go to Extensions and then Extension Manager and click the X to close the Install from Web message at the top of the Extension Manager.

5. This takes you to a page named "Installer configuration." Click the "Hide message" button for Joomla Extensions Directory.

To enable the Install from Web feature again, simply enable the plugin.

Developing for Joomla

Joomla development is driven by contributors of both the Joomla CMS and Joomla Framework. The Joomla Extension Directory (JED) is full of hundreds of developers who have extended Joomla in many ways and made it even more powerful. If you want to contribute to make Joomla better or develop your own extensions, here are a few resources and bits of information.

Joomla Framework and API

The Joomla Framework (*http://framework.joomla.org*) is the underlying scaffolding the Joomla CMS is built upon (and replaces the Joomla Platform). They are really separate pieces, but together they make up what is installed with Joomla. This lightweight framework enables developers who are interesting in building their own application via an API (*http://bit.ly/joom-api*) to leverage the power and benefits of Joomla, even if they don't want to use the CMS. It also enables Joomla Framework developers to implement and take advantage of the most modern trends in web application development. The framework is developed independently from the CMS, so the version numbers are different. When the CMS team is planning their next release, they decide which version of the framework is appropriate for their needs, and that's what is incorporated.

It is licensed under the LGPL (the CMS is still licensed under the GPL), which allows for more flexibility in how it can be used and integrated with other applications. This should greatly help increase enterprise adoption.

If you're interested in contributing to the Joomla Framework API, visit these sites:

- Contributing to the Joomla Framework on Github (*http://bit.ly/joom-contribute*)
- Joomla Framework on the JDN (*http://bit.ly/joomla-frame*)

Developer Resources

As a developer, you have a great opportunity to contribute new features to Joomla and help fix bugs. The Project can always use more code contributions, especially from highly skilled PHP developers.

Before you get started developing on Joomla core code, you need to sign the Joomla Contributor Agreement (*http://bit.ly/contrib-agree*). It takes only a few minutes online and basically says you agree to distribute your contribution under the same license used by Joomla. Once you do that, you're ready to go, but there are a few basic requirements:

1. All code has to meet the Joomla Coding Standards (*http://bit.ly/j-code-stand*).
2. It has to include automated tests (unit and/or system) and pass those tests.
3. Any new functionality needs at least some basic documentation.

We also recommend you get some background on development before you dive right in. Some developers just start writing what they think is cool before finding out if it's really something that can be used in the Joomla codebase. It's a good idea to visit the Developer Network (*http://developer.joomla.org*), understand the Joomla Development Strategy (*http://bit.ly/j-strategy*), and view the latest updates to the roadmap (*http://developer.joomla.org/cms/roadmap.html*) before you spend time on something you think fits with the team's strategy. Talk to team members and see what they think about your ideas.

If you're interested in developing your own extensions for Joomla, the documentation wiki has a few tutorials on how to create a basic component, module, and plugin. Templates are also considered extensions (though they aren't allowed in the Joomla Extensions Directory) and are easy to create once you know the basics.

All Joomla code is managed on GitHub (*https://github.com/joomla*), so if you're not familiar with distributed revision control, you should read up on how it works (it's a very unique, but far superior, approach to source code management). If you prefer a free SVN-based code repo for your project, you can use JoomlaCode (*http://joomlacode.org*) for code management—it includes a robust tracker, download manager, and a few other handy features.

How to Get Involved and Give Back to the Community

There are a lot of things you can do to give back to the Joomla Project, no matter how limited or deep your technical knowledge is. Here are a few ways:

Answer Questions on the Joomla Discussion Forum
> Participating on the Joomla forums (*http://forum.joomla.org*) is probably the easiest way to get involved in Joomla and where most people get their start. There's no time

commitment beyond what you dedicate, and it's a good way to make a name for yourself.

Join the Joomla Bug Squad (JBS)

The JBS (*http://bit.ly/j-bugsquad*) is the heart of software development, and it's responsible for testing, reporting, and fixing bugs in Joomla. You can help verify bugs, browse the forums and report bugs in the tracker, and more.

Report Bugs and Test Fixes

All software has bugs. You can help find them and add them to the bug tracker (*http://bit.ly/j-bugtracker*). Make sure you provide as much information as possible about the bug, and also be sure to search the tracker before you post to see if your bug has already been found or fixed.

Join a Joomla Mailing List

Mailing lists (*http://www.joomla.org/mailing-lists.html*) are used for communication in many areas of the Joomla Project. Join one (or all!) to see the latest developments in the framework, CMS, Leadership Team, and more.

Share Your Ideas for Improving Joomla

Do you have great ideas for how to make Joomla even better? You can add your ideas to the idea portal (*http://ideas.joomla.org*).

Translate Joomla

Joomla might not be in your language, and if you speak multiple languages, the Project could use your help—you can join or create a Translation Team (*http://bit.ly/translate-team*).

Organize a Joomla Event

JoomlaDays and other events are a great way to meet other Joomla fans from all over the world. See current events and find out how you can host your own on the Joomla Community Portal (*http://community.joomla.org/events.html*).

Sponsor Development

If you are a business, you can help by sponsoring new features for upcoming releases. Get in touch with David Hurley, Community Development Manager, at *david.hurley@joomla.org* or Open Source Matters (*http://opensourcematters.org*) for details on how to get started.

Tips and Tricks

Having used Joomla since its inception, we've collected a variety of helpful tips along the way. Here are a few we think are pretty important to have in our tool bag.

How to Recover Your Admin Password

Yes, it happens to all of us at some point or another. We get locked out of our own home and need to find a way back in. The procedure for Joomla 2.x and 3.x is a little different than it was in Joomla 1.5. There are two ways to do it, and we'll start with the easier of the two. You'll need FTP access to get to the *configuration.php* file.

1. Use an FTP application to connect to your site and go to the root folder. You should see all your Joomla files there, including the *configuration.php* file.

2. Download this file and open it up in a text editor (e.g., Notepad++, TextWrangler, or Sublime Text). Make sure this is a plain text editor that doesn't convert the file to RTF or some other text format (don't use something like Microsoft Word for this).

3. Add the following line to the end:

   ```
   public $root_user='myname';
   ```

    Replace *myname* with a username for which you know the password and save the file.

4. Delete the *configuration.php* file on the server and upload this new file. You will now be a Super Administrator and can log in to make any necessary changes, including resetting the Super Administrator password.

5. Once you've completed your changes and gained access, try the automatic removal of the line you added to the *configuration.php* file. This has mixed reliability, so it's probably best to edit the file, remove the line, and reupload the original file.

 Be careful about setting your file permissions, and make doubly sure they are set to 444 on the *configuration.php* file. This file has important access information for your site and database, so protect it with the correct file permissions!

If changing your *configuration.php* was unsuccessful, you'll have to edit the database directly using a tool such as phpMyAdmin. If you don't have access to it (it's usually available in most hosting packages and setups), ask your hosting provider to set it up or help you accomplish the following steps:

1. Go to phpMyAdmin and open the database for your site. You will see a list of tables in the left column.

2. Find the "_users" table and click on it to view the users. The actual name of this table will depend on the prefix defined during the Joomla installation.

3. Find the user you want to give access to in the list and click the Edit link in the left column to edit that record. Enter the following sequence into the password field:

    PD3Y0MClapAvHimedwAq8KHQ7/byH6F0

4. Click the Go button at the bottom to save the record.

You can now log in with that user account and use **help** as the password.

If neither of these methods work, you will need a SQL statement to insert a new record, which requires more advanced skills. Consult the Joomla Help documentation (*http://bit.ly/j-help-docs*) for instructions on how to do this. You will need to scroll a good way down the page to locate the instructions for Joomla 3.x.

How to Tell If a Website Is Running Joomla

With Joomla 1.5 it was easier to tell if a website was running Joomla, but that's changed with Joomla 2.x and 3.x. Here are a few ways you can tell:

1. Look at the source code for the page to see if you can find the meta tag within the <head>:

   ```
   <meta name="generator" content="Joomla - Open Source Content Management" />
   ```

2. Check the source code and see if known Joomla template names (e.g., *beez_20*, *protostar*) are in use within the <head> to call CSS and JavaScript files.

3. Add */administrator* to the end of the top-level URL to see if the Joomla administrator login page comes up.

4. Look for common file paths to libraries Joomla needs to work:

   ```
   /media/system/js/mootools-core.js
   /media/system/js/core.js
   /media/system/css/system.css
   ```

5. Use the Chrome Sniffer plugin in Chrome.

Index

Symbols

.htaccess file, 260
404 pages, custom, 42

A

About menu items, 51–55
Absolute Beginners Guide to Joomla, 30
Access Control Lists, 17
    content access with, 248
    in Users menu, 246
access level, setting, 277
ACL Manager extension, 249, 305
ACLs, 17
    migrating, 305
    viewing/modifying, 27
Acyba, 231
AcyMailing, 231–236
    integrating with contact forms, 187
    mailing lists, 232
    sending newsletters with, 233
    subscription management, 235
AddThis module, 222
administrator modules, 32
administrator panel, 23–35
    components menu, 29
    content menu, 28
    control panel, 23
    extensions menu, 29

    help menu, 30
    in other languages, 152
    menus menu, 27
    personal information settings menu, 32
    system menu, 25
    users menu, 26
Adobe Dreamweaver, 3
Advanced tabs, 72
AdWords, 241
Afterburner2 templates, 20, 58–72
Akeeba Admin Tools, 256
    PHP File Change Scanner, 260
Akeeba Backup, 56, 263, 290
    migrations and, 301
Akeeba Kickstart, 263, 290
Akismet, 212
Alias field (Category Manager), 42
Amazon, 197
AmeriCommerce, 197
Android, 257
Apache, 239
Apple iCal, 221
archiving articles, 123
Article Manager
    display, 33
    filtering, 33
    footer menu, 34
    top toolbar, 33
Article Options, 86

We'd like to hear your suggestions for improving our indexes. Send email to index@oreilly.com.

articles
  adding contact forms to, 185
  adding media to, 131–137
  archiving, 123
  blogs as, 155–157
  checking in, 26
  creating, 43–46
  customizing, 97–105
  deleting, 123
  displaying, 12
  embedding image galleries in, 142
  filtering, 33
  management, 119–124
  option hierarchy, 85–93
  ordering, 121
  permissions, 122
  planning, 15
  publishing, 46
  setting schedules for, 156
  unpublishing, 46
  versioning/revisions and, 119–121
Assignments tabs, 72
Atomic template, 19
attributes, 186
  filtering, 284
Azrul, 211

B

Backend Administrator Control Panel
  Footer menu and, 34
  template parameters, 58–72
backups, 56–58
  migrations and, 301
  recovering from security breaches with, 259
bak_, 271
BlackBerry, 257
blogs, 155–163
  adding comments, 157–163
  adding modules, 157–163
  adding tags, 157–163
  articles as, 155–157
  creating posts for, 156
  editing layouts globally, 90
  latest posts modules, 162
  scheduling articles, publish/unpublish, 156
Blue Eagle template (Kunena), 231
Blueprint framework, 19
Bootlicker template (Kunena), 231
Bootstrap, Twitter, 19

broken links, 307
Brute Force Stop plugin, 254
bugs, reporting, 323
buttons, 8

C

cache, 286
  clearing, 26, 286
  purging, 287
  settings, 280
Captcha, 26
  adding to forms, 188
  clearing files, 158
  setting default, 277
Cart Module (HikaShop), 208
categories
  copying, 42
  creating, 38–40
  editing globally, 90
  of contacts, 181
  of User Notes, 27
  planning, 14
  publishing/unpublishing, 40
  setting up, 37–43
  uncategorized, 42
Category Blog menu item, 15, 51–55
  ordering, 121
Category List menu type, 55
  ordering, 121
Category Manager, 37–43
  Save as Copy button, 42
  Status column, 40
ccNewsletter, 236
check-in, 121
  from System menu, 26
  global, 284–286
Claverie, Nicolas, 202
CMS, 3
  check-in, 121, 284–286
  editing articles and, 119–121
CodeMirror, 93
ColorZilla, 64
comments, 159
Community Builder, 222, 229
Community Portal, 31
components menu, 29
Constant Contact, 236
  integrating with contact forms, 187

Contact Enhanced (Ideal Extensions)
    configuring, 185
    installing, 180
contact forms, 179–189
    adding fields to, 186
    adding to articles, 185
    adding to menu, 184
    creating, 180–183
    testing, 188
contacts, categories of, 181
content, 85–125
    article options hierarchy, 85–93
    copying, 98–99
    customizing articles, 97–105
    embedded HTML code, 112–116
    heading lists, 102–104
    hyperlinking, 105–112
    keywords, 118
    menu item options, 91–93
    Meta Description, 118
    modules, adding, 124
    Page Break, 117–118
    pasting, 98–99
    pasting lists, 100–101
    Read More button, 117–118
    tables, 105
    text color, 104
    text, filtering, 112–116
    translating, 149–151
    underlining, 104
    WYSIWYG editors, 93
content management system (see CMS)
Content menu, 28
Control Panel, 23
    Add New Article link, 43–46
    quick links in, 24
cookie settings, 279
cPanel, 263
    Password Generator, 265
credit cards, 210
CSS
    heading tags, 102–104
    in WYSIWYG editors, 97
    overriding, 67–69
custom HTML modules, 64, 73–79
    creating, 74
custom messages, 276
customizing articles, 97–105

D
database
    configuration, 269–272
    settings for, 282
    setup, 263–266
Database Fix tool, 237
debug settings, 279
default editor, 277
default list limit, 277
Developer Network, 322
developer resources, 322
display, 33
documents, linking, 137
donation forms, 191–193

E
Easy Social, 222
eBay, 197
editors, changing globally, 93
email
    configuration for, 272
    hyperlinking to, 110–112
    security and, 283
    settings for, 282
error reporting, 281
event calendars, 165–177
    adding events to, 169
    adding from frontend, 176
    adding to menu, 167–168
    categories, 167–168
    creating, 166
    from other pages, 176
    installing/configuring, 165
Eventbrite, 170
events
    adding from frontend, 176
    in JomSocial, 218–222
    one time, 169
    recurring, 171–175
    title formatting, 166
Extension Manager, 25, 29
    languages, installing with, 147
extensions
    choosing, 18, 311–319
    developing, 322
    encryption of, 315
    licenses for, 313
    packaging of, 318

security of, 314
support for, 313
Extensions menu, 29
external hyperlinks, 109–110

F

Facebook, 211, 222, 257
    AddThis module, 222
Favicon, 241
Featured button (Add New Article), 44
featured layouts, editing globally, 90
Featured Menu Item types, 121
Features tab, 69
Federal Express, 202
Feed component (Joomla), 90
feed email, 277
file size, limiting, 140
File Transfer Protocol (see FTP)
FileZilla, 58, 266
filtering, 33
Finish Publishing parameter, 156
Firebug add-on, 66
flood protection, 229
follow buttons, 222
Font setting, 65
footer menu, 34
Footer Style, setting, 64
formatting, removing, 100
forms, 179–195
    adding Captcha to, 188
    adding fields to, 186
    adding to menu, 193
    contact, 179–189
    creating contact pages with, 180–183
    donation, 191–193
    RSForms Pro and, 190–195
forums, 159
    creating categories for, 225–228
    for user engagement, 224–231
    Joomla community, 322
    permissions, 228–229
    spam, preventing, 229
Free Software Foundation, 3
frontend layout, 82
FTP, 263, 266–274
    clients, 58
    settings for, 281

G

Gantry Framework, 61
Gimp, 139
GitHub, 322
Global Article Options, 85
    setting, 87–91
Global Check-in feature, 284–286
Global Configurations, 275–284
    Server tab, 280–284
    Site tab, 276–279
GNU General Public License (GPL), 1, 313
Golden Gate Kennel Club, 221
Good Password, 265
Google
    Authenticator, 257
    Calendar, 221
    Checkout, 197
    Maps, 182
    placement scams, 241
    Presentations, 10
    ReCaptcha, 188, 212, 229
    Spreadsheet, 189
    Website Optimizer, 205
GroupJive, 229
GZIP page compression, 281

H

hacking, recovering from, 259
Header Style, setting, 64
heading tags, 102–104
health checks, performing, 254–256
help
    files, 279
    guide, 30
Help menu, 30
HikaMarket Multivendor, 203
HikaShop, 198
    categories, adding, 204
    characteristics, adding, 204
    configuring, 200
    installing, 199
    modules, adding, 208
    products, adding, 204
homepage
    as uncategorized page, 42
    layouts, 20–20
hosting control panel, 263

hosting services, 262
    changing during migration, 309
HTML code
    attributes, 186
    embedding, 112–116
human-friendly URLs, 238
Hurley, David, 323
hyperlinking, 105–112
    documents, 137
    email addresses, 110–112
    external, 109–110
    images, 136
    internal content, 106–109

I

ICS file support, 221
Ideal Extensions, 179
IgniteGallery, 144
iJoomla, 211
image galleries, 140–144
    creating, in module, 141
    embedding in articles, 142
    sigplus, 141
Imageoptimizer, 139
images, 131–137
    adding to articles, 131
    changing, 136
    linking, 136
    moving in Media Manager, 130
    naming, 139
    optimizing, 139
    organizing, 132
    removing, 136
    resizing, 139
    uploading, 132
Inspect Element function (Chrome), 66
Install from Web feature, 56
    disabling, 318
internal
    links, 106–109
    pages, 22
iOS, 257
iSEO extension (iJoomla), 240
Itemid parameters, 53

J

J2XML, 299
J2XML Importer, 299

JCE, 94–96
    downloading, 93
    uploading images with, 132
JED, 31, 311
JEvents extension, 165–177
    adding events to, 169
    adding to menu, 167–168
    installing/configuring, 165
    third party tagging tools and, 161
JEvents Latest Events module, 176
JFBAlbum, 144
JMASS (Joomla Anti Malware Scan Script), 254
jNews, 236
JomSocial, 211–222
    custom user profiles, 213
    events in, 218–222
    installing/configuring, 211
    integrating with Kunena Forum, 221
    user groups in, 216–218
Joo ReCaptcha plugin, 255
Joomla, 1–5
    administrator panel, 23–35
    CMS and, 3
    database setup, 263–266
    designing with, 4
    developer resources, 322
    downloading, 267
    evolution of, 1
    FTP, transferring files with, 266–274
    hosting services for, 262
    installing, 261–288
    migrating, 293–309
    on local web servers, 262
    one-click installers, 263
    open source and, 3
    release history of, 3
    Security Center, 253–260
    System Information tab, 287
    system requirements for, 261
    translating, 323
    updates, 289–293
    web installer, 268–274
Joomla Anti Malware Scan Script (JMASS), 254
Joomla Bug Squad (JBS), 323
Joomla CMS versions, 2
Joomla Content Editor (see JCE)
Joomla Developer Network, 31
Joomla Development Strategy, 322
Joomla Extensions Directory (JED), 31, 311

Joomla Framework and API, 321
Joomla Production Leadership Team (PLT), 297
Joomla Security and Performance FAQs, 256
Joomla Security Checklist, 256
Joomla Security Checklist - Getting Started, 256
Joomla Security News Feed, 256
Joomla Technical Requirements, 261
Joomla Translation Working Group, 25
Joomla User Group (JUG), 293
Joomla Vulnerable Extensions Feed, 256, 315
JoomlaDays, 323
JooStrap template, 19
JTicketing, 170
JUpgrade, 299

K

K2, third party tagging tools and, 161
keywords, 118
    in System menu, 26
Komento, 157
Kunena Forum, 159
    creating categories, 225–228
    customizing look of, 231
    discussion forums with, 224–231
    integrating with JomSocial, 221

L

Language Code plugin, 151
Language Filter system plugin, 151
Language Manager, 30
language support, 145–154
    adding, 147
    in administrator panel, 152
    installing, 145–147
    uninstalling, 149
Language Switcher module, 151
languages
    overriding, 241–243
    translating content between, 149–151
    Unicode aliases and, 279
Latest Events module (JEvents), 176
Latest News module, 162
layouts
    editing globally, 90
    frontend, 82
    homepage, 20–20
    internal pages, 21, 22
    multiple, 22

of contact forms, 186
Layouts tab, 71
leading spaces, 78
Link & Accent Color, setting, 64
lists
    editing layouts globally, 90
    pasting, 100–101
local web servers, 262
location settings, 281
log files, 279
login module, 249

M

Mac, 262
MagentoGo, 197
mail options, setting, 26
MailChimp, 236
    integrating with contact forms, 187
mailing lists, 232
Maintenance side bar, 292
Mambo Steering Committee, 1
MAMP, 262
media
    adding to articles, 131–137
    deleting, 128–130
    organizing, 137
    uploading, 128–130
Media Manager, 127–144
    deleting images, 136
    global options for, 140
    Style tab, 62–66
    Thumbnail View, 128
menu item aliases, 5
Menu Item Article Options, 86
menu items
    About, 51–55
    Category Blog, 51–55
    Category List, 55
    changing types of, 51
    checking in, 26
    creating, 47–55
    drawing out, 9
    forms, 193
    JEvents, 167–168
    maximum number of, 9
    options, changing, 91–93
    planning, 8–14
    Shop, 205
    single article, 49–51

Testimonials, 51–55
text separator, 47–49
Menu Style, setting, 64
Menu tab, 70
menus menu, 27
Meta Description
content, 118
setting, 277
Meta Keywords, 118
in System menu, 26
setting, 278
metadata, 240
settings for, 277
Microsoft Outlook, 221
Microsoft Word, copy/pasting content from, 98–99
Migrate Me, 300
migrations, 293–309
case study, 300
full, 299–309
mini-, 297–299
planning for, 294–297
tools for, 299
Miro, 1
mobile devices
tables, formatting for, 105
templates and, 22
moderating forum users, 228–229
ModSecurity (Apache), 209
Module Class Suffix, 78
Module Manager, 30, 72, 79
modules
adding content to, 124
adding to blogs, 157–163
applying to selected pages, 78
checking in, 26
creating, 72–82
creating image galleries in, 141
deleting, 81
duplicating, 79
for social media, 222
frontend layouts, 82
HikaShop, adding, 208
latest posts, 162
login, 249
ordering, 79
Placeholder Custom HTML, 73–79
spacing in, 20
mod_rewrite (Apache), 278

MyJoomla security audit tool, 260
MySQL, 260, 269, 282

N

newsletters, 231–236
mailing lists, 232
sending, 233

O

OCR (Optical Character Recognition), 255
offline message, 276
OmniGraffle, 9
one-click installers, 263
online stores, 197–210
payments, 200
planning for, 197–199
products, adding, 204
security of, 208–210
shipping fees, 201–203
taxes, 203
zones for, 201
open source, 3
Open Source Initiative, 3
Open Source Matters fork, 1
Optical Character Recognition (OCR), 255
ordered lists, pasting, 100–101
OS Content extension, 272
Outlook (Microsoft), 221

P

Page Break button, 117–118
Parent window, 53
Password Bird, 260
Password Generator (cPanel), 265
passwords, securing, 260
recovering admin, 325
pasting
content, 98–99
lists, 100–101
payments
in HikaShop, 200
in JEvents, 170
shipping fees, 201–203
zones for, 201
PayPal, 170, 197
icon for, 193
payment integration, 191–193

RSForm Pro and, 190
PCI compliance, 210
performance
    cache settings and, 280
    GZIP page compression and, 281
    images and, 139
permissions
    directory, 288
    editing globally, 90
    embedding HTML code and, 113
    limiting file sizes with, 140
    on articles, 122
    on forums, 228–229
permissions settings, 283
personal information settings menu, 32
Photoshop (Adobe), 139
Photoshop Elements (Adobe), 139
PHP
    manipulation, 190
    settings, 287
PHP File Change Scanner, 260
Pintrest, 211
Placeholder Custom HTML modules, 73–79
planning, 7–22
    an online store, 197–199
    article layout, 12
    articles, 15
    choosing extensions, 18
    choosing templates, 18
    for migration, 294–297
    for multiple users, 16
    goal setting, 7
    layouts, 20–22
    menu items, 8–14
Plugin Manager, 30
popular tags module, 161
POST limits, 129
PostgreSQL, 269
PowerPoint, 10
previewing, 34
publishing categories, 40
purging cache, 26

Q

QR Codes, 189

R

Random Products module (HikaShop), 208

Read More button, 117–118
ReCaptcha (Google), 188, 212, 229
    Joo ReCaptcha plugin, 255
Recently Added Articles module, 32
recurring events
    adding, 171–175
    editing, 176
redMIGRATOR, 299
release cycles, updating within, 289–291
Remove Formatting button, 100
robots, 278
RocketTheme, 20
RSForms Pro, 190–195
    configuring, 190
    installing, 190
    plugins and modules, installing, 190

S

SalesForce, 189
    RSForm Pro and, 190
script kiddie, 259
search engine
    crawlers, 278
    indexing, 106
Search Engine Friendly URLs, 26, 238, 278
search engine optimization, 240
    activating, 239
    settings for, 278
SecuImage captcha plugin, 188
security, 253–260
    best practices for, 254
    breaches, recovering from, 259
    email settings for, 283
    file types, limiting, 140
    health checks, performing, 254–256
    Install from Web feature and, 318
    of extensions, 314
    of online shops, 208–210
    on forums, 228
    tools for, 254–256
    two-factor authentication, 257–259
    updates, 289–291
Security Center, 31, 253–260
SEF URLs, 26, 238, 278
SEO basics, 240
Server tab (Global Configurations), 280–284
    database settings, 282
    email settings, 282
    FTP settings, 281

location settings, 281
permissions settings, 283
text filter settings, 283
session settings, 280
setting up, 37–82
articles, creating, 43–46
backups, 56–58
categories, 37–43
modules, 72–82
multilanguage support, 145–147
template parameters, 58–72
sharing buttons, 222
shipping fees, 201–203
zones for, 201
Shopify, 197
shopping carts, third-party/hosted, 197
sidebars on contact forms, 182
sigplus, 141
downloading, 141
image gallery plugin, 142
Simonsen, Matt, 208
Single Article menu items, 49–51
site map, 4
site name setting, 276
site navigation, 4
site offline setting, 276
site settings, 276
Site tab (Global Configurations), 276–279
cookie settings, 279
metadata settings, 277
site settings, 276
Slideshow CK, 144
smart layers, 222
SMTP settings, 283
social media, 222
software piracy, 312
spaces, leading, 78
spacing in modules, 20
spam, preventing, 212, 229
with user options, 250
spambots, 255
Split Menus (Menu tab), 70
sponsoring development, 323
spreadsheets, designing menu items with, 9
SPUpgrade, 299, 301
SSL, 209
forcing, 281
Start Publishing parameter, 156
stickies, organizing with, 10

Stop Forum Spam service, 231
Strong Password Generator, 260, 265
Style tab, 62–66
subscription management, 235
System Information tab, 287
System menu, 25
system requirements, 261
system settings, 279
System tab (Global Configurations)
cache settings, 280
debug settings, 279
session settings, 280

T

Table Prefix, 270
tables, 105
tabs, 8
removing, 99
tags, 160–161
filtering, 284
taxes, 203
zones for, 201
Taylor, Phil, 260
temp folder path, setting, 280
Template Manager, 30
Edit Style screen, 62–66
template parameters, 58–72
Advanced tabs, 72
Assignments tabs, 72
CSS overrides, 67–69
Features tab, 69
Layouts tab, 71
Menu tab, 70
Style tab, 62–66
templates
choosing, 18
custom, 19
included, 18
Media Manager and, 128
mobile devices and, 22
third-party, 18
Testimonials menu items, 51–55
text
filtering, 26, 112–116
formatting, 104
text filtering, 26, 112–116
settings for, 113, 283
Text Separator menu item, 47–49
third-party templates, 18

Thunderbird (Mozilla), 221
time zone, 281
TinyMCE, 93
top toolbar, 33
Tor Tags, 161
tp parameter, 73
Twitter, 211, 222
    AddThis module, 222
Twitter Bootstrap, 19
two-factor authentication, 257–259

U

uncategorized categories, 42
underlining, 104
Unicode aliases, 279
United States Postal Service, 202
unordered lists, pasting, 100–101
unpublishing categories, 40
updates, 289–293
    third party extensions and, 291–293
    within release cycle, 289–291
uploads, limits on size of, 129
UPS (United Parcel Service), 202
user engagement, 211–236
    AddThis module for, 222
    discussion forums for, 224–231
    JomSocial and, 211–222
    newsletters for, 231–236
    social media, 222
    subscription management, 235
user groups, 16
    creating, 245
    forum permissions for, 228–229
    implementing ACLs with, 246–248
    in JomSocial, 216–218
    text filters based on, 283
users
    ACLs and, 17
    adding events by, 176
    creating, 244
    custom profiles for, 213

in multiple groups, 248
moderating, 228–229
newsletter subscription management for, 235
planning for, 16
setting options for, 250
Users menu, 26
USPS, 202

V

Vulnerable Extensions List, 254

W

watchul.li service, 260
Web Installer (Joomla), 268–274
Webresizer, 139
website
    planning, 7–22
    setup, 37–82
Widgetkit (YooTheme), 144
Windows, 262
wireframing tools, 9
word processors, copy/pasting from, 98–99
Wright template, 19
WYSIWYG editors, 93
    assigning to users, 96
    JCE, 94–96

X

XAMP, 262

Y

YouTube videos, embedding, 115–116
yTiger, 190
YubiKey authentication, 258

Z

zones, 201

About the Authors

Ron Severdia is Chief Technology Officer of the award-winning ebook company Metrodigi in the San Francisco Bay Area and has been a creative director on interactive branding projects—from websites and brand identities to interactive campaigns—for clients such as HP, Verizon, Electronic Arts, Yahoo!, Visa, Walmart.com, and Apple. His prior experience includes stints as a senior designer and then creative director at Young & Rubicam, DDB, Glow, and Landor Associates. Fluent in several languages, he worked for seven years in Europe, where he's won several awards for successful creative work. Ron has been using Joomla since 2006 to build sites for companies large and small, including a worldwide branding site for Citibank and a Big Data portal for eBay.

Jennifer Gress (*www.snapdragonservices.com*) has been working with Joomla since 2006 with its beginnings in corporate America for employers. Clients began approaching her to build websites for them in January of 2010. Jennifer's skills from corporate life—project management, training, and more—combined with her knowledge and experience with Joomla make her a well-rounded website builder, implementer, trainer, and consultant. Jennifer has worked with Joomla 1.0.x, 1.5.x, 2.5.x, and Joomla 3.x. She has executed many migrations from Joomla 1.5 to 2.5 and 3. Jennifer is co-leader for the Joomla Users Group in the San Francisco Bay Area. She also helps other Joomla users in the Joomla Community Forum.

Colophon

The animal on the cover of *Using Joomla* is a white stork (*Ciconia ciconia*). According to legends that originated in northern Germany, white storks are a symbol of fertility and prosperity. Found throughout Europe, the Middle East, and west-central Asia, white storks are long-necked wading birds whose bodies are mostly white except for their black flight feathers. Their bills and legs are red. Nothing but size (males are slightly larger than females) distinguishes the sexes from each other.

Monogamous during the breeding season, couples build their nests together, although finding materials is primarily the male's responsibility. The nests are large and usually made up of twigs, grass, sod, and paper. Pairs will often reuse their nests year after year, adding new material each breeding season. To signify the completion of the next, they will often plant a leafy branch on one side.

Since the Middle Ages, white storks have built their nests on man-made structures like rooftops, chimneys, and telephone poles. Nests can also be found in trees and sometimes even on the ground. Females usually lay between three and five eggs. Both parents are responsible for feeding their young until the babies reach eight or nine weeks of age and leave the nest, after which time the young are known to return to their parents on occasion to beg for food.

The white stork's diet is quite varied and includes frogs, fish, snakes, lizards, earthworms, crustaceans, and even sometimes the eggs and chicks of small ground-nesting birds. Storks are visual hunters, so when foraging, they walk with their eyes and bill pointed toward the ground. Once they spot their prey, they cock their necks back and then jab their bills back and forth until they catch their victim.

Over the last 50 years, the white stork population has seen a steady decline, particularly in Western Europe. In 1910, there were 500 breeding pairs in the Netherlands, but in 1985 there were only 5. This extreme change is mostly due to habitat destruction, but pesticide use and wetland drainage have limited the availability of food as well.

The cover image is from Cassell's *Natural History*. The cover fonts are URW Typewriter and Guardian Sans. The text font is Adobe Minion Pro; the heading font is Adobe Myriad Condensed; and the code font is Dalton Maag's Ubuntu Mono.

Get even more for your money.

Join the O'Reilly Community, and register the O'Reilly books you own. It's free, and you'll get:

- $4.99 ebook upgrade offer
- 40% upgrade offer on O'Reilly print books
- Membership discounts on books and events
- Free lifetime updates to ebooks and videos
- Multiple ebook formats, DRM FREE
- Participation in the O'Reilly community
- Newsletters
- Account management
- 100% Satisfaction Guarantee

Signing up is easy:

1. Go to: oreilly.com/go/register
2. Create an O'Reilly login.
3. Provide your address.
4. Register your books.

Note: English-language books only

To order books online:
oreilly.com/store

For questions about products or an order:
orders@oreilly.com

To sign up to get topic-specific email announcements and/or news about upcoming books, conferences, special offers, and new technologies:
elists@oreilly.com

For technical questions about book content:
booktech@oreilly.com

To submit new book proposals to our editors:
proposals@oreilly.com

O'Reilly books are available in multiple DRM-free ebook formats. For more information:
oreilly.com/ebooks

CPSIA information can be obtained at www.ICGtesting.com
Printed in the USA
LVOW03s1723090315

429800LV00026B/114/P